American Outrage

A Testamentary

AMERICAN OUTRAGE

A TESTAMENTARY

H. L. HIX

BLAZEVOX[BOOKS]
Buffalo, New York

American Outrage
by H. L. Hix

Published by BlazeVOX [books]

Printed in the United States of America

Interior design and typesetting by Geoffrey Gatza
Cover Art: "Double Pistol" by Sarah Kabot, Carbon Paper double transfer process on kozo, reproduced here by kind permission of the artist.

Special thank you to the **Wyoming Institute for Humanities Research** for its vibrant support of this book.

First Edition
ISBN: 978-1-60964-472-7
Library of Congress Control Number: 2024932233

BlazeVOX [books]
131 Euclid Ave
Kenmore, NY 14217
Editor@blazevox.org

publisher of weird little books

BlazeVOX [books]

blazevox.org

23 22 21 20 19 18 17 16 15 14 13 01 02 03 04 05 06 07 08 09 10 11 12

BlazeVOX

Contents

AMERICAN OUTRAGE

A TESTAMENTARY

American Outrage

I didn't write every single name down; I wrote perhaps 1,000.

This tragic list could go on.

Jessica Rekos liked books about whales, horses, and fairies.

Ethel Lee Lance liked to make bacon and grits
for her grandkids for breakfast.

Ryan Clark played baritone in the marching band.
Friends called him "Stack."

Satwant Singh Kaleka worked at someone else's gas station
until he'd saved enough money to buy his own.

Sonam Choedon, born in India to Tibetan parents in exile,
was studying nursing.

Carole Robertson took Saturday dance lessons,
played clarinet, and was in the science club.

Angel Candelario-Padro worked as an opthalmic technician
and as a Zumba instructor.

Garrett Swasey, a police officer,
had been a competitive ice dancer.

Stephanie Works, who liked fly fishing,
had been born with six toes on each foot, like her father.

William Kinney was an avid baseball player.

5,586: between 1969 and 2009, the total number of people killed in terrorist attacks against the U.S. or its interests, including the attacks of September 11, 2001. **More than 30,000**: between 1986 and 2010, the number of people killed by guns in the U.S. every single year.

Violence results *from* violence. □ Violence results *in* violence. □ Commitment *of* violence is commitment *to* violence.

Stephon Clark had played on his school football team.

Karla Holcombe and Bryan Holcombe, high school sweethearts,
had been married for forty years.

Melvin Wax, even at 88, parked far from his synagogue,
to leave closer spaces for others.

Nevaeh Bravo played softball and was a cheerleader.
Her name is "heaven" spelled backward.

Rhonda LeRocque worked at a design agency,
and was active in her Jehovah's Witnesses chapter.

Andre Mackniel, a cook and a stay at home dad,
wrote poems and played guitar.

Tralona Bartkowiak had recently gotten engaged.
She had a chihuahua named Opal.

Maribel Hernández Loya kept a garden,
and liked going to the casino.

Chia Ling Yau, who went by "Charlie,"
had dual citizenship, in Taiwan and the U.S.

Phillip High Bear had one son and one daughter.

650,000,000: number of firearms held by civilians in 2006. **875,000,000**: number of firearms held by civilians in 2017. **35**: percentage increase in civilian firearms held by civilians in the 11 years from 2006 to 2017.

Guns aren't the only way to inflict violence, but they have become the paradigmatic way. □ What guns symbolize might not exhaust what a given gun symbolizes. □ Guns don't have to *provide* safety to *symbolize* safety.

James Cho loved elephants, and wore elephant bibs and shirts.

Ahmaud Arbery worked at a truck washing company
and for his father's landscaping business.

Quintonio LeGrier was studying electrical engineering
at Northern Illinois University.

Madeleine Hsu played piano,
and read books about fairies, princesses, and Pinkalicious.

Clementa Pinckney, a seminary graduate,
was a member of the South Carolina Senate.

Caitlin Hammaren sang and played violin,
and served as a resident advisor in her dorm.

Katleen Ping had a young child,
and worked as a receptionist at a nursing school.

Carol McNair played baseball,
and was a member of a Brownie troop.

Simon Carillo worked at McDonald's,
and liked dancing, biking, and water skiing.

Sita Singh had four children, and liked music and reading.

17: in the year of the Columbine shooting, the number of students killed at school.
2,500+: in the same year, the number of young people (ages 5-19) who were murdered outside of school.

Individual-level explanations of violence oversimplify complex phenomena: they are reductive. □ Assigning violence to individual choice gives cover to the violence of systems. □ As long as we *think* of gun ownership as exclusively individual, we'll keep *treating* it as if it were.

Emily Garcia was seven years old, and in second grade.

Ke'Arre Stewart, an Army vet, liked sports and movies,
and playing the video game "Assassin's Creed."

Rachel Works loved dance and music,
and liked to make up stories with video clips.

Hallie Scruggs liked ninjas and unicorns,
and played soccer and basketball.

Irving Younger had two children,
and had coached little league and high school JV baseball.

Uziyah Garcia loved running and swimming.
He liked football, jumping on trampolines, and gorilla tag.

Pearl Young, at 77, still taught Sunday school
and substituted in Buffalo Public Schools.

Teri Leiker held a job for 31 years
at her local chain grocery store.

Margie Reckard worked at Walmart,
and had been married to her second husband for 22 years.

Brennan Stewart was an amateur singer/songwriter.

14,157: number of McDonald's restaurants in the United States. **37,053**: number of grocery stores in the United States. **58,794**: number of retail gun stores and pawn shops selling guns in the United States.

"[S]omething more than objective threat is at work in police killings." □ Racial disparities in police killing will not decrease until structural racism is mitigated. □ Reducing the number of police killings will require many changes, not just one change.

Christian Escobedo, 22, was a high school graduate.

Julisa Molina Rivera was 31 years old.
She had been born in Honduras, but lived in Texas.

Shawn Jackson liked making music videos
and had just graduated from high school.

Pedro Cortez, who was legally blind,
worked for his stepfather in a moving company.

Beatrice Dotson was 95,
and had recently moved in with her daughter.

Destiny Howard, a Black trans woman,
was a high school graduate and loved fashion.

Walter Scott was behind in child-support payments,
and drove a twenty-year-old car.

Avielle Richman, who often went barefoot,
liked to be told stories at bedtime.

Myra Thompson was retired from her career
as an eighth-grade English teacher and guidance counselor.

Kenneth Mills-Tucker worked at his local U-Haul.

71: of firearm deaths among children aged 0-4, percentage that are by intent, not unintentional. **80**: of firearm deaths among children aged 5-9, percentage that are by intent, not unintentional. **90**: of firearm deaths among youth aged 10-14, percentage that are by intent, not unintentional. **97**: of firearm deaths among youth aged 15-19, percentage that are by intent, not unintentional.

Fear immunizes against influence by fact. □ Numb to others' pain, dishonest to oneself. □ Traumatic events cause trauma *and* fear.

Noah Holcombe, her parents' only child, was 17 months old.

Rachael Hill had played volleyball in high school.
She played piano, and was studying biology.

Ranjit Singh worked odd jobs in the U.S.
to send money back to his family in India.

Grace Eunhae Kim used the intercom where she worked
to sing and joke with her co-workers.

Addie Mae Collins had six siblings.
She played softball and liked making art.

Akyra Murray had graduated third in her class,
and scored over 1,000 points for her school basketball team.

Jennifer Markovsky liked baking, arts and crafts.
and taking her young children on hikes.

Philip Crouse had been a skinhead in his youth,
but wanted to do missionary work.

Cynthia Peak had a daughter and two sons,
and worked as a substitute teacher.

Richard Rodriguez was a retired railroad worker.

18: number of bullets an average shooter could fire in one minute with a six-shot revolver.
100: number of bullets an average shooter could fire in one minute with an assault rifle equipped with a one-hundred-round drum.

War declared against an abstract concept ("crime") produces very concrete collateral damage. □ Militarizing police weaponry increases the distance from which officers can target suspects. □ Expansion of the criminal justice system expands state predation.

Carlos LaMadrid, 19, loved music and soccer.

Alexander Mikhail Gusev had come to the U.S. from Belarus
to earn his degree in civil engineering.

Omarian Banks worked at McDonald's,
and wanted to become an electrician like his father.

Sarah Lee Circle Bear, a 24-year-old Lakota woman,
was the mother of two young children.

DeAunta Farrow, nicknamed "Tae Tae," was 12,
and had just completed sixth grade.

Punjab Singh had served for 19 years
in the Indian Army as a Sikhi chaplain.

Sharonda Coleman-Singleton coached a high school girls track team,
and served as a lay minister in her church.

Henry Lee knew no English when he arrived in the U.S. at age 5,
but graduated as salutatorian of his high school class.

Lydia Sim served as a babysitter at her church,
and wanted to become a pediatrician.

Anne Marie Murphy, a special education aide, liked taking walks.

3: number of times the phrase "God-given right" was used in the *American Rifleman* in the ten-year period from 1975 through 1984. **22**: number of times the phrase "God-given right" was used in the *American Rifleman* in the nine-year period from 2010 through 2018. **2**: references to evil as an unseen or disembodied force in the *American Rifleman* in the ten-year period from 1975 through 1984. **37**: references to evil as an unseen or disembodied force in the *American Rifleman* in the four-year period from 2015 through 2018.

"Privatizing violence removes it from the sphere of public rhetoric." □ Privatizing violence precludes redress of white supremacy. □ The state's coercive powers are being militarized *and* privatized.

Alejandro Barrios Martínez had recently immigrated from Cuba.

Cynthia Morris was raised by a single mother,
and in school excelled in math, reading, and band.

Tiffany Johnson enjoyed snowboarding and skateboarding,
and planned to study international business and Japanese culture.

Mike Hill worked as a custodian at an elementary school,
and did the greeting for services at his church.

Joyce Fienberg worked for 25 years as a research specialist
at a university Learning Research and Development Center.

Alithia Ramirez liked to play soccer,
and wanted someday to go to art school in Paris.

Hannah Ahlers, a stay-at-home mom, liked country music,
and loved getting manicures and pedicures.

Margus Morrison collected sneakers, and made a good tuna salad.
He liked the songs of Donell Jones.

Rikki Olds enjoyed hiking and camping and golf.
Her favorite animal was the octopus.

Megan Hill was nine. Her family had nicknamed her "Megacute."

55: of homes in the U.S. with children and firearms, the percentage with one or more firearms in an unlocked place. **43**: of homes in the U.S. with children and firearms, the percentage with one or more firearms not in a locked place and not locked with a trigger lock or other locking mechanism.

"[I]n addition to being protected by guns, we can also be, and too often are, tyrannized by them." □ Maybe guns *would* protect my freedom, if what threatened it were something that could be shot. □ Maybe police would shoot fewer persons if *fighting* crime were a less prevalent metaphor.

Daniel Enrique Laso-Guzmán was 9, and in third grade.

Destinee Thompson was 27, and the mother of three children.
She was seven months pregnant with her fourth child.

Javier Rodriguez played soccer and liked video games.
He was starting his sophomore year in high school.

Muoi Dai Ung was a refugee from Vietnam
who loved dance enough that she was taking ballroom lessons.

Renzo Smith was an Army veteran
whose service had included deployment in Iraq.

Christopher Rapp played in a bagpipe band.
He loved line dancing, ballroom dancing, and Filipino dances.

Rumain Brisbon wanted to get a barber's license.
He liked to take his four daughters roller skating and bowling.

Deion Fludd was in high school in Brooklyn
and played on a traveling basketball team.

Olivia Engel liked to dance.
She helped potty train her little brother by giving him stickers.

Larry Jackson, Jr. was a 32-year-old father of four.

$76.4 billion: U.S. Department of Education Budget. **$557 billion**: annual economic cost to the U.S. of gun violence. **2.6**: percent of the U.S. Gross Domestic Product to which the annual economic cost of gun violence is equal.

"[R]acial prejudice predicts police militarization." □ Militarized policing exacerbates racialization of policing. □ More police = less white risk of police killing, more Black risk.

Karen Marshall was a master sergeant in the Air National Guard.

Tywanza Sanders went fishing with father,
and went to Bible study with his mother and his great aunt.

Nicole White worked as a lifeguard and swimming instructor,
and volunteered at a women's shelter and an animal shelter.

Prakash Singh had just brought his wife and two children
from India to join him in the U.S.

Doris Chibuko was studying nursing
and working part-time at a mental health rehabilitation center.

Rodolfo Ayala-Ayala liked Latin dancing
and "could rock a bow tie. He was famous for the bow tie."

Evelyn Dieckhaus had two dogs, Mable and Birdie,
and a collection of stuffed tigers all named Tony.

Rose Mallinger was 97 but did not use a cane or walker,
and still cooked family meals for high holidays.

Jailah Silguero, 10 was the youngest of four siblings.
She liked dancing and making TikTok videos.

Rekia Boyd lived in a Chicago suburb. She was 22.

20,000+: number of suicides by gun every year in the United States.

The harm guns cause is not surprising; our acceptance of the harm is. □ Events that warn us to change the system are swallowed by the system. □ No understanding the offense without recognizing the role of the system as offender.

Alexia Christian was a 26-year-old mother of two young sons.

Andrea Castilla, whose mother had died of cancer,
wanted to work as a makeup artist for cancer survivors.

Katherine Massey went by "Kat,"
and was retired from her work at Blue Cross Blue Shield.

Eric Talley enjoyed drones and collected board games.
He and his wife had seven children.

Guillermo Garcia coached his daughter's soccer team.
His friends called him "Tank" or "Memo."

Sonia Argentina Guzmán was 25 years old.
She had been born in Honduras, but lived in Texas.

Michelle Langer loved the beach.
She was 60, went by "Missy," and had just adopted a puppy.

Nicholas Heyward, Jr., 13, an honor student,
had just made his school basketball team.

Bettie Jones had four daughters and a son,
and was experiencing ovarian cancer.

Jacob Hall was in first grade, and loved superheroes.

34: of female victims of murder and nonnegligent manslaughter in 2021, the percentage who were killed by an intimate partner. **6**: of male victims of murder and nonnegligent manslaughter in 2021, the percentage who were killed by an intimate partner.

Military performance of law enforcement contradicts democracy. □ Consolidation of military and police threatens human rights. □ Militarization disfigures and destroys.

Tarika Wilson was 26, and had six children.

Victoria Soto taught first grade,
and sometimes brought snacks for her students.

Depayne Middleton-Doctor had four daughters.
She sang alto, and her favorite song was "I Really Love the Lord."

Ross Alameddine played piano, loved rollerblading,
and played games competitively, especially "Company of Heroes."

Suveg Singh Khattra farmed in India into his seventies,
then moved to the U.S. to live with his son and daughter-in-law.

Judith Seymour was studying nursing,
and had two adult children, a daughter and a son.

Paul Henry worked at a call center.
He played piano and organ, and liked singing and dancing.

Katherine Koonce, an elementary-school principal,
liked traveling, art, music, and playing pickleball.

Carlin Holcombe was not yet born, was due in a month,
and already had the nickname "Billy Bob."

Jeffrey Osborne ran a poultry farm, and liked motorcycling.

78: percentage of homicide cases in the U.S. solved when the person killed was white.
67: percentage of homicide cases in the U.S. solved when the person killed was Black.
16: percentage of homicide cases in the U.S. solved when the person killed was trans.

Every person shot in a mass shooting is a *person.* □ Violence attacks a person, and personhood. □ "Violence, like other traumas, fragments the self and removes the ground from below us."

Tracy Gaeta lived in California, and was a grandmother.

Bernard Whitehurst worked as a janitor.
He and his wife had four children.

Brooke Ward loved the movie *Frozen*,
and liked to dress up like characters in the film.

Cecil Rosenthal and David Rosenthal were brothers,
and attended services together at their synagogue.

Amerie Garza loved was protective of her 3-year-old brother,
and kissed him every morning before she went to school.

Heather Alvarado ran an at-home day care center.
She loved fishing, camping and vacationing in Cancun.

Roberta Drury went by "Robbie"with family and friends.
She enjoyed walking with her sister through the Buffalo Zoo.

Denny Stong worked extra shifts at his grocery store job
to save for plane fuel while he pursued his pilot's license.

Angie Englisbee, 86, did her shopping each Saturday morning,
and liked watching TV sports and "General Hospital."

Jalen Randle was 29, and had a 5-year-old daughter.

100: percentage of Board members of the Remington Society of America who are white males.

Open carry is equally open to all carriers, but more equally open to some carriers than to others. □ What made cars less lethal would do the same for guns. □ Consistent rules, effective rules.

Jayland Walker worked as a DoorDash driver in Akron, Ohio.

Diana Man Ling Tom had worked as a pharmacy technician
while she and her husband raised their children.

Aishwarya Thatikonda worked as an engineer.
She was about to turn 27.

José Jonathan Casárez was 18 years old.
He had been born in Honduras, but lived in Texas.

Katherine Nixon, who went by "Kate," worked as an engineer.
Her grandmother had taught her how to quilt.

Kelly Loving, a trans woman, had just turned 40.
She liked travel. Friends called her "Jenna Sno."

Tyshon Anderson was looking into alternative schools,
and planning to get a state ID so he could apply for a job.

Danroy Henry, 20, went by "DJ."
At his university he was on the football team and the Dean's List.

Charleena Lyles was pregnant with her fifth child.
She lived unhoused, but worked at a coffee company.

Emily Hill loved horses, karate, cooking, and being with her family.

17: of news stories about mass shootings between 1997 and 2012, the percentage that mentioned dangerous people with SMI (serious mental illness) as causes of gun violence.
9: of news stories about mass shootings between 1997 and 2012, the percentage that mentioned dangerous weapons as causes of gun violence.

Black men are targeted disproportionately; dark-skinned Black men even more so. □ Inhibit the activation of stereotypes; suspend their application to behavior. □ To end hate crimes against minorities, end discrimination against minorities.

Rayshard Brooks was 27, and had three daughters and a stepson.

Deana Eckert and her husband had two children.
She worked in a bank as an executive assistant.

Reat Underwood loved to camp and hunt.
He was a high school freshman and an Eagle Scout.

Randolph Evans went by "Randy."
He was 15, and a high school freshman.

Belinda Galde worked as a probation officer,
and had operated a hairdressing business from her home.

Grace McDonnell loved the beach,
and wanted to become a painter when she grew up.

Susie Jackson had two children and eight grandchildren.
She sang soprano in her church choir.

Jeremy Herbstritt was a marathon runner,
and loved to hike, ski, and kayak.

Paramjit Kaur worked 11 hours a day, 6 days a week,
in production at a medical devices firm.

Casey Goodson was 23, and lived with his grandmother.

9: in 2015, how many times more likely a Black man between 15 and 34 was than any other American to be killed by a police officer. **2**: of the U.S. population, the percentage that are Black males between 15 and 34. **15**: of persons killed by the use of deadly force by police officers in 2015, the percentage that were Black males between 15 and 34. **17**: in 2015, the percentage of white persons killed by police who were unarmed. **25**: in 2015, the percentage of Black persons killed by police who were unarmed.

Police protect what, and who, policing was created to protect. □ Bad officers sometimes make police violence actual; bad policy makes it inevitable. □ More policing harms the most policed.

Henry Green lived with his aunt, and went by "Bub."

Tshering Rinzing Bhutia was studying nursing.
He worked the overnight shift as a custodian.

Edward Sotomayor Jr., wore a top hat to events,
so his friends nicknamed him "Top-Hat Eddie."

Haley Krueger was in ninth grade, and loved babies.
She wanted to become a nurse in a neonatal intensive care unit.

Daniel Stein was active in his synagogue community,
and served as president of his congregation.

Jayce Luevanos loved dinosaurs and ninjas.
He made his grandparents a pot of coffee every morning.

Dorene Anderson lived in Anchorage,
and rooted for the Alaska Aces minor league hockey team.

Geraldine Talley had a degree in secretarial science,
and loved to bake, especially cheesecake and carrot cake.

Kevin Mahoney enjoyed walking, hiking, skiing, and camping.
He volunteered in his local Meals on Wheels program.

Julius Tate, Jr. was 16, and lived in Columbus, Ohio.

25.6: in 1984, percentage of towns between 25,000 and 50,000 people with a SWAT team. **52.1**: in 1990, percentage of towns between 25,000 and 50,000 people with a SWAT team. **80**: in 2005, percentage of towns between 25,000 and 50,000 people with a SWAT team.

From any one death, devastation; to the many deaths, disregard. □ We only count as real deaths the ends of lives we can *see.* □ Recognition as active, full human beings reduces a group's vulnerability to violence.

Bernice and Sylvan Simon had been married for over 60 years.

Cornelius Fredericks, 16, lived in a facility
for teenagers with behavioral problems.

Herman Whitfield III, 39, had degrees from Oberlin.
He was a pianist and composer.

Nicholas Cumer had been in band in high school and college.
He had a Yorkie-poo named Maxie.

Jesse Lewis was good with animals,
and especially loved horseback riding.

Daniel L. Simmons was awarded a purple heart
for his Army service in Vietnam.

Maxine Turner, who went by Max, liked swing dancing,
and was a red belt in Tae Kwan Do.

Franky Dejesus Velazquez went by "Jimmy,"
and worked as a professional Jíbaro folk dancer.

Therese Rodriguez liked thrift shopping.
She was active in her church, and an avid gardener.

Isaiah Lewis was two weeks away from his high school graduation.

45: percentage of Americans who believed that Black persons are treated less fairly than white persons in dealing with the police, such as in traffic incidents, in 2016. **52**: percentage of Americans who believed that Black persons are treated less fairly than white persons in dealing with the police, such as in traffic incidents, in 2018. **77**: percentage of Black Americans who believe that Black persons are treated less fairly than white persons in dealing with the police, such as in traffic incidents. **45**: percentage of white Americans who believe that Black persons are treated less fairly than white persons in dealing with the police, such as in traffic incidents.

The state's primary use-of-force entities, once kept distinct, are increasingly allied. □ What we learned in war against others, we apply in war against ourselves. □ Make America Violent Again.

Dreasjon Reed was a high school graduate and an Air Force veteran.

Tess Mata played second base in softball,
and in gymnastics she could do a backbend or the splits.

Austin Davis played fast-pitch softball,
and worked as a journeyman pipe fitter.

Ruth Whitfield and her husband had four children,
and had been married for 68 years. She was 86.

Neven Stanišić enjoyed anime.
He worked with his father repairing coffee machines.

Sarita Regalado, 66, grew up in Juarez.
She and her husband had an adult daughter.

Valentino Alvero, a 68-year-old Filipino American,
loved ballroom dancing, and was a devout Catholic.

Sofia Mendoza, 8 years old and in second grade,
described herself in a school scrapbook as "sassy."

Diana Velázquez Alvarado had been born in Honduras,
and was a permanent resident of the U.S.

Ryan Twyman and his wife had three children, ages 1, 2, and 3.

14: for the period 2007-2012, the percentage of deaths by lethal violence in direct conflicts (wars). **74**: for the same period, the percentage of deaths by lethal violence that were intentional homicides.

Different patterns of killing invite different methods of prevention. □ Urban gun use *does* differ from rural; urban gun regulation *could.* □ Violence may vary across demographics, but we are all of us involved.

Alison Cienfuegos-Vasquez was a 21-year-old college student.

Alberta Spruill rode the bus each weekday to her job.
She had worked as a city employee for 29 years.

Byron Williams volunteered at a nonprofit foundation
that helps underserved families receive food and medical care.

Jim Tutt had four children,
and had worked in banking for over forty years.

William Lewis Corporon wore boots and suspenders to work
for the 25 years he practiced family medicine in Oklahoma.

Megan Betts collected shells and sea glass,
and made personalized gifts for her friends on their birthdays.

Joshua Higbee worked in a factory,
and took on extra handyman jobs to support his family.

Charlotte Bacon had a large collection of stuffed animals,
and liked to imitate her older brother.

Cynthia Graham Hurd worked as a librarian.
In her youth, her first job had been at an ice cream parlor.

Ahjah Dixon was a 23-year-old college student.

4.46: in an assault, times more likely a person in possession of a gun is to be shot than a person who is not in possession of a gun. **4.23**: in an assault, times more likely a person in possession of a gun is to be *fatally* shot than a person who is not in possession of a gun. **5.45**: in an assault in which the person assaulted has a chance to resist, times more likely a person in possession of a gun is to be shot than a person who is not in possession of a gun.

Everything you buy is regulated for health and safety, except guns. □ Exemption from regulation keeps guns embedded in the market. □ Only the gun is made specifically for the purpose of killing.

Ronell Foster was 33, and the father of two children.

Partahi Lumbantoruan liked to cook. Friends called him "Mora."
He was studying for his Ph.D. in civil engineering.

Amanda Alvear was studying to be a nurse.
She had lost 180 lbs. through gastric bypass surgery and exercise.

Shani Corrigan married her high school sweetheart,
and as a military spouse raised their three children.

Richard Gottfried was a dentist, as was his wife.
He was a past president of his synagogue congregation.

Eliahna Garcia went by "Ellie," and wanted to be a cheerleader.
She loved basketball and making TikToks.

Brett Schwanbeck was a retired over-the-road truck driver.
He loved to go Razor riding.

Celestine Chaney was 65. She had learned to sew
at the girls vocational high school from which she graduated.

Lynn Murray liked to sit on her patio
to drink wine, smoke cigarettes, and stare at the mountains.

Tyisha Miller was 19, and lived in Riverside, California.

26: as of early April 2023, the number of states that allow permitless concealed carry of guns.

"[P]olicing is a way of doing gender in our society." □ *Militarizing* police is a way of doing race. □ Police militarization reinforces racial hierarchies.

Renee Benjamin worked at a factory. She was 30.

Andre and Jordan Anchondo had recently celebrated
their first wedding anniversary.

Melissa Ventura had three children, including a two-month-old.
She had a history of mental illness.

Natasha Skorczewski had completed sixth grade.
She played Junior Olympics volleyball and other sports.

Terri LaManno worked as an occupational therapist.
She and her husband had three children.

Saeed Saleh had fled Eritrea with his wife and young daughter.
He worked as a forklift operator for DHL.

Brian Sadowsky liked heavy metal concerts and his pet Dachshunds.
He was a fan of the Pittsburgh Steelers and the KC Royals.

Aiken Smith was in Junior ROTC at school,
and wanted to join the Air Force when he was old enough.

Jillian Johnson had a B.F.A. in ceramics,
and sang lead vocals for a band called the Figs.

Zachary Bearheels suffered from bipolar disorder and schizophrenia.

1887: year in which Smith & Wesson introduced the "New Departure" safety grip designed to increase "the safety of the arm in the hands of children, as no ordinary child under eight years of age can possibly discharge it." **2000**: year in which the NRA called for a boycott of Smith & Wesson as "the first gun maker to run up the white flag of surrender," for an agreement with the U.S. government that would have included putting locks on handguns.

Hiding the killing completes the erasure of the killed. □ Pushed aside in life, shrugged off after death. □ "Violence disrupts our relations to the dead, not simply our relation to the living."

Michelle Cusseaux suffered from bipolar disorder and schizophrenia.

Sandra Bland graduated from Prairie View A&M,
where she majored in agriculture and played in the band.

Kathryn Johnston was 92. She lived alone,
and still did her own cooking and cleaning.

James Mattioli could ride his bike without training wheels.
He liked to sing, and he liked to spike his hair.

Liviu Librescu had lived as a child in World War II
in a Jewish ghetto in Romania.

Mercedez Flores worked at Target,
and was studying literature at her local community college.

Keith Braden was recovering from chemotherapy.
He worked in the dairy department of his local grocery store.

Jerry Rabinowitz was a primary care physician,
known for wearing a bowtie.

Jacklyn Cazares loved animals, especially her four dogs,
and wanted to become a veterinarian.

Phillip Pannell was 16 years old, and lived in New Jersey.

80: in incidents of gunfire on school grounds, approximate percentage of shooters under age 18 who got the gun from their own home or from the home of a friend or relative.

Seeing civilian affairs in military terms sanctions treating civilian affairs with military methods. □ "War on crime" institutionalizes militarism in U.S. culture. □ Law enforcement as "war" (on drugs, crime, etc.) turns citizens into enemy combatants.

Pamela Turner had two children, and suffered from schizophrenia.

Candice Bowers was a single mother, with three children,
two by birth and one a niece she adopted.

Aaron Salter Jr. was retired from his career as a police officer,
and was working as a security guard.

Suzanne Fountain, a prolific gardener,
was especially fond of a peach tree she had planted.

David Johnson worked in sales for Texas Lighting,
and enjoyed golfing on weekends.

Yu Lun Kao went by "Andy Kao" in his work as a contractor.
Evenings at home, he played the saxophone.

Daniela Mendoza was 11, and in the fourth grade.
She was once named Most Likely to Become a Teacher.

Laquita Brown was a Jehovah's Witness,
and had preached in Haiti and in West Africa.

Daniel Aston had participated in drama in high school.
He often performed at the club where he worked tending bar.

Martin Angel Hernandez was 21, and had a 2-year-old son.

0: In 2016-17, the number of persons fatally shot by police in Switzerland. **3**: In 2016-17, the number of persons fatally shot by police in Finland. **26**: In 2016-17, the number of persons fatally shot by police in France. **36**: In 2016-17, the number of persons fatally shot by police in Canada. **996**: In 2016-17, the number of persons fatally shot by police in the U.S.

The history of violence does not enforce pessimism but does urge specificity. □ It might take different questions about violence, to elicit more effective answers to violence. □ We can move on from gun violence only by *not* moving on from incidents of gun violence.

Heriberto Godinez Jr. was engaged. He went by "Junior."

Josh Barrick worked in banking.
He enjoyed golfing, and was a Xavier University basketball fan.

Beatrice Warren-Curtis went by her middle name, Nicole.
She worked for a health insurance company, and enjoyed travel.

Kenna Guardipee worked in the kitchen
of an assisted living center across the street from her home.

Mayci Breaux was in college, studying
for a career as an ultrasound and radiology technician.

Dymir Stanton was 29, and liked sports.
He and his girlfriend had a 4-year-old daughter.

Ma'Khia Bryant had three younger siblings,
and liked to make TikTok videos, dance, and go skating.

Terence Crutcher sang in his church choir for 25 years,
and was majoring in music at his local community college.

David McAtee, who went by "Yaya,"
owned and operated a barbecue business in Louisville.

Omar Gonzalez Jr. had two sons, and worked construction.

1: number of handguns sold every thirteen seconds in the U.S.

"Each of the techniques of the armed body articulates an important aspect of the gun culture." □ Mode of attempted defense conforms to perceived danger. □ We would be wise to correlate our fear with what actually threatens us.

Ajewan Jones was 18, and lived in Charlotte, North Carolina.

Mary Sherlach worked as a school psychologist,
and was a Miami Dolphins fan.

Matthew La Porte had been drum major of his high school band.
He liked heavy metal, *Finding Nemo*, and science fiction novels.

Antonio Brown was a Captain in the Army Reserves,
and had served a tour in Kuwait.

Marc Holcombe went by "Danny," from his middle name, Daniel.
He lived on the family farm.

Irma Garcia taught at the same elementary school
for her entire career of more than twenty years.

Nicol Kimura worked for a tax agency, and loved hiking.
She went for nightly runs with her dog, Sadie.

Heyward Patterson drove a taxi for his living.
He enjoyed singing at his church, where he was a deacon.

Jody Waters always kept and cared for rescue dogs,
often those with disabilities.

Alexsandra Olmo lived in Chicago with her adult daughter.

$7.79 million: amount U.S. taxpayers, survivors, families, and employers pay per day in health care costs related to gun violence. **$147.32 million**: amount U.S. taxpayers, survivors, families, and employers lose per day from work missed due to injury or death from gun violence. **$1.47 million**: amount U.S. employers lose daily in productivity, revenue, and costs required to recruit and train replacements for victims of gun violence.

Categorizations of killer and killed inflect understandings of culpability. □ Conceptions of violence have moral and material consequences. □ Erasure of race from accounts of violence is a form of violence.

Aura Rosser was an artist and the mother of three children.

Tyre Nichols worked second shift at FedEx, and each evening
he returned to his mother's house for his meal break.

Jeanetta Riley and her husband were living out of a car.
She had three daughters, and was pregnant with another child.

Arturo Benavides worked as a city bus driver.
He liked gambling and pineapple upside-down cake.

Ming Wei Ma had immigrated to the U.S. from China,
where he had been part of a professional touring dance troupe.

Christian LaCour worked as a security guard at an outlet mall.
He loved music, SciFi, comics, and anime.

Mary Louise Gayle made gingerbread houses every Christmas
for each household in her extended family.

Derek Walker was 26, and had a five-year-old son.
He was training to be a mortician.

Jose de la Trinidad and his wife had two daughters.
He worked two jobs to provide for his family.

Ricardo Diaz Zeferino worked as a cook at an Asian restaurant.

27: in 2013, the number of police officers killed in the line of duty by firearms. **82**: in 2013, the number of preschoolers killed by firearms. **42**: in 2017, number of law enforcement officers killed with guns in the line of duty. **93**: in 2017, number of preschool children killed with guns.

Racialization of police violence was not *spontaneous*; it has a *genealogy*. □ Present patrolling resembles past patrolling. □ Incidents of racialized police violence *recur* because systemic state racialization *persists*.

Johnathan Cuevas and his fiancée had a four-year-old son.

Derrick Rump was 38, and part owner of a club
in which he also tended bar.

Juliana Farmer worked in banking as a loan analyst.
Friends and family called her "J." She enjoyed travel.

Gary Anderson liked to fix bicycles.
He wore his hair braided, and had a cat named Mocha.

Lois Oglesby was in nursing school and worked at a daycare.
Her nickname, "Nae Nae," came from her middle name, Lenae.

Devin Smith had recently graduated from high school,
and struggled with a learning disability and social cues.

Ralph Moralis worked in restaurants.
He was preparing for his oldest daughter's wedding.

Brian Fraser was studying business,
and was president of the campus chapter of his fraternity.

Scott Beigel worked as a high school geography teacher,
cross country coach, and summer sleep-away camp counselor.

Ernest Duenez Jr. was 34, and had a 1-year-old son.

54: percentage of gun owners who do not lock all their weapons. **4.6 million**: number of children in the U.S. who live in a home with at least one unlocked and loaded firearm.

This conversation, too, only on condition of listening. □ Testimony supports solidarity. □ To reveal a nonviolent vista, reinvent a vocabulary.

Jesus Huerta went by "Chuy." He was 17.

Megan Waterman was 22, and had a 4-year-old child.
She earned her living as a sex worker.

Nasratullah Ahmad Yar and his wife had four children.
He was working as a Lyft driver to support his family.

Jamar Clark worked at a trucking firm,
and hoped to attend college, but had not yet enrolled.

Noah Pozner replied to his mother's declarations of love for him
with "Not as much as I love you, Mom."

Jocelyne Couture-Nowak loved gardening and hiking.
On hikes, "she touched and smelled and felt everything."

Stanley Almodovar worked as a pharmacy technician,
and frequently changed his hair color and style.

Sara Johnson had worked for her county tax office for years.
She volunteered in her church nursery.

Maite Rodriguez loved the TV show "Attack On Titan."
She wanted to be a marine biologist when she grew up.

Anastasio Hernández Rojas a Mexican national and father of five.

4.3: in 2016, the percentage of the global population in the U.S. **35.3**: in 2016, the percentage of global suicides by firearm that occurred in the U.S.

We blame for murder what we exonerate for suicide. □ Framing gun harm as "crime" gives it a different look than framing it as "public health." □ Judges wouldn't need to punish as much violence if we let doctors cure some of it.

Patricio Arroyo was 13 years old, and lived in Albuquerque.

Jessica Klymchuk worked for a school in Ontario
as an educational assistant, librarian, and bus driver.

Maria Flores and Raul Flores first met in Juarez, Mexico.
They had 3 children, 11 grandchildren, and 12 greatgrandchildren.

Hongying Jian liked to sing, play volleyball, dance, and play piano.
She also liked to make food for friends and neighbors.

Elio Cumana-Rivas had applied for asylum in the U.S.
He worked delivering food.

Tara Welch Gallagher had worked as an engineer
in her city's public works department for six years.

Jeanette Anaya had managed an optical shop for five years.
When it closed, she worked in various Santa Fe restaurants.

Janisha Fonville lived with her girlfriend and her girlfriend's child.
She had a mood disorder and a history of self-harm.

Kareem Ali Nadir Jones was 30, and had four children.
He loved music, and sang in his church choir.

Ernesto Canepa, a Mexican national, was 28, and a father of four.

1 month: length of time it takes for the number of American civilians who die from gunfire to exceed the number of deaths of U.S. military personnel in the first ten years of the war in Afghanistan.

Violence "has a way of scattering narratives and people across time, space, and consciousness." □ "It is possible that there is no other memory than the memory of wounds." □ Memory re-members.

Lisa German had three children and lived in upstate New York.

Corey Kanosh was a traditional pow wow dancer
and the father of a newborn son.

Paul Monroe was 23, and a community leader
who helped care for youth without families.

Ashley Paugh worked for a nonprofit.
She loved hunting, fishing and riding four-wheelers.

Tommy Elliott's "goofy" side included telling "Dad jokes,"
watching Andy Griffith, and listening to Susan Boyle while ironing.

Monica Brickhouse worked for a health insurance company,
and volunteered with Toys for Tots.

Kenneth Guardipee went by "Kenny."
He helped his daughter, a single mother, raise her two sons.

Lashyd Merritt was the youngest of five siblings.
His nieces and nephews called him "Shyd."

Unique Banks was a 21-year-old Latinx transgender woman.
She lived in Chicago with her mother.

Craig McKinnis was 44, and lived in Kansas City, Kansas.

48: of 64 8-12-year-old boys in a study, the number who found a concealed handgun within 15 minutes of being in a room with it. **30**: of the 48 boys who found the gun, the number who handled it. **16**: of those who handled the gun, the number who pulled its trigger. **1**: of the 64 boys, the number who left the room to inform an adult of the presence of the gun. **74**: percent of parents of 4-12-year-old children in another study who said that if their child encountered a gun, he or she would not touch the gun or would tell an adult. **52**: of parents in the second study who own guns, the percent who reported keeping at least one gun stored either loaded or unlocked. **13**: of parents in the second study who own guns, the percent who reported keeping at least one gun stored both loaded *and* unlocked.

Guns redefine the boundaries of their bearers' bodies. □ Guns redefine the rights accorded their bearers. □ Guns confer power, and command attention.

Areli Rodriguez was 18, and lived in Albuquerque.

Freddie Gray had suffered lead poisoning as a child.
He never held a "steady" job.

Shem Walker served for seven years in the Army,
then worked for a utility company, and later as a handyman.

Alexandria Verner was studying biology and anthropology,
intending to become a forensic scientist.

Jaime Guttenberg loved dance.
She wanted to become a pediatric physical therapist.

Valerie Mack had entered foster care at a young age.
She lived in Philadelphia with a boyfriend.

Jack Pinto had names for his stuffed sharks,
including Sharkey Jr. and Sharkey Hunter.

Jamie Bishop kept a ponytail,
and regularly cut his long hair to donate it to Locks of Love.

Luis Conde and his husband ran a salon.
They had been in high school together in Puerto Rico.

Eduardo Edwin Rodriguez had a girlfriend, and children.

3.49: number of times higher the probability is of being {Black, unarmed, and shot by police} than of being {white, unarmed, and shot by police}.

Hegemonic masculinity in policing does not begin on the job but in training *for* the job. □ Forgiving police violence sustains the system that generates the violence. □ Police violence is a *symptom.*

Christopher Williams Jr. lived in Houston. He was 2 years old.

Greg Hill had a reputation in his extended family
as a "baby whisperer" who could rock any baby to sleep.

Alexandria Rubio liked fishing with her dad
and playing Rock Paper Scissors with her mom.

Jennifer Irvine ran her own law firm.
She was a black belt in Taekwon-do, and an avid snowboarder.

Adolfo Cerros Hernández grew up in Aguascalientes,
and lived in Ciudad Juarez. He was 68.

Xiujuan Yu loved to cook,
especially soy sauce duck, soy sauce chicken, and sticky rice.

Ryan Cox went by his middle name, Keith.
He worked in his city's public utilities department.

Raymond Green Vance had just gotten a new job at FedEx.
He and his girlfriend had been together since middle school.

Logan Turner worked at a precision machining company.
Previously, he had managed a pizzeria and tended bar at a pub.

Jesse Romero was a 14-year-old, in middle school in Los Angeles.

<1.4 million: as of 2015, number of U.S. war deaths since 1775. **>1.45 million**: number of gun deaths in the U.S. between 1970 and 2015.

Murder epitomizes ignorance. □ Deadly force preempts deliberation. □ The language of civility hides the fact of violence.

David Smith was 28, and suffered from mental illness.

Joseph Wamah, Jr. had a twin sister, and was 31.
He enjoyed cooking and drawing.

Arielle Diamond Anderson was studying to become a surgeon.
She liked photography, concerts, tubing and roller-skating.

Peter Wang wanted to attend West Point and become a pilot.
He liked video games, anime, and basketball.

Maureen Brainard-Barnes had held cashier and telemarketing jobs
before taking on sex work to support her children.

Sarena Dawn Moore was a Seventh-Day Adventist,
and had three adult sons.

Ana Grace Marquez-Greene preferred dancing to walking.
She liked to sing the hymn "Come Thou Almighty King."

G.V. Loganathan liked cricket, badminton, and James Bond films,
and he often wore a pocket protector under a sweater vest.

Cory Connell liked to play football and basketball.
He wanted to become a firefighter.

Valarcia Blair had 13 siblings, and 3 children. She was 19.

18: number of 6-deaths-or-more mass shootings in the U.S. per decade in the four decades from 1966-2005. **115**: number of casualties per decade from those shootings. **39**: number of 6-deaths-or-more mass shootings in the U.S. in the decade from 2006-2015. **349**: number of casualties in that decade from those shootings.

The crimes of the system are necessary to the system; the system is not necessary. □ Blurring the contrast between internal and external threats blurs the limits of state power. □ Maybe the state monopoly on the use of force *should* be broken up.

Maria Eugenia Legarreta Rothe lived in Chihuahua, Mexico.

Annabelle Pomeroy liked to go to the pool,
and to ride with her father on his motorcycle.

Tanisha Anderson wanted to become a broadcast journalist.
She was 37, and had a 16-year-old daughter.

Ezell Ford, the oldest of seven siblings, was 25,
and had been diagnosed with schizophrenia and bipolar disorder.

Mark McMullen liked 80s movies and board games.
He worked as a chef. He and his wife had a 1-year-old son.

Eliahna Torres poured her grandfather a glass of ice water
to be waiting for him when he came home from work.

Chris Hazencomb worked as a cashier at Walmart,
and often brought coffee to his coworkers.

Elsa Mendoza Marquez worked as a school teacher and principal.
She and her husband had two grown children.

Wen Tau Yu, at 64, was retired from one career,
and in pharmacy school studying for another.

Fifty Bandz was a trans woman who lived in Baton Rouge.

2: worldwide, the percentage of firearms owned by law enforcement agencies. **13**: worldwide, the percentage of firearms in military arsenals. **85**: worldwide, the percentage of firearms in civilian hands.

Guns carried for protection don't protect their carriers. □ "Protective gun ownership" might shore up one's masculinity but does not protect one's family. □ "[W]hen gun owners believe that owning a gun will make them feel safer, little else may matter."

JoJo Striker was a 23-year-old trans woman who lived in Toledo.

Herbert Snelling worked as a project manager.
He and his wife had two children and eight grandchildren.

Philando Castile worked as a nutrition services assistant
at one school, then as a kitchen supervisor at another.

Jordan Edwards, a high school freshman, made the honor roll,
and played quarterback and receiver on the football team.

Eric Garner once held a seasonal job as a horticulturalist
with the New York City Parks Department.

Roxsana Hernández was seeking asylum,
hoping to open a beauty salon to support her family Honduras.

Thomas McNichols worked at a factory in Dayton, Ohio.
He had four children. Friends called him "TeeJay."

Da'Juan Brown loved making TikToks with friends,
and he played point guard on his basketball team.

Carmen Schentrup planned to study medicine in college.
She wanted to find a cure for ALS.

Jose Nieves loved dogs. He worked in construction and security.

10: of the 17 deadliest mass shootings since 2012, the number that involved AR-15 semiautomatic rifles. **1**: of every 20 U.S. adults, the number who own at least one AR-15. **13.7 million**: number of AR-15s manufactured between the Sandy Hook Elementary School shooting and the end of 2020. **$11 billion**: revenue from sales of AR-15s between the Sandy Hook Elementary School shooting and the end of 2020. **1.2**: of all guns produced in 1990, the percentage that were AR-15s. **23.4**: of all guns produced in 2020, the percentage that were AR-15s. **8.5 million**: estimated number of AR-15s in circulation when the federal assault weapons ban expired in 2004. **19.8 million**: estimated number of AR-15s in circulation by 2020.

Police use excessive force because they *can.* □ Police are *rewarded* for using force. □ Law enforcement is *enforcement.*

Jose Ocampo was 33, and had been born in Honduras.

Amber Lynn Costello was 27, and had been married twice.
She made her living as a sex worker.

Lucas Eibel was an FFA member,
and volunteered at his local animal shelter.

Mah-hi-vist Goodblanket was 18, liked basketball,
and had graduated from high school a year early.

Ousmane Zongo immigrated to the U.S. from Burkina Faso,
and worked repairing furniture and musical instruments.

Allison Wyatt often helped her mother garden.
She liked reading and math and art.

Brian Bluhm was a Detroit Tigers fan,
and often posted on the Motownsports.com message board.

Jerry Wright grew up in Miami, and worked
first at Universal Orlando, then at Walt Disney World.

Tara McNulty, a single mother,
worked bartending shifts in addition to her desk job.

Nathaniel Pickett II went by "Nate," and lived alone in a motel.

685,724: number of times NYPD officers stopped and interrogated people in 2011. **87**: percent of those stopped who were Black or Latino. **90**: percent of those stopped who neither arrested nor charged. **55.7**: percent of those stopped who were frisked. **1.9**: of frisks conducted by NYPD officers in 2011, percentage in which a gun was found. **160,851**: number of NYPD stops in 2003. **685,724**: number of NYPD stops in 2011. **266**: number of stops made for every gun recovered in 2003. **3,000**: number of stops made for every gun recovered in 2011.

We assign *persons* to *roles* in the morality play we make of violence. □ The go-to rationale for police violence: cultural myth. □ As long as the weaponed hero is a story *type*, we'll have weaponed-hero stories.

John Kohler had two teenage children, a son and a daughter.

Jose Flores Jr. loved baseball and video games.
He wanted to be a police officer when he grew up.

Javier Ambler II served in the U.S. Army, as his father had.
He worked as a rural postal carrier and an independent caterer.

Mesha Caldwell was a 41-year-old trans woman
who worked as a hair and makeup artist.

José Antonio Elena Rodríguez liked cloudy days,
chocolate cookies, and spending time with his sisters.

Brian Fraser was a father of four.
He liked boating, hunting, fishing, and snowboarding.

Teresa Sanchez had retired from her career as a biology teacher.
To her family, she was known as Tía. She was 82.

My My Nhan had emigrated from Vietnam to the U.S.
She took ballroom dancing lessons for years.

Pearlie Golden was known as "Miss Sully."
She was 93, and lived in Hearne, Texas.

Quindell Lee had two brothers, and lived in Dallas. He was 7.

2: of the 15 on-duty officers killed in police-on-police shootings (shootings in which police officers mistook other officers for crime perpetrators and fatally shot them) over a 29-year period, the number who were Black. **1**: of those 15 on-duty officers, the number who were Hispanic. **12**: of those 15 on-duty officers, the number who were white. **8**: of the 10 off-duty officers killed in police-on-police shootings over the same period, the number who were Black. **1**: of those 10 off-duty officers, the number who were Hispanic. **1**: of those 10 off-duty officers, the number who were white.

Stored or not, having a gun in the home increases risk of homicide and suicide. □ Who most gun owners most fear suggests who is more endangered by more gun carrying. □ Guns sound a racial dog whistle.

Tariq Morris had a brother and a sister. He was 3 months old.

Anthony Lowe Jr. used a wheelchair for mobility
after both his legs were amputated.

Jasmine Mack lived in D.C., and went by "Star."
She was a trans woman, 36.

Robert Williams had worked as a special projects coordinator
in his city's public utilities department for 41 years.

Derrick Fudge and his only child, a son,
enjoyed fishing together and playing cards.

Alex Schachter wanted to attend the University of Connecticut.
He played trombone and baritone in his school marching band.

Tyler Dunn liked to fish in the creek behind his family's house,
and he liked four-wheeling, dirt-biking, and sledding.

Roy Nelson Jr. was 42, and had a wife and son.
He suffered from schizophrenia.

Antonio Zambrano-Montes was unemployed and unhoused
since falling off a ladder at work and breaking both wrists.

Denali Berries Stuckey was a 29-year-old trans woman.

65: in 1989, the percentage of Americans who favored stricter gun control laws. **28**: in 1989, the percentage of Americans who opposed stricter gun control laws. **50**: in 2015, the percentage of Americans who favored stricter gun control laws. **50**: in 2015, the percentage of Americans who opposed stricter gun control laws.

"A day doesn't go by that you don't see violence." □ Hard to conceal targeted killings that the targeted can expose. □ Hard to keep guns out of minors' hands, with so many guns ready to hand.

Noel Aguilar was 23, lived in Long Beach, and had a daughter.

Marvin Booker lived unhoused in Denver.
He worked as a street preacher.

Emilie Parker liked to draw and paint.
Her mother was teaching her Portuguese.

Cashay Henderson also went by the name Gemini Shanti.
She loved makeup, fashion, hip hop, and restaurants.

Carrie Barnette entered her basset hound, Lucy,
in a calendar contest to raise money for a local animal shelter.

Sheneque Proctor had recently graduated from high school,
and also recently given birth to her first child.

Peggy Warden lived on the family farm
that had been established by her grandparents.

Carlos Alcis worked at a department store as a stockman.
He had eight children.

Mario Woods had once, as a child, given his new winter coat
to a schoolmate who didn't have a coat.

MaKayla Walker had 11 siblings. She was 24.

2: of the 11 times that Demaris Turner was shot by a Lauderhill, Florida police officer, the number that were to his head. **2**: number of times David Kassick was shot in the back by a police officer while lying face down, unarmed. **4**: of the 23 bullets fired by police officers at Tyisha Miller, the number that hit her in the head.

Long histories of violence develop inertia that can be slowed only by real counterforce. □ "Breaking with the violent past demands paying intimate attention to its often-erased figures." □ Until killing *does* stop, resistance can't.

Sarah Gonzalez was 19, and lived in Tulsa.

Kyam Livingston worked as a security guard,
and had a son who wanted to learn to cook like her.

Kate Armand was 24, and had two children.
She worked as a med tech at an Oregon senior living center.

Royal Poetical Starz worked as a masseuse and singer,
and was a graduate of Florida Career College Vocational School.

Catherine Hubbard loved animals of all kinds, including pets,
stuffed animals, and worms and frogs she found in her yard.

Daunte Wright and his fiancée had a 1-year-old son.
He was 20, and liked to play basketball.

John Phippen had gone to the L.A. Trade College,
and ran his own home remodeling company.

Julio Joseph Bald Eagle planned to attend the University of Utah.
He was 19, and had one child.

Makenna Elrod loved to write notes to her family
and leave them in hidden places to be found later.

Rocio Lissette Vasquez was 46, and lived in East Los Angeles.

>$7 billion: the monetary value of surplus military equipment transferred to police departments through the 1033 program in its first 20 years. **12,440**: as of 2014, additional assaults on police officers each year due to increased police militarization. **2,653**: as of 2014, additional injuries to police officers each year due to increased police militarization. **0.76 per million inhabitants**: increase in the rate of killings by the police for every dollar spent on militarization.

Gun carriers assign themselves a citizenship status upgrade. □ Gun owners aren't the only citizens with rights. □ Guns influence how frequently we *kill* one another, yes, but also how we *see* one another.

Stephen Young was 41, and living unhoused in Mesa, Arizona.

Tyianna Alexander loved to dance,
and sometimes used the moniker Barbie the Dance Diva.

Josephine Gay liked to play with her Barbie dolls,
and swim, swing, and be with her sisters.

Dominique Franklin Jr. had been named a deacon in his church
at age 9, and preached his first sermon at age 10.

Michelle Vo worked as an insurance agent.
Her hobbies included golf, paddle boarding, and surfing.

Antonio Guzman Lopez had a son and a stepdaughter,
and lived in San Diego.

Annabell Rodriguez was ten. Her favorite color was blue,
especially when it was on butterflies' wings.

Jamal Rollins was 21, and lived in Miami.
He was a new father, and an avid dirtbiker.

Loreal Tsingine was placed in Child Protective Services
after her father's death when she was 10.

Christian Siquieros was 25, and lived in Montclair, California.

11: percentage of violent crimes that take place at a store, restaurant, or office. **14**: percentage of violent crimes that take place at a school or college. **21**: percentage of violent crimes that take place by a road or highway. **35**: percentage of violent crimes that take place in a home or residence. **103**: number of homicides of persons ages 5 through 19 outside of school, for every one homicide in school.

Brutal enforcement has always and everywhere invited resistance. □ Police use of deadly force is systemic, but is not homogeneous. □ The higher the Social Vulnerability Index, the more often police use deadly force.

Julian Cox was 41, and lived in Mesa, Arizona.

Whispering Wind Bear Spirit loved cooking and Skor chocolate bars,
wrote poetry and could play several instruments.

Daniel Barden's teachers buddied him with a special needs student
because he had already befriended her.

Jack Beaton had played football in high school.
He worked for a roofing company.

Xavier Lopez loved dancing to Colombian songs,
and his favorite school subject was art.

Timothy Dawkins-El worked as an electrician,
and was studying to become an ordained minister.

Antash'a English was a regular performer at a local club,
and had won many pageants.

Osmar Hernandez worked as an agricultural laborer.
He was born in El Salvador, and lived in Salinas, California.

Shayla Martin worked for twenty-five years
as a makeup artist at Macy's.

Derrick Scott was 41, and lived in Oklahoma City.

15: maximum number of seconds of Taser shocks to which any person should be subjected, according to the Taser manual. **74**: number of seconds of Taser shocks to which Chance Ross was subjected by police officers within less than one hour. **2**: number of times officers Tasered Ross using the "probe" mode. **8**: number of times officers Tasered Ross using the "drive-stun" mode. **17**: number of minutes Ross lay immobile and unclothed on the floor of a prison cell before officers called EMTs to the scene. **0**: attempts at CPR performed by the officers. **0**: charges filed against the officers involved.

The heroic loner frontier gunfighter is as real as SpongeBob or Santa Claus. □ Good guys killing off bad guys one by one won't get the job of stopping evil done. □ Owning a gun doesn't make you a good guy or a bad guy, just more likely to die.

Sergio Navas, a 35-year-old father of three, lived in L.A.

Dawn Hochsprung was studying for a Ph.D.
and raising two daughters and three stepdaughters.

Victor Link worked in financial services.
He enjoyed music, especially going to concerts with his fiancée.

Layla Salazar liked to swim in the river with her parents.
On her fourth-grade field day, she won six first-place ribbons.

Wendell Allen was working for Richard's Disposal,
a garbage removal company. He was 20 years old.

Chavis Carter wanted to be a veterinarian.
He liked shopping for sneakers and playing basketball.

Savannah Graziano enjoyed camping, skateboarding,
playing video games, and playing with her dog Aurora.

Pooh Johnson was also known as "Titanizer Mua,"
her brand for her glamour-centered make-up artist business.

Frank Shephard III was 41, and went by "Trey."
He worked as a barber, and had three children.

Ricky Cobb II was 33, and the father of five children.

2.6: how many times higher the non-firearm homicide rate is in the U.S. than in other high-income countries. **24.9**: how many times higher the firearm homicide rate is in the U.S. than in other high-income countries. **7.5**: in 2003, how many times higher the overall firearm death rate was in the U.S. than in other high-income countries. **11.4**: in 2015, how many times higher the overall firearm death rate was in the U.S. than in other high-income countries. **13.5**: how many times higher the firearm homicide rate is in low-gun U.S. states than in other high-income countries. **36**: how many times higher the firearm homicide rate is in high-gun U.S. states than in other high-income countries.

Militarization nudges police decision-making in the direction of violence. □ "[P]olice militarization *decreases* police safety." □ Routine use of militarized policing does not increase safety but does decrease trust.

Caroline Ireland was 8 months old, and had two older brothers.

Lauren Rousseau called her boyfriend "Worker Bee,"
and he called her "Busy Bee."

Neysa Tonks was a single mother of three sons,
and enjoyed traveling with them.

Tamir Rice liked soccer, football, and basketball.
He liked to draw, and was active in the art program at his school.

Maranda Mathis loved unicorns and mermaids,
and her favorite color was purple.

Bennie Edwards was 60, and lived with bipolar schizophrenia.
He lived unhoused, and sold flowers.

Danielle Keyes enjoyed listening to music,
and spending time with her three children.

Kirk Mattson was a member of Boilermakers Union Local 647.
He loved boating, fishing, hunting, and gardening.

Jaylow McGlory was a 29-year-old trans woman.
She had one sister and one brother.

Brandon Jones was 18, lived in Cleveland, and had seven siblings.

953,613: number of NCIS Background checks performed during the week of 17-23 December 2012, the week after the shooting at Sandy Hook Elementary School. **50**: percentage higher that number is than the number of the second highest week that had previously been recorded. **43**: in sales by Smith and Wesson, percentage rise in the fiscal year ending after the Sandy Hook shooting over the previous year. **76**: percent increase in gun sale revenue of Walmart during the first six months of 2013. **3**: limit placed on number of boxes of ammunition per individual purchase at Walmart when it rationed ammunition sales in February 2013 due to limited supply.

Cool violence does its work insidiously. □ Invisible violence exceeds visible violence. □ "Acceptable 'defensive' violence is the cultural condition for spectacular aggressive violence."

Jason Ireland was 4 years old, and in preschool.

Tracy Single loved Louisiana bounce music,
and wanted to become a part of Houston's rap music scene.

Rachel D'Avino sometimes took her dog Diezel with her
when she met with special needs children in her work.

Steve Berger worked as a financial planner, and loved to fish.
He was the father of three children.

Timothy Stansbury worked at McDonald's.
He was working on a documentary film about gun violence.

Rojelio Torres went by "Rojer." He had three siblings,
and loved Pokémon, board games, Lotería, and playing football.

Jaquarrius Holland was unemployed and housing insecure.
She loved the R&B singer K. Michelle.

Lewis DeWayne Green was 44,
and lived in Springfield, Missouri his entire life.

Briseis Aljumaily went by "Bri."
She was a 15-year-old high school freshman with a 4.0 GPA.

John Paul Quintero was 23, and lived in Wichita, Kansas.

57: in 1989, the percentage of Americans who considered it more important to control gun ownership than to protect the right to own guns. **34**: the percentage who considered it more important to protect the right to own guns than to control gun ownership. **2001**: year in which the NRA passed the AARP as the most powerful Washington lobby. **$2 million**: expenditures of Mayors Against Illegal Guns in 2010. **$277 million**: expenditures of the NRA and its affiliates in 2010. **50**: in 2015, the percentage of Americans who considered it more important to control gun ownership than to protect the right to own guns. **47**: the percentage who considered it more important to protect the right to own guns than to control gun ownership.

Gun owners are a varied group, but they're a *group*. □ Gun owners are not homogeneous, and gun culture is not uniform. □ There is queer gun ownership, too.

Billy Collins was 56, and had one son and three daughters.

Troy Boyd had been a Boy Scout as a child,
and loved the outdoors, especially fishing, hunting, and gardening.

Caroline Previdi liked to color and draw,
and she loved to twirl, sing, and dance.

Calla Medig worked as a bartender and server
at a restaurant in Edmonton, Alberta.

Eva Mireles worked as a fourth-grade teacher,
and had taught in the same school district for 17 years.

Muhammad Abdul Muhaymin was Muslim,
and had three older sisters. He was 43.

Tyre King was in his STEM Academy's young scholars program.
He played football, hockey, and soccer and did gymnastics.

Jon Stoffel worked as a journeyman carpenter.
He liked the outdoors, especially fishing.

Gabriella Aljumaily was 5 years old, and had Down Syndrome.
She could sing "Jesus Loves Me" and "Father Abraham."

Salome Rodriguez Jr. was 23, and lived in Ontario, California.

3: On average, the number of U.S. citizens fatally shot by police officers per day. **50**: of the fifty U.S. states, the number in which in 2015 there was at least one death caused by police. **8-10**: of all homicides in the U.S., the percentage perpetrated by police. **1/3**: of all American homicide victims killed by people they don't know, the approximate proportion killed by police.

"Racial/ethnic disparities in police violence and brutality exceed what is covered by the media." □ "Police homicide risk is higher than suggested by official data." □ The policed trust the police less with each shooting.

Andy Lopez was 13, and the second child of an immigrant family.

Ben Wheeler wanted to be an architect, a paleontologist,
and a lighthouse keeper, all at once.

George Floyd had once worked as an automotive customizer
and been part of the hip hop group Screwed Up Click.

Bill Wolfe Jr. loved outdoor activities:
hunting, fishing, boating, camping, gardening, and jogging.

Li Lan Li was 63, a mother and grandmother.
She enjoyed taking ballroom dancing lessons.

April Ireland had attended the cosmetology program
at her local community college in North Carolina.

Michael Sabbie was a 35-year-old stay-at-home dad.
He and his wife had four children.

Olivia Stoffel liked to write notes and stories,
and wanted to be a writer when she grew up.

Audrie Quinn Cooper-Fortner was 9.
She enjoyed being outside and loved rocks, seashells and sticks.

Phillip White lived in Vineland, New Jersey, and had two children.

1: in the 2012 election cycle, the percentage of political advertisements making reference to guns. **3.4**: in the 2014 election cycle, the percentage of political advertisements making reference to guns. **6.2**: in the 2016 election cycle, the percentage of political advertisements making reference to guns. **11.5**: in the 2018 election cycle, the percentage of political advertisements making reference to guns.

E pluribus unum. The one story of guns is the many stories. □ *The shooter's mental illness caused the shooting*: convenient story, deadly lie. □ Our *stories* secure our violent *policies*, or inhibit them.

Ivy Webster was 14. She played softball and loved animals.

Chase Kowalski was a Cub Scout. He liked running,
and won his age group in the first triathlon he entered.

Denise Cohen had two sons, both in their thirties.
She was a country music fan, and loved to attend concerts.

Leonardo Campos and his wife had lived in El Paso for ten years,
and he had recently returned to college to finish his degree.

Bryson Ireland was his 4-year-old brother's "little shadow,"
and slept next to him every night.

Jamie Lee Wounded Arrow worked as a customer service agent.
She loved spending time at the library.

Adam Bentdahl worked at a Mediterranean restaurant,
and loved to watch campy horror movies with his sister.

Trayvon Martin wanted to fly or repair airplanes.
He washed cars, babysat, and cut grass to earn his own money.

Evelyn Rose Cooper-Fortner was "Evie" to her family.
She liked to go outside and blow bubbles.

Tiara Banks was a 24-year-old trans woman who lived in Chicago.

4: for every time a gun in the household is used for self-defense or justifiable reasons, the number of unintentional shootings. **7**: for every time a gun in the household is used for self-defense or justifiable reasons, the number of criminal assaults. **11**: for every time a gun in the household is used for self-defense or justifiable reasons, the number of homicides.

Opportunities for harmful gun use will always exceed opportunities for socially beneficial use. □ If I need a gun to be safe, having a gun won't make me safe. □ If taking up arms is the answer, what's the question?

Gavin Haight was 4, and loved to give and get tickles.

Jacqueline Salyers was a Puyallup tribal member, 32 years old.
She was the mother of four children, pregnant with her fifth.

Dylan Hockley liked plain spaghetti with garlic bread,
and his favorite color was purple.

Melissa Ramirez had a degree in business administration,
and had just received a promotion at her employer.

Juan Velazquez was born in the Mexican state of Zacatecas,
but became a U.S. citizen. He was 77.

Michael Barrera was 30.
He had one daughter, and another on the way.

Breonna Taylor worked as an ER medical technician.
She liked muscle cars.

John Leehey's passions included the blues, golf, and poker,
and playing guitar and harmonica.

Tausha Haight was active in her church,
and enjoyed spending time with her five children.

Muhlaysia Booker was a 23-year-old trans woman from South Dallas.

8: number of rounds fired by an Arvada, Colorado police officer at unarmed, five-foot-tall, 7-months pregnant Destinee Thompson. **8**: of the 10 bullets from a Border Patrol agent's gun that hit José Antonio Elena Rodríguez, the number that hit him in the back. **9**: of the 16 shots fired by a police officer at Laquan McDonald, the number that hit his back.

"No duty to retreat" changes violence from last resort to point of pride. □ "Stand your ground" kills more adults, and kills more kids. □ Tell me again what makes it *yours*, the ground you're standing your ground on.

Joseph Slater was 28, and had one son and one daughter.

Austin Cloyd had worked four summers with a service project
that helped repair homes in rural Appalachia.

David Werblow was an entrepreneur,
and an advocate of the Seeds of Peace Organization.

Denise Burditus worked as a bank teller.
She liked to RV with her husband and their grandchildren.

Hector Arreola was born into a military family,
and had lived in numerous places in his childhood and youth.

Jorge Calvillo was the general manager
for a dairy import export cross border business.

Andrew Finch was passionate about drawing,
and was studying to be a tattoo artist.

Tonya Clark was a single mother with a 13-year-old son.
She loved live music and Red Bull with vodka.

Macie Haight was the oldest of 5,
and helped care for her younger siblings.

Alexus Braxton lived in Miami and worked as a hairstylist.

4: murder rate (number of persons murdered per 100,00) that the U.S. never got *down* to for even a single year at any point between 1900 and 2006. **3**: murder rate that Australia, Canada, and England never got *up* to for even a single year at any point between 1900 and 2006. **>7**: the average murder rate over the period 1900-2006 in the U.S. **<2**: the average murder rate over the period 1900-2006 in Australia, Canada, and England.

State violence is not the only possible means of addressing and minimizing citizen violence. □ "[I]ntergenerational transmission of violence is not inevitable." □ "We are not bound to this cycle of violence and inaction."

Alonzo Bagley was a longtime resident of Shreveport, Louisiana.

Julia Pryde was researching water quality, working on
a masters degree in biological systems engineering.

Derrick Taylor worked as a corrections officer,
and was in charge of inmates who volunteer to fight forest fires.

Eleanor Bumpurs was four months behind in her rent,
but had been denied city HRA emergency rent funds.

Gloria Irma Márquez worked as a health care assistant
for elderly patients.

Michael Lembhard went by "Jones." He was 22.
He had developed lead poisoning during childhood.

Brooklyn Deshuna lived in Shreveport, Louisiana,
and was studying cosmetology at her local community college.

Glen Sprowl described himself as a "contraptionist,"
someone who could build or make anything.

Briley Haight loved to read,
and wanted to be a librarian so she could read all day.

DaJuan Graham had two children, and went by "PeeWee."

920,000: approximate number of National Instant Criminal Background Check System (NICS) background checks per month in 1999. **1,200,000**: approximate number of NICS background checks per month in 2009. **2,100,000**: approximate number of NICS background checks per month in 2018. **11**: percentage increase in handgun carry permit application rates after high-profile mass shootings.

Police use of excessive force makes Black men into involuntary martyrs. □ Crime is not the only factor that shapes police use of fatal force. □ Racial bias in police shootings does not track crime rate, but does track financial inequality.

Amaree'ya Henderson worked making DoorDash deliveries.

Kevin Granata was a professor who taught biomechanics
and researched movement dynamics in cerebral palsy.

Sandy Casey lived in southern California,
and had worked as a special education teacher for nine years.

Alexander Gerhard Hoffman had been stationed at Fort Bliss
during service in the German Air Force.

Luis Góngora Pat was living unhoused in San Francisco.
He was 45. His family nickname was "Sapo."

Ariella Bell's family called her "Ella." She was 18 months old,
and lived with her mother in Franklin, New Hampshire.

Timothy Owens was an Army Sergeant,
a heavy vehicle driver who had served in both Kuwait and Iraq.

Ammon Haight loved to build Legos
and had just finished constructing the Titanic Lego kit.

Che Taylor had a history of felony convictions,
and had been incarcerated. He was 47.

Yenitza Arroyo Torres was 44, and had a daughter and two sons.

6.75: average number of children and teens killed by guns per day in 2013. **2**: number of children killed or wounded by a bullet in the U.S. every hour. **350**: average number of children per year who unintentionally shoot themselves or someone else. **35**: of homes with children in the U.S., the percentage that also have firearms.

"Public health and prison abolition are interwoven projects." □ Our advanced society: walled and weaponed like the medievals. □ Border Patrol is out of bounds.

Darryl Tyree Williams was 32, and lived in Wendell, North Carolina.

Mary Read played clarinet in her university's concert band.
She liked to wear flip-flops, even in cold weather.

Lisa Patterson and her husband of thirty years
operated a hardwood flooring company.

Ivan Filiberto Manzano was born in Ciudad Juárez.
He and his wife had two children.

Amia Tyrae Berryman was a 28-year-old trans woman.
She was employed as a sex worker.

Carlos Lazaney-Rodriguez was a Staff Sergeant
whose Army service included three deployments to Iraq.

Sienna Haight loved to take pictures with her camera
and apply funny filters to them. She was 7 years old.

Gwen Grimmette once made the space under the stairwell
in her small apartment into a playroom for her daughter.

Jeremy Lett worked in an auto detailing shop,
and was a volunteer coach for his step-son's T-ball team.

Jordan Davis was a 17-year-old high school student.

56.6: of firearm deaths in 2018 among those aged 15 to 24 years, the percentage that were homicides. **91.2**: of firearm deaths in 2018 among those older than 65 years, the percentage that were suicides. **48,830**: in 2021, the total number of gun deaths in the U.S. **26,328**: of those deaths, the number that were suicides. **54**: percentage that represents.

"Violence is a form of entitlement." □ White privilege can be secured only by a police state. □ White male anger wants *political*, not *therapeutic*, remedy.

Julius Hamilton enjoyed fishing, and was good at fixing cars.

Serenity Hollis worked at a corporate chicken farm,
and had recently moved into her first apartment.

Matthew Gwaltney was studying environmental engineering,
completing a masters thesis on methods of predicting droughts.

Kurt Von Tillow owned a trucking company.
He and his wife loved to golf.

Luis Alfonzo Juarez was 90, and still in such good health
that he had recently painted the eaves of his house.

Korryn Gaines was a 23-year-old hairstylist
and the mother of two young children.

Daniel Ferguson was a Sergeant First Class whose Army service
had included deployments to Iraq, Afghanistan, and Kuwait.

Gail Earl was the youngest of seven children,
and she and her husband had seven children. She was 78.

Danton Munoz had an older sister. His nickname was "Mister."
He was nearing his second birthday.

Shakiie Peters was a performance artist and community organizer.

101,970: in the six years 2005-2010, number of people of all nationalities, worldwide, killed by terrorist attacks. **187,426**: in the six years 2005-2010, number of people killed by guns in the U.S.

Better state laws, fewer gun deaths. □ Accurate records and effective laws: a bonded pair. □ Different polities, different policies.

Candace Towns lived in Macon, Georgia, and had five siblings.

Reema Samaha was studying Tae Kwon Do.
She was in the contemporary dance ensemble at her university.

Laquan McDonald was taken into protective custody at age 3,
and had three psychiatric hospitalizations by 13.

Thomas Day Jr. coached little league baseball,
and he had a Pittsburgh Steelers tattoo on his leg.

Ashley Atwell was 38, and lived in Tulsa.
She was a stay at home mother of four children.

Jack Keewatinawin was 21, and had schizophrenia.
He was physically large, approximately 300 pounds.

Michael Cahill was a civilian employee at Fort Hood,
where he worked as a physician assistant.

Miguel Flores and Kelly Baltazar had recently married.
He was 44 and she was 42. They lived in Woodbridge, Virginia.

Jor'Dell Da'Shawn Richardson was 14,
and had just completed eighth grade in Aurora, Colorado.

Keri Washington went by "Bobo," and lived in Clearwater, Florida.

5: multiplier by which access to a firearm increases the risk of intimate partner homicide. **<20**: of intimate partner homicides, the percentage of persons killed who were identified as husband, common-law husband, ex-husband, or boyfriend. **>80**: of intimate partner homicides, the percentage of persons killed who were identified as wife, common-law wife, ex-wife, or girlfriend.

If only violence *were* confined to aberrant behavior by deviant individuals. □ Abnormal violence won't stop until we change what is normal. □ We don't have to change human nature, to reduce the number of gun deaths.

Gustav Montag immigrated to the U.S. from Cold War Hungary.

Alton Sterling had five children.
He liked to cook for everyone at the shelter where he lived.

Emily Hilscher loved horses,
and rode on her university equestrian team.

Erick Silva worked as a security guard,
and wanted one day to work for the Las Vegas PD.

Annaway Mackey lived in Tulsa.
She was 20, and a recent high school graduate.

Jamarion Robinson sat out one year of college
to help support the family when his mother was laid off.

Eduardo Caraveo was a Major in the U.S. Army,
and was preparing for deployment to Iraq.

Karrie Sotelo was a K-Pop fan,
and liked to memorize dance routines to her favorite songs.

Shai Vanderpump worked at a fashion retailer and a nursing facility.
She wanted to become a personal stylist.

Hector Morejon had applied for certification as a forklift driver.

3.8: for the five-year period 1976-1980, the ratio of killings by police to killings of police.
7.8: for the five-year period 2008-2012, the ratio of killings by police to killings of police.

Agreement that the gun is an icon exacerbates disagreement over what it is an icon *of.* □ As pacifiers console, so guns. □ To sell guns, flatter gun buyers.

Kawaski Trawick worked as a personal trainer and dancer.

Asia Jynaé Foster often did volunteer community activist work
finding homeless youth who needed HIV and STD testing.

Waleed Shaalan was working on his Ph.D. in civil engineering.
He was married, and the father of a young child.

Christiana Duarte went by "Chrissy,"
and worked for the Los Angeles Kings hockey team.

Richard Nettleton and his wife enjoyed day trips,
and walking through botanical gardens.

John T. Williams was a seventh generation Nitinaht carver
of the Nuu-chah-nulth First Nations.

Justin DeCrow and his wife had been high school sweethearts.
They had a teenage daughter.

Richard Corrales had come to the U.S. from Peru,
and loved to cook Peruvian food for family and friends.

Ahtalia Crayton had three sons and two daughters.
She had served in the U.S. Army as a heavy equipment mechanic.

Warren Bowman worked maintenance for an apartment complex.

76: of female victims of murder and nonnegligent manslaughter in 2021, the percentage who were killed by someone known to the victim. **56**: of male victims of murder and nonnegligent manslaughter in 2021, the percentage who were killed by someone known to the victim.

To protect whom, and serve whom? □ To protect how, and serve how? □ The streets are not a war zone from which the police secure us.

Laura Ann Carleton owned and operated a clothing store.

Demixica Dunnette Coleman-Gipson went by "Misha."
She and her two daughters loved to cook and dance together.

Jarrett Lane was valedictorian of his high school class,
and had been on the tennis, football, basketball, and track teams.

Kelsey Meadows worked as a substitute teacher
in the same high school from which she had graduated.

Joshua Hardy had been named Dennis Hoskins at birth,
but had changed his name to honor his grandfather.

Bianca "Muffin" Bankz grew up in foster care
and did not have a relationship with her biological family.

John Gaffaney was an avid baseball card collector
who liked to read military novels and ride his Harley.

Bernadette Steadman worked as a salesperson at JCPenney
for 34 years until her retirement.

Kasim Crayton was an 18-year-old high school student,
already the co-owner and co-founder of a business.

William Chapman wrote poetry, and loved to read. He was 18.

3.1: the number of times more likely it is for a Native American than for a white American to be killed by police. **515**: number of words devoted in the *Washington Post* and *New York Times* to the killing of Suquamish tribal member Daniel Covarrubias by police. **0**: number of words devoted in the *Washington Post* and *New York Times* to the other twenty-eight police killings of Native Americans during the period May 2014 – October 2015.

"Most mass shootings are related to domestic violence." □ More mass shootings than not include the killing of a family member of the perpetrator. □ In intimate partner homicides, the intimate partner often is not the only person killed.

Keke Collier had two sisters and a brother. She loved to dance.

Cindy Clouse had two daughters,
and was also raising chickens, 2 goats, a pig, and dogs.

Leslie Sherman liked to play basketball,
and was training for a marathon.

Stacee Etcheber loved horses and water sports,
and hiking and snow skiing in Tahoe.

Shannan Gilbert grew up in foster care,
and graduated from high school at age 16.

Jonathan Ferrell lived in Charlotte, North Carolina with his fiancée,
and worked at Best Buy.

Frederick Greene was from Mountain City, Tennessee,
and had worked for a lumber and truss company there.

Lisa Steadman enjoyed music, lighthouses, and knitting.
She had recently read through the entire Bible.

Nyla Crayton was a 16-year-old high school student
who loved drawing and crafts.

Derek Cruice was a fan of live-action role playing games.

10: number of times Osmar Hernandez was shot by two police officers. **11**: of the 13 shots fired at Ernest Duenez Jr., the number that struck him. **14**: of the 48 bullets fired by three police officers at Alex Nieto, the number that struck him.

Good guys with guns rush in where institutions failed to hold. □ Guns don't kill people, gun culture kills people. □ "People without guns *injure* people; guns *kill* them."

TeeTee Dangerfield had just bought her own house.

Lauren McCain was a member of the Choctaw Nation.
She liked science fiction movies but disliked country music.

Jordyn Rivera was majoring in health care management,
and had recently turned 21.

Melissa Barthelemy grew up in upstate New York.
She wanted to own and operate a salon.

Julian Lewis worked as a carpenter, and volunteered
to do work for senior citizens and a local church.

Autumn Hagger played percussion in her school band,
and was on the cheer team.

Jason Hunt joined the Army immediately out of high school,
and re-enlisted after a first two-year assignment.

Matthew Steadman shared a birthday with one of his aunts,
and always greeted her with, "Hi, my twin!"

Nasir Crayton was a 10-year-old elementary school student.
His family nicknamed him "Fat Fat" and "Fats."

Brendon Glenn went by "Dizzle," and had a black lab named Dozer.

1,189: number of persons killed by police in 2017. **147**: of those, the number who were unarmed.

"Violence is not generated by isolated individuals but by an entire emotional attention space." □ Thinking about violence poses conceptual challenges *and* emotional challenges. □ Violence reifies the fraudulence of power and the partiality of understanding.

Chyna Gibson was a touring stage performer as "The Dancing Doll."

Mackenzie Hagger wanted to be a police officer
and have a police dog when she grew up.

Daniel O'Neil played piano and guitar, and wrote songs.
He liked backpacking and skateboarding.

Keri Galvan had three children,
and had worked for ten years as a server at a steakhouse.

Lucero Alcaraz was 19, and loved to draw.
She was studying to be a pediatric nurse.

Layleen Xtravaganza Cubilette-Polanco was a trans woman
who was active in New York City's ballroom scene.

Yvette Smith was a high school graduate,
and had worked for the State of Texas.

Amy Krueger enjoyed spending time with family and friends,
shooting pool, playing sheepshead, and playing softball.

Mary Beth Bergum played soccer, softball, and basketball,
and had recently begun playing Gaelic football.

Deven Guilford wanted to become a welder or a stock broker.

76.5: percentage of gun owners who indicate that "protection" is a major reason for their gun ownership. **72**: percentage of persons who do not own guns who indicate that "for protection" would be a major reason they would consider owning a gun in the future. **2011**: year in which, in *Guns* magazine, advertising space devoted to personal protection/self-/home and family defense and concealed carry themes exceeded advertising space devoted to themes of hunting and sports/recreation.

"The sexualization of guns arms deeper desires." □ Gun use has been gendered and racialized since its origins, and continues to be. □ After one masculinity is lost, guns can help find another to substitute for it.

Sheldon Haleck served 15 years in the Hawai'i Air National Guard.

Queasha Hardy worked for some time at Popeye's,
but had recently opened her own hair salon.

Juan Ortiz was born in Puerto Rico, and played the timbal
in his family music group, and his church choir.

Dana Gardner had worked for San Bernardino County
for 26 years, most recently as Deputy Recorder.

Lawrence Levine was 67.
He had a masters in creative writing, and wrote novels.

Steven Eugene Washington had autism and learning disabilities,
but was taking classes at a community college.

Aaron Nemelka came from a Mormon family,
but joined the Army rather than going on a mission.

Jeremy McDole went by "Bam Bam," and had used a wheelchair
since being shot in the back when he was 18.

Nancy Bergum owned and operated Tape Group USA,
a provider of adhesive liners and products.

Angelina Harrison wanted to become a lawyer or cosmetologist.

4 million: the population of the state of Oklahoma. **3.9 million**: the number of people on probation in the U.S. **70 million**: approximate number of U.S. citizens with criminal records. **70 million**: approximate number of U.S. citizens with four-year college degrees. **37 million**: in the 2021 census, the entire population of Canada.

Police threaten with what they are threatened with. □ Guns are used to *kill* intimate partners, but also to *threaten* and *intimidate* them. □ The more effective the tool for inflicting harm, the more harm inflicted.

José Mendez had 8 siblings. He was living in a rehab facility.

Sean Bell dreamed of becoming a professional baseball player,
and also studied acting.

Minal Panchal liked mint chocolate ice cream.
She was in graduate school, studying architecture.

Susan Smith loved country music.
She worked as an office manager at an elementary school.

Treven Anspach was in community college,
studying to become a fire fighter/paramedic like his father.

Melvin Pérez was a masonry worker, nearing his 31st birthday.
He and his wife had 3 children.

Michael Pearson played the guitar,
and enjoyed "horsing around" with his nieces and nephews.

Mark Bergum and his wife enjoyed hiking,
and had four grandchildren. He was 65.

Gigi Eugene-Pierce lived unhoused in Portland, Oregon,
where she was using and selling drugs.

Don Myrick played sax as a member of Earth, Wind, and Fire.

16 October 1860: the date on which B. Tyler Henry was granted US Patent #30,446 for a semiautomatic "magazine fire arm." **9,800**: Winchester Repeating Arms Company gun sales in 1875. **292,400**: Winchester Repeating Arms Company gun sales in 1914. **3,363,537**: number of boys aged ten to sixteen that in 1922 the Winchester Repeating Arms Company planned to reach with its "boy plan" for marketing. **225 million +**: number of firearms purchased by U.S. citizens during the twentieth century.

Punitive ≠ preventive. □ Detained by a police officer and tried in a court of law ≠ shot and killed by a police officer. □ Dangerous + accessible to children = dangerous to children.

Irvo Otieno was working to become a hip-hop artist.

Daniel Pérez loved his year-old basset hound, Shiloh.
He spoke Spanish, English, and Italian, and was learning French.

Angela Gomez, who went by "Angie," was a nursing student,
only recently graduated from high school.

Medgar Evers served in the U.S. Army in WWII,
and earned a B.B.A. from Alcorn A&M.

Rebecka Ann Carnes was as an avid hunter.
She had just started a new job at Walmart.

Mayra Pérez and some friends had once climbed "the Incline,"
a hiking trail that climbs 2,000 vertical feet in roughly a mile.

George Jackson was born in Chicago, but made summer visits
to his grandmother and aunt in rural southern Illinois.

Russell Seager was a psychiatrist and an Army Captain,
preparing for deployment to Afghanistan.

Carlos Mejia was born in El Salvador,
and lived in Salinas, California. He was 44.

Marcus-David Peters had 11 siblings, and taught high school biology.

16: number of times Hector Arreola told police he couldn't breathe before he died.

Violence can't just be skimmed off life's surface. □ Violence is complex; reducing it is not simple. □ The question is not whether intervention is needed but what interventions work.

Nina Pop was a lifelong resident of Sikeston, Missouri.

Elijah McClain worked as a massage therapist,
and taught himself to play both the guitar and the violin.

Erin Peterson was a fan of 50 Cent,
and was majoring in international studies at college.

Bailey Schweitzer was 20 years old.
She had a tattoo of her motto, "Saved by Grace."

Jason Johnson was in community college
studying to become an EMT. He was 33.

Joana Cruz owned her mobile home,
and was nearing her 54th birthday.

Francheska Velez was a Private in the U.S. Army.
She wrote poetry and loved dancing.

Duanna Johnson lived in Memphis,
but planned to return to Wisconsin to live with her mother.

Ta'Kiya Young was the mother of two sons, ages 6 and 3,
and was pregnant with a daughter.

Richard Ramirez lived in Billings, Montana, and had a son.

9: of the 10 U.S. cities with the highest gun death rate in 2020, the number that were also among the fifty most segregated cities in the U.S. that year.

It is not self-evident what connection holds between gun violence and gun rights. □ Gun rights and gun control share family resemblances. □ Between compromising rights and sanctioning harm, no simple choices.

Walter Wallace was newly married, and his wife was pregnant.

Kayla Moore, a Black trans woman,
had been named Xavier at birth, but identified as female.

Mike Pohle had a black belt in karate.
He was putting himself through school by tending bar.

Rocio Guillen was the daughter of immigrants,
and worked as a restaurant manager.

Quinn Cooper was physically large and strong:
he wore size 14 shoes, and could deadlift 400 pounds.

Jose Gutierrez loved the outdoors,
and liked to spend time with family and friends.

Juanita Warman was preparing for deployment to Iraq.
She was 55, and had two daughters and six grandchildren.

Russell Sharrer was a lifelong resident of Kennewick, Washington.
He was 54, and worked as a dishwasher.

Tamara Wilson-Seidle liked to wear white clothes
and a peach shawl to special church events.

Samuel Brightmon wanted to become a police officer.

251,000: estimated number of people who died from firearm injuries in 2016. **50.5**: percentage of those deaths that occurred in six countries: Brazil, U.S., Mexico, Colombia, Venezuela, and Guatemala. **<10**: percentage of the global population represented by those six countries.

Persons killed in shootings are not the only ones irreparably harmed by shootings. □ Lives ended by police violence are not the only lives harmed by police violence. □ Harm from police killings extends even to the health of pregnant women and unborn children.

Calvin Cains went by "Trey." He was 18, and lived in New Orleans.

Jessica Hernandez was 17, and the oldest of six siblings.
She took on odd jobs to save money to buy a puppy.

Oscar Aracena-Montero played piano and sang.
He and his partner had pet chihuahas.

Cameron Robinson worked as a legal records specialist,
and had recently received a promotion.

Kim Dietz and her husband worked as caretakers of a winery.
She loved mermaids and gardening and animals and the ocean.

Kalief Browder, the youngest of seven siblings,
passed the GED and enrolled in Bronx Community College.

Sandra Ibarra was born in Dallas,
but had lived in Colorado Springs for 26 years.

Kham Xiong was 23, and was an Army Private First Class,
preparing to deploy to Afghanistan.

Valeria Tachiquin Alvarado, who went by "Munique,"
was a 32-year-old mother of five who lived in San Diego.

Amadou Diallo was 23, and worked as a street peddler.

>300: number of companies in the United States that are in the business of small arms production.

If blaming you is wrong, I don't want to be right. □ Cultural anesthesia abets blame-mongering for violence. □ We're killing each other *because* we agreed to disagree.

Shelly Frey was 27. Her 2-year-old daughter had sickle-cell anemia.

Willie McCoy went by "Willie Bo,"
and rapped as part of the group FBG (Forever Black Gods).

Darryl Burt had recently been nominated
for the Board of a local young professionals organization.

Charleston Hartfield was an Army veteran
and a Sergeant 1st Class in the Nevada National Guard.

Nicholas Arnstad went by "Nick."
He had 2 sisters, and 5 nieces and nephews.

Mary Stanton was born in Kenya, and lived in Louisville.
She was the mother of two daughters.

Jose Ibarra lived his whole life in Colorado Springs, Colorado.
He liked to spend time with his family.

Carson Holmquist was 25. He and his wife had a son,
and were expecting another child.

Jasleen Kaur handled the books for her family's trucking business.
She and her husband had one daughter.

Anthony Hill was a 27-year-old Air Force vet and aspiring musician.

19: number of 6-deaths-or-more mass shootings in the U.S. in the decade preceding the Assault Weapons Ban. **155**: number of casualties from those shootings. **12**: number of 6-deaths-or-more mass shootings in the U.S. in the decade of the Assault Weapons Ban **89**: number of casualties from those shootings. **34**: number of 6-deaths-or-more mass shootings in the U.S. in the decade after the Assault Weapons Ban ended. **302**: number of casualties from those shootings.

"School shootings are very rare, but fear is very common." □ A school shooting is a *shooting*. □ Another child shot, another unprevented preventable death.

Michael Brown wanted to get a job as an HVAC technician.

Idriss Stelley was an avid chess player,
and for a year had studied massage.

Juan Chevez-Martinez worked as a housekeeping supervisor
for a resort staffing company.

Laura Shipp loved the L.A. Dodgers and country music.
She moved to Las Vegas after her son moved there.

John Swain had for the past three or four years
struggled with substance abuse and homelessness.

Samuel DuBose was 43 years old, and a father of 13.
He was the founder of a motorcycle club, Ruthless Riders.

Miriam Carey had an 18-month-old daughter,
and had been hospitalized for postpartum depression.

Randall Smith and his wife had three daughters.
He was a Petty Officer 2nd Class in the Navy.

Aroohi Dheri lived with her parents and extended family
in Merced, California. She was 8 months old.

Kiwane Carrington enjoyed coding and playing basketball.

<1%: increase in the S&P 500 on 25 March 2022, the day after the Uvalde school shooting. **>4%**: the increase in share price for Sturm, Ruger & Co. that day. **>6%**: the increase in share price that day for Smith & Wesson Brands. **>6%**: increase in the share price for both Sturm, Ruger & Co. and Smith & Wesson Brands on the day after the Orlando mass shooting, when broader market averages all decreased.

No single remedy for the many forms of illness, or the many forms of violence. □ No simple solution for the complex problems of gun violence. □ Violence, like any other public health disorder, invites intervention strategies.

Naeschylus Carter worked construction, and liked rap and jazz.

Tevin Crosby started his own business, running ad campaigns
for corporations from kiosks in big box stores.

Carly Kreibaum lived with her husband and two children
on a farm just outside a small town in northwest Iowa.

Barbara Hawthorne was a VISTA volunteer in Alabama in the '60s,
and later taught special education in Illinois for ten years.

Jonny Gammage had been an organizer
for a group participating in the Million Man March.

Danyale Johnson was a 35-year-old trans woman.
She was born and raised in Memphis.

Richard Linyard Jr. was a rapper who went by Afrikan Richie,
and with his brother had released an album.

Thomas Sullivan was a Marine Gunnery Sergeant,
and a fan of the Irish punk-rock band the Dropkick Murphys.

Jasdeep Singh came to the U.S. from Punjab, India.
He and his wife had one daughter. He was 36.

Reginald Clay Jr. lived in Chicago, and worked for Amazon.

11: number of times Anthony Lowe Jr. was shot in the back by police officers while in his wheelchair. **17**: number of times Eduardo Edwin Rodriguez was shot by sheriff's deputies. **34**: number of rounds fired at Ryan Twyman by two sheriff deputies. **39**: number of rounds fired at 92-year-old Kathryn Johnston by undercover police officers.

Bullets kill because of their size *and* their speed. □ "The most effective guns are the ones that never get fired." □ "[W]here there are no guns, there is no gun violence."

Nicholas Dyksma liked music, and wanted to learn to play drums.

Joseph Murphy served in the National Guard,
and was deployed to Iraq in 2005 as a machine gunner.

Deonka Drayton worked at a nightclub, and went by "DeeDee."
She and her partner had a young son.

Christopher Roybal served five years in the U.S. Navy,
including 11 months in Afghanistan as a dog handler.

Tyler Smith was studying marketing
to help start a family business with his father, sister, and cousin.

CoCo Chanel Wortham, originally from Kansas City, Kansas,
was a "master cosmetologist."

Dante Parker worked as a newspaper pressman for seven years.
He loved to sing on the job.

Squire Wells left college after two years to join the Marines,
and became a field artillery cannoneer.

Amandeep Singh worked warehouse jobs
until he earned a commercial truck driver's license.

Shereese Francis helped with her family's child care business.

4: how many times more children and teens have been killed with guns on American soil than U.S. soldiers killed in action in wars abroad. **15**: how many times more likely U.S. children and teens are to die from gunfire than their peers in 31 other high-income countries combined.

L'état, c'est la police. □ Police shooting: the ultimate state coercion. □ It is a *task* to come to see state violence for what it is.

Kaylin Gillis wanted to become a veterinarian or a marine biologist.

Leroy Fernandez worked as a leasing agent at an apartment complex,
and "filled the office with music," especially songs by Adele.

Alprentice Carter went by the nickname "Bunchy,"
which he explained as "Bunchy … like a bunch of greens."

Jordan McIldoon worked as a heavy-duty mechanic apprentice,
and planned to enter trade school in his native British Columbia.

Mary Lou Nye was 62, and Mary Jo Nye was 60.
They were sisters-in-law, and had been college roommates.

Jessica Nelson Williams had grown up in Sacramento,
but was living unhoused in San Francisco.

Edwin Rajo was a picky eater, slender in build.
His girlfriend called him "McLovin," after a movie character.

David Wyatt had been an Eagle Scout in his youth,
and as a career Marine achieved the rank of Staff Sergeant.

Monica Delgado was a 38-year-old stay-at-home mother.
She enjoyed cooking and baking for her children and family.

Ramarley Graham loved his grandmother's Jamaican stewed peas.

51.6: in a North Carolina survey, of adults who had loaded firearms in or around the home, the percentage who kept their loaded firearms unlocked. **50.6**: in the same survey, of adults with loaded and unlocked firearms in or around the home, the percentage who did not keep their firearms in a secure place. **31**: percentage of accidental deaths caused by firearms that might be prevented by adding child-proof safety locks and loading indicators.

The myth of heroic power through violence has never solved the problems it claims to solve. □ Rampant violence, extreme responses. □ The violence we use to solve problems *is* a problem.

Aiyana Jones was 7, and had two siblings and four stepsiblings.

Novaa Watson often rapped on social media,
and shared quotes from his favourite artists, such as Drake.

Peter Gonzalez-Cruz worked at UPS,
and with friends went by the nickname "Ommy."

Tara Roe enjoyed boating, hiking, biking,
and camping in the Rockies with her husband and two sons.

Richard Smith volunteered with Girl Scouts of America,
helping scouts learn a skill or trade.

Andrew Alan Myers served for ten years in the U.S. Army.
He and his ex-wife had two children.

Denis Reyes had seven children,
and had been diagnosed with bipolar disorder and schizophrenia.

William Love and his wife were nearing their 55th anniversary.
He enjoyed dancing, and fixing old cars.

Miguel Avila helped his grandfather cut yards after school,
and they had plans on buying his first car.

Marquiisha Lawrence loved hair, nails, travel, and cooking.

60: of all homicides and suicides in the U.S., the approximate percentage that are committed with a firearm. **2/3**: of firearm-involved deaths in the U.S. annually, the proportion that are suicides rather than acts of violence against others.

Communities pay less for larger schools; students pay more. □ Patterns of violence in society recur in schools. □ To cut down on school shootings, cut out toxic masculinity.

Chyna Carrillo was 24, and worked at a nursing home.

Keaton Farris was a three-sport athlete in high school.
In his 20s, he aspired to be a writer.

Juan Guerrero was studying finance.
He liked video games, working out, and travel.

Sonny Melton was an RN. He lived with his wife, an MD,
for whom he worked as a surgical assistant.

Dorothy Brown served as Secretary of the Board of her church,
and often shared herbs from her garden with her neighbors.

Sinthanouxay Khottavongsa grew up in a farming village in Laos
and came to the U.S. in the 1970s after the Vietnam War.

Christy Galella was 34. She was studying cosmetology
and working as a telemarketer.

Preston Phillips had a degree from Harvard Medical School,
and volunteered frequently at a local free clinic.

Natallie Avila was shy, but she loved being a big sister,
and helped care for her younger siblings.

Kenneth Chamberlain was 68, and had a chronic heart condition.

55: how many times more likely a U.S. citizen is to be killed by a law enforcement officer than by a terrorist.

Violence is not essence, but accident: a complex accident actively maintained. □ Violence is *made* inevitable. □ Being legitimated does not make violence legitimate.

Alvin Haynes had a longstanding addiction to heroin.

Victor Villalpando was 16, and had been adopted in infancy.
He taught hip-hop and studied ballet.

Frank Hernández had a tattoo on his left bicep
that read "Love has no gender."

Lisa Romero-Muniz had worked for 14 years
at the school district in Gallup, New Mexico.

Leonard Deadwyler and his wife first met
when they were in kindergarten. They had two children.

Kellie Pyle grew up in Norfolk, Virginia, and had returned there
after reconnecting with her high school sweetheart.

Jennifer Vasquez had two daughters. She loved cooking,
doing her makeup, and spending time with her family.

Stephanie Husen was a doctor of osteopathic medicine
who worked as a sports medicine physician in Tulsa.

Lorena Aviles went by "Lori" with friends and family.
She was an associate pastor at her church.

Vickie Lee Jones was retired from working at a VA hospital.

68.2: between 2014 and 2019, the percentage of mass shootings involving domestic violence. **83.7**: the case fatality rate for mass shootings involving domestic violence. **36.9**: the case fatality rate for mass shootings not involving domestic violence.

"[G]uns transform those who choose to use them." □ "Gun and gunner are co-constituting subjectivities." □ Its being *strong* does not prevent a person's identification with gun culture from being *selective.*

Anthony Lee and his ex-wife had practiced Nichiren Buddhism.

Miguel Honorato and his wife had three children.
He helped manage the family businesses begun by his parents.

Deborah Danner had schizophrenia, and had written an essay,
"Living With Schizophrenia," about the experience.

Pati Mestas was partly retired from her job as a deli manager
at a Shell convenience store in Corona, California.

Randy Blevins was 70. He watched professional wrestling
and Washington Commanders football games on TV.

Jose Romero had migrated from Mexico,
and worked at a mushroom farm in California.

LaVena Johnson was a 19-year-old PFC in the U.S. Army.
She played the violin, and wanted to be a movie producer.

Amanda Glenn worked as a receptionist at a hospital clinic,
and had worked as a registered medical assistant before that.

Natalie Aviles was studying to be a doctor.
She was known for the banana bread she baked.

Jesse LePore participated in BMX bike racing and won many races.

25: number of homicides of trans persons in the U.S. in 2019. **43**: number of homicides of trans persons in the U.S. in 2020. **51**: number of homicides of trans persons in the U.S. in 2021.

The more wars the state fights against its citizens, the more militarized it makes police. □ Police *have* partnered with soldiers, but *could* partner with doctors. □ To end police violence, reimagine public safety.

Donovan Lewis loved art and music. He was an expecting father.

Javier Jorge-Reyes loved doing drag, and one year dressed
for his city's Pride Parade as Alice from *Alice in Wonderland.*

Quinton Robbins coached ninth-grade basketball
at the same high school where he himself had played basketball.

Brian Pendleton was born with a congenital brain disorder.
He lived in Chesapeake, Virginia, where he had grown up.

Marciano Martinez-Jimenez worked at a farm,
and volunteered at a free clinic.

Rikkey Outumuro lived in Centralia, Washington.
She was crowned the first Miss Gay Lewis County in 2008.

Melissa Dunham was active with the Girl Scouts,
and loved walking her dogs and camping with her family.

Abdoulaye Thiam was a 20-year-old high school graduate
who enjoyed playing soccer.

Douglas Dulmage loved golfing and fishing with his 3 daughters,
and loved hunting ducks, geese, turkeys, deer, and coyotes.

Keith Lamont Scott and his wife of twenty years had seven children.

21: how many times more likely a Black man is to be shot by police than a white man. **1.47**: from 2010-2012, number of white males per million who were killed by police. **31.17**: from 2010-2012, number of Black males per million who were killed by police. **28**: in 2012, average number of hours between one police shooting of a Black person and the next.

Gun violence is shameless, not in that shame is *absent* but in that shame is *repressed.* □ Tragedy resists mistaking assignment of blame for a solution to the problem. □ Exclusive attention to guilt and innocence aggravates violence.

Alberto Sepulveda taught bike tricks to his neighbor across the street.

Jason Josaphat was born in Florida to Haitian parents,
and was studying computer science in a community college.

Austin Meyer was studying transportation technologies
at a community college in Reno.

Fernando Jesus Chavez was 16, and worked
the overnight shift at Walmart to help his family.

Yetao Bing and his wife lived in a trailer
on the farm where he worked.

Sean LePore was active in Bandolero racing,
and had won the Alabama state championship.

Renee Dunham was a Girl Scout,
and played in her high school marching band and jazz band.

Bich Cau Thi Tran was born in Vietnam in 1978.
She and her boyfriend had two sons, ages 4 and 2.

Justin Bracken worked for a farming family for 14 years,
and his dream was to own his own farm.

Joseph Taylor had two children. He loved to play spades.

44: from 2008-2012, average number of executions per year. **404**: from 2008-2012, average number of officially reported police killings per year.

Mass murder: ultimate simulation as ultimate reality. □ Violence feeds entertainment gluttony. □ Too much too-visible violence hides the violence of violence.

Patrick Warren had three children, and ran a landscaping business.

Eddie Justice owned his own accounting business,
drove a Mercedes, and lived in a high-rise.

Jennifer Parks worked as a kindergarten teacher,
and had just completed her masters in education.

Chance Ross was a 34-year-old high school graduate.
He had two brothers, and lived in Sulphur Springs, Texas.

Tyneka Johnson loved music and dancing,
and putting together different outfits and styling her hair.

Zhishen Liu and Aixiang Zhang had one daughter,
and lived and worked on a farm in California.

Amber Dunham was 12, and in the seventh grade.
She loved sequins, glitter and sparkles, and creating fashion.

Valerie Jackson and Dwayne Jackson. Nathaniel Conley.
Dewayne, Honesty, Caleb, Trinity, and Jonah Jackson.

Richard Bracken lived his whole life in Leeds, North Dakota.
He and his wife had two daughters. He loved onion rings.

Dan Brown liked to go hunting and auctioning.

43: in 1989, the percentage of Americans who believed that having a gun in the house made it a safer place to be. **42**: in 1989, the percentage of Americans who believed that having a gun in the house made it a more dangerous place to be. **63**: in 2014, the percentage of Americans who believed that having a gun in the house made it a safer place to be. **30**: in 2014, the percentage of Americans who believed that having a gun in the house made it a more dangerous place to be.

Anger ≠ violence. □ Ability + desire + opportunity = violence. □ Fewer guns toted = fewer shots fired.

John Collado was 43, and had six children, including a two-year-old.

Anthony Laureano Disla had majored in education in college.
He performed in drag as Alanis Laurell.

Adrian Murfitt loved his dog Paxson,
and was rebuilding a 1970 Camaro he'd bought in high school.

Lorenzo Gamble had worked for 15 years at Walmart,
where he was a custodian on the overnight shift.

Mya Hall made her living by sex work,
and lived insecurely housed in Baltimore.

Qizhong Cheng had been born in China
but worked at a farm in California.

Evan Dunham was 9, and in the third grade.
He could solve a Rubix cube in two minutes.

Cameron Tillman had started 9th grade, and was good at math.
He enjoyed watching SpongeBob with his younger cousins.

George Keene had three children and two stepchildren.
He worked as an electrician, and liked to fish.

Daniel Covarrubias made beadwork lanyards and medallions.

46: number of times Jayland Walker was shot by police. **48**: number of times Idriss Stelley was shot by police. **55**: number of rounds fired by 6 police officers at Willie McCoy in under 3.5 seconds. **59**: number of times Jamarion Robinson was shot by police.

Polarizing approaches to firearm-related issues interfere with evidence-based approaches. □ Introducing the binary of gun-owners vs. non-gun-owners diverts from any issue related to guns. □ The gun culture war, one head of a hydra.

David Dehmann was 33, and had autism and Tourette's Syndrome.

Christopher Leinonen was a vegetarian,
and loved electronic music, especially the artist deadmau5.

Rachael Parker lived in Long Beach, California.
She loved her two rescue dogs, traveling, and volunteer work.

Rexdale Henry had been active in his Choctaw tribal community,
coaching stickball and running for tribal council.

Jingzhi Lu was born in China but immigrated to the U.S.
and worked at a farm in California.

A.J. Laguerre was a high school graduate
with plans to attend college to study cybersecurity.

Clayton Doerman was 7, and loved making Lego creations,
riding his go kart, telling jokes, singing and laughing.

Bryan Gradney went by "Big G," and worked as a truck driver.
He enjoyed hunting, fishing, and cooking.

Alonzo Smith worked as a teacher's aide at a therapeutic school.
He had two sisters, and was the father of a 6-year-old son.

Chuck Eagan worked at Boeing in the commercial airplanes division.

<200: number of people on probation per 100,000 adults in Denmark. **<300**: number of people on probation per 100,000 adults in England. **<400**: number of people on probation per 100,000 adults in France. **>1,500**: number of people on probation per 100,000 adults in the U.S.

Capital keeps itself safe by keeping its violence secret. □ Rampage killers epitomize financial capitalism. □ Violence brings financial benefits, physical and emotional costs.

Andre Hill wanted one day to own his own restaurant.

Maurice Stallard was a retired GE employee and military veteran.
He and his wife had two children and three grandchildren.

Brenda McCool loved salsa dancing,
and had survived two bouts with cancer.

Carrie Parsons loved country music,
and one of her favorite musicians was Eric Church.

Yitzian Torres Garcia was seven years old.
His nickname was "Bootie."

John Crawford III went by "Trey." He worked
telemarketing and manual labor jobs through a temp agency.

Angela Michelle Carr worked as an Uber driver.
She had 3 children and 14 grandchildren.

Hunter Doerman liked going to the creek and catching frogs,
and he loved baseball. He was 4 years old.

Scott Nolet worked as a tattoo artist,
and enjoyed tubing down the Guadalupe River and camping.

Eddie Irizarry worked as a mechanic, and loved reggaetón.

9: percentage of firearms with large-capacity magazines recovered by Virginia police in 2004, the last year during which the 1994 ban on assault weapons and high-capacity magazines applied, before its expiration. **20**: percentage of firearms with large-capacity magazines recovered by Virginia police in 2010.

Free rein to police loosens the reins on politicians. □ Racialized police violence is a failure of the individual officer(s), *and* of the state. □ Police killings, eruptions; societal association of blackness with criminality, the molten core.

Prince Jones Jr. worked as a personal fitness trainer.

Maxwell Emerson taught social studies and coached wrestling
in the same school from which he had graduated.

Gilberto Silva Menéndez worked at Speedway,
and was studying health care management.

Alyssa Alhadeff was on her high school debate team,
and wanted to become a doctor.

Gustin Hinnant's first name is pronounced with a soft G,
as if it were spelled Justin.

Jerrald Gallion was 29. He worked two to three jobs
to provide for his 4-year-old daughter.

Chase Doerman loved swinging on swings, playing with Dinos,
and pretending to be a superhero. He was 3.

Donald Ivy suffered from paranoid schizophrenia,
and had a heart condition. He went by "Dontay."

Violet Parrish enjoyed camping and playing softball,
and was an artist and musician.

Charly Leundeu Keunang lived unhoused in Los Angeles.

27: number of miles between Sandy Hook Elementary School and the headquarters of gun manufacturer Sturm, Ruger & Co. **56**: percent increase in the profits of Sturm, Ruger & Co. in the year following the Sandy Hook shooting.

Men disproportionately bear arms. Women disproportionately bear the brunt of arms. □ Violence: masculinity wannabe. □ Make America Masculine Again.

Larry Kobuk was 33, and had lived in Anchorage for about 10 years.

Kendrec McDade was a student athlete at Citrus College,
whose sports included football, track, and swimming.

Jean Méndez Pérez liked working out at the gym,
and he worked at a Perfumania store.

Cara Loughran enjoyed Irish dancing, ice skating,
and shopping with her mother and grandmother.

Katherine Goldstein loved bird watching and travel.
She enjoyed cooking, and visiting the Chicago Botanic Garden.

Stephen Romero loved to wear pressed shirts and cologne,
earning him the nickname "el Romántico."

John Sawyer was employed in the construction business
and also worked as a handyman with his "Poppa."

Rob Hiaasen had the nickname "Big Rob" because of his height.
He and his wife had three children. He was 59.

Glenn Edward Bennett was a Korean War veteran.
He was an avid movie lover and he also loved classic cars.

Michael Stewart's signature graffiti tag was "RQS."

3,410: number of children and teens killed with guns in 2017. **9**: average number of children and teens killed per day with guns in 2017. **1**: how many children and teens were killed or injured with a gun every 24 minutes in 2017. **2020**: year in which firearm-related injuries passed motor vehicle crashes to become the leading cause of death among children and adolescents (persons 1 through 19 years old).

Even violence that happens for no reason (serves no purpose) happens for a reason (has causes). □ Proximate causes of killing cause killing when and where ultimate causes are at work. □ Power the exercised, violence the exercise.

Stanley Taylor played bass drum in his school's marching band.

Kimberly Morris worked as a bouncer at a nightclub.
Her drag king personality was "Daddy K."

Helena Ramsay played the clarinet,
and loved watching Alex Trebek host "Jeopardy!"

Reggie Doucet Jr. worked as a model
and had plans to build a training facility for athletes.

Irina McCarthy was born in Moscow
and moved with her family to Chicago when she was 2 ½.

Christina Tahhahwah loved to listen to powwow music,
sing Comanche hymns, and play cards.

Keyla Salazar had a chihuahua named Lucky.
She liked to make digital videos and animations.

Gerald Fischman was a University of Maryland graduate,
and was married to a Mongolian opera singer he had met online.

Donald Ray Surrett Jr. served in the Army for 20 years
as a Drill Sergeant, Infantryman, and Combat Engineer.

Donnell Thompson, Jr. was nicknamed "Little Bo Peep."

15: of white persons killed by police in the first five months of 2015, the percent who were unarmed. **25**: of Latinx persons killed by police in the first five months of 2015, the percent who were unarmed. **32**: of Black persons killed by police in the first five months of 2015, the percent who were unarmed.

No gun rights without gun responsibilities. □ What of your violence you don't pay for, your children will. □ "Gun control" and "gun violence prevention" might not be identical.

Ashley Carpenter liked playing video games and football.

Clifford Glover went with his stepfather on weekends
to the junkyard at which his stepfather worked.

Jean Nieves Rodriguez loved the beach and cars.
He had recently bought a house for himself and his mother.

Martin Duque Anguiano was a JROTC Cadet,
and wanted to become a Navy SEAL.

Stephen Straus was 88.
He and his wife had two sons and four grandchildren.

Dominique Lucious was a 26-year-old trans woman
who loved red lipstick and red nails.

Trevor Irby grew up in Romulus, New York.
He worked as a medical technician in Scotts Valley, California.

John McNamara worked for more than 20 years
at the Capital Gazette newspaper in Annapolis, Maryland.

Deborah Martinez-Garibay served in the U.S. Army for 16 years,
and later worked as a Constable in her hometown of Tucson.

Dominique Jackson hoped one day to have her own salon.

9.1: of NYPD officers who retired before 1995, percentage who reported having experienced, during their active duty, high pressure to conduct forcible stops. **35.1**: of NYPD officers who retired between 2002 and 2012, percentage who reported having experienced, during their active duty, high pressure to conduct forcible stops. **44.6**: of NYPD officers who retired before 1995, percentage who reported having experienced, during their active duty, high pressure to uphold citizens' constitutional rights. **35.7**: of NYPD officers who retired between 2002 and 2012, percentage who reported having experienced, during their active duty, high pressure to uphold citizens' constitutional rights.

In use of force, the ideal for *legitimacy* should be *justice*. □ To diminish police brutality, diminish economic injustice. □ The number of police killings *can* be reduced.

David Carpenter-Kohler played in his school band.

Francisco Serna was married and had five children.
He was retired from his work at a cotton gin.

Ke'Yahonna Stone was a 32-year-old trans woman
who worked at warehouse jobs in Indianapolis and Chicago.

Luis Ocasio-Capo went by his middle name, Omar.
He loved dancing: salsa, bachata, hip-hop, or any other kind.

Gina Montalto played soccer and flag football.
She was a Girl Scout and a member of her school color guard.

Eduardo Uvaldo and his wife had four daughters,
13 grandchildren and seven great-grandchildren.

Aaliyah Gonzalez had just graduated with honors from high school,
and planned to study sports medicine at community college.

Rebecca Smith was a sales assistant at a newspaper,
and a survivor of endometriosis.

Angela Fox worked as the property manager
at an apartment complex in Tucson, Arizona.

Jeremy Linhart had worked for five years as a service technician.

53: in 1999, after Columbine, the percentage of Americans who believed that government and society can take action that will be effective in preventing such shootings in the future.
43: in 1999, after Columbine, the percentage of Americans who believed that such shootings will happen again regardless of what action is taken by government and society.
35: in 2015, after Charleston, the percentage of Americans who believed that government and society can take action that will be effective in preventing such shootings in the future.
64: in 2015, after Charleston, the percentage of Americans who believed that such shootings will happen again regardless of what action is taken by government and society.

Depicted aggression does increase performed aggression. □ Action films mythologize guns, and idealize gun combat. □ "Violence as entertainment is a pop-cultural sure shot."

Taylin Roland worked as a Supervisor at a YMCA Family Shelter.

Manuel Ellis was recovering from addiction, and was active
in his church, playing drums in services four times a week.

Fred Hampton was deputy chair of the Black Panther Party,
and founded the Rainbow Coalition.

Geraldo Ortiz-Jimenez went by "Drake," and maintained
his five-days-a-week workout routine even when traveling.

Meadow Pollack liked cats, the color pink, and working out.
She wanted to become a lawyer.

Kevin McCarthy and his wife had a 2-year-old son,
and lived in Highland Park, Illinois.

Kylis Fagbemi had recently signed up
for a certification course to become an ultrasound technician.

Wendi Winters had a fashion design degree from VCU,
and volunteered with the Girl Scouts and Red Cross.

Elijah Miranda worked the late-night shift at McDonald's,
and had recently been promoted to manager.

Diamond Sanders went by "Kyree," and liked travel and fashion.

50: percent increase in the odds of a person's having a gun in the home, with every 1 point increase (on a scale of 1 to 5) in that person's symbolic racism. **106.3**: percentage increase in the incidence of police-caused homicide with a one-standard-deviation increase in Black dissimilarity index (degree of racial segregation). **44.4**: percentage increase in the ratio of Black to White fatal police shooting rates with a one-standard-deviation increase in Black dissimilarity index (degree of racial segregation). **24**: percentage increase in the Black-White disparity ratio of unarmed police shooting rates, for every 10-point increase (on a 100-point scale) in the overall state racism index.

Toward reducing violence: listen to those most affected by it. □ Toward reducing gun violence: enhance imagination. □ Violence is everywhere and always, but so is resistance.

Adrianna Stanton was a 17-year-old high school senior.

Anthony Lamar Smith worked at McDonalds.
He and his fiancée had a 1-year-old daughter.

Eric Ivan Ortiz-Rivera worked at Party City and Sunglass Hut.
He liked to cook traditional Puerto Rican foods.

Nicholas Dworet was on his school swim team,
and had been offered a college swimming scholarship.

Jacki Sundheim was a congregant
and also a staff member at her local synagogue.

Sean Adler was a coffee enthusiast,
and had recently opened a coffee shop called Rivalry Roasters.

Shirly Voita worked as a school nurse until her retirement.
She enjoyed skiing trips, tennis, and pickleball.

Natasha McKenna had been diagnosed at age 12
with bipolar disorder and schizophrenia.

Clyde and Sally Knox had been married for 60 years,
and had two children and seven grandchildren.

Brianna Stanton was an 11-year-old junior high student.

7,391: in 2009, the number of hospitalizations of U.S. children and adolescents for firearm-related injuries. **20**: the number that averages to per day. **89.2**: of those hospitalized, the percentage who were male. **35.1**: out of those hospitalizations, of the ones resulting from suicide attempts, the percentage who died in the hospital.

Effective preventive measures for gun violence will elude us as long as effective inquiry does. □ About guns, too, it matters not only *what* one thinks but also *how* one thinks. □ My perceiving threat might reveal *what* I perceive, but certainly reveals *how* I perceive.

Bryant Tennell kept an aquarium, and raised chickens.

Malcolm Ferguson was 23, and had earned his GED
during an eight-month incarceration on drug charges.

Botham Jean did volunteer work with at-risk-youth,
and sang in a Christian a cappella group.

Joel Rayon Paniagua worked in gardening and construction
to earn money to send home to his family in Mexico.

Luke Hoyer loved basketball
and chicken nuggets and macaroni and cheese.

Nicolas Toledo-Zaragoza liked fishing and taking walks.
He had eight children. He was 78.

Cody Coffman had three younger brothers,
and liked to go fishing with his father.

Melody Ivie enjoyed taking morning walks with her dogs,
and tending the vegetables and flowers in her garden.

Sarah Anderson was a high school graduate
who worked at Premier Health and was active in her church.

Ben A. C de Baca lived in Santa Fe his whole life. He had 7 children.

20: number of gunshot wounds in Mario Woods's body, according to the coroner's report. **6**: number of those that were in the back. **27**: number of shell casings recovered at the scene.

With every push to regulate gun sales, gun sales increase. □ Guns compensate for economic precarity with perceived moral security. □ Guns help the rich get richer.

JoAnna Cottle lived with her 3 children in Chester, Virginia.

Jared Forsyth worked as a police officer in Ocala, Florida.
He liked camping, fishing, and relaxing near the water.

Enrique Rios liked to dance, and liked to cook.
He was studying for a degree in social work.

Aaron Feis was a security guard and an assistant football coach
at the same high school he had attended twenty years before.

Patrick Dorismond worked as a security guard
in midtown Manhattan, and was a part-time DJ.

Blake Dingman loved fixing up cars
and driving them around in the desert.

Gwendolyn Schofield kept a large garden
and was known for her canning, especially her dill pickles.

Kayla Anderson was a 15-year-old high school sophomore.
She loved sports, music, gymnastics, and dancing.

Jonathan Pierce had studied electronics in college.
He enjoyed hunting and fishing.

Lorenzo Hayes had attended technical college for welding.

15: of homicide victims, the percentage who are women. **7**: of homicide victims, the percentage who are children. **64**: of mass shooting victims, the percentage who are women or children.

The spread of violent behavior resembles the spread of a communicable disease. □ Violence-proneness is not spontaneously generated but is self-reinforcing. □ We must be ever ending violence, because violence is never-ending.

Kaelyn Person loved to draw, and expressed herself through her art.

Juan Pablo Rivera Velázquez and his husband ran a salon.
He had a miniature schnauzer named Juicy Couture.

Chris Hixon was a Navy veteran who served in the Persian Gulf.
He was then in the Naval Reserves for over twenty years.

Kiwi Herring was a Black trans woman.
She and her spouse were raising three sons, ages 2 to 8.

Tierramarie Lewis was a 36-year-old trans woman
who loved dancing, singing, and spending time with her sister.

Miles Hall was a self-taught musician who played guitar and piano,
and composed music on his computer.

Jake Dunham was 21, and lived in Newbury Park, California.
He loved off-roading, and liked fixing cars.

Hilda Marshall and Susie Arnold, mother and daughter,
lived next door to one another. Hilda was 74, and Susie was 50.

Tyler Schmidt liked camping and canoeing,
board and card games, hiking and snowshoeing, and cooking.

Zachee Imanitwitaho worked at a meat-processing plant in Louisville.

26: percentage of police shootings in relation to which the involved officer reported afterward experiencing sadness. **29**: percentage of police shootings in relation to which the involved officer reported afterward experiencing elation.

Guns exist in context, and operate in context. □ Police decide in context, and act in context. □ Assign the use of deadly force, but don't neglect it.

KC Johnson worked as a manager at a Domino's franchise.

Yilmary Rodriguez Solivan went by Mary.
She was the mother of two young children.

Joaquin Oliver went by "Guac."
He was a fan of the Venezuelan national soccer team.

Matthew Ajibade was a student at Savannah Technical College.
He was 22, and had bipolar disorder.

Alaina Housley was a first-year student at Pepperdine,
and planned to study law. She was 18.

Kinsey Cottle and Jayson Cottle were 4-year-old twins
who loved to start a conversation by saying, "I have a question."

Antwon Rose Jr. was a 17-year-old high school honor student.
He took AP classes, and played basketball and the saxophone.

Amia Smith was working as a manager at McDonald's.
She had worked previously as a live-in nanny.

Sarah Schmidt worked at the public library in Cedar Falls, Iowa.
She was in the handbell choir at her church.

Nicole Kelly was a stay-at-home mother for her two daughters.

15, 16, 22: standard and optional magazine capacities of the Glock 22, "[b]y far the most popular police service pistol in the United States." **16**: number of shots fired at Jeanette Anaya by the police officer who killed her. **16**: number of shots fired at Laquan McDonald by the police officer who killed him.

"America is a gun-horny nation." □ Americans are no more hotheaded than anyone else, we just pack more heat. □ The U.S. does not keep its policing methods to itself.

Nancy Lanza enjoyed gardening, and was a Red Sox fan.

Jarrell Garris had been diagnosed with schizophrenia.
He had a full-time job as a caretaker for older people.

Christopher Joseph Sanfeliz liked working out at the gym,
and enjoyed dancing, especially bachata.

Alaina Petty, the youngest of four siblings,
was a high school freshman and a JROTC Cadet.

Dominique Fells was a dancer and artist,
and planned to go back to school to become a fashion designer.

Daniel Manrique was 33,
and dreamed of launching his own brewing business.

Holly Guess was the mother of three children.
She worked from home, most recently by selling insurance.

Alex Nieto worked as a bouncer at a nightclub,
and was a practicing Buddhist.

Lula Schmidt was 6. She loved her stuffed animals
and her Barbie and Our Generation dolls.

David Lynch owned and operated a trucking business.

92,000: average number of firearm sales per day in the U.S. in January and February of 2020. **120,000+**: average number of firearm sales per day in the U.S. in the 12 days following the 13 March 2020 declaration of a national emergency concerning the outbreak of COVID-19. **29.3**: percentage increase in incidents of firearm violence during the COVID pandemic. **3.8 million**: number of Americans who became first-time gun owners in 2020.

Gun ownership is not demographically neutral. □ "[W]hat matters most is who owns guns rather than how many guns are owned." □ No demographic innocent, no demographic immune.

Thomas May Jr. went by "T.J." He coached Little League.

Malice Green worked for ten years at a steel mill in Chicago
before returning home to Detroit.

Rhiannon Layendecker loved animals, and on social media
she frequently posted photos of rescue dogs and cats.

Xavier Serrano Rosado was born in Puerto Rico.
He worked in a shoe store.

Dennis Johnson and his wife had six children,
and had just celebrated their 44th wedding anniversary.

Oscar Grant earned his GED while incarcerated,
and planned to become a barber.

Justin Meek worked for a social services nonprofit
helping children with developmental disabilities.

Rylee Allen liked to paint, and wanted to be an artist.
She also wanted to be a doctor. She was 17.

Pedro Piñeda was born in El Salvador, and lived in Indianapolis.
He worked in construction, repairing and painting homes.

Feras Morad was a champion debater in high school and college.

79: in 1999, after Columbine, the percentage of Americans who believed that such events indicate that there is something seriously wrong in the country today. **17**: in 1999, after Columbine, the percentage of Americans who believed that such events are isolated incidents that do not indicate anything about the country in general. **24**: in 2012, after the Aurora CO theatre shooting, the percentage of Americans who believed that such events indicate that there is something seriously wrong in the country today. **67**: in 2012, after the Aurora CO theatre shooting, the percentage of Americans who believed that such events are isolated incidents that do not indicate anything about the country in general.

The most visible mass shooting may not be the most typical mass shooting. □
Complete prevention of mass shooting is not possible; reduced opportunity is. □
More mass shootings occur in private than in public.

Alfred Olango hoped one day to open his own restaurant.

Martin Benitez Torres liked to design costumes for parties.
He was studying to become a pharmacy technician.

Tony Terrell Robinson Jr. graduated high school a semester early,
but was on probation for armed robbery.

Crystal Holcombe homeschooled the five children
she had with her first husband before he passed away.

Atatiana Jefferson was working as a pharmaceutical sales rep
to save money for medical school.

Mark Meza was active on YouTube,
posting videos of music on his channel.

Michael Mayo played football on his high school team,
and ran cross-country and track.

Rosa Mirian Rivera de Piñeda was 37, and worked as a babysitter.
Family members called her "Rosie."

Akai Gurley was born in the Virgin Islands.
He and his fiancé had a two-year-old daughter.

Melissa Perez enjoyed cooking, especially lasagna and enchiladas.

92: from 2009-2011, the percentage of persons against whom tasers were used by Chicago police who were Black or Latinx. **32.9**: the percentage of Chicago's population who are Black. **75.3**: from 2009-2013, of persons shot by Chicago police, the percentage who were Black. **10**: number of times more likely a Black citizen is than a white citizen to be shot by a Chicago police officer.

Gun violence has analogies with disease epidemics, and disanalogies. □ Meaningful early preventive intervention against violence *is* possible. □ If gun violence is an epidemic, let's treat it like one.

Frank Petro owned and operated a gun and taxidermy shop.

Sarai Lara was a high school sophomore.
She enjoyed going out with friends, texting and shopping.

Shane Tomlinson was a graduate of East Carolina University,
and was the lead vocalist for a cover band, Frequency.

Robert Marshall was retired from the Air Force,
and worked as a civilian contractor and mechanic.

Franklin Lynch was a 24-year-old singer
who had just released a single, "Young Girl."

Amilcar Perez-Lopez was Ch'orti' Mayan, from Guatemala.
Friends and family called him "Mica."

Kristina Morisette was 20, and worked as a cashier at a bar.
She liked to hike, draw, and do makeup.

Tiffany Guess ran cross-country on her school team.
She was also in the choir, and had tried out for cheerleading.

Victor Gomez was a high school graduate
who owned and operated a marble and granite business.

Egypt Powers liked to wear blue, green, yellow, and pink braids.

28: of gun owners, the percentage best described as "family protectors who go to the shooting range and feel empowered by their guns." **19**: of gun owners, the percentage best described as "incidental gun owners motivated by protection or family tradition." **18**: of gun owners, the percentage best described as "Second Amendment activists who engage in multiple gun-related activities and are resistant to social change." **13**: of gun owners, the percentage best described as "target shooters." **12**: of gun owners, the percentage best described as "hunters." **11**: of gun owners, the percentage best described as "self-protectors."

"Peaceful violence" can take place as "confinement, degradation, ill health, and early death." □ Obedience can be as violent as disobedience. □ Violence overpowers and undervalues. Violence is as malleable as it is persistent.

Calvon Reid went by "Andre," and worked as a meat salesman.

Janet Harrison was 83. She enjoyed singing to family and friends,
and the "occasional" spin of a slot machine.

Jonathan Camuy Vega liked to take his nieces to the pool,
and to go dancing with his friends.

Joann Ward had two dogs,
a great dane named Zena and yellow lab named Bubbles.

Jonathon Salcido worked as a Teachers Assistant for over a year,
but from age 18 had lived with mental illness.

Telemachus Orfanos was a Navy veteran,
and worked at a car dealership. Friends called him "Tel."

Henry James Hunter loved to play his guitar,
listen to gospel music, and practice martial arts.

Brittany Brewer was a 16-year-old high school student
who wanted to become a teacher or a veterinarian.

Ryan Bolinger liked to do lawn work and fish.
He worked maintenance at the Iowa State Fair grounds.

Daniel Prude worked in warehouses and factories in Chicago.

75,000+: the number of individuals in state and federal prisons held in solitary confinement. **10**: of individuals in solitary confinement, the percentage who have been held in that way for 3 or more years. **11**: of all Black men in Pennsylvania born between 1986 and 1989, the percentage who have been held in solitary confinement by age 32.

How one thinks about guns and how one feels about guns do not pull apart. □ How we talk about guns and how we make decisions about guns do not pull apart. □ The rubber band's snap is sudden, but the stretching that results in it is not.

Kindra Chapman identified as gay from the seventh grade on.

Edward Morris Jr. was 21, and had been employed
as a packer with a confection company.

Luis Vielma was studying to become an EMT. He worked
at Universal Studios at the Wizarding World of Harry Potter.

Robert Corrigan retired from the Air Force
as a Chief Master Sergeant, after nearly 30 years of service.

Phillip Vallejo went by "Flip."
He and his wife had three sons and a daughter.

Noel Sparks was a youth camp leader
and a youth volunteer at her church.

Tracy Martinez earned a pharmacy technician license,
and worked at a hospital for 15 years.

Darrell Mattson enjoyed vegetable gardening,
and was in the Color Guard at his VFW Post.

Cassandra Geschke went by "Cassie."
She was 21, and worked as a cashier at Kroger's.

Jaiden Dixon played Little League. His coaches called him "Smiley."

7: gun deaths of children and teens per day in the United States. **2**: of gun deaths of children and teens per day in the United States, the number that are suicides.

Militarization of law *enforcers* implicates law *makers* and law *interpreters*. □ In a militarized world, "crime consists in not killing if orders insist on it." □ Enemies are not the enemy.

David Felix could dance salsa, bachata, cha cha, and merengue.

Luis Daniel Wilson-Leon was "Dani" to close friends and family.
He and his partner were together for eight years.

Lula White was active in her church, and liked travel.
She had recently taken a fishing trip with a grandson.

Meagan Hockaday was a stay-at-home mom
with three daughters, ages 8 months, 2 years, and 4 years.

Rubén García Villalpando was 31, and worked as a welder.
He and his wife had four children.

Ron Helus was Sgt. in the Ventura County Sheriff's Office,
and had been on the force for 29 years.

Bianca Roberson had worked through school
as a Dietary Aide at a retirement center.

Denise Mattson enjoyed crocheting,
and was President of her VFW Post's Auxiliary.

Kiér Laprí Kartier lived with her grandmother in Dallas.
She was between jobs, and looking for employment.

Jennifer LePore worked as a special needs assistant teacher.

40: percentage of Americans who know someone who was fatally shot or who committed suicide with a gun. **22**: percentage of Americans who know someone who was killed by another person with a gun.

Empathy after violence does not relieve withholding of rights and protections before. □ Forgiveness may supplement, but cannot replace, justice. □ Recognition of the life that has been ended *is* a call for justice.

Parerga

• [Title

Violence need not express rage to be outrageous. "Outrage" *looks* like a compound: base "rage" modified by prefix "out," the same way, say, "outcry" works. Not so. In its origin, the word "outrage" has no connection at all to the word "rage." "Outrage" entered English around 1300, as a borrowing from the Old French *outrage* (harm, damage, insult, presumption, overweening), itself derived from the verb *oultrager* (to go to excess, to act immoderately). The Old French words come from the Latin *ultra* (beyond), which came from the Proto-Indo-European root **al-* (beyond).

Over time, the folk etymology from "out + rage" shifted the meaning of the English word toward association with violence, but the original borrowing was not about being angry: it was about being outside of customary or reasonable limits. "Outrage" originates not from rage-ness but from beyond-ness, not from the emotions or attitude of the doer but from the nature of the done, not from being out of sorts but from being out of bounds.

Any *feelings* of rage are of secondary importance to the nexus of problems *American Outrage* laments. Persons performing the violence attested to here might or might not feel rage: a shooter might feel righteous or dutiful or proud or confused or who knows how. The focus here is on the outrageousness of the violence performed, on its being out of bounds.

Similarly, the surviving persons most immediately and profoundly affected by the violence attested to here (such as family members of persons killed, and members of demographic groups disproportionately targeted) might or might not feel rage: a person whose spouse or child has been killed might feel grief or despair or who knows what. The focus here is on the outrageousness — the out-of-bounds-ness — of the deed that evoked whatever feelings surviving persons experience.

Title] • [Epigraphs

The first epigraph, "I didn't write …," quotes Percival Everett, from "A Different Language: A Conversation with Percival Everett," by George Makari. *Los Angeles Review of Books*, 7 August 2023.
https://lareviewofbooks.org/article/a-different-language-a-conversation-with-percival-everett/

The second epigraph quotes Michelle Alexander, from p. xii of her preface to the tenth anniversary edition of *The New Jim Crow*.

Everett delivers the quoted sentence during a portion of the interview in which he and Makari are discussing Everett's novel *The Trees*. Makari draws attention to a character in the novel, a young professor who finds a filing cabinet full of information about "a group of people" who have been reduced to "one category — they are *the lynched*." In response, the character "decides that he is going to write every single name down." Makari reports his understanding that Everett himself did what the fictional character did: "You wrote those names down yourself." Everett amends Makari's understanding by saying, "I didn't write every single name down; I wrote perhaps 1,000, until my hand cramped."

Posting Everett's words on the lintel of *American Outrage* announces that it *does* share with Everett's project a procedure (writing down names) and a total ("perhaps 1,000"), but also, and more importantly, indicates that it *aspires* to share a disposition. About the writing-down, Makari asks Everett, "To give them names?" Everett refines the suggestion. He did the writing-down, he says, to "give those names some meaning to me," and to enable him to go a step beyond the character in his novel. The character says "They're not statistics anymore," but for Everett himself the names become in the writing-down *not simply* not statistics: "they did become real for me." That is the aspiration here. May *American Outrage* testify that these names bear meaning, and that what they mean is real: real lives really ended, of real human persons.

Appealing immediately after Everett's words to Alexander's recognizes — admits — that 1,000 names may be exhaust*ing* but it is far from exhaust*ive.* The list Alexander refers to, of vigilante killings and police killings of Black persons, shares with the list in *American Outrage* the feature that its tragic-ness is amplified by its incompleteness. It is tragic that these persons *were* killed, and tragic that more persons *are being* killed.

Epigraphs] • [Situation

We're killing ourselves. That sentence is used most often as a figure of speech, to mean something like *we collectively are faltering because we individually are failing.* A coach exhorting her team at halftime, for instance, might mean it in that way: "We're killing ourselves. If we stop making mistakes and play the way we practice, we'll win this game." The figurative usage derives, though, from a literal usage that means *some individuals among us are killing other individuals among us.* A political officeholder during the U.S. Civil War, for instance, might have used it in that way: "We're killing ourselves. We must find a way to end the slaughter."

This testamentary does not *deny* the figurative usage: I take it that we *are* figuratively killing ourselves, and that the fact urgently concerns us all. *American Outrage* attends directly, though, not to the figurative usage of "we're killing ourselves," but to the literal usage from which the figurative usage derives. Americans *literally* kill one another more often — much more often — than people kill one another in any other "developed" nation in the world. It is in response to this situation, the literal killing, that *American Outrage* undertakes its remembrance, registry, and reflection.

Situation] • [Desideratum

May this testamentary be, as Allen Grossman says poetry is, "one means by which human beings engage, as they can, in the maintenance of a human world in which they can meet one another, affirm one another, remember, see, and foresee one another," because it is just such a human world that the kinds of violence lamented here — rampage shootings, police shootings of unarmed civilians, and so on — compromise, and it is against such compromises that the humanity of such a human world must be maintained.

Desideratum] • [Principles

American Outrage would *join* the work of the very many testaments (websites, articles, books, sculptures, songs, …) that remember persons violently killed and resist violent killing, but it would *replicate* the work of none. It has *something* in common with each such project, but *everything* in common with no one of them. Among the principles it tries to fulfill are these:

1. *Each description pertains to the person's life, not to the person's death.*

A person's having been killed by an act of violence is a criterion for inclusion in the listing, but one important purpose of the listing is to assert that a violent death is not the only memorable fact about, and not the ultimately defining feature of, the person. This testamentary attests to lives ended, not to the ending of lives.

2. *The description given of the person* excludes *the reason for the person's being described here.*

A person might be included here because of having been shot to death by a police officer, say, but that fact is *not* included in the description. Violent death severs possibility from actuality: what a person might be is cut off from what a person has been. Remembering who a person was prior to death restores continuity with what the person might have been. Each description pertains to how the person *lived*, not to how the person *died.*

3. *Each description emphasizes the specific over the generic.*

Memory tends toward abstraction and reduction. Much of what is said in moments of grief is generic: "she was such a caring person"; "he was always helping others"; and so on. Such formulations *are* used widely because they *can be*: they might apply to any number of persons. The comfort they offer comes from their familiarity, and their value lies in declaring the speaker's love or esteem for the spoken-of. This testamentary does not contradict that way of speaking, but complements it with a different way of speaking, favoring descriptions much more like "she had a cross tattooed on her left arm, to commemorate her father, who had been killed in active duty" or "he kept two rescue mutts as pets, and volunteered at the animal shelter." That is, it de-emphasizes general qualities or characteristics imputed to the deceased by others, instead foregrounding as much as possible what it can learn of the person's own particular decisions and tastes and actions in life.

4. *A "round" number of descriptions are given.*

More than a thousand persons in the U.S. die from firearm injury every month, and more than a thousand are killed by police every year. One thousand persons are named and described here, then, not to tally how many there are, but to tell how many *more* there are, not to be exhaustive but to be indicative. As, say, the *Iliad* is when it reports the Trojan War lasted ten years, not to specify how many days the war lasted but to suggest how much suffering it brought about. The present incantation continues not *ad nauseum* but *ad vigilium*, not until one's stomach is on edge but until one's attention is on alert, until a counter-norm shows out the harm of accepting as norm what has been normalized.

5. *A* small *"round" number of descriptions are given.*

A listing need not be comprehensive to aid comprehension. (As in the figure of speech "I get the idea.") From their being too *many* to remember or repeat, I understand that these thousand persons here included are only a *few* of those who merit inclusion. (As in the familiar metaphor "the tip of the iceberg.") That the listing *could not be* comprehensive is part of what I must attempt to comprehend. By analogy with Simone Weil's insight that "We know by means of our intelligence that what the intelligence does not comprehend is more real than what it does comprehend," I understand by means of this listing that those who are not included here far outnumber those who are.

6. *Persons are not grouped by incident or category.*

Persons killed in rampage shootings often are grouped by incident. We humans readily substitute place names for events that occurred at those places (as with Pearl Harbor, for example, or Watergate). Numerous place names have come to function in this way in regard to violent events such as mass shootings: Virginia Tech, Columbine, Uvalde, and so on. Substituting the place for the event in that way has the limitation that it recognizes only the singularity, not the multiplicity, of what took place. "Sandy Hook," used metonymically, identifies as *one* event, *one* tragedy, what was also *twenty-six* tragedies. The present testamentary seeks to recognize each *life*, not only each *place*. It seeks to emphasize the singularity of each person over the singularity of the event.

7. *Only persons killed, not killers, are named.*

Our characteristic way of telling stories reifies a familiar but violence-valorizing vision of agency, by devoting more attention to the one who perpetrates an act of violence than to the one against whom the violence is perpetrated. In each narration, the perpetrator becomes the agent, understood as active, and the perpetrated-against becomes the patient, understood as passive. The perpetrator is seen as doing something, and the perpetrated-against is seen as doing nothing. The perpetrated-against is seen, that is, as *merely* being done to: a judgment of relative value is smuggled in with the narrative structure. In an event involving violence, our prevailing imaginary construes only the violence as a deed, an act. The perpetrator ingests the agency of the perpetrated-against as surely as, in a cannibalistic society, the eater ingests the soul of the eaten. This testamentary works to counter that pervasive tendency to treat perpetrators of violence as stars, and those against whom violence is perpetrated as extras.

8. *No description here includes the word "victim."*

"Victim" is the customary category term for persons who have been killed in acts of violence, but identifying a person as a "victim" accepts as definitive the person's membership in a group in which the person has been placed by the agency of another/others, rather than foregrounding the person's self-definition through the person's own agency, so no one whose life is recognized here is labeled a "victim."

9. *Entries emphasize* de*scription over* pre*scription.*

Praise does honor a person who has died, but so does simple description. To honor one who has died, it is well to tender praise ("his smile could light up a room"; "she was a born leader") but well also to give description. It is well, that is, to say what the person's virtues were, but it is well also to say who the person was. Persons are included here not for their *merits* but for their *humanity.*

10. *The listing recognizes persons killed by various forms of violence.*

Some persons whose names are included in this testamentary died when a hate crime was perpetrated against them, others from a violent action performed by a mentally ill person. Some died by themselves, others among multiple persons killed in a single event. Some died from acts of violence perpetrated by private citizens, others from acts perpetrated by officers of the state. The great majority died from gunshot wounds, but some few died from other forms of physical violence. Those contrasts exemplify one feature of the tragedy lamented here, namely that it has no single source. Apparently, there is no one exacerbating factor the elimination of which by itself would end the ongoing disaster: nothing sets a limit to it. No simple, single change would draw the outrage back within bounds, end its outrageousness.

Principles] • [Focus

By prevailing customs of scholarship, this testamentary is unfocused. Is it about violence? guns? gun culture? gun control? police brutality? police militarization? racial profiling? structural racism? misogyny? mass incarceration? carceral capitalism? toxic masculinity? predatory sexuality? domestic violence? hate crime? school shootings? mass shootings? The answer is *yes*. Jennifer Carlson ends her *Policing the Second Amendment* with this sentence: "There is an alternative to the reductive, unproductive debate about gun violence in the United States, and it starts by refusing to see the gun debate and police reform as isolated political projects." Any one of us, and we all of us, would do well to heed her counsel, and even to add political projects to the pair she names, which are not isolated from each other, or from a whole cadre of interconnected concerns.

Focus] • [Limitation

In the sciences and social sciences, prevailing standards for presenting results include explicitly identifying limitations of the research being reported. Here is one limitation of the research presented in *American Outrage*: in some ways it reproduces and reinforces precisely what it would resist. It would contest the underreporting of certain types of violence (e.g. domestic violence), but it relies methodologically on existing reports. It would shift the emphasis in testimony away from familiarizing ("he had a heart of gold") and toward particularizing ("she taught history at the same high school she had attended"), but it can only give particulars already given by others. Though *American Outrage* has not *sought* to be limited in these ways, it cannot but *suffer* such limitations.

Limitation] • [Structure

Episodes of violence manifest systems of violence and realize violent conceptions. The names in this testamentary emphasize that violence is episodic, the numbers and notices that violence is not *only* episodic. The numbers emphasize that violence is systemic, the names and notices that violence is not *only* systemic. The notices emphasize that violence is conceptual, the names and numbers that violence is not *only* conceptual. Together, the three recognize that violence occurs *in* episodes, but not only *as* episode; *in* systems, but not only *as* system; *in* conceptions, but not only *as* conception.

Emphasis on one aspect of violence, far from *denying* the other aspects, actually *confirms* them. Emphasizing by the listing of names here the episodic character of violence does not *obscure* the systemic character of violence but *demonstrates* and *illuminates* it. Violence is episodic, yes, and episodes can be enumerated, but the fact that there have been so *many* episodes that even an *extensive* list is not an *exhaustive* list indicates that violence is also *structural.* The many episodes do not *hide* patterns, they *create* patterns and *fulfill* them and *reveal* them. The problems that contribute to the many episodes of violent death memorialized here are not confined to anomalous personalities — "bad guys" — operating independently from other factors.

Structure] • [13

Jessica Rekos kept a journal, and named her pet fish Betty. http://www.jessicarekos.org/about-jessica/. 0223.

Ethel Lee Lance worked as a custodian for more than thirty years at her city's municipal auditorium and for five years at her church. She loved gospel music, and her favorite song was "One Day at a Time." https://www.fallenheroesproject.org/post/ethel-lee-lance. 0223.

Ryan Clark was triple majoring in psychology, biology, and English, and working at a restaurant part-time to put himself through school. https://www.weremember.vt.edu/biographies/clark.html. 0223.

Satwant Singh Kaleka had been a farmer in India; he immigrated to the U.S. in his thirties. He had two children. http://sikhtempleofwisconsin.com/memorial. 0223.

Sonam Choedon enjoyed babysitting her two nieces, and she volunteered with the local Tibetan community center working with orphans whose parents had been killed. https://www.sfgate.com/crime/article/Oikos-shooting-victim-Sonam-Choedon-3456742.php. 0323.

Carole Robertson was a Girl Scout, and participated in a national service organization, Jack and Jill of America. https://www.ourbiography.com/carole-robertson/. 0323.

Angel Candelario-Padro had been born in Puerto Rico, and attended optometry school in Chicago. He lived in Florida. https://www.nytimes.com/interactive/projects/cp/us/orlando-shooting-victims/angell-candelario-padro. 0323. https://people.com/crime/orlando-pulse-shooting-tributes-to-49-victims/. 0323.

Garrett Swasey was born in Melrose, Massachusetts, but in his youth moved to Colorado Springs to train at the U.S. Olympic Training Center. He was an elder in his church, and sometimes played guitar as part of its worship services. He was the father of two children, a daughter and a son. https://www.cnn.com/2015/11/28/us/colorado-springs-police-officer-garrett-swasey/index.html. 0423.

Stephanie Works was home schooled, and was active in the college-age ministry at her family's church. She loved writing, music, and travel. She played chess every day with one of her younger sisters. https://www.findagrave.com/memorial/25654357/stephanie-pauline-works. 0423.

William Kinney went by "Will."
https://www.tennessean.com/story/news/local/2023/03/30/nashville-shooting-victim-will-kinney-covenant-student/70060282007/. 0423.

5,586: Diaz, *The Last Gun*, 1. Diaz adds the qualification that there were four exceptional years "in which the number of deaths fell slightly below 30,000 — 1999, 2000, 2001, 2004."

Violence results *from* violence: W. H. Auden, "September 1, 1939."
https://poets.org/poem/september-1-1939. 0423.
"Those to whom evil is done / Do evil in return."

Violence results *in* violence: Arendt, *On Violence*, 79-80:
"No doubt, 'violence pays,' but the trouble is that it pays indiscriminately.... The practice of violence, like all action, changes the world, but the most probable change is to a more violent world."

Commitment *of* violence: Berry, *Imagination in Place*, 30.
Violence "is its own way, which is entirely unlike the ways of thought or dialogue or work or art or any manner of caretaking. Once you have committed yourself to the way of violence, you can only suffer it through to exhaustion and accept the always unforeseen results."

13] • [14

Karla Holcombe worked as the assistant secretary at her church, and also taught Sunday school. Bryan Holcombe had a canvas shop and worked in a volunteer associate pastor role at his church.
https://people.com/crime/holcombe-family-killed-texas-church-shooting/. 0523.

Melvin Wax was retired from his work as an accountant.
https://www.cnn.com/2018/10/28/us/pittsburgh-synagogue-shooting-victims/index.html. 0523.

Nevaeh Bravo was ten years old, and had two brothers and a sister.
https://www.hillcrestmemorialfuneralhome.com/obituaries/Nevaeh-Bravo/#!/Obituary. 0523.
https://www.pressreader.com/usa/san-antonio-express-news-sunday/20230521/281715503978500. 0523.

Rhonda LeRocque lived near Boston, with her husband and daughter.
https://www.bustle.com/p/who-was-rhonda-lerocque-the-las-vegas-victim-42-attended-route-91-harvest-festival-with-her-family-2761775. 0523.

Andre Mackniel and his fiancée had one son. He loved basketball, collecting books, and listening to music. https://www.legacy.com/us/obituaries/buffalonews/name/andre-mackniel-obituary?id=34902559. 0523.

Tralona Bartkowiak went by "Lonna." She managed and was a co-owner of a clothing store and artist collective in Boulder, Colorado.

https://www.findagrave.com/memorial/224796290/tralona-lynn-bartkowiak. 0523.
https://www.nytimes.com/2021/03/23/us/boulder-victims.html. 0523.

Maribel Hernández Loya enjoyed getting together with friends and barbequing, especially ribs. She had a favorite motto: "shaa-shhinggg!!!" She had a favorite plant in her garden, a bougainvillea. https://www.elpasotimes.com/obituaries/tnm018121. 0523.

Chia Ling Yau loved music, dance, and travel. https://news.yahoo.com/11-victims-were-killed-monterey-023802697.html. 0623.

Stephon Clark was a high school graduate.
https://en.wikipedia.org/wiki/Killing_of_Stephon_Clark. 0523.

Phillip High Bear was 33. https://www.charlesrooksfuneralhome.com/obituaries/Phillip-High-Bear/#!/Obituary. 0523.

650,000,000: As estimated by the Small Arms Survey.
https://www.smallarmssurvey.org/database/global-firearms-holdings. 0323.

Guns aren't the only way: Springwood, "The Social Life of Guns: An Introduction," 11.
"Clearly, violence, even mass murder, existed before the invention of firearms…. And without a doubt, weapons far more powerful than firearms, from missile launchers to explosives to chemical agents, prevail in many conflicts around the world. Yet it is impossible to attempt an insightful analysis of patterns of armed violence, in global perspective, without accounting for the persistence and power of guns."

What guns symbolize: Taylor, *American Gun Culture*, 1-2.
Prior studies of the symbolic value of guns in the U.S. "have proceeded with the incomplete premise that gun owners assign a universal meaning to all of their guns: protection, patriotism and freedom. This limited view overlooks a world of ritual activity and human emotion that determines how guns are defined and ultimately used. In order for social policy pertaining to the use of objects and ideas to be meaningful and effective, the symbolic values assigned to these objects, in motion, must first be understood, as these symbolic meanings will come to determine how objects — such as guns — are used in practice."

Guns don't have to: Herbert, "Arming the Settler Colony," 26.
"Much like the racially based fears associated with US gun culture, suburbia emerged as a safe haven for wealthy and middle-class white families that harbored anxieties over the racial and ethnic diversity found within the migrating working poor found in newly urbanizing spaces. This spatial management of the nonwhite poor parallels the spatial relationship that white settlers maintained between white settlements and nonwhite land and labor in the foundation of the United States. Given the low crime rates and heavy police surveillance found in most contemporary American suburbs, a gun within the home likely functions as a visual symbol of freedom and dominance with little feasible utility: it rejuvenates the historical relationship between violence and land ownership while relying upon the proxy means of protection afforded by police departments, security companies and insurance policies."

James Cho was 3 years old, but could read and was writing his own name. https://abcnews.go.com/US/mom-dad-3-year-son-killed-texas-mass/story?id=99201272. 0623.

Ahmaud Arbery ran every day, and lifted weights. He often sang freestyle rap. He had played linebacker for his high school football team. He wanted to become an electrician, and was saving money to continue his coursework at South Georgia Technical College. https://www.reuters.com/legal/government/who-was-ahmaud-arbery-2021-11-18/. 0623.

Quintonio LeGrier was nineteen years old. He had a history of mental health issues. https://www.newsweek.com/bettie-jones-and-quintonio-legrier-two-black-people-shot-and-killed-chicago-409207. 0623.

Madeleine Hsu liked to sing along with the radio. https://mysandyhookfamily.org/. 0223.

Clementa Pinckney was pastor of "Mother Emanuel" AME Church, and understood religious devotion to extend beyond a given congregation to "the life and community in which our congregation resides." https://obamawhitehouse.archives.gov/the-press-office/2015/06/26/remarks-president-eulogy-honorable-reverend-clementa-pinckney. 0223. https://www.blackpast.org/african-american-history/pinckney-clementa-c-1973-2015/. 0223.

Caitlin Hammaren was events chair for her chapter of Kappa Kappa Gamma sorority. She was majoring in international studies and French. At her high school junior prom, she had worn a hand-made Renaissance dress, and gone with a boy who wore a purple kilt. http://vt-memorial.org/profiles/Hammaren.html. 0223. https://www.weremember.vt.edu/biographies/hammaren.html. 0223.

Katleen Ping was born in the Philippines and had been studying nursing there. She continued nursing study after emigrating to the U.S. https://www.sfgate.com/crime/article/Oikos-shooting-victim-Katleen-Ping-3455757.php. 0323.

Carol McNair helped raise money for charity by staging plays, dance routines, and poetry readings in the family carport. https://www.findagrave.com/memorial/6433280/carol-denise-mcnair. 0323.

Simon Carrillo and his partner had recently bought their first house, and had just returned from a vacation trip to Niagara Falls. https://www.npr.org/sections/thetwo-way/2016/06/12/481785763/heres-what-we-know-about-the-orlando-shooting-victims. 0323.

Sita Singh was born in India, and had lived in England and Canada before moving to the U.S. http://sikhtempleofwisconsin.com/memorial. 0223.

17: Borum et al., "What Can Be Done," 27. The researchers add that more than 9,700 young people were killed in accidents that year, and observe that "The fear of school shootings is greatly exaggerated in comparison with other risks such as riding in a car."

Individual-level explanations: Marganski, "Making a Murderer," 3.
"Pointing to individual pathologies may be favorable to those who are uncomfortable confronting social and cultural forces at play. However, it hinders understanding because it overlooks the context that drives and produces violent offending. In order to understand mass murder and similarly egregious acts, it is imperative that we contextualize violence and explore risk across a wide range of levels. To reduce events to individual-level explanations neglects relationship and institutional factors that impact offending as well as the larger society and culture where concerning behaviors are able to grow and thrive."

Assigning violence: Nicholas Mirzoeff, in Evans and Lennart, *Violence*, 88.
"Where there is violence, there is a message. Because so many forms of human action can be defined as violent, it is always a key political moment when a particular group or person is identified [as having 'turned violent']. Defining violence as a personal choice, as if it were a consumer purchase, hides systemic or structural violence, such as poverty or racism. It presents the state as the only legitimate user of violence, in an implied social contract in which citizens renounce violence in exchange for protection. To be violent, in defiance of the state's monopoly on violence, is therefore to be a kind of traitor."

As long as we: Mahmood, "Gun Cultures," 276.
"For Americans, the idea of owning a gun is a highly individualized concept. One applies in person for the license to purchase and carry a gun, just as one applies personally for a driver's license or a fishing license. Even if one later joins a group like a militia, it is not the militia that is seeking the guns; it is individuals. It is believed at this point that the Wisconsin shooter who killed Sikhs worshipping at a Wisconsin *gurudwara* acted alone; if so, he probably felt he was heroically protecting American society as a lone, courageous man. School shootings all too frequent in the US society point to lonely and bullied teens, not to organized or political groupings."

15] • [16

Emily Garcia. https://www.findagrave.com/memorial/184994516/emily-rain-garcia. 0523. https://www.nytimes.com/2017/11/07/us/sutherland-springs-texas-victims.html. 0523.

Ke'Arre Stewart once quit a job because his boss wouldn't give him time off to attend his daughter's ballet recital. https://www.cbsnews.com/texas/news/iraq-veteran-killed-in-colorado-shooting-leaves-behind-children-in-texas/. 0423. https://obits.gazette.com/us/obituaries/gazette/name/ke-arre-stewart-obituary?id=15603837. 0423. https://www.cnn.com/2015/11/30/us/colorado-planned-parenthood-shooting-victims/index.html. 0423.

Rachel Works was home schooled, and was active in her family's church. She had been to Brazil, Mexico, and China on youth mission trips.

https://obits.gazette.com/us/obituaries/gazette/name/rachel-works-obituary?id=24472013. 0423.

Hallie Scruggs. https://www.tennessean.com/story/news/crime/2023/03/30/family-of-hallie-scruggs-9-mourns-loss-we-are-heartbroken/70057467007/. 0423.

Irving Younger was retired from his work as a real estate agent. https://www.cnn.com/2018/10/28/us/pittsburgh-synagogue-shooting-victims/index.html. 0523. https://jewishchronicle.timesofisrael.com/irving-younger/. 0523. https://people.com/crime/synagogue-shooting-victims-names-photos/. 0523.

Uziyah Garcia was known to his family as "Uzi." He loved playing Nintendo Switch and Oculus. His favorite color was red. He liked vacationing with his aunt and uncle. https://www.gosanangelo.com/obituaries/sas021354. 0523.

Pearl Young worked for many years as a missionary at her church's food pantry and soup kitchen. She earned a college degree while she was in her thirties and raising three children. https://www.wkbw.com/news/local-news/buffalos-mass-shooting-victim-pearl-young-devoted-to-her-church-community. 0523.

Teri Leiker, despite her mild cognitive differences, had graduated from her high school's special education program, and then was able to live independently. She was a loyal fan of the University of Colorado sports teams. https://www.dignitymemorial.com/obituaries/boulder-co/teri-leiker-10125506. 0523.

Margie Reckard had three children. https://abcnews.go.com/US/thousands-expected-attend-funeral-el-paso-shooting-victim/story?id=65014173. 0623.

Brennan Stewart was 30, and lived in Las Vegas. https://people.com/crime/las-vegas-shooting-victims-names-photos-tributes/. 0523.

14,157: In 2012, as reported in Boss, *Guns and College Homicide*, 36.

"[S]omething more than: Holmes, Painter, and Smith, "Race, Place, and Police-Caused Homicide," 781.

Racial disparities: Mesic et al., "The Relationship between Structural Racism," 114. "Future efforts to reduce the deeply rooted racial disparities in firearm violence cannot succeed unless the role of structural racism is directly confronted."

Reducing the number: Phelps, Robertson, and Powell, " 'We're Still Dying Quicker," 898. "Dramatically reducing the number of people killed by the police… will require many kinds of transformations in tandem, including addressing the high rates of gun violence in low-income communities of color; reducing the prevalence of discriminatory police stops in those same communities; and altering the policies, training, and accountability structures that guide officers' decisions. In other words, we need alternatives to the police, we need to invest in addressing root causes, and we need transformative changes in policing."

16] • [17

Christian Escobedo. https://www.fightbacknews.org/2018/2/19/angry-chicano-community-protests-lapd-killing-christian-escobedo. 0523.

Julisa Molina Rivera. https://abcnews.go.com/US/5-victims-texas-shooting/story?id=98960747. 0623.

Shawn Jackson was 18. He liked rap music, and he played sports, including football, basketball, and baseball. https://www.nbcnews.com/news/us-news/family-mourns-father-son-killed-hs-graduation-shooting-police-name-sus-rcna88164. 0623. https://www.usatoday.com/story/news/nation/2023/06/07/richmond-graduation-shooting-updates-victims/70296703007/. 0623.

Pedro Cortez went by "Junior" or "Moko." His favorite drink was Hennessy. (Younge, *Another Day in the Death of America.*)

Beatrice Dotson. https://www.seattletimes.com/seattle-news/law-justice/burlington-mall-shooting-victims-officially-identified/. 0323.

Destiny Howard had been born into a family of five brothers and five sisters. https://www.them.us/story/destiny-howard-trans-woman-killed-in-georgia. 0323.

Walter Scott worked in a warehouse. (Hill, *Nobody.*)

Avielle Richman. https://www.cuanschutz.edu/centers/national-mental-health-innovation/the-avielle-initiative/history. 0223.

Myra Thompson, a mother of two, had earned two masters degrees, and was a licensed AME minister, working toward ordination. https://emanuelnine.epistles.faith/the-emanuel-nine/myra-thompson/. 0223. https://www.postandcourier.com/myra-thompson/article_4b6ced36-c878-11e6-a4ee-cf86ef5610f9.html. 0223.

Kenneth Mills-Tucker was a high-school graduate. (Younge, *Another Day in the Death of America.*)

71: of firearm deaths among children: Andrews et al., "Pediatric Firearm Injury Mortality Epidemiology," 39.

Fear immunizes: AlAmmar, *Silence Is a Sense*, 53-54.
"It's [an error] you see repeated on the news, in op-eds, in documentaries, in social media posts. There's this idea that if only you bombard bigots with enough facts and data and statistics, you can cure them. This notion that their hatred comes from a place of ignorance is one people have a hard time shaking. It's not lack of education…. It's fear; fear of the unknown, the Other, fear

that things are changing in ways he can't predict or control. Fear doesn't waver in the face of facts." These are the words of the first-person speaker in the novel.

Numb to others' pain: George Yancy, in Evans and Lennart, *Violence*, 41.
"The fact that we don't hear cries of pain doesn't let us off the hook. Ethical discourse and practice must be imbued with an effort to remain honest, especially about one's own ethical shortcomings and the pain and suffering that we cause others."

Traumatic events: Wallace, "Responding to Violence," 165.
"[M]ass shootings are associated with a jump in the number of Federal background checks. This increase is delayed and short-term. However, this effect raises important questions about the effects of gun ownership and acquisition for violence as well as the impact of the media on individual decision-making. While this study cannot speak to individual-level processes or explain why a person may purchase a gun following a shooting, it is clear that traumatic events have far-reaching consequences for outcomes besides crime itself."

17] • [18

Noah Holcombe. https://people.com/crime/holcombe-family-killed-texas-church-shooting/. 0523. https://heavy.com/news/2017/11/sutherland-springs-texas-church-shooting-victims-list-names-photos-pictures/. 0523.

Rachael Hill was an only child. She intended eventually to get a Ph.D. in biochemistry, with a specialization in nanotechnology. https://www.weremember.vt.edu/biographies/hill.htm. 0223. http://www.vt-memorial.org/profiles/Hill.html. 0223.

Ranjit Singh had four siblings. He and his wife had three children. http://sikhtempleofwisconsin.com/memorial. 0223.

Grace Eunhae Kim was studying nursing, and worked as a waitress at a restaurant/brewpub. https://www.sfgate.com/crime/article/Oikos-shooting-victim-Grace-Eunhea-Kim-3457417.php. 0323.

Addie Mae Collins "happily went door-to-door in white neighborhoods of Birmingham to sell aprons and potholders her mother had stitched together, to make ends meet." https://gunviolencememorial.org/apple/. 0323.

Akyra Murray went by "Kira." She had signed a letter of intent to play basketball at Mercyhurst University on a full scholarship. https://www.orlandoweekly.com/news/remembering-the-orlando-49-4833144. 0323.

Jennifer Markovsky was born in Hawai'i, and moved to Colorado when her husband was stationed there in the military. https://www.cnn.com/2015/11/30/us/colorado-planned-parenthood-shooting-victims/index.html. 0423.

Philip Crouse had been raised in Alaska, and in his youth had been involved with drugs and drinking, but after a religious conversion he became a staff member for the nonprofit organization "Youth with a Mission." https://www.southcoasttoday.com/story/news/nation-world/2007/12/11/a-look-at-colorado-church/52713200007/. 0423.

Cynthia Peak grew up in Louisiana, and went to college in Texas. She taught swim lessons and tutored outside of school. https://www.cnn.com/2023/03/28/us/victims-covenant-school-shooting-nashville/index.html. 0423. https://williamsonsource.com/obituary-cynthia-peak/. 0423.

Richard Rodriguez. https://www.cbsnews.com/news/texas-shooting-massacre-victims-sutherland-springs-first-baptist-church/. 0523.

18: number of bullets: Klarevas, *Rampage Nation*, 211-12.

War declared against: Skolnick and Fyfe, *Above the Law*, 133.
"Most important, street cops should not be encouraged to see themselves as soldiers locked in a war.

In fact, police brutality is inevitable when, as has happened in some places, officers describe themselves as *ghetto gunslingers* or as troopers assigned to isolated outposts of civilization."

Militarizing police weaponry: Hayes, "The Thriving Life of Racialized Weaponry," 119.
"Enhanced militarization efforts by police in the US more generally point to a trend in which police officers are increasingly outfitted with not only more potent and military-grade weaponry but also weaponry that allows them to enjoy increased distance from the suspects they target as well as the weapons themselves…. [I]n the necropolitical logic that marks the social life of weapons, this distance mirrors the same distance found in the relationship of the drone operator from their insurgent targets and from the weapon itself. And, those targets, in both cases, are disproportionately people of color."

Expansion of the criminal: Davis, "Predation in State and Nation," 206.
"My central argument here is that the predatory state exists and operates at all levels of government and through all its institutions…. Crime and punishment are institutional outputs and more importantly, punishment is not directly correlated with criminal activity. McNeely and Pope (1981) find that race has a direct impact on the ecology of justice and on the organizational characteristics of the institution of criminal justice. The expansion of the criminal justice system represents an unprecedented expansion of predaceous governmental power into the everyday lives of—some—Americans, which produces severe adverse consequences for those individuals, their families, and communities."

18] • [19

Carlos LaMadrid was married to Nydia Valenzuela. https://www.alipac.us/f12/carlos-lamadrids-family-speaks-out-about-border-patrol-shoo-221721-print/. 0523.

Alexander Mikhail Gusev had worked for nine years as a right of way agent in his city's public works department. He played soccer with friends every Sunday morning. https://time.com/5599393/victims-viginia-beach-shooting/. 0623. https://people.com/crime/virginia-beach-mass-shooting-victims-identified/. 0623.

Omarian Banks. https://www.nytimes.com/2023/04/20/us/wrong-house-shootings-guns.html. 0423.

Sarah Lee Circle Bear. https://ebwiki.org/cases/sarah-lee-circle-bear. 0523.

DeAunta Farrow. https://www.learntheirstories.com/#/deaunta-farrow/. 0623.

Punjab Singh was known in his community as "Baba ji." http://sikhtempleofwisconsin.com/memorial. 0223.

Sharonda Coleman-Singleton was the mother of two sons and a daughter. She was studying for a doctoral degree. https://emanuelnine.epistles.faith/the-emanuel-nine/rev-sharonda-coleman-singleton/. 0223.

Henry Lee was born in Vietnam, the ninth of ten children. Henry Lee was his chosen name, echoing his given name, Hehn Ly. He was majoring in computer engineering, and liked origami and photography, raquetball and Frisbee. http://www.vt-memorial.org/profiles/Lee.html. 0223. https://www.weremember.vt.edu/biographies/lee.html. 0223.

Lydia Sim was studying nursing, and wanted eventually to attend medical school. She lived with her parents and brother. https://www.sfgate.com/crime/article/Oikos-shooting-victim-Lydia-Sim-3456234.php. 0323.

Anne Marie Murphy. https://www.newstimes.com/news/article/paraprofessional-Anne-Marie-Murphy-Sandy-Hook-17590216.php. 0223. https://www.legacy.com/us/obituaries/newstimes/name/anne-murphy-obituary?id=18736368. 0223.

3: number of times: Dawson, "Shall Not Be Infringed," 6, 9.

"Privatizing violence: Wilkes, "This Is America On Guns," 119.
Later in the same paragraph, Wilkes expands on the quoted sentence. "Privatizing gun violence, silencing those who would discuss gun control policy as violators of decorum, and privileging individual rights over collective rights forcefully maintain a deadly status quo that, for the most part, garners only fleeting engagement in media environments. When firearm-related deaths remain a daily occurrence and the collective response, underwritten by discourses of privatization, amounts to short-lived 'thoughts and prayers,' a majority of Americans have acquiesced to gun violence as the status quo. This is America on guns."

Privatizing violence precludes: Gage, "National News Coverage," 180.

News media customarily engage in "displays of mass shooters as aberrant individuals, and with those displays, representations of gun violence as expressions of individual deviance rather than expressions of dominant social structures and cultures…. In this reporting, national media strategically reveal white supremacy to be a form of direct violence inflicted by deranged individuals while simultaneously concealing white supremacy as a form of structural and cultural violence. Concealing white supremacy's structural and cultural functions attempts to curtail interrogations of its 'systemic roots.' Without such interrogation, white supremacy, and its attendant gun violence, is allowed to persist, for white supremacy cannot be redressed if it is understood as a violence limited to individual actors."

The state's coercive powers: Kautzer, "Good Guys with Guns," 174.
"The rapid liberalization of open- and concealed-carry laws, the proliferation of guns in public spaces and institutions, the reinterpretation of the Second Amendment of the US Constitution, and the abstraction and individuation of the Castle Doctrine in Stand Your Ground laws all contribute to the legalization of nonstate violence to defend extra-legal relations of domination…. Since the state is accused of being unwilling to exercise its coercive powers to stabilize these relations of domination as it has in the past, individuals have sought to arrogate such powers to themselves; a privatization of state violence through the quasi-deputization of certain groups."

19] • [20

Alejandro Barrios Martínez was still learning English. https://tdn.com/alejandro-barrios-martinez/article_a73da83e-3eea-5f80-b0a9-55d23915f732.html. 0323.

Cynthia Morris stayed during the week with a couple, Claude and Gertrude Wesley, who were unable to have children, in order to attend a better school. https://abc3340.com/archive/family-of-16th-st-bombing-victim-says-a-name-has-been-wrong-for-decades. 0323. https://www.splcenter.org/news/2020/09/15/four-girls-forever-lost-57-years-ago-16th-street-baptist-church-bombing-awakened-nation. 0323.

Tiffany Johnson was a staff member of the nonprofit organization "Youth with a Mission." She planned to attend university in her home state, Minnesota. https://tiffanyjohnsonmemorialfund.com/story.php. 0423.

Mike Hill had seven children and fourteen grandchildren. The students at the school where he worked called him "Big Mike." He enjoyed cooking. https://www.cnn.com/2023/03/28/us/victims-covenant-school-shooting-nashville/index.html. 0423. https://www.tennessean.com/story/news/2023/03/29/big-strong-mike-nashville-shooting-victim-mike-hill-remembered/70057251007/. 0423.

Joyce Fienberg had two sons and six grandchildren. https://abcnews.go.com/US/pittsburgh-synagogue-shooting-portraits-11-victims/story?id=58823835. 0523.

Alithia Ramirez had one brother and one sister. https://www.legacy.com/us/obituaries/name/alithia-ramirez-obituary?id=34946650. 0523.

Hannah Ahlers married her high-school sweetheart; she and her husband had three children. https://www.cheerstohannah.com/. 0523. https://www.nytimes.com/2017/10/02/us/vegas-victims-names.html. 0523.

Margus Morrison had worked as a school bus aide for three years. https://spectrumlocalnews.com/nys/central-ny/news/2023/05/06/family-members-remember-margus-morrison. 0523. https://www.cnn.com/2022/05/15/us/buffalo-shooting-victims-what-we-know/index.html. 0523.

Rikki Olds worked as store manager for a grocery chain. Her favorite color was pink. Work colleagues had nicknamed her "Wendy" because she often wore her hair in braids. https://www.findagrave.com/memorial/226359297/rikki-lyn-olds. 0523. https://www.denver7.com/news/boulder-king-soopers-shooting/the-light-of-our-family-uncle-of-rikki-olds-killed-in-boulder-shooting-shares-her-story. 0523.

Megan Hill. https://www.arbormemorial.ca/preview/mountlawn/megan-gail-hill/13992. 0523. https://www.mysanantonio.com/news/local/article/Services-honor-Holcombe-family-killed-in-12359588.php. 0523.

55: of homes in the U.S.: 1994 and 2000 data. Schuster et al., "Firearm Storage Patterns," 590.

"[I]n addition to being protected: Stroud, "Guns Don't Kill People," 6.
The quoted passage completes Stroud's argument that the anti-reform position of "the most visible and vocal segment of gun owners" is "not first and foremost about guns—it is instead an assertion of patriarchal white domination. After all, there is no reason that a gun owner's identity should be threatened by gun control laws."

Maybe guns *would* protect: Horwitz and Anderson, *Guns, Democracy, and the Insurrectionist Idea*, 1, 223.
In the view we call *Insurrectionism*, "unfettered access to firearms is the key ingredient in protecting individual rights from overreaching by government. [Insurrectionists] argue that the best way — in fact, the only way — to keep centralized authority in check is to ensure that individual citizens retain the capability to confront the government with force of arms.... If we believed that the highest gun-death rate of any mature democracy were really the price of freedom, as some Insurrectionists have suggested, we have no doubt that the price would be worth paying. The problem is that the Insurrectionist idea has left us with the worst of both worlds — a society where firearm violence is all too prevalent even as democratic safeguards are under attack."

Maybe police would shoot: Barlow and Barlow, *Police in a Multicultural Society*, 19.
"Media portrayals of police tend to perpetuate a one-dimensional perspective on police as crime fighters, and police officers and their leadership are quick to embrace this perspective. Researchers consistently demonstrate that the police themselves define their role in terms of fighting crime and catching criminals, despite the research evidence to the contrary.... Police officers struggle to maintain their vision of themselves as 'fighters of crime,' even when they are

engaged in the daily work of controlling the whereabouts and activities of those who are homeless or deemed disorderly."

20] • [21

Daniel Enrique Laso-Guzmán lived in Cleveland, Texas. https://abcnews.go.com/US/5-victims-texas-shooting/story?id=98960747. 0623. https://www.click2houston.com/news/local/2023/05/01/family-shares-photos-of-san-jacinto-county-shooting-victims/. 0623.

Destinee Thompson. https://www.cbsnews.com/news/destinee-thompson-family-lawsuit-pregnant-mother-3-fatally-shot-by-police-denver-suburb-arvada/. 0923.

Javier Rodriguez was 15. https://apnews.com/article/texas-shootings-immigration-us-news-el-paso-texas-mass-shooting-1aa03c4a153f4f6d9881f0f11cd2e89a. 0623.

Muoi Dai Ung liked to gamble. https://news.yahoo.com/11-victims-were-killed-monterey-023802697.html. 0623.

Renzo Smith was 36 years old. He had served in the Army Reserve from 2005 to 2006 as a motor transport operator before serving in the regular Army from 2006 to 2010. https://www.nbcnews.com/news/us-news/family-mourns-father-son-killed-hs-graduation-shooting-police-name-sus-rcna88164. 0623.

Christopher Rapp had worked as Stormwater Management Regulatory Engineer in his city's public works department for 11 months. He had a masters in civil and environmental engineering. He enjoyed nature, biking, and hiking. https://time.com/5599393/victims-viginia-beach-shooting/. 0623. https://people.com/crime/virginia-beach-mass-shooting-victims-identified/. 0623. https://www.dignitymemorial.com/obituaries/virginia-beach-va/christopher-rapp-8730264. 0623.

Rumain Brisbon frequently initiated living-room dance parties. He was 34 years old. https://www.learntheirstories.com/#/rumain-brisbon/. 0623.

Deion Fludd was 17, and had been raised in the Red Hooks projects. He had two older siblings and two younger siblings. https://www.learntheirstories.com/#/deion-fludd/. 0623.

Olivia Engel. https://www.nhregister.com/news/article/Newtown-victim-Olivia-Engel-comforted-by-police-11505396.php. 0223.

Larry Jackson. https://www.learntheirstories.com/#/larry-jackson-jr/. 0623.

$76.4 billion: https://www2.ed.gov/about/overview/budget/budget23/budget-highlights.pdf. 0323. **$557 billion**: https://everytownresearch.org/report/the-economic-cost-of-gun-violence/. 0323.

"[R]acial prejudice predicts: Jimenez, Helm, and Arndt, "Racial Prejudice Predicts," 2009.

Militarized policing exacerbates: Lindsay-Poland, "Understanding Police Militarization," 154. "When police departments adopt more militarized practices and increased firepower, the impacts of racial discrimination are escalated."

More police = less white risk: Siegel et al., "The Interaction of Race and Place," 260. "Also in contrast to the results for black victims, the likelihood of the victim being white decreased as the per capita number of police officers in a city increased. This latter finding is important because it argues against the hypothesis that the probability of a police shooting occurring is simply a function of the police presence in a city. While a greater police presence increases the risk of a fatal police shooting of a black person, it reduces the risk of a fatal police shooting of a white victim."

21] • [22

Karen Marshall planned to retire soon. https://www.nytimes.com/2017/11/07/us/sutherland-springs-texas-victims.html. 0523.

Tywanza Sanders performed in poetry slams. He worked as a licensed barber, and was about to begin graduate school for a degree in Media and Communication. https://emanuelnine.epistles.faith/the-emanuel-nine/tywanza-sanders/. 0223.

Nicole White was studying international relations. Her favorite movie was *Napoleon Dynamite*, and her favorite musicians included Bob Marley, Janis Joplin, and Outkast. http://www.vt-memorial.org/profiles/White.html. 0223.
https://www.weremember.vt.edu/biographies/white.html. 0223.

Prakash Singh was born in New Delhi. He had worked in the U.S. for seven years before receiving a green card. http://sikhtempleofwisconsin.com/memorial. 0223.

Doris Chibuko was born in Nigeria, and had been a lawyer there before emigrating to the U.S. She and her husband had three children. https://www.sfgate.com/crime/article/Oikos-shooting-victim-Doris-Chibuko-3457262.php. 0323.

Rodolfo Ayala-Ayala worked as a platelet supervisor at the nonprofit blood donation center OneBlood. The quoted words are a co-worker's. https://people.com/crime/orlando-pulse-shooting-tributes-to-49-victims/. 0323.
https://www.nytimes.com/interactive/projects/cp/us/orlando-shooting-victims/rodolfo-ayala-ayala. 0323.

Evelyn Dieckhaus liked to play with her older sister, and they liked to hold hands when they walked. She liked crafting and drawing. She wanted a pet rat for her next birthday, and wanted to be an occupational therapist when she grew up, like her mother.
https://www.nbcnews.com/news/us-news/evelyn-dieckhaus-9-remembered-beacon-light-hope-

first-nashville-school-rcna77575. 0423. https://www.tennessean.com/obituaries/ten252284. 0423.

Rose Mallinger had three children, five grandchildren and one great grandchild. She was known to her family and friends as "Bubbie," Yiddish for Grandma. https://abcnews.go.com/US/pittsburgh-synagogue-shooting-portraits-11-victims/story?id=58823835. 0523. https://www.cnn.com/2018/10/28/us/pittsburgh-synagogue-shooting-victims/index.html. 0523. https://people.com/crime/synagogue-shooting-victims-names-photos/. 0523.

Jailah Silguero. https://www.cnn.com/interactive/2023/05/us/victims-uvalde-school-shooting/. 0523.

Rekia Boyd was born in Chicago, and had moved with her family from Chicago's Southside to Dolton, Illinois. https://www.blackpast.org/african-american-history/boyd-rekia-1989-2012/. 0623.

20,000+: Extrapolating to "every year" from data for the years 2014 through 2019. https://www.gunviolencearchive.org/. 0323.

The harm guns cause: Diaz, *Making a Killing*, 8.
"Each of the millions of firearms that the gun industry produces, imports, and sells in the United States every year is lethal. Every type of gun sold in this country… can kill a human being…. Given the inherent lethality of firearms, it is no wonder that guns cause so much mayhem in the United States every year. The wonder is that our society has become so inured to firearms violence that we hardly pay attention to the casualties that mount steadily, day after day and year in and year out."

Events that warn us: Pawlett, *Violence, Society and Radical Theory*, 117.
"Horror and death suspend the routines of everyday life; suspend 'reality' — but only for a moment. Events that might provoke re-evaluations of the nature of society and community are buried, quickly, by the twittering banalities of consumer-driven culture where everything becomes entertainment, then disappears. We might respond to the suspension of reason in death and horror in more profound ways, resisting the re-production of consumer capitalism, pushing against the system, seeking new social and collective forms."

No understanding the offense: Bubar and Thurman, "Violence Against Native Women," 84.
"Native women emphasize the impact of the 'system as offender' upon battered women and the need for culturally based, meaningful research and effective programming."

22] • [23

Alexia Christian. https://www.wsbradio.com/news/news/woman-killed-in-shootout-with-atlanta-police-ident/nk7Jq/. 0623. https://www.lhamar.org/say-their-names-biography/alexia-christian. 0623.

Andrea Castilla worked as a sales associate at a Sephora store. Her mother had died when Andrea was 13. https://www.nytimes.com/2017/10/02/us/vegas-victims-names.html. 0523. https://www.latimes.com/nation/la-na-andrea-castilla-20171014-story.html. 0523.

Katherine Massey was the president of her block club, among other activities in her neighborhood. She never had children but was the family matriarch, a mother figure to her nieces and nephews. https://www.nbcnews.com/news/us-news/community-mourns-victims-buffalo-supermarket-shooting-rcna28935. 0523.

Eric Talley was a Star Wars fan. He was known for his Mountain Dew "habit." He left an IT job in cloud communications at age 40 to become a police officer. https://www.denverpost.com/2021/03/30/boulder-police-eric-talley-funeral/. 0523. https://www.nytimes.com/2021/03/23/us/boulder-victims.html. 0523.

Guillermo Garcia volunteered with his son's tee-ball team. He and his wife had met in high school, and he proposed to her by giving her a box of chocolates with the ring inside, wrapped as if it were a chocolate. https://cbs4local.com/news/local/wife-of-latest-walmart-shooting-victim-to-die-describes-memo-garcia-as-resilient-loving. 0523.

Sonia Argentina Guzmán. https://abcnews.go.com/US/5-victims-texas-shooting/story?id=98960747. 0623.

Michelle Langer worked as an administrative assistant in her city's public utilities department for 12 years. She liked working in her yard and watching football. She loved Paul McCartney and was a fan of the Michigan Wolverines and the Pittsburgh Steelers. https://time.com/5599393/victims-viginia-beach-shooting/. 0623. https://people.com/crime/virginia-beach-mass-shooting-victims-identified/. 0623. https://www.legacy.com/us/obituaries/pilotonline/name/michelle-langer-obituary?id=15314599. 0623.

Nicholas Heyward, Jr. https://www.learntheirstories.com/#/nicholas-heyward-jr/. 0623.

Bettie Jones was 55. Her children ranged in age from 19 to 38. https://abc7chicago.com/quintonio-legrier-bettie-jones-chicago-police-shooting/1148775/. 0623. https://www.newsweek.com/bettie-jones-and-quintonio-legrier-two-black-people-shot-and-killed-chicago-409207. 0623.

Jacob Hall was active in the Good News Club at his elementary school. https://www.legacy.com/us/obituaries/independentmail/name/jacob-hall-obituary?id=17607726. 0323. https://www.huffpost.com/entry/pictures-jacob-hall-superhero-funeral_n_57f56537e4b002a731209793. 0323.

34: https://bjs.ojp.gov/female-murder-victims-and-victim-offender-relationship-2021. 0323.

Military performance: Dunlap, "The Thick Green Line," 34.

"What we have seen in the last twenty years is a growing tendency to look to the armed forces to perform tasks that are essentially law enforcement.... Notwithstanding the seeming acquiescence of the public, this growing trend bears further analysis. In truth, there are few instances in modern times where the military effectively conducted a police-like internal security mission consistent with both the maintenance of an authentic combat capability and democratic values."

Consolidation of military and police: Dunn, "Waging a War on Immigrants," 79.
"The U.S.-Mexico border has served as a contemporary proving ground for the militarization of law enforcement: it has been implemented largely out of public view against subordinate groups in this peripheral region on a broader scale than anywhere else within the United States during the contemporary era.... This collaboration between the state's main corporal bureaucratic power structures does not bode well for the vulnerable status of subordinated groups.... The security of our human rights may hang in the balance."

Militarization disfigures: González, *Militarizing Culture*, 173.
"The end result of a militarized society is a greater propensity for war and its consequences: death, disfigurement, disease, depression, destruction.

Many Americans have forgotten this reality."

23] • [24

Tarika Wilson. https://www.learntheirstories.com/#/tarika-wilson/. 0623.

Victoria Soto's favorite color was green. https://people.com/human-interest/victoria-soto-connecticut-teacher-died-protecting-her-students/. 0223.

Depayne Middleton-Doctor was ordained as a minister in the Baptist and AME churches, both. https://emanuelnine.epistles.faith/the-emanuel-nine/rev-depayne-middleton-doctor/. 0223.

Ross Alameddine had worked, prior to college, as a home-computer repair specialist. https://www.weremember.vt.edu/biographies/alameddine.html. 0223.

Suveg Singh Khattra had two brothers and three sisters. http://sikhtempleofwisconsin.com/memorial. 0223.

Judith Seymour worked for years as a senior tax analyst, but had been laid off from that job. Nursing had been the occupation of both of her parents, who were Guyanese. https://www.sfgate.com/crime/article/Oikos-shooting-victim-Judith-Seymour-3457241.php. 0323.

Paul Henry had a daughter and a son. https://www.chicagotribune.com/os-orlando-mass-shooting-victim-paul-terrell-henry-20160613-story.html. 0323.

Katherine Koonce grew up in Baton Rouge, Louisiana, and had a master's degree from Georgia State and a doctorate from Trevecca University. https://www.cnn.com/2023/03/28/us/victims-

covenant-school-shooting-nashville/index.html. 0423.
https://www.tennessean.com/obituaries/ten252379. 0423.

Carlin Holcombe's nickname was given by the other children in the family without their yet knowing Carlin's gender. https://www.nytimes.com/2017/11/07/us/sutherland-springs-texas-victims.html. 0523.

Jeffrey Osborne had three children.
https://www.independentmail.com/story/news/local/2016/10/02/funeral-held-school-shooting-suspects-slain-father/91440080/. 0323.

78: Citing a Scripps Howard News Service study of data from 1980-2008. https://www.vox.com/2015/6/10/8757163/homicide-race. 0323. **16**: https://www.businessinsider.com/insider-investigation-5-years-of-transgender-homicides-2022-12#insider-compiled-a-comprehensive-account-of-the-rising-fatal-violence-targeting-transgender-people-1. 0323.

Every person shot: Schildkraut and Elsass, *Mass Shootings*, 159-60.
"The most abhorrent mistake in the wake of a mass shooting is the lack of emphasis on the victims of these tragedies by the media, politicians, pundits, and the general public alike. In the midst of all the inaccurate reporting and generation of myths, the most important topic — those who lost their lives — often largely is left out of the conversation…. The media's focus on only certain victims of these tragedies is a travesty. Every life matters, and in the case of mass shootings, each victim is equally important and represents a heartbreaking loss."

Violence attacks a person: Evans and Lennart, "Introduction," 3.
"Violence is always an attack upon a person's dignity, sense of selfhood, and future. It is nothing less than the desecration of one's position in the world. And it is a denial and outright assault on the very qualities that we claim make us considered members of this social fellowship and shared union called 'civilization.' In this regard, we might say violence is both an ontological crime, insomuch as it seeks to destroy the image we give to ourselves as valued individuals, and a form of political ruination that stabs at the heart of a human togetherness that emerges from the ethical desire for worldly belonging."

"Violence, like other traumas: Dawn Lundy Martin, as quoted in Kearney, *Optic Subwoof*, 110.

24] • [25

Tracy Gaeta was 54. https://www.nbcnews.com/news/us-news/california-woman-fatally-shot-police-was-victim-shocking-excessive-for-rcna24340. 0623.

Bernard Whitehurst was 32. https://www.learntheirstories.com/#/bernard-whitehurst/. 0623.

Brooke Ward was five years old. https://www.findagrave.com/memorial/184994553/brooke-bryann-ward. 0523. https://www.mysanantonio.com/news/local/article/Shooting-victim-Joann-Ward-s-life-was-all-about-12338429.php. 0523.

Cecil Rosenthal and David Rosenthal both were developmentally disabled. David was employed by Goodwill Industries. At their synagogue, both participated at each service in taking the Torahs out. https://www.schugar.com/obituaries?id=1714. 0523. https://time.com/5437123/victims-tree-of-life-synagogue-shooting-pittsburgh/. 0523.

Amerie Garza loved to swim, draw, and spend time with her family. She liked vanilla bean frappes and Chick-fil-A. She wanted to become an art teacher. https://www.npr.org/2022/05/27/1101286508/what-we-know-about-the-victims-of-the-uvalde-school-shooting. 0523. https://www.texastribune.org/2022/05/25/uvalde-school-shooting-victims/. 0523.

Heather Alvarado had three children. Her favorite color was hot pink. https://www.reviewjournal.com/crime/homicides/las-vegas-shooting-victim-heather-alvarado-remembered-for-kind-spirit/. 0523. https://www.thespectrum.com/story/news/local/cedar-city/2017/10/13/las-vegas-shooting-victim-heather-alvarado-remembered-her-love-family/761904001/. 0523.

Roberta Drury had moved from Syracuse to Buffalo to help her brother through his treatment for leukemia. https://cnycentral.com/news/local/sister-of-roberta-drury-reflects-on-her-death-one-year-after-buffalo-mass-shooting. 0523. https://www.npr.org/2022/05/21/1100560941/the-youngest-of-the-10-buffalo-shooting-victims-was-laid-to-rest. 0523.

Denny Stong was a dirt biker and remote-controlled airplane hobbyist. He was an avid supporter of the National Foundation for Gun Rights. https://www.nytimes.com/2021/03/23/us/boulder-victims.html. 0523.

Angie Englisbee had raised all of her seven children by herself, often working multiple jobs to support them, after her husband died of a heart attack. She had a routine of going to church daily. https://people.com/crime/el-paso-mass-shooting-remembering-victims/. 0523. https://www.koat.com/article/one-year-later-remembering-the-santa-fe-native-killed-in-el-paso-mass-shooting/33503782#. 0523. https://apnews.com/article/texas-shootings-immigration-us-news-el-paso-texas-mass-shooting-1aa03c4a153f4f6d9881f0f11cd2e89a. 0623.

Jalen Randle. https://abc13.com/jalen-randle-unarmed-man-shot-and-killed-houston-police/11805083/. 0623.

100: Witkowski, "Mythical Moments in Remington Brand History," 63. Witkowski's obervation was made in 2015. My visit to the website in late May of 2023 suggested that Witkowski's observation still applied at that time.

Open carry is equally open: Neville-Shepard and Kelly, "Whipping It Out," 468. "The open carry of firearms is emblematic of the political radicalization of White men in response to the relative social and economic gains of women, people of color, and other marginalized groups."

What made cars: Goldstick et al., "Current Epidemiological Trends," 242.
"Successful public health approaches have been applied to reverse worsening mortality trajectories for other mechanisms of injury, such as motor vehicle crash. If a similar road map is followed with regard to firearm mortality, it may be possible to reverse the current trend and reset to a new, lower, endemic firearm mortality rate."

Consistent rules: Vizzard, "Our Gun Laws Are Fine," 189.
"Because more than 100 million Americans do own guns, the laws applying to them should be clear, consistent, and easy to understand and follow. This is a more difficult goal than it might seem. In addition to federal law, each state, city, and county can pass laws and ordinances applying to gun ownership, transportation, sales, or purchase. We should make every effort to follow the pattern of laws relating to automobiles, which provide uniform rules that are easy to follow."

25] • [26

Jayland Walker was 25. https://www.usatoday.com/story/news/nation/2023/06/26/bci-report-jayland-walker-life-before-shooting/70352022007/?gnt-cfr=1. 0623.

Diana Man Ling Tom loved to dance. https://www.pasadenastarnews.com/2023/01/29/the-victims-seniors-who-found-joy-in-a-monterey-park-dance-studio/. 0623.

Aishwarya Thatikonda had come to the U.S. from Hyderabad, India. Her employer was a Dallas, Texas general contracting firm. https://news.yahoo.com/know-victims-mass-shooting-allen-003821790.html?guccounter=1&guce_referrer=aHR0cHM6Ly9kdWNrZHVja2dvLmNvbS8&guce_referrer_sig=AQAAADuwXbClvnVozi5EYSSS9kZdxGxoUqCI1NbE9xkjNlyFItOcF9I4_Skpt34TyOJnI8c_oV7WTln2l5LpdBwSAti6cy7ro6eLhWd5Gv7JGTO27Qk6Tpb773jPprJq5qV00-ifMhi7ZKN4S4UAh8dWoIkyToxs4pwqdgKf6PCPmjT2. 0623.

José Jonathan Casárez. https://abcnews.go.com/US/5-victims-texas-shooting/story?id=98960747. 0623.

Katherine Nixon had worked in her city's public utilities department for 10 years, overseeing the department's regulatory compliance. She and her husband had three daughters, ages 1, 6, and 12. She loved the seaside. https://time.com/5599393/victims-viginia-beach-shooting/. 0623. https://people.com/crime/virginia-beach-mass-shooting-victims-identified/. 0623.

Kelly Loving had been born in Batesville, Mississippi, but had recently moved from Memphis to Denver. https://www.denverpost.com/2022/11/21/club-q-shooting-victim-kelly-loving-obit/. 0623. https://www.cpr.org/2022/12/06/kelly-loving-funeral-club-q-shooting/. 0623. https://www.nytimes.com/article/victims-colorado-springs-shooting.html. 0623.

Tyshon Anderson went by "Lakesidegangsta" on Instagram. He liked the movies *Rambo* and *The Hills Have Eyes*, and the TV shows *Futurama* and *Family Guy*. (Younge, *Another Day in the Death of America*.)

Danroy Henry was the oldest of three siblings. He had played soccer in junior high, and been a three-sport athlete in high school. https://www.learntheirstories.com/#/danroy-henry/. 0623. https://djdreamfund.org/who-we-are/. 0623.

Charleena Lyles had found her job through the work of a nonprofit that helps homeless persons find work. https://www.blackpast.org/african-american-history/lyles-charleena-1987-2017/. 0423.

Emily Hill. https://www.nytimes.com/2017/11/07/us/sutherland-springs-texas-victims.html. 0523.

17: McGinty et al., "News Media Framing," 409.

Black men are targeted: Russell-Brown, "Making Implicit Bias Explicit," 152.
"While black men as a group face a particular threat of criminalization and disparate levels of lethal force when compared with white men, darker-skinned men are disproportionately targeted by the police. The majority of the high-profile cases involving police killings of black men bear out these findings. Case examples include Michael Brown (Missouri), Freddie Gray (Maryland), Walter Scott (South Carolina), Alton Sterling (Louisiana), Sam DuBose (Ohio), Philando Castile (Minnesota), and Corey Jones (Florida)."

Inhibit the activation: Fridell, "Racial Aspects of Police Shootings," 482-83.
Two processes linked to the manifestation of Black-crime implicit bias "are activation and application. Activation refers to the existence of the stereotype in an individual's head; a person sees another person from a particular group (e.g., gender group or racial group) and associates that person with a stereotype that is associated with that group. But, importantly, this activation does *not necessarily* impact behavior. A person could have an implicit bias activation but not *apply* that activation to behavior.... These two processes are linked to two sets of interventions to address implicit biases, and these interventions can help us further understand the disparate findings and the implications of them for police. First, there are ways that individuals can reduce their biases; that is, there are mechanisms that can reduce the activation of the stereotypes. Second, there are ways that individuals can manage their biases; that is, even if *activation* occurs, people can still thwart the *application* of bias to behavior."

To end hate crimes: Settembrino, "Mass Shootings as Hate Crimes," 60.
"Social sciences research suggests that negative attitudes about minorities do not come out of thin air. Rather, they are produced by the norms and values within a society. This means that in order to understand hate crimes, the influences of institutionalized oppression in our society must be examined, including white supremacy, negative attitudes, and discrimination against racial and ethnic minorities and homophobic and transphobic attitudes, actions, policies, and laws hostile toward LGBTQ people.... If we truly want to end mass shooting hate crimes, we also need to end discrimination against and abuse of minorities in the United States."

26] • [27

Rayshard Brooks's daughters were 8, 2, and 1, and his stepson was 13. https://www.11alive.com/article/news/local/rayshard-brooks-atlanta-police-case/85-8d17ac5a-e819-40dc-adb1-5febd0eb55a4. 0723.

Deana Eckert was 57. https://www.courier-journal.com/story/news/2023/04/10/louisville-old-national-bank-shooting-deana-eckart-identified-as-victim/70101708007/. 0623.

Reat Underwood, 14, participated in debate and theater at school. https://www.nbcnews.com/storyline/jewish-center-shootings/eagle-scout-his-grandfather-killed-jewish-center-shooting-n79496. 0623.

Randolph Evans was born and raised in East New York. https://www.learntheirstories.com/#/randolph-evans/. 0623.

Belinda Galde had two daughters. https://www.seattletimes.com/seattle-news/law-justice/burlington-mall-shooting-victims-officially-identified/. 0323.

Grace McDonnell wanted to live on Martha's Vineyard when she grew up. https://www.twentysixbells.com/index.php/twenty-six-bell-angels/grace-mcdonnell. 0223.

Susie Jackson worked as a beautician and home health care provider. She was on the board of trustees of her church. https://www.live5news.com/story/29365278/susie-jackson-oldest-victims-memory-to-live-on/. 0223. https://www.fallenheroesproject.org/post/susan-j-susie-jackson. 0223.

Jeremy Herbstritt was working toward a masters degree in civil engineering, conducting research on the Lower Roanoke River in North Carolina. https://www.weremember.vt.edu/biographies/herbstritt.html. 0223. http://vt-memorial.org/profiles/Herbstritt.html. 0223.

Paramjit Kaur was born in India, and moved to the U.S. in her thirties. She had recently made a visit to India with her two children. http://sikhtempleofwisconsin.com/memorial. 0223. https://www.cbsnews.com/news/the-sikh-temple-shooting-victims/. 0223.

Casey Goodson had a 5-year-old brother. https://www.cnn.com/2020/12/09/us/ohio-police-shooting-casey-goodson-autopsy/index.html. 0623.

9: https://www.theguardian.com/us-news/2015/dec/31/the-counted-police-killings-2015-young-black-men. 0423.

Police protect what: Williams, *Our Enemies in Blue*, 396-97.
"The modern police institution is at its core racist, elitist, undemocratic, authoritarian, and violent. These are the institution's major features, and it did not acquire them by mistake. The order that the police preserve is the order of the state, the order of capitalism, the order of White supremacy. These are the forces that require police protection. These are the forces that created

the police, that support them, sustain them, and guide them. These are the ends the police serve."

Bad officers sometimes make: Butler, *Chokehold*, 2-3.
"[R]acist cops are not the main problem. Most police officers are decent working-class men and women with no more racial hang-ups than teachers, doctors, or anyone else.... [T]he crisis in law and order in the United States stems from police work itself rather than from individual cops.... The problem is the criminal process itself. Cops routinely hurt and humiliate black people because that is what they are paid to do. Virtually every objective investigation of a U.S. law enforcement agency finds that the police, as *policy*, treat African Americans with contempt.... The police kill, wound, pepper spray, beat up, detain, frisk, handcuff, and use dogs against blacks in circumstances in which they do not do the same to white people. It is the moral responsibility of every American, when armed agents of the state are harming people in our names, to ask why."

More policing harms: Cobbina-Dungy and Jones-Brown, "Too Much Policing," 15.
"History has provided evidence time and again that there are significant harms associated with using police to enforce control in times of rising social inequality."

27] • [28

Henry Green was 23, and had two siblings.
https://www.legacy.com/us/obituaries/dispatch/name/henry-green-obituary?id=16588571. 0623. https://psmag.com/social-justice/racism-institutionalized-cpd. 0623.

Tshering Rinzing Bhutia was born in India, and practiced Buddhism. He worked cleaning the food court at the San Francisco Airport, after previous work as a waiter in an Indian restaurant. https://www.sfgate.com/crime/article/Oikos-shooting-victim-Tshering-Rinzing-Bhutia-3457013.php. 0323.

Edward Sotomayor Jr. worked as the brand manager for an LBGTQ travel agency.
https://people.com/crime/orlando-pulse-shooting-tributes-to-49-victims/. 0323.

Haley Krueger was active in her church youth group. In junior high, she had sung in her school choir. She had three siblings. She liked the TV show *Grey's Anatomy*.
https://www.nbcnews.com/storyline/texas-church-shooting/texas-church-shooting-who-were-victims-sutherland-springs-massacre-n818356. 0523. https://www.huffpost.com/entry/texas-shooting-grieving-mother_n_5a04f296e4b0e37d2f3690af. 0523.
https://www.legacy.com/us/obituaries/sanantonio/name/haley-krueger-obituary?id=11915423. 0523.

Daniel Stein had two children and one grandchild. He provided services to the elderly community in his congregation. https://abcnews.go.com/US/pittsburgh-synagogue-shooting-portraits-11-victims/story?id=58823835. 0523.

Jayce Luevanos made his grandparents a pot of coffee every morning. His favorite colors were blue and green, and he would write love letters for his loved ones and sign them with "I love you!" https://www.texastribune.org/2022/05/25/uvalde-school-shooting-victims/. 0523. https://latino.si.edu/exhibitions/healing-uvalde/twenty-one-healing-uvalde-murals/jayce-carmelo-luevanos. 0523.

Dorene Anderson, a stay-at-home mother of two daughters, was treasurer of her hockey team fan club's cowbell crew. https://www.nytimes.com/2017/10/02/us/vegas-victims-names.html. 0523.

Geraldine Talley lived in Buffalo. She and her fiancé had a ritual of going on a picnic once a week at the waterfront. https://people.com/crime/buffalo-mass-shooting-geraldine-talley-remembered/. 0523.
https://www.democratandchronicle.com/story/news/2022/05/17/buffalo-shooting-victim-geraldine-talley-helped-those-need/9796684002/. 0523.

Kevin Mahoney had retired as the COO of a hotel development and hospitality management company. He and his wife had two children, with their first grandchild on the way. https://www.dignitymemorial.com/obituaries/boulder-co/kevin-mahoney-10124789. 0523. https://www.nytimes.com/2021/03/23/us/boulder-victims.html. 0523.

Julius Tate, Jr. https://abc6onyourside.com/news/local/a-year-later-julius-tates-family-still-looking-for-justice-in-deadly-police-shooting. 0723.

25.6: Balko, *Rise of the Warrior Cop*, 308.

From any one death: Younge, *Another Day*, xiv.
"Firearms are the leading source of death among black children under the age of nineteen and the second leading cause of death for all children of the same age group, after car accidents. Each individual death is experienced as a family tragedy that ripples through a community, but the sum total barely earns a national shrug."

We only count: Butler, *Precarious Life*, xx-xxi.
"The public sphere is constituted in part by what can appear, and the regulation of the sphere of appearance is one way to establish what will count as reality, and what will not. It is also a way of establishing whose lives can be marked as lives, and whose deaths will count as deaths. Our capacity to feel and to apprehend hangs in the balance."

Recognition as active: Ramirez, "Healing, Violence, and Native American Women," 109.
"Once Indian women are seen as rightful inheritors and tillers of the soil, who are active, full human beings, and no longer represented as passive receptacles for male penetration, these damaging assumptions are undermined. As a result, Indian women become less vulnerable to violence and assault."

28] • [29

Bernice and Sylvan Simon had three stickers on the front door of their home: "Support Our Troops," "God Bless America," and "America the Beautiful." https://abcnews.go.com/US/pittsburgh-synagogue-shooting-portraits-11-victims/story?id=58823835. 0523.

Cornelius Fredericks had been placed in the facility after his mother died and his stepfather was incarcerated. https://www.howmyvoiceisheard.com/lives/cornelius-fredericks. 0723.

Herman Whitfield III held a B.A. in Politics and a B.M. in both Composition and Piano Performance. He worked for seven years at The Ancient Spanish Monastery in Miami as an accompanist and composer. He had twice won the Detroit Symphony Orchestra's "emerging African-American composers" competition. https://www.indystar.com/story/news/local/2022/10/25/herman-whitfield-iii-family-mourns-loss-as-40th-birthday-approaches/69511100007/. 0623. https://www.wrtv.com/news/local-news/crime/people-weve-lost/musical-genius-of-herman-whitfield-iii-was-a-gift-to-the-world. 0623.

Nicholas Cumer had a bachelor's degree in exercise physiology and a master's in cancer care. He volunteered in the physical therapy department of his local hospital. https://www.legacy.com/us/obituaries/observer-reporter/name/nicholas-cumer-obituary?id=12354083. 0723.

Jesse Lewis liked math. https://nypost.com/2012/12/15/fathers-anguish-after-losing-his-son-in-connecticut-shooting/. 0223.

Daniel L. Simmons became one of the first Black drivers for Greyhound, and worked for the VA as a counselor for disabled veterans. He earned both a Master of Social Work and a Master of Divinity, and was Senior Pastor for several different AME churches over a thirty-year span. https://emanuelnine.epistles.faith/the-emanuel-nine/rev-daniel-simmons-sr/. 0223.

Maxine Turner volunteered at an animal shelter. At her university, she had helped found a campus chapter of Alpha Omega Epsilon, a sorority for female engineering students. Her favorite video game was Zelda. http://www.vt-memorial.org/profiles/Turner.html. 0223. https://www.weremember.vt.edu/biographies/turner.html. 0223.

Franky Dejesus Velazquez was born in Puerto Rico. https://www.nytimes.com/interactive/projects/cp/us/orlando-shooting-victims/franky-jimmy-dejesus-velazquez. 0323. https://people.com/crime/orlando-pulse-shooting-tributes-to-49-victims/. 0323. https://www.npr.org/sections/thetwo-way/2016/06/12/481785763/heres-what-we-know-about-the-orlando-shooting-victims. 0323.

Therese Rodriguez. https://www.nytimes.com/2017/11/07/us/sutherland-springs-texas-victims.html. 0523. https://www.mysanantonio.com/news/local/article/Family-friends-of-Therese-and-Richard-Rodriguez-12350556.php. 0523.

Isaiah Lewis was 17. https://newsone.com/3852038/oklahoma-edmond-police-kill-isaiah-mark-lewis/. 0723.

45: https://news.gallup.com/poll/246866/americans-less-satisfied-treatment-minority-groups.aspx. 0323.

The state's primary use-of-force: Kraska and Kappeler, "Militarizing American Police," 2.
"The military and police comprise the state's primary use-of-force entities, the foundation of its coercive power. A close ideological and operational alliance between these two entities in handling domestic social problems usually is associated with repressive governments. Although such an alliance is not normally associated with countries like the United States, reacting to certain social problems by blurring the distinction between military and police may be a key feature of the post-cold war United States."

What we learned in war: Grossman, *On Killing*, 308.
"In Vietnam a systematic process of desensitization, conditioning, and training increased the individual firing rate from a World War II baseline of 15 to 20 percent to an all-time high of up to 95 percent. Today a similar process of systematic desensitization, conditioning, and vicarious learning is unleashing an epidemic, a virus of violence in America."

Make America: Spina, "When the Smoke Clears," 229.
"Violence is about power. The United States is unrivaled in institutionalizing violence to the point where it is acceptable behavior."

29] • [30

Dreasjon Reed went by Sean, and was 21 years old.
https://www.nytimes.com/2020/05/07/us/sean-reed-indianapolis-shooting.html. 0723.

Tess Mata liked soccer. She loved the Nickelodeon show "Victorious," the Houston Astros, and her cat, Oliver. In a jar in her bedroom, she was saving money for a family vacation to Disney World. https://www.rekfunerals.com/obituaries/Tess-Mata. 0523.
https://nowcastsa.com/obituary/tess-marie-mata. 0523.
https://www.nytimes.com/article/uvalde-shooting-victims.html. 0523.

Austin Davis was 29 years old. He and his father often went fishing or watched sports together. https://www.reviewjournal.com/crime/homicides/las-vegas-shooting-victim-austin-davis-colton-california/. 0523. https://www.nytimes.com/2017/10/02/us/vegas-victims-names.html. 0523.

Ruth Whitfield, for eight years, had visited her husband daily in the nursing home where he lived, tending to such caretakings as ironing his clothes, clipping his nails, and grooming his mustache. https://www.nbcnews.com/news/us-news/community-mourns-victims-buffalo-supermarket-shooting-rcna28935. 0523.

Neven Stanišić was 23. His parents had fled Serbia as refugees in the 1990s, prior to his birth. https://www.nytimes.com/2021/03/23/us/boulder-victims.html. 0523.

Sarita Regalado. https://www.oxygen.com/crime-time/these-are-the-22-victims-who-died-in-el-paso-walmart-shooting. 0523.

Valentino Alvero had two children, three grandchildren, and many nieces and nephews. https://news.yahoo.com/11-victims-were-killed-monterey-023802697.html. 0623. https://www.pasadenastarnews.com/2023/01/29/the-victims-seniors-who-found-joy-in-a-monterey-park-dance-studio/. 0623.

Sofia Mendoza was an honor roll student, and was learning about fractions, weather patterns and organisms. She had been memorizing lines for the lead role in her drama class' upcoming play *Pirate Jane*. https://news.yahoo.com/know-victims-mass-shooting-allen-003821790.html?guccounter=1&guce_referrer=aHR0cHM6Ly9kdWNrZHVja2dvLmNvbS8&guce_referrer_sig=AQAAADuwXbClvnVozi5EYSSS9kZdxGxoUqCI1NbE9xkjNlyFItOcF9I4_Skpt34TyOJnI8c_oV7WTln2l5LpdBwSAti6cy7ro6eLhWd5Gv7JGTO27Qk6Tpb773jPprJq5qV00-ifMhi7ZKN4S4UAh8dWoIkyToxs4pwqdgKf6PCPmjT2. 0623. https://thebrunswicknews.com/news/national_news/remembering-allen-shooting-victims-sisters-daniela-and-sofia-mendoza/article_b90c6ee3-f33b-53b6-abfc-8c19acf2e38c.html. 0623.

Diana Velázquez Alvarado was 21 years old, and had been living with her partner for six years. https://abcnews.go.com/US/5-victims-texas-shooting/story?id=98960747. 0623.

Ryan Twyman. https://www.theguardian.com/us-news/2019/aug/15/police-shootings-los-angeles-sheriffs-department-ryan-twyman. 0723.

14: http://www.genevadeclaration.org/measurability/global-burden-of-armed-violence/gbav-2015/executive-summary.html. 0523.

Different patterns of killing: Van Horne, "Institutional Correlates," 106-7.
"What works in urban communities to reduce intimate partner gun homicides may not work in rural communities."

Urban gun use: Blocher, "Firearm Localism," 91-92.
"Americans in cities are, and apparently always have been, less likely to own, use, or approve of guns than those in rural areas. City-dwellers are victimized by gun crime at much higher rates, and are far more likely to support stringent gun control. Rural residents, by contrast, are more likely to grow up with guns, to have positive role models with regard to their responsible use, and to oppose gun control. These differences are historically consistent, and they tend to be obscured by doctrinal analysis that focuses solely on states and the federal government."

Violence may vary: Lane, *Murder in America*, 329.
"The fact that there are large numbers of citizens who somehow share in the American Dream but see no legitimate way of making it a reality in their own lives is a deeply disturbing social development. Their violence is far more dangerous to themselves and each other than to the

dominant majority…. But increasingly murderous self-destruction among those left behind does sometimes spill over into other lives and places. And if present trends continue, with the postindustrial economy continuing to swell the numbers of these jobless people, the rest of us may have to recognize that we are all in trouble together."

30] • [31

Alison Cienfuegos-Vasquez was studying at Montgomery County Community College in Maryland. https://www.washingtonpost.com/dc-md-va/2023/07/06/dc-killings-lyft-driver-refugee-teacher/?utm_campaign=wp_post_most&utm_medium=email&utm_source=newsletter&wpisrc=nl_most. 0723.

Alberta Spruill was 57. https://digitalcommons.law.uga.edu/cgi/viewcontent.cgi?article=1050&context=fac_pm. 0623.

Byron Williams was 50. https://people.com/crime/byron-williams-las-vegas-homicide-police/. 0623.

Jim Tutt was 64, had an MBA, and was active in his church. https://www.courier-journal.com/story/news/local/2023/04/10/louisville-bank-shooting-victims-what-to-know-about-james-jim-tutt/70100357007/. 0623.

William Lewis Corporon was 69. He and his wife had 3 children and 9 grandchildren, to whom he was known as "Popeye." https://www.oklahoman.com/story/news/nation-world/2014/04/14/friends-family-mourn-former-oklahoma-physician-killed-in-suburban-kansas-city-shooting/60831982007/. 0623. https://www.legacy.com/us/obituaries/kansascity/name/william-corporon-obituary?id=4149030. 0623.

Megan Betts had been on her high school swim team and had played trumpet in marching band. At college, she sang in her university's chorale, and was a semester away from completing her degree in Earth Science. She hoped to work for NASA to be a part of exploring the viability of life on other planets. https://www.cnn.com/2019/08/06/us/megan-betts-remembered/index.html. 0723. https://www.legacy.com/us/obituaries/dayton/name/megan-betts-obituary?id=2217682. 0723.

Joshua Higbee had been adopted as a child. He was 31. https://www.theguardian.com/us-news/2016/feb/27/kansas-shooting-police-identify-victims-josh-higbee-renee-benjamin-brian-sadowsky. 0723.

Charlotte Bacon liked shrimp and fried chicken. https://charlottehelenbaconfoundation.org/who-we-are/meetcharlotte/. 0223.

Cynthia Graham Hurd lived as an adult in the house she grew up in as a child, and her love of gardening included tending flower boxes on the home's picket fence. https://today.cofc.edu/2015/10/21/storybook-life-cynthia-graham-hurd/. 0223.

Ahjah Dixon was studying at Navarro College in Texas. https://www.corsicanadailysun.com/news/navarro-student-s-last-days-troubled/article_d1bc78e5-fdf8-5bb4-a6b7-cde1d335b30a.html. 0723.

4.46: Branas et al., "Investigating the Link," 2037.

Everything you buy: https://vpc.org/regulating-the-gun-industry/regulate-htm/. 0323.
"Guns are the only consumer products manufactured in the United States that are not subject to federal health and safety regulation. All other products that Americans use or come into contact with are regulated by a federal health and safety agency."

Exemption from regulation: Haag, *The Gunning of America*, xii-xiii.
"We became a gun culture not because the gun was symbolically intrinsic to Americans or special to our identity, or because the gun was something exceptional in our culture, but precisely because it was not. From the vantage point of business, the gun was a product of non-exceptionalism…. Although the gun industry produced an exceptional product — designed to injure and kill — it followed the ordinary trends and practices of the corporate industrial economy in the nineteenth and twentieth centuries. In short: the gun was no exception."

Only the gun is made: Dunbar-Ortiz, *Loaded*, 15.
"Gun-love can be akin to non-chemical addictions like gambling or hoarding, either of which can have devastating effects, mainly economic, but murder, suicide, accidental death, and mass shootings result only from guns. Guns are made for killing, and while nearly anything, including human hands, may be used to kill, only the gun is created for the specific purpose of killing a living creature. The sheer number of guns in circulation, and the loosening of regulations on handguns especially, facilitate deadly spur-of-the-moment reflex acts."

31] • [32

Ronell Foster. https://www.npr.org/2021/01/25/956177021/fatal-police-shootings-of-unarmed-black-people-reveal-troubling-patterns. 0723.

Partahi Lumbantoruan had been raised in a military family, and liked war movies. He grilled beef and chicken satay at a local street fair to raise money for a student organization at his university. http://vt-memorial.org/profiles/Lumbantoruan.html. 0223.

Amanda Alvear worked at a pharmacy, and had recently been promoted to lead pharmacy technician. https://people.com/crime/orlando-pulse-shooting-tributes-to-49-victims/. 0323. https://www.orlandosentinel.com/news/pulse-orlando-nightclub-shooting/victims/os-orlando-nightclub-shooting-victim-amanda-alvear-20160613-story.html. 0323.

Shani Corrigan and her husband lived in Texas after his Air Force career. https://www.nytimes.com/2017/11/07/us/sutherland-springs-texas-victims.html. 0523.

Richard Gottfried and his wife volunteered at a free clinic that treated refugees and immigrants, many of whom had never been to a dentist. https://abcnews.go.com/US/pittsburgh-synagogue-shooting-portraits-11-victims/story?id=58823835. 0523.

Eliahna Garcia was only 10, but she had already picked out a quinceañera dress. https://www.rekfunerals.com/obituaries/Eliahna-Garcia. 0523. https://www.texastribune.org/2022/05/25/uvalde-school-shooting-victims/. 0523.

Brett Schwanbeck had three children and five grandchildren. He loved any outdoor activity, especially going to the lake, swimming, and camping. https://www.williamsnews.com/news/2017/oct/10/community-mourns-loss-brett-schwanbeck-victim-las-/. 0523. https://www.cnn.com/2017/10/02/us/las-vegas-shooting-victims/index.html. 0523.

Celestine Chaney worked at manufacturing companies as her career, making men's suits and baseball caps, until a series of brain aneurysms forced her to retire. She had one son and six grandchildren. https://www.legacy.com/us/obituaries/buffalonews/name/celestine-chaney-obituary?id=34899229. 0523. https://www.nytimes.com/2022/05/28/nyregion/buffalo-shooting-celestine-chaney-family.html. 0523.

Lynn Murray earned her college degree in photography in Ohio, then worked in New York as a photo director for several magazines. After her marriage, she and her husband raised their two children in Boulder, Colorado. https://www.9news.com/article/news/local/boulder-shooting/lynn-murray-king-soopers-victim/73-c4b3c2a8-0137-46b0-a1ba-0e43bc2af0ea. 0523. https://www.nytimes.com/2021/03/23/us/boulder-victims.html. 0523.

Tyisha Miller. https://www.howmyvoiceisheard.com/lives/tyisha-miller. 0723.

26: https://www.forbes.com/sites/katharinabuchholz/2023/04/06/which-states-allow-the-permitless-carry-of-guns-infographic/?sh=701bfa5b4e85. 0523.

"[P]olicing is a way: Farrell et al., " 'There's No Crying…,'' 223.

Militarizing police: Ramey and Steidley, "Policing Through Firepower," 839.
Acquisition of surplus military equipment increases with Black population, but *faster* than Black population. "[T]he presence of minority populations is associated only with LEA acquisitions of militarized equipment (e.g., weapons, vehicles, and fatigues) from the 1033 Program but not of nonmilitarized equipment (e.g., tools and medical supplies). This finding, specific to combat equipment, provides support for the argument that police militarization is, in part, a product of racial threat mechanisms. Specifically, as the relative size of the Black population in places increases, police departments are more likely to acquire surplus military equipment, and as both Black and Hispanic populations increase, the supplies LEAs successfully acquire are worth more money."

Police militarization reinforces: Gamal, "The Racial Politics of Protection," 982.
Police militarization is "a race-making process — that is, patterns of police militarization have constructed and reinforced race and racial hierarchies in America.... [P]olice militarization both reflects and reinforces a system of white supremacy and black subordination.... [P]olice militarization reifies the idea that some lives — black and brown lives — will be subject to military-like state control and some lives — white lives — will be the beneficiaries of militarized state protection. In what I call the racial politics of protection, the process of police militarization allows the State to construct race by selectively assembling two groupings — those who will be marginalized through heightened surveillance and control and those who will be advantaged by their access to state protection."

32] • [33

Renee Benjamin worked at a factory. She was 30. https://www.theguardian.com/us-news/2016/feb/27/kansas-shooting-police-identify-victims-josh-higbee-renee-benjamin-brian-sadowsky. 0723.

Andre and Jordan Anchondo together were raising three children, two of them Jordan's by a previous relationship. Andre owned and operated his own business installing granite countertops and renovating kitchens, and Jordan was a stay-at-home mother for their children. https://people.com/crime/el-paso-mass-shooting-remembering-victims-2-year-later/. 0523. https://www.houstonpublicmedia.org/articles/news/texas/2019/08/08/342266/the-couple-killed-saving-their-baby-in-el-paso-had-just-found-a-future-together/. 0523.

Melissa Ventura was 24. https://www.univision.com/univision-news/united-states/what-we-know-about-the-five-latinos-killed-by-police-last-week. 0723. https://time.com/4396699/melissa-ventura-yuma-county-arizona-shooting/. 0723.

Natasha Skorczewski liked school, and her favorite subject was math. She liked camping, reading, and bicycling. https://www.pipestonestar.com/articles/natasha-skorczewski/. 0323.

Terri LaManno helped children with visual impairments develop fine motor skills, eye-hand coordination and sensory-system strategies. She served as an Extraordinary Minister of Holy Communion at her Catholic church. She was 53. https://www.kcur.org/community/2014-04-17/occupational-therapist-terri-lamanno-warmly-remembered. 0623.

Saeed Saleh had been in the U.S. only three years. He was 38. https://www.nbc4i.com/news/daytonshooting/remembering-the-victims-saeed-saleh/. 0723.

Brian Sadowsky worked at a factory. He was 44. https://www.theguardian.com/us-news/2016/feb/27/kansas-shooting-police-identify-victims-josh-higbee-renee-benjamin-brian-sadowsky. 0723.

Aiken Smith was 16. https://www.spokesman.com/stories/2023/jun/20/sweet-and-kindhearted-friends-remember-kellogg-fam/. 0723.

Jillian Johnson owned and ran a gift boutique with her husband, and also ran a clothing line with her brother and a friend. Her favorite film was *Coal Miner's Daughter*, and she was a fan of Fats Waller, Tina Turner, and John Steinbeck. https://news.yahoo.com/remembering-the-victims-of-the-louisiana-theater-shooting-182925421.html. 0723.

Zachary Bearheels was 29. https://www.dominalaw.com/legal-blog/2017/june/mentally-ill-man-shocked-12-times-with-a-stun-gu/. 0723.

1887: Younge, *Another Day*, 112-13.

Hiding the killing: Alfredo Jaar, in Evans and Lennart, *Violence*, 173.
"It is not that I specialize in violence. I just think violence is our present condition. And it is not only physical violence that concerns me here, it is also psychological and political forms of violence. Some forms of violence suffer from total invisibility. Let us consider the case of killing drones, for example.... We are killing thousands of people, most of them innocent, and they are dying in complete invisibility. Sadly, nobody is demanding that we stop this carnage. The casualties are always people without names. Will we ever know their names?

That violence might be invisible to us, but it exists out there, and we will see the consequences of it sooner or later."

Pushed aside in life: Shanafelt and Pino, *Rethinking Serial Murder*, 179.
"During transactions, or the actual violent act itself, victims tend to come from marginalized groups; and attacks are based on various forms of opportunity, such as a serial killer meeting a perceived attractive target in time and space, or from militaries, police, or other organizations locating civilian and other targets deemed dangerous (though vulnerable) by those in power. The marginalized status of victims influences the aftermath of criminal events, as well. In the case of victims of serial offenders, there is often a weak criminal justice system response."

"Violence disrupts: Stewart, *The Open Studio*, 55.

33] • [34

Michelle Cusseaux was 50, and lived in Phoenix. https://exhibits.stanford.edu/saytheirnames/feature/michelle-cusseaux. 0623.

Sandra Bland returned after college for a few years back in her native Chicago, and then was hired by her alma mater as a program associate. Hill, *Nobody*.

Kathryn Johnston lived in northwest Atlanta. https://www.blackpast.org/african-american-history/people-african-american-history/kathryn-johnston-1914-2006/. 0723.
https://www.nytimes.com/2006/11/23/us/23atlanta.html. 0723.

James Mattioli answered to "J." He preferred shorts to long pants even in cold weather. https://www.newstimes.com/news/article/james-mattioli-sandy-hook-17635983.php. 0223.

Liviu Librescu was a professor of engineering who did research on strong, lightweight materials for aircraft and ships. http://www.vt-memorial.org/profiles/Librescu.html. 0223. https://www.weremember.vt.edu/biographies/librescu.html. 0223.

Mercedez Flores was born in Queens. She loved music, and wanted to do party planning with her two older brothers, who are DJs. https://www.romper.com/p/who-is-mercedez-marisol-flores-the-orlando-victim-was-a-hardworking-student-12439. 0323. https://www.npr.org/sections/thetwo-way/2016/06/12/481785763/heres-what-we-know-about-the-orlando-shooting-victims. 0323.

Keith Braden came from a military family, had served in the Army National Guard, and as a veteran delivered death notices to the relatives of soldiers who died in combat. He and his wife had three children. https://www.nbcnews.com/storyline/texas-church-shooting/texas-church-shooting-who-were-victims-sutherland-springs-massacre-n818356. 0523. https://www.cnn.com/2017/11/06/us/texas-church-shooting-victims-list/index.html. 0523. https://www.nytimes.com/2017/11/07/us/sutherland-springs-texas-victims.html. 0523.

Jerry Rabinowitz was remembered by one former patient for defying stigma in the early days of HIV treatment: he "held our hands (without rubber gloves) and always hugged us as we left his office." https://www.cnn.com/2018/10/28/us/pittsburgh-synagogue-shooting-victims/index.html. 0523.

Jacklyn Cazares loved to sing, make videos on TikTok and interact with her friends on Snapchat. Her favorite color was sage green. She wanted someday to visit Paris. https://www.rekfunerals.com/obituaries/Jacklyn-Cazares. 0523.

Phillip Pannell. https://www.blackpast.org/african-american-history/phillip-pannell-jr-1973-1990/. 0723.

80: https://everytownresearch.org/solution/responsible-gun-storage/. 0323.

Seeing civilian affairs: Kraska, "Crime Control as Warfare," 24.
"The war metaphor, more than just a cliché, reflects the ideological underpinnings of post-Cold War crime control efforts. Metaphors mirror the values we harbor. The tendency of our society to adopt the values embodied in the military model to solve internal problems such as crime and drugs signals the degree to which the tenets of high-modern militarism are institutionalized in our civilian affairs, our government, and our culture.... [T]he real-world manifestations of this ideological framework are dauntingly real."

"War on crime": Caulfield, "Militarism, Feminism, and Criminal Justice," 131.

"Criminal justice engages in a war on crime. It is no accident that we engage in a war, rather than a campaign or an effort. The rhetoric of war is the language of militarism…. It is not overstating the case, then, to suggest that criminal justice has become the institutionalization of militarism in U.S. culture."

Law enforcement as "war": Fisher, *SWAT Madness*, ix.
"American law enforcement has become zero tolerant, more violent, and militarized…. The barrier between the U.S. military and domestic law enforcement has broken down. The police have become soldiers and military personnel now function as civilian law enforcers. Paramilitary police officers wear combat gear, are transported in army-surplus armored personnel carriers, receive special-forces training, and view criminal suspects as enemy combatants. Federal, state, and local law enforcement agencies field teams of military-trained snipers. In many jurisdictions, the 'public servant' concept of policing has been replaced by the 'occupying force' model."

34] • [35

Pamela Turner was 44. https://www.nbcnews.com/news/us-news/woman-had-several-bad-experiences-texas-officer-who-fatally-shot-n1006176. 0723.

Candice Bowers loved country music, and worked as a waitress.
https://www.bustle.com/p/who-was-candice-bowers-the-las-vegas-shooting-victim-loved-country-music-2808591. 0523. https://time.com/4965896/las-vegas-shooting-victims-names/. 0523.

Aaron Salter Jr. and his wife had three children, and had opened a dry cleaning business before her death. He was working to invent a technology to enable cars to run off of water rather than gasoline. https://www.blackenterprise.com/beloved-security-aaron-salter-jr-killed-by-gunman-tried-to-save-lives-hes-a-hero/. 0523.

Suzanne Fountain had studied acting in New York, and been active in the Denver and Boulder Colorado theater communities. She operated a business to advise people newly turned 65 about how to apply for Medicare.
https://www.legacy.com/us/obituaries/poughkeepsiejournal/name/suzanne-fountain-obituary?id=8316995. 0523. https://www.nytimes.com/2021/03/23/us/boulder-victims.html. 0523.

David Johnson and his wife had four children and four grandchildren.
https://www.elpasotimes.com/story/news/2019/08/12/el-paso-shooting-victim-david-johnson-family-remembers/1987671001/. 0623.

Yu Lun Kao sold materials to make windows and gates. He was not married, and had no children. He liked sports and dancing, and his friends at dance lessons called him "Mr. Nice."
https://news.yahoo.com/11-victims-were-killed-monterey-023802697.html. 0623.
https://www.pasadenastarnews.com/2023/01/29/the-victims-seniors-who-found-joy-in-a-monterey-park-dance-studio/. 0623.

Daniela Mendoza wore black-framed glasses and bows in her hair. She and her sister won awards for perfect attendance. https://news.yahoo.com/know-victims-mass-shooting-allen-003821790.html?guccounter=1&guce_referrer=aHR0cHM6Ly9kdWNrZHVja2dvLmNvbS8&guce_referrer_sig=AQAAADuwXbClvnVozi5EYSSS9kZdxGxoUqCI1NbE9xkjNlyFItOcF9I4_Skpt34TyOJnI8c_oV7WTln2l5LpdBwSAti6cy7ro6eLhWd5Gv7JGTO27Qk6Tpb773jPprJq5qV00-ifMhi7ZKN4S4UAh8dWoIkyToxs4pwqdgKf6PCPmjT2. 0623. https://thebrunswicknews.com/news/national_news/remembering-allen-shooting-victims-sisters-daniela-and-sofia-mendoza/article_b90c6ee3-f33b-53b6-abfc-8c19acf2e38c.html. 0623.

Laquita Brown was 39, and had worked as a right of way agent in her city's public works department for four years. She enjoyed traveling, amusement parks, karaoke, dancing, playing games and cooking. https://people.com/crime/virginia-beach-mass-shooting-victims-identified/. 0623. https://www.legacy.com/us/obituaries/pilotonline/name/laquita-brown-obituary?id=15274729. 0623.

Daniel Aston was a 28-year-old trans man, and had recently moved to Colorado Springs, to be closer to his parents. He was 4 when he told his mother he was a boy, and a decade later came out as transgender. He wrote poetry, and loved to dress up. https://www.cnn.com/2022/11/21/us/club-q-colorado-shooting-victims/index.html. 0623. https://www.nytimes.com/article/victims-colorado-springs-shooting.html. 0623.

Martin Angel Hernandez. https://www.ocweekly.com/new-account-emerges-of-how-martin-angel-hernandez-died-at-the-hands-of-anaheim-cops-6447657/. 0723.

0: Peeples, "What the Data Say," 25.

The history of violence: Richard Bernstein, in Evans and Lennart, *Violence*, 133.
"I don't think that violence will ever completely disappear from the world. In the future we will become aware of new forms of violence that we can't anticipate now. But I am certainly not pessimistic. What we learn from the history of violence is that we need to be specific and concrete when we speak about violence."

It might take different: Moeller, "Cycle Breakers," 198.
"Criminal justice — more aptly called the legal system by some as justice is rarely found in it — is punitive and offender driven, asking the questions of what law is broken, who is to blame and what do they deserve as punishment. RJ ['Restorative Justice'] is victim driven and restorative, asking who has been hurt, what are their needs to be made whole and healed, and whose obligations is it to provide the necessary actions to fulfill those needs."

We can move on: Rood, *After Gun Violence*, 142-43.
"When life has been overturned by gun violence, it is common to assert order, virtue, and hope by saying, in effect, This awful thing happened, but people demonstrated heroism in response to it. Some public officials and reporters even imply that the communities directly affected by this recent violence in Nevada, Texas, and Florida will become stronger as a result. Maybe that's true.

But maybe not. In any case, innocent people were injured and killed. We should not forget that or move past it so quickly…. At some point, if we're being honest, those of us who have not been directly impacted by gun violence need to acknowledge the brutality of what happened and dwell with the horror…. If there is any hope of interrupting the cycle of violence and inaction, we need to find the courage, strength, and resolve not to move on so quickly."

35] • [36

Heriberto Godinez Jr. was 24. https://peoplestribune.org/2015/09/justice-for-heriberto-godinez-jr-1988-2015/. 0723.

Josh Barrick held the title of Senior Vice President. He and his wife had two children, and he enjoyed Sunday breakfast with them. https://www.ratterman.com/obituaries/Joshua-Barrick/#!/Obituary. 0623.

Beatrice Warren-Curtis was 36. https://www.delawareonline.com/story/news/2019/08/05/delaware-native-beatrice-warren-curtis-killed-dayton-shooting/1924915001/. 0723.

Kenna Guardipee had two sons. She was 41. https://www.spokesman.com/stories/2023/jun/20/sweet-and-kindhearted-friends-remember-kellogg-fam/. 0723.

Mayci Breaux was working at a women's clothing store to put herself through college. She had been captain of the cheerleading team during her junior and senior years in high school. She was active in pro-life causes and once had traveled to Washington, D.C. to participate in a march protesting abortion. https://news.yahoo.com/remembering-the-victims-of-the-louisiana-theater-shooting-182925421.html. 0723.

Dymir Stanton. https://www.nytimes.com/article/philadelphia-shooting.html. 0723.

Ma'Khia Bryant was 16, and had been in foster care for two years. She had a speech impediment. https://www.nytimes.com/2021/05/08/us/columbus-makhia-bryant-foster-care.html. 0623.

Terence Crutcher lived in Tulsa, and was 40 years old. Friends called him "Big Crutch." He had a twin sister, and he had four children, ages 4 to 17. https://www.learntheirstories.com/#/terence-crutcher/. 0623.

David McAtee was 53. https://www.npr.org/sections/live-updates-protests-for-racial-justice/2020/06/12/875463084/louisville-hosts-public-viewing-for-david-mcatee-as-details-of-his-shooting-emer. 0723.

Omar Gonzalez Jr. was 36. https://homicide.latimes.com/post/omar-gonzalez/. 0723.

1: Spina, "Introduction," 1.

"Each of the techniques: Shapira, "How to Use the Bathroom with a Gun," 206.
Shapira continues: "In the process of looking at the technique for loading a gun, we see how gun culture is invested with hegemonic masculinity and how those ideas become inscribed in the way men and women use their bodies when they load ammunition and carry guns on their bodies."

Mode of attempted defense: Kaminer, "Second Thoughts," 499.
"If the war against crime has replaced the Cold War in popular culture, a private storehouse of guns has replaced the fallout shelter in the psyche of Americans who feel besieged."

We would be wise: Patrick Ball, "Violence in Blue." https://granta.com/violence-in-blue/. 0623.
"America is a land ruled by fear. We fear that our children will be abducted by strangers, that crazed gunmen will perpetrate mass killings in our schools and theaters, that terrorists will gun us down or blow up our buildings, and that serial killers will stalk us on dark streets. All of these risks are real, but they are minuscule in probability: taken together, these threats constitute less than three per cent of total annual homicides in the US. The numerically greater threat to our safety, and the largest single category of strangers who threaten us, are the people we have empowered to use deadly force to protect us from these less probable threats."

36] • [37

Ajewan Jones. https://www.legacy.com/us/obituaries/charlotte/name/ajewan-jones-obituary?id=12280382. 0723.

Mary Sherlach and her husband planned to spend more time at their cabin in the Finger Lakes once she retired from her job. https://patch.com/connecticut/newtown/mary-sherlach-ct-school-shooting-victim-looked-ahead-5824f865ed. 0223.

Matthew La Porte played tenor drum. He was studying political science in college on an Air Force ROTC scholarship, intent on being commissioned as an intelligence officer after graduation. http://www.vt-memorial.org/profiles/LaPorte.html. 0223.
https://www.weremember.vt.edu/biographies/laporte.html. 0223.

Antonio Brown earned a degree in criminal justice from Florida A&M. He worked as a human resource manager at his local Lowe's.
https://www.nytimes.com/interactive/projects/cp/us/orlando-shooting-victims/antonio-davon-brown. 0323.

Marc Holcombe lived in his own house but near his grandfather, who described him as "a self-made engineer" who "could make anything out of nothing."
https://people.com/crime/holcombe-family-killed-texas-church-shooting/. 0523.

Irma Garcia was married to her high-school sweetheart, with whom she had four children. She was named teacher of the year at her school in 2019. She liked to BBQ and listen to music.

https://www.npr.org/2022/05/27/1101286508/what-we-know-about-the-victims-of-the-uvalde-school-shooting. 0523. https://www.bbc.com/news/world-us-canada-61593071. 0523.

Nicol Kimura was 38, and had a tight-knit group of close friends who called themselves a "framily." https://www.cbsnews.com/sacramento/news/friends-mourn-loss-of-southern-california-woman-killed-in-las-vegas-shooting/. 0523.

Heyward Patterson had three children. He enjoyed telling jokes, and he liked to "dress to impress." Some friends and family still called him "Teeny," a nickname he had been given as a child. https://www.cnn.com/2022/05/15/us/buffalo-shooting-victims-what-we-know/index.html. 0523.
https://www.democratandchronicle.com/story/news/2022/05/17/buffalo-shooting-victim-heyward-patterson-remembered/9796527002/. 0523.

Jody Waters owned a clothing store called Applause, beginning it in one location and ultimately expanding it to three. Her care for rescue dogs was a characteristic she inherited from her mother and passed on to her two daughters.
https://www.legacy.com/us/obituaries/dailycamera/name/jody-waters-obituary?id=35274282. 0523. https://www.9news.com/article/news/local/boulder-shooting/boulder-king-soopers-shooting-victim-jody-waters-foundation-dogs/73-f45adaf5-4cfa-4852-abae-fc70b47dc6ab. 0523.

Alexsandra Olmo was 43; her daughter was 21. https://www.hrc.org/news/remembering-unique-banks-latina-transgender-woman-killed-in-chicago-illinois. 0723.
https://www.msn.com/en-us/news/crime/father-mourns-after-transgender-daughter-slain-in-south-shore-mass-shooting-i-still-can-t-believe-it/ar-AA16HNw3. 0723.

$7.79 million: https://everytownresearch.org/report/the-economic-cost-of-gun-violence/. 0323.

Categorizations of killer: Shrikant and Sambaraju, " 'A Police Officer Shot…,'" 1212.
"Overall, the analysis above shows how news media attend to racism as an explanation for the violation of police-civilian moral obligations. Media have traditionally presented officers as heroic people who protect communities from criminals and used routine categorization in news reports to construct the device of law enforcement as normatively expected to engage in the moral activities of protecting communities through arresting criminals. Through providing racism as an explanation for police shootings, news media alter normative expectations for activities and predicates associated with police (from hero to racist perpetrator) and those who are shot (from criminals to upstanding victims)."

Conceptions of violence: Rutherford et al., "Violence: A Glossary," 680.
"Defining violence in different ways has both moral and material consequences, such as whether or not a perpetrator is prosecuted, whether or not a prevention program is funded, or how a victim understands their situation."

Erasure of race: Mingus and Zopf, "White Means Never," 73.

"Through the process of racial formation, race is either totally erased from official media accounts of the shootings or else takes center stage as a fundamental issue. Drawing on white privilege, a privilege so taken-for-granted that it is virtually unrecognized by its beneficiaries, focus is diverted from the race of white shooters. Instead, these individuals are labeled as aberrations, anomalies within society, or psychopaths who represent the antithesis of mainstream America. Without the benefits of white privilege, shooters who are not white are forever doomed to be the blackguards of their race, a permanent shadow to those who bear a cultural or phenotypical similarity. In short, whites are able to successfully disassociate themselves from massacres perpetrated by whites, whereas non-whites feel obligated to apologize for crimes committed by someone from their race or to be vigilant against potential irrational retaliation or retribution from a color-blind public who nonetheless seems unable to distinguish between a mass murderer and someone who bears some resemblance to that murderer."

37] • [38

Aura Rosser was 40, and lived in Michigan. https://www.michigandaily.com/news/ann-arbor/community-members-hold-vigil-honor-three-year-death-anniversary-aura-rain-rosser/. 0723.

Tyre Nichols liked to skateboard. https://www.nytimes.com/2023/01/26/us/who-was-tyre-nichols.html. 0323.

Jeanetta Riley was 35. She was addicted to alcohol and meth. https://www.theguardian.com/us-news/2015/apr/03/idaho-police-shootings-jeanetta-riley-justice-for-arfee. 0723.

Arturo Benavides was an Army veteran who served more than 15 years in the National Guard. He loved his dog, and was a Dallas Cowboys fan. He and his wife of 33 years had a routine of doing their weekly grocery shopping after church on Sundays. https://taskandpurpose.com/news/arturo-benavides-el-paso-shooting/. 0523. https://www.insider.com/el-paso-shooting-victims-walmart-2019-8#arturo-benavides-59-2. 0523. https://apnews.com/article/texas-shootings-immigration-us-news-el-paso-texas-mass-shooting-1aa03c4a153f4f6d9881f0f11cd2e89a. 0623.

Ming Wei Ma was the manager at a dance studio, where his students called him "Mr. Ma." In an interview about his studio, he had once said, "Having a place where people from all over the world can come together and communicate through dance is how I can help." https://news.yahoo.com/11-victims-were-killed-monterey-023802697.html. 0623.

Christian LaCour was 20. His favorite colors were red and black. https://www.nbcdfw.com/news/local/loved-ones-hold-celebration-of-life-service-for-security-guard-killed-in-allen-mass-shooting/3258430/. 0623.

Mary Louise Gayle went by "Mary Lou." She had worked as a right of way agent in the public works department for 24 years. She was 65. She had two children and two grandchildren. She had grown up along the Lynnhaven River in Virginia, and as an adult worked to preserve space in it for new oyster reefs. She also participated in a bunco group, enjoyed craft projects including crochet and knitting. https://www.vpm.org/news/2021-05-31/virginia-beach-shooting-victim-loved-the-lynnhaven-river-now-her-name-is-part. 0623. https://www.findagrave.com/memorial/199728062/mary-louise-gayle. 0623.

Derek Walker lived in Durham, North Carolina. https://www.wral.com/story/man-killed-in-durham-police-standoff-snapped-close-friend-says/12899940/. 0723.

Jose de la Trinidad. https://socialistworker.org/2013/12/19/they-killed-jose-twice. 0723.

Ricardo Diaz Zeferino was 34. https://www.dailybreeze.com/2013/06/06/man-killed-by-gardena-police-was-trying-to-help-friends-attorney-says/. 0723. https://homicide.latimes.com/post/ricardo-diaz-zeferino/. 0723.

27: https://www.nytimes.com/2015/10/04/opinion/sunday/nicholas-kristof-a-new-way-to-tackle-gun-deaths.html. 0423. **42**: Children's Defense Fund, *Protect Children, Not Guns 2019.*

Racialization of police violence: Garza, "Foreword," vii.
"Police violence is not a new phenomenon in Black communities. Modern-day policing locates its origins in the slave economy, which helped build the wealth and the industrialized economy of this nation and of other nations around the world. Policing in the context of slavery was intended to ensure the protection of private property owners — with the private property being Black human beings."

Present patrolling: Robertson and Chaney, *Police Use of Excessive Force*, 22.
W. Marvin Dulaney's description of eighteenth-century slave patrols in the American South, as "authorized to stop, search, whip, maim, and even kill any African slave caught off the plantation without a pass, engaged in illegal activities, or running away," is "eerily similar to the role and function of twenty-first century police officers and their treatment of African Americans. Primarily, White police officers today appear to be able to brutalize persons of African descent and, by extension, other poor persons of color, with impunity."

Incidents of racialized police violence: Rosa, Trinidad, and May, "We Charge Genocide," 122.
"Police violence is and always has been state-sanctioned violence. We must understand police violence to be rooted in historical and systemic anti-Blackness that seeks to control, contain and repress Black bodies through acts of repeated violence."

38] • [39

Johnathan Cuevas was 20. https://ebwiki.org/cases/johnathan-cuevas. 0723.

Derrick Rump grew up in Kempton, Pennsylvania, but had lived in Colorado Springs for ten years. https://www.cnn.com/2022/11/21/us/club-q-colorado-shooting-victims/index.html. 0623. https://6abc.com/colorado-springs-shooting-club-q-muders-derrick-rump-victim-lgbtq-nightclub/12478735/. 0623. https://www.colefh.com/obituary/Derrick-Rump. 0623.

Juliana Farmer, 45, had three children and four grandchildren. She had been in a new job for less than three weeks. https://www.tomblinsonfuneralhome.com/obituaries/Juliana-Maria-Farmer?obId=27719733. 0623.

Gary Anderson had the same name as his father, so in his family he was known as Junior. He liked dogs, and was in process of applying to work for his local Humane Society. Younge, *Another Day in the Death of America.*

Lois Oglesby had two children, a newborn and a 7-year-old. She was 27. https://time.com/5643666/what-to-know-dayton-ohio-shooting-victims/. 0723. https://www.npr.org/2019/08/07/749163924/remembering-lois-oglesby-a-victim-of-the-dayton-shooting. 0723.

Devin Smith lived with his mother, grandfather, and younger brother in the lower floor of a duplex. He was 18. https://www.spokesman.com/stories/2023/jun/20/sweet-and-kindhearted-friends-remember-kellogg-fam/. 0723.

Ralph Moralis was 59. https://www.nytimes.com/article/philadelphia-shooting.html. 0723.

Brian Fraser was 20. He had one sister. His eyes were blue. He had been on his high school swimming and diving teams. https://www.nytimes.com/2023/02/14/us/michigan-state-shooting-victims.html?searchResultPosition=4. 0723. https://www.verheyden.org/obituaries/Brian-Anthony-Fraser?obId=28395707. 0723.

Scott Beigel was 35. https://sjbmf.org/meet-scott/. 0723.

Ernest Duenez Jr. lived in Manteca, California. https://www.indybay.org/newsitems/2011/07/18/18685224.php. 0723.

54: https://everytownresearch.org/solution/responsible-gun-storage/. 0323.

This conversation: Waugaman, "Understanding America's Obsession," 451.
"People also have to find ways to keep the dialogue going. In the course of conversations over several months with gun advocates, they eventually revealed that they are afraid in their homes and on their streets, that some were bullied in school and may even have suffered abuse, that they fear they are not being listened to or heard, and that if they compromise, they will lose everything. Once it is made clear that they are being listened to, that their opinions are being sought, that there is more than all or nothing to choose from, a conversation can begin."

Testimony: Rascon-Canales, "'Brokenheartedness,'" 163.
"*Testimonios* can thus be a bridge that merges epistemologies by women of color and that may be able to retrospectively help us understand the many implications of police killings but also their proliferating impact on the family and the collateral killings of caregivers and loved ones.

The number of collateral deaths does not validate or invalidate our community's suffering; however, shared *testimonios* may be crucial to our understanding of collective survival and solidarity across communities."

To reveal a nonviolent vista: Berardi, *The Uprising*, 157.
"Only an act of language can give us the ability to see and to create a new human condition, where we now only see barbarianism and violence."

39] • [40

Jesus Huerta lived in North Carolina.
https://www.wral.com/news/local/asset_gallery/13305031/. 0723.

Megan Waterman. https://www.oxygen.com/true-crime-buzz/lost-girls-who-were-the-victims-of-the-long-island-serial-killer. 0723.

Nasratullah Ahmad Yar was a military interpreter from Afghanistan who escaped the Taliban and sought refuge in the U.S. He started working at Bagram air base north of Kabul when he was 10 or 11, raking leaves and picking up stones. He learned English and became an interpreter, living on the base with the military. He was 31, and had spent 18 of those years working for the U.S. Special Forces. https://www.washingtonpost.com/dc-md-va/2023/07/06/dc-killings-lyft-driver-refugee-teacher/?utm_campaign=wp_post_most&utm_medium=email&utm_source=newsletter&wpisrc=nl_most. 0723. https://www.washingtonpost.com/dc-md-va/2023/07/08/nasrat-ahmadyar-lyft-driver-killed-dc/?utm_campaign=wp_post_most&utm_medium=email&utm_source=newsletter&wpisrc=nl_most. 0723.

Jamar Clark, 24, had been adopted at age four, and had 14 siblings. He had been incarcerated, and was on probation. https://en.wikipedia.org/wiki/Killing_of_Jamar_Clark. 0723.

Noah Pozner liked to play with Legos and with superhero figurines.
https://noahpozner.com/about/. 0223. https://abcnews.go.com/US/newtown-connecticut-school-shooting-victims/story?id=17984685#5. 0223.

Jocelyne Couture-Nowak had two daughters. She taught French, and had helped develop a school for francophone families in rural Nova Scotia. https://www.washingtonpost.com/wp-srv/metro/vatechshootings/victims/Jocelyne_Couture-Nowak.html. 0223.
https://www.weremember.vt.edu/biographies/couturenowak.html. 0223.

Stanley Almodovar affirmed in one social media post that, "Yes I wear makeup and I'm still a man about it tho." https://www.nytimes.com/interactive/projects/cp/us/orlando-shooting-victims/stanley-almodovar-iii. 0323.

Sara Johnson worked for a home and garden business. She and her husband had six children, and had just celebrated their 44th wedding anniversary. https://www.cnn.com/2017/11/06/us/texas-church-shooting-victims-list/index.html. 0523.

Maite Rodriguez loved the color green. Her favorite meal was #13 from Whataburger with a side of sliced jalapeños. https://www.cbsnews.com/news/texas-school-shooting-maite-rodriguez-19-kids-killed-elementary-mom-wants-the-world-to-know/. 0523.

Anastasio Hernández Rojas. https://www.huffpost.com/entry/anastasio-hernandez-rojas-death-complaint_n_56fd4893e4b0daf53aeef92d. 0723.

4.3: Naghavi et al., "Global Mortality from Firearms," 804.

We blame for murder: Swanson et al., "Mental Illness and Reduction of Gun Violence," 375. "Evidence is clear that the large majority of people with mental disorders do not engage in violence against others, and that most violent behavior is due to factors other than mental illness. However, psychiatric disorders, such as depression, are strongly implicated in suicide, which accounts for more than half of gun fatalities."

Framing gun harm: Carlson and James, "Conspicuously Concealed," 211.
"Crime and criminal justice have not just dominated the American imagination; our findings suggest that they have also dominated the American intellect. We expect that further inquiry will reveal that 'governing through crime' (Simon 2007) has impacted not just how guns are addressed as a public policy concern but also as an object of scientific inquiry—that is, the process we describe as 'knowing through crime.'"

Judges wouldn't need to punish: Rutherford et al., "Violence: A Priority," 769-70.
"Traditionally the domain of the criminal justice system, violence has only recently attracted a multi-sectoral approach. Public health practitioners have a role in identifying and documenting the range of forms of violence that exists in communities, especially many of the hidden or 'private' forms of violence, including child maltreatment, intimate partner violence and elder abuse. Identifying the determinants of these patterns and establishing the scope for intervention is paramount. As more knowledge about violence and its causes emerges, public health must seek to intervene with new and creative solutions that increase policy makers' confidence in, and understanding of, violence as a preventable problem."

40] • [41

Patricio Arroyo. https://www.krqe.com/news/crime/13-year-old-shot-and-killed-in-northeast-albuquerque/. 0723.

Jessica Klymchuk was a single mother of four children. https://www.bustle.com/p/who-was-jessica-klymchuk-the-las-vegas-attack-victim-was-visiting-the-city-with-her-fiance-2759445. 0523.

Maria Flores and Raul Flores first met when he was working at a tailor shop and made a point of being outside, sweeping, when she passed by on the sidewalk. They had been married for 60 years and had moved back from California to El Paso to retire. https://www.theguardian.com/us-news/2019/aug/12/god-decided-to-take-them-together-el-paso-funeral-for-couple-married-for-60-years. 0523.

Hongying Jian also went by her married name, Nancy Liu, but friends had nicknamed her "Sister Sunshine." She and her husband had one child. https://news.yahoo.com/11-victims-were-killed-monterey-023802697.html. 0623. https://www.insider.com/shooting-monterey-park-victims-identified-lunar-new-year-party-2023-1. 0623. https://www.pasadenastarnews.com/2023/01/29/the-victims-seniors-who-found-joy-in-a-monterey-park-dance-studio/. 0623.

Elio Cumana-Rivas was 32. He was a refugee from Caracas, Venezuela. He was working to raise the $3,000 a friend had lent him to pay the smuggler who helped him cross Mexico. He loved car racing and dreamed of seeing the Daytona International Speedway. https://www.dallasnews.com/news/crime/2023/05/11/allen-shooting-victim-elio-cumana-rivas-fled-violence-in-venezuela-seeking-asylum-in-us/. 0623.

Tara Welch Gallagher had a masters degree in environmental engineering from Old Dominion University. She and her husband were fixing up their home. They had a son who was not quite two years old. https://people.com/crime/virginia-beach-mass-shooting-victims-identified/. 0623.

Jeanette Anaya was 39. She had been raised in Santa Fe, and had recently returned to live with her mother in her childhood home. She doted on her nieces and nephews, taking them swimming, on picnics and outings to places such as Bandelier National Monument. https://www.santafenewmexican.com/news/local_news/mother-of-jeanette-anaya-speaks-out-on-daughter-s-death-at-hands-of-police/article_72eb7e0f-e885-5c5d-b003-e359a70b969c.html. 0723.

Janisha Fonville was 20. https://www.nycshutitdown.org/janisha-fonville. 0723.

Kareem Ali Nadir Jones liked sports, especially basketball. https://www.findagrave.com/memorial/208880200/kareem-ali_nadir-jones. 0623.

Ernesto Canepa. https://www.ocweekly.com/protesters-plan-march-for-ernesto-canepa-a-year-after-santa-ana-police-shot-and-killed-him-7002415/. 0723.

1 month: Gabor, *Confronting Gun Violence*, 6.

Violence "has a way: Hana Rivers, "The Afterlives of Violence." https://lareviewofbooks.org/article/the-afterlives-of-violence-on-brandon-shimodas-hydra-medusa/. 0623.

"It is possible: Milosz, *Nobel Lecture*, 20.

Memory: Kierkegaard, *Eighteen Upbuilding Discourses*, 210.
"… one who is dead is made not of flesh and blood but of the holiest and best thoughts of a thankful memory…"

41] • [42

Lisa German was 52, and her children were 20, 17 and 13. https://www.theglobaldispatch.com/lisa-german-killed-by-husband-christopher-german-in-new-york-murder-suicide-91706/. 0723.

Corey Kanosh was a 35-year-old Paiute man. https://ictnews.org/archive/natives-call-for-attention-to-police-killing-of-paiute-corey-kanosh. 0723.

Paul Monroe had a 4-month-old daughter. https://www.learntheirstories.com/#/paul-monroe/. 0623. https://www.vox.com/first-person/2020/8/14/21362387/police-brutality-black-lives-matter-protests-george-floyd. 0623.

Ashley Paugh worked for an organization that helps find homes for foster children. She was 35. She was married to her high school sweetheart and had an 11-year-old daughter. https://www.cnn.com/2022/11/21/us/club-q-colorado-shooting-victims/index.html. 0623. https://www.nytimes.com/article/victims-colorado-springs-shooting.html. 0623.

Tommy Elliott had a B.A. in Business Administration, and worked in banking for 42 years, eventually as a Senior Vice President. He and his wife had four daughters. He was 63. He served on the boards of several charities. https://www.legacy.com/us/obituaries/name/thomas-elliott-obituary?id=51625220. 0623.

Monica Brickhouse was 39. She and her husband had three children. Before her insurance work as a "recovery specialist," she had worked at a bank call center. https://www.legacy.com/us/obituaries/dayton/name/monica-brickhouse-obituary?id=2216455. 0723. https://www.nbc4i.com/news/daytonshooting/dayton-shooting-victims/remembering-the-victims-monica-brickhouse/. 0723.

Kenneth Guardipee was 65, and had been recovering from a recent heart attack. https://www.spokesman.com/stories/2023/jun/20/sweet-and-kindhearted-friends-remember-kellogg-fam/. 0723.

Lashyd Merritt worked for the IRS from home. He was 21. https://abcnews.go.com/US/philadelphia-mass-shooting-5-victims/story?id=100717829. 0723. https://6abc.com/philadelphia-mass-shooting-july-2023-lashyd-merritt-kingsessing/13463038/. 0723. https://www.wbaltv.com/article/philadelphia-july-3-shooting-victims/44453927#. 0723.

Unique Banks. https://www.hrc.org/news/remembering-unique-banks-latina-transgender-woman-killed-in-chicago-illinois. 0723. https://www.msn.com/en-us/news/crime/father-mourns-after-transgender-daughter-slain-in-south-shore-mass-shooting-i-still-can-t-believe-it/ar-AA16HNw3. 0723.

Craig McKinnis. https://www2.ljworld.com/news/2016/oct/02/lawsuits-claim-kck-police-killed-one-man-during-tr/. 0723.

48: Jackman et al., "Seeing Is Believing," 1248.
74: Farah, Simon, and Kellerman, "Firearms in the Home," 1061.

Guns redefine the boundaries: Springwood, "Gunscapes," 22.
"The symbolic interaction that frames the relationship between guns and those who carry them turns on embodiment, or a redefinition of the boundary of the body in terms of the objects that surround it and the ideas it creates. The complex *relationship of embodiment* a gun has with its owner is a very useful starting-point for understanding the interpenetration of the cultural and the political, of the local and the global, and of the ideological and the material. Guns *too easily* merge with bodies, dissolving into one's self as unconsciously as a cell-phone or purse."

Guns redefine the rights: Corrigan "The Gun as (Race/Gender) Technê," 77-78.
"Rhetorically central to the normalization of the gun as a technê of whiteness (and masculinity) has been the 'Good Guy with a Gun' narrative.... [I]nalienable property rights have been conferred upon the gun as a *symbol of whiteness*, but also as a badge of masculinity. In this case, given the rates of gun ownership, guns' status in the courts, and their use (especially in the South) as a tool to secure property and safeguard white generational wealth, the gun functions as a racial and gendered technology.... The gun becomes the technology that elevates or subordinates rights based on the presence of whiteness and the way in which it is exercised through lethal force."

Guns confer power: Kriegel, "A Loaded Question," 152.
"The man with the gun decides whether or not to shoot, just as he chooses where to point his gun. It is not political power that stems from the barrel of a gun.... It is individual power, the ability to impose one's presence on the world, simply because guns always do what language only sometimes does: Guns command! Guns command attention, guns command discipline, guns command fear."

42] • [43

Areli Rodriguez. https://www.abqjournal.com/news/local/man-charged-in-connection-with-fatal-shooting-of-girlfriend/article_70abd70b-8cf9-5ed3-bf0e-1cc94590b56b.html. 0723.

Freddie Gray brought in money by selling drugs on the street. Hill, *Nobody*.

Shem Walker was born in Guyana, and moved to the U.S. with his family when he was 16. He had two daughters. He was 49. https://www.learntheirstories.com/#/shem-walker/. 0623.

Alexandria Verner was 20. She had gone by Al or Alex since she was in kindergarten, and had played high school volleyball, softball, and basketball. https://www.nytimes.com/2023/02/14/us/michigan-state-shooting-victims.html?searchResultPosition=4. 0723. https://www.detroitnews.com/story/news/local/oakland-county/2023/02/14/msu-victim-clawson-native-alexandria-verner-leaves-a-happy-loving-legacy/69903506007/. 0723.

Jaime Guttenberg was a 14-year-old high school freshman. She was active in her local dance theater organization. She wanted to attend the University of Florida and room with her cousin. https://www.jta.org/2020/02/21/united-states/fred-guttenberg-whose-daughter-was-killed-in-parkland-believes-2020-is-the-most-crucial-year-in-this-countrys-history. 0723. https://abcnews.go.com/US/parkland-families-give-emotional-statements-penalty-phase-gunmans/story?id=87742310. 0723.

Valerie Mack was 24. She was employed as a sex worker. https://www.oxygen.com/true-crime-buzz/lost-girls-who-were-the-victims-of-the-long-island-serial-killer. 0723.

Jack Pinto had lost one front tooth in wrestling practice. He was a New York Giants fan, and was looking forward to being old enough to play tackle football. https://www.fallenheroesproject.org/post/jack-pinto. 0223.

Jamie Bishop had taught English in Germany, and German in the U.S. He liked woodworking and film, and was an Atlanta Braves fan. https://www.weremember.vt.edu/biographies/bishop.html. 0223.

Luis Conde did makeup and managed the business for the salon he and his husband ran. https://www.romper.com/p/who-is-luis-daniel-conde-the-puerto-rican-business-owner-died-with-his-partner-12622. 0323.

Eduardo Edwin Rodriguez was 29. https://abc7.com/eduardo-edwin-rodriguez-lawsuit-filed-la-county-sheriffs-department-lasd-east-man-killed-by-deputies/1416509/. 0723.

3.49: Ross, "A Multi-Level Bayesian Analysis," 1.

Hegemonic masculinity in policing: Prokos and Padavic, " 'There Oughta Be a Law," 439. "Academy training teaches female and male recruits that masculinity is an essential requirement for the practice of policing and that women do not belong…. [T]he masculinity that is characteristic of police forces and is partly responsible for women's low representation on them is not produced exclusively on the job, but is taught in police academies as a subtext of professional socialization."

Forgiving police violence: Pearl, "Staying Angry," 286. "This is an ongoing crisis, and one that apologies and forgiveness cannot now suture as the underlying racism of the system become ever more explicit. Black women should not be expected to perform forgiveness to save society as it is currently structured…. For many—namely, the perpetrators and beneficiaries of White supremacy—racism not only is not a problem but also is the necessary condition for the orderly functioning of the state. The crisis for those people is that the authority of the police is being challenged, not just in individual cases but as part of an ongoing national conversation…. Racialized forgiveness requests underscore the problem of structural oppression, attempting to silence Black women's anger and obscuring their voices while asking them to absolve and save the system."

Police violence: Holmes, Painter, and Smith, "Race, Place, and Police-Caused Homicide," 781. "The differential incidence of police-caused homicide undoubtedly reflects both objective (criminal) and subjective (stereotypical) threats arising from the challenging conditions confronted by both the citizens of minority communities and the police officers who patrol them. Ultimately, then, the problem of police violence in minority communities is symptomatic of the endemic social and economic inequalities that plague American cities."

43] • [44

Christopher Williams Jr. https://www.chron.com/news/houston-texas/article/Child-shot-in-Acres-Homes-13058120.php. 0723.

Greg Hill liked to cook. https://www.nytimes.com/2017/11/07/us/sutherland-springs-texas-victims.html. 0523.

Alexandria Rubio went by "Lexi." In her first season playing youth basketball, her team, the Spurs, won the championship. She liked to bake cookies – chocolate chip or sugar cookies with sprinkles – with her maternal great-grandmother. https://www.rekfunerals.com/obituaries/AlexandriaLexi-Rubio. 0523.

Jennifer Irvine was a graduate of California Western School of Law, and specialized in family law and criminal defense. https://www.bustle.com/p/who-was-jennifer-irvine-the-las-vegas-shooting-victim-was-a-shining-light-2781499. 0523.

Adolfo Cerros Hernández and his wife had one daughter. https://www.oxygen.com/crime-time/these-are-the-22-victims-who-died-in-el-paso-walmart-shooting. 0523.

Xiujuan Yu emigrated from China to the U.S. in the early 2010s. She had two children. She would often drop off food at her relatives' homes unasked. Because her father liked reading the newspaper but sometimes had trouble walking, she would buy him a paper and drop it off for him. https://news.yahoo.com/11-victims-were-killed-monterey-023802697.html. 0623.

Ryan Cox worked as an accounting clerk. He was active in his church, and had been working on his first sermon, with the intention of becoming a pastor. https://time.com/5599393/victims-viginia-beach-shooting/. 0623.

Raymond Green Vance was 22, and was saving to get his own apartment. He played video games and hoped to turn that into an online career. https://www.cnn.com/2022/11/21/us/club-q-colorado-shooting-victims/index.html. 0623.

Logan Turner had been an offensive lineman on his high school football team. He was 30. https://www.dignitymemorial.com/obituaries/franklin-oh/logan-turner-8803712. 0723.

Jesse Romero. https://www.ibtimes.com/who-jesse-romero-after-lapd-shoots-teen-everything-we-know-2399977. 0723.

<1.4 million: https://www.nytimes.com/2015/10/04/opinion/sunday/nicholas-kristof-a-new-way-to-tackle-gun-deaths.html. 0423.

Murder: Camus, *The Plague*, 131.
"On the whole, men are more good than bad; that, however, isn't the real point. But they are more or less ignorant, and it is this that we call vice or virtue; the most incorrigible vice being that of an ignorance that fancies it knows everything and therefore claims for itself the right to kill."

Deadly force: Palmiotto, "Use of Deadly Force," 47.
"Unlike the middle ages, our modern society has many crimes considered a felony and only one punishable by death. First-degree murder is the only crime punishable by death. The police who use deadly force against a felony suspect while apprehending them are exercising more authority and power than a judge or jury."

The language of civility: Ahmed, *The Promise of Happiness*, 86.
"Feminist consciousness can thus be thought of as consciousness of the violence and power that are concealed under the languages of civility and love, rather than simply consciousness of gender as a site of restriction of possibility."

44] • [45

David Smith lived in Minneapolis. https://www.npr.org/2020/05/29/865341322/minneapolis-police-were-sued-a-decade-ago-in-similar-restraint-case. 0723.

Joseph Wamah, Jr. was involved in his local acting community, and had gotten a role as an extra in one of the "Creed" movies. https://abcnews.go.com/US/philadelphia-mass-shooting-5-victims/story?id=100717829. 0723. https://www.wbaltv.com/article/philadelphia-july-3-shooting-victims/44453927#. 0723.

Arielle Diamond Anderson was 19. She was planning to graduate from college early. She enjoyed attending Michigan State basketball games.
https://www.nytimes.com/2023/02/14/us/michigan-state-shooting-victims.html?searchResultPosition=4. 0723.
https://www.detroitnews.com/story/news/local/michigan/2023/02/21/funeral-held-for-arielle-anderson-one-of-msu-students-killed-in-shooting/69925884007/. 0723.

Peter Wang was a 15-year-old high school student, and a JROTC Cadet. https://people.com/crime/florida-school-shooting-peter-wang-funeral/. 0723. https://sinceparkland.org/people/peter-wang/. 0723.

Maureen Brainard-Barnes was a 25-year-old single mother of two children, ages 8 and 1. She had grown up in Groton, Connecticut, and lived in Norwich. https://www.oxygen.com/true-crime-buzz/lost-girls-who-were-the-victims-of-the-long-island-serial-killer. 0723.

Sarena Dawn Moore was in community college, studying toward her dream of starting a therapeutic horse ranch for people with disabilities. She used a wheelchair for mobility, and had a service dog named Bullet. https://www.oregonlive.com/pacific-northwest-news/2015/10/oregon_shooting_sarena_dawn_mo.html. 0723.

Ana Grace Marquez-Greene sang to her older brother's piano accompaniment. https://anagraceproject.org/ana-grace/. 0223. https://www.fallenheroesproject.org/post/ana-marquez-greene. 0223.

G.V. Loganathan worked as a professor of civil engineering; his research and teaching was focused on hydrology and water resources systems. He had two daughters. He liked chess and reading. http://vt-memorial.org/profiles/Loganathan.html. 0223.

Cory Connell worked stocking shelves in a grocery store to put himself through college. https://people.com/crime/orlando-pulse-shooting-tributes-to-49-victims/. 0323.

Valarcia Blair lived in Youngstown, Ohio. https://www.statonborowskifuneralhome.com/obituary/Valarcia-Blair. 0723.

18: Klarevas, *Rampage Nation*, 75.

The crimes of the system: Morales, "Too Many Stolen Lives," 173.
"[T]he police murder and mass incarceration of Black and Brown people; the patriarchal degradation and dehumanization of women everywhere; the U.S. wars for empire; the criminalization and deportation of immigrants; the environmental destruction of the planet — all this and many other crimes are the workings of an industrial-capitalist system. We do not have to live this way. It is only because of this system, and we can change it. A better world is possible. We need a revolution. And all the struggles against the crimes of this system need to be part of getting to that revolution: *En el movimiento para la revolución…*"

Blurring the contrast: Kraska, "The Military-Criminal Justice Blur," 11
"[A] central feature of our government is fading: the clear delineation in form and function between internal security forces (civilian police) and external security forces (the military). This transformation signals a historic shift in the nature of the state, how it secures (or attempts to secure) compliance, and the overall character of modern social control."

Maybe the state monopoly: Harmon, "U.S. Gun Culture," 529.

"Political thought about state power distribution lies at the heart of gun culture. The basis for this… is that political power is intrinsically a question of monopoly of force. Gun culture's ambivalence requires us to rethink the standard model of it as a purely individualistic praxis but, rather, one interested in networks of power relations; a social movement whose social-narcissistic compensations make it, in specific and limited ways, collectivist, and, insofar as it is prone to nationalism, not entirely estranged from the state." Gun culture is an "attempt to contest state power by disrupting its monopoly on force."

45] • [46

Maria Eugenia Legarreta Rothe had driven across the border to pick up her teenage daughter from the El Paso airport. https://people.com/crime/el-paso-mass-shooting-remembering-victims-2-year-later/. 0623.

Annabelle Pomeroy was a preacher's kid, who went by "Belle." https://www.nytimes.com/2017/11/07/us/sutherland-springs-texas-victims.html. 0523. https://heavy.com/news/2017/11/sutherland-springs-texas-church-shooting-victims-list-names-photos-pictures/. 0523.

Tanisha Anderson had been diagnosed with bipolar disorder and placed on medication. For six years while she was raising her daughter, she had run a daycare from her mother's home, where she lived. https://www.theguardian.com/us-news/2015/jun/05/black-women-police-killing-tanisha-anderson. 0723.

Ezell Ford, when he was a child, had wanted to become a professional athlete and a doctor. https://www.blackpast.org/african-american-history/ford-ezell-1988-2014/. 0723.

Mark McMullen was 44. https://www.legacy.com/us/obituaries/bostonherald/name/mark-mcmullen-obituary?id=21736685. 0623. https://www.learntheirstories.com/#/mark-mcmullen/. 0623.

Eliahna Torres went with her grandfather after his heart attack on the walks his doctor prescribed. She liked to sing along with the Taylor Swift song "You Belong With Me." She loved her cat and her goldfish. https://www.nytimes.com/article/uvalde-shooting-victims.html. 0523.

Chris Hazencomb lived with his mother, and they had a Wednesday ritual of dinner together and watching an episode of "The Little Couple." https://www.reviewjournal.com/crime/homicides/las-vegas-shooting-victim-chris-hazencomb-camarillo-california/. 0523. https://www.nytimes.com/2017/10/02/us/vegas-victims-names.html. 0523.

Elsa Mendoza Marquez had as a favorite saying, "Things done with love are done better." https://www.oxygen.com/crime-time/these-are-the-22-victims-who-died-in-el-paso-walmart-shooting. 0523.

Wen Tau Yu was a citizen of Taiwan, living in the U.S. on a green card. In his first career he was a manager for an agricultural company. https://www.pasadenastarnews.com/2023/01/29/the-victims-seniors-who-found-joy-in-a-monterey-park-dance-studio/. 0623.

Fifty Bandz was 21. https://www.pghlesbian.com/2021/02/21-year-old-black-trans-woman-shot-to-death-in-baton-rouge/. 0723.

2: As estimated by the Small Arms Survey. Data is for the year 2017. https://www.smallarmssurvey.org/database/global-firearms-holdings. 0323.

Guns carried for protection: Branas et al., "Investigating the Link," 2037.
"After we adjusted for numerous confounding factors, gun possession by urban adults was associated with a significantly increased risk of being shot in an assault. On average, guns did not seem to protect those who possessed them from being shot in an assault. Although successful defensive gun uses can and do occur, the findings of this study do not support the perception that such successes are likely."

"Protective gun ownership": Warner et al., "To Provide or Protect?" 115.
"Americans broadly, and gun owners specifically, may need to accept that 'protective gun ownership' is more about protecting masculine identities and masculine hierarchies and less about protecting one's family."

"[W]hen gun owners believe: Pierre, "The Psychology of Guns," 3.

46] • [47

JoJo Striker. https://www.13abc.com/2022/03/31/mother-reacts-arrest-suspect-2017-murder/. 0723.

Herbert Snelling went by "Bert." His project manager work was at a construction company. https://people.com/crime/virginia-beach-mass-shooting-victims-identified/. 0623. https://www.dignitymemorial.com/obituaries/virginia-beach-va/herbert-snelling-8732892. 0623.

Philando Castile was a high school graduate. https://www.nbcnews.com/news/us-news/philando-castile-killed-police-during-traffic-stop-remembered-gentle-man-n605581. 0523. https://www.blackpast.org/african-american-history/castile-philando-divall-1983-2016/. 0523.

Jordan Edwards was 15. He lived in a suburb of Dallas. https://www.learntheirstories.com/#/jordan-edwards/. 0623.

Eric Garner was tall enough, about 6'3", and solid enough, north of 300 pounds, that friends had nicknamed him "Big E." Hill, *Nobody*.

Roxsana Hernández was a 33-year-old trans woman. https://www.newsweek.com/who-was-roxsana-hernandez-transgender-woman-who-died-ice-custody-was-beaten-1234721. 0723.

Thomas McNichols was 25. His children were aged 2 through 8. https://www.legacy.com/us/obituaries/hamilton/name/thomas-mcnichols-obituary?id=2216810. 0723. https://www.daytondailynews.com/news/dayton-shooting-victim-father-four-called-gentle-giant/3mRupzosrvz9RBD165EAbK/. 0723.

Da'Juan Brown was 15, and had finished his freshman year of high school. His two siblings and 16 cousins called him "Juan Juan." When he was young, he and his grandfather went often to the park together to feed the ducks. https://www.inquirer.com/news/kingsessing-shooting-victims-dajuan-brown-philadelphia-20230706.html. 0723.

Carmen Schentrup was a high school student, about to turn 17. She enjoyed singing in her church choir. She was a National Merit Finalist, and had been accepted to the University of Florida honors program. https://sinceparkland.org/people/carmen-schentrup/. 0723. https://www.cnn.com/2018/02/21/us/florida-shooting-carmen-schentrup/index.html. 0723.

Jose Nieves was known to family as "Cheo." He was 38. https://www.chicagotribune.com/news/ct-off-duty-chicago-cop-shooting-met-20170106-story.html. 0723.

10: https://www.washingtonpost.com/nation/interactive/2023/ar-15-america-gun-culture-politics/. 0323.
8.5 million: https://www.businessinsider.com/us-20-million-ar-15-style-rifles-in-circulation-2022-5?op=1. 0523.

Police use excessive: Dubber, *The Police Power*, xi, 211.
"Among the powers of government none is greater than the power to police, and none less circumscribed.... The history of American law and government can profitably be seen as a continuing attempt to resolve, and to submerge, the inherent tension between police and law, between public welfare and individual rights, and between heteronomy and autonomy.... The project of critically analyzing the power to police is a crucial part of the general project of critically analyzing state power.... The basic question is whether police within the limits of law is possible."

Police are *rewarded*: Art Lurigio, as quoted in Macaraeg and Flowers, "Amid Shootings," 35.
"Police departments are quasi-military organizations. The police are authorized to use force in ways that no other citizen is authorized to act. Police are rewarded for exercising force and sometimes engaging in violent behaviors, including shooting at the suspects, including shooting dead the suspects, including tasing the suspects. They are not credited for performance that's passive."

47] • [48

Jose Ocampo lived in Durham, North Carolina. https://ebwiki.org/cases/jose-adan-cruz-ocampo. 0723.

Amber Lynn Costello had been raised in Wilmington, North Carolina, and lived in New York City. She experienced substance misuse issues. https://www.oxygen.com/true-crime-buzz/lost-girls-who-were-the-victims-of-the-long-island-serial-killer. 0723.

Lucas Eibel was studying chemistry in community college. He was a quadruplet. He liked hiking, building driftwood forts at the beach, skiing, and playing catch and having airsoft battles in the backyard with siblings and friends. https://umpqua.edu/we-remember/lucas-eibel-we-will-always-remember/. 0723.

Mah-hi-vist Goodblanket was from Clinton, Oklahoma. In school, he had been chosen to be a Youth Ambassador to Europe. He was named for his great-great-great grandfather, and his given name translates into English as Red Bird. He had a sister and four brothers. He had been diagnosed with oppositional defiant disorder.
https://www.findagrave.com/memorial/122239256/mah-hi-vist-goodblanket. 0723.

Ousmane Zongo had two young children, ages 5 and 3, who lived with their mother in Yako, a village in Burkina Faso. According to his brother, he supported 70 people in that village.
https://www.learntheirstories.com/#/ousmane-zongo/. 0623.
https://www.nytimes.com/2003/08/01/nyregion/slain-immigrant-s-family-here-asking-why.html. 0623.

Allison Wyatt. https://www.ctpost.com/news/article/Allison-Wyatt-liked-to-garden-with-her-mother-4122893.php. 0223. https://screeningsandyhook.net/2018/01/10/allison-noelle-wyatt/. 0223.

Brian Bluhm was an active member of Baptist Collegiate Ministries while studying for his masters degree in civil engineering, and had accepted a job at an engineering firm to begin after graduation. https://www.weremember.vt.edu/biographies/bluhm.html. 0223.

Jerry Wright grew up in a Colombian-American family. He studied at Florida International University. At Walt Disney World, he worked first at Tomorrowland and then at Main Street.
https://www.nytimes.com/interactive/projects/cp/us/orlando-shooting-victims/jerald-arthur-wright. 0423. https://www.orlandoweekly.com/news/remembering-the-orlando-49-jerald-arthur-wright-3049287. 0423.

Tara McNulty was raising two children on her own.
https://www.nytimes.com/2017/11/07/us/sutherland-springs-texas-victims.html. 0523.

Nathaniel Pickett II suffered from mental illness.
https://www.howmyvoiceisheard.com/lives/nathaniel-pickett. 0723.
https://www.nhp2foundation.org/our-vision. 0723.

685,724: https://www.nyclu.org/en/press-releases/new-nyclu-report-finds-nypd-stop-and-frisk-practices-ineffective-reveals-depth-racial. 0423. https://www.nyclu.org/en/stop-and-frisk-data. 0423.

We assign *persons* to *roles*: Spencer, *The Paradox of Youth Violence*, 16-17.
"[P]erpetrators and victims of violence are fashioned by media discourse into a type of morality play, with offenders as the evil, predatory villains and their targets as innocent victims. Typecasting of offenders and victims facilitates the fashioning of these morality plays. For example, news discourse focuses disproportionately on women, children, and the elderly as victims of violence, likely because they are more easily presented as vulnerable and weak. Further, victims are typically portrayed as morally pure — not responsible for their plight and deserving of our sympathy and assistance.

Violent offenders, however, are often demonized. For example, media discourse focuses on violence committed by men and youth. Violence by strangers garners more attention than violence between friends, acquaintances, or family members. Quite often in this discourse, victimizers lack conscience and act without remorse."

The go-to rationale: Perry, *In the Name of Hate*, 216.
"The cultural myths that have come to signify people of color inform police violence against minorities. They provide the context within which law enforcement officers can rationalize their own relational enactment of white masculinity through brutal acts. Skin color alone marks the 'other' as deviant, criminal, potentially violent."

As long as the weaponed hero: Poudrier, "The Virtue of the Weaponed Hero," 37.
"[U]ntil and unless firearms can be written out of the American psyche as a suitable weapon for the hero, the guns in our theaters won't be silenced."

48] • [49

John Kohler was 42. He lived in Barberton, Ohio.
https://www.legacy.com/us/obituaries/ohio/name/john-kohler-obituary?id=13895775. 0723.

Jose Flores Jr. was in fourth grade. He had three brothers and two sisters.
https://www.npr.org/2022/05/27/1101286508/what-we-know-about-the-victims-of-the-uvalde-school-shooting. 0523. https://www.texastribune.org/2022/05/25/uvalde-school-shooting-victims/. 0523.

Javier Ambler II was 40, and had two sons, ages 4 and 15. https://www.blackpast.org/african-american-history/people-african-american-history/javier-ambler-ii-1979-2019/. 0723.

Mesha Caldwell lived in Canton, Mississippi.
https://www.independent.co.uk/news/world/americas/mesha-caldwell-first-transgender-woman-us-mississippi-american-person-killed-in-2017-lgbtq-a7513576.html. 0723.

José Antonio Elena Rodríguez was 16, and lived in Nogales, Mexico. He wanted to be a soldier.
https://www.theguardian.com/world/2015/may/31/jose-antonio-us-mexico-border-shooting-constitutional-rights. 0723.

Brian Fraser worked as a vice president of sales at a mortgage firm. https://apnews.com/article/1427720179. 0523.

Teresa Sanchez had been living in El Paso for 30 years. https://people.com/crime/el-paso-mass-shooting-remembering-victims-2-year-later/. 0623. https://www.findagrave.com/memorial/201868147/teresa-trinidad-sanchez. 0623.

My My Nhan liked at social dances to sit near the speakers, and sip tea between dances. Her mother, for whom she had been the caretaker, had only recently passed away. https://news.yahoo.com/11-victims-were-killed-monterey-023802697.html. 0623. https://www.pasadenastarnews.com/2023/01/29/the-victims-seniors-who-found-joy-in-a-monterey-park-dance-studio/. 0623.

Pearlie Golden's late husband had been an officer in the Hearne, Texas Police Department. https://www.theatlantic.com/national/archive/2014/05/police-officer-who-killed-93-year-old-woman-has-killed-before/361969/. 0723.

Quindell Lee. https://usgunviolence.wordpress.com/2013/11/23/killed-boy-quindell-lee-dallas-tx/. 0723.

2: Charbonneau, Spencer, and Glaser, "Understanding Racial Disparities," 745.

Stored or not, having a gun: Dahlberg, et al., "Guns in the Home," 929.
"Results show that regardless of storage practice, type of gun, or number of firearms in the home, having a gun in the home was associated with an increased risk of firearm homicide and firearm suicide in the home."

Who most gun owners: Couch, "A Qualitative Analysis," 406.
"[T]his study reveals a critical aspect of student gun rights advocates – most construct their vulnerability in relation to people of color. Therefore, this must be taken into account when campus administrators are deliberating on decisions to allow concealed carry on college campuses."

Guns sound: Schutten et al., "Are Guns the New Dog Whistle?" 108-9.
"[R]acial resentment conditions the effect of gun-related candidate characteristics on voter evaluations. Racially resentful voters express greater willingness to vote for election candidates when those candidates receive NRA funding and when they do not support gun control. Therefore, not only does racial prejudice affect gun control attitudes these racialized attitudes can be activated by gun rights politics and may affect vote choice."

49] • [50

Tariq Morris lived in Youngstown, Ohio. https://www.findagrave.com/memorial/205668488/tariq-morris. 0723.

Anthony Lowe Jr. was 36, and lived in California. https://news.yahoo.com/police-killing-anthony-lowe-double-163346472.html. 0723.

Jasmine Mack. https://www.lgbtqnation.com/2023/01/beloved-transgender-woman-stabbed-death-d-c/. 0723.

Robert Williams went by "Bobby." He was planning to retire soon. He and his wife had two children and four grandchildren. He had served in the Navy in Vietnam aboard the USS America. https://time.com/5599393/victims-viginia-beach-shooting/. 0623. https://people.com/crime/virginia-beach-mass-shooting-victims-identified/. 0623. https://www.legacy.com/us/obituaries/pilotonline/name/robert-williams-sr-obituary?id=15277356. 0623.

Derrick Fudge had four brothers, two sisters. He was 57. He volunteered for the Salvation Army. He liked cooking and painting, and was good at fixing cars. https://fudgefoundation.org/. 0723. https://www.wlwt.com/article/derrick-fudge-well-known-salvation-army-volunteer-among-dead-in-dayton-mass-shooting/28614470#. 0723. https://people.com/crime/dayton-shooting-victim-died-sons-arms-laid-to-rest/. 0723.

Alex Schachter was a 14-year-old high school freshman. He hoped to qualify for DECA States, and looked forward to being old enough to drive his father's red Tesla. https://www.dignitymemorial.com/obituaries/north-lauderdale-fl/alexander-schachter-7763952. 0723. https://sinceparkland.org/people/alexander-schachter/. 0723.

Tyler Dunn's favorite TV show was *Duck Dynasty*, and his favorite video game was *Call of Duty*. Younge, *Another Day in the Death of America.*

Roy Nelson Jr. lived in Hayward, California. He was physically large, weighing approximately 350 pounds. He was living at a court-mandated halfway house because of his history of drug use and mental issues. https://www.ktvu.com/news/this-is-the-west-coast-eric-garner-case-father-dies-after-telling-hayward-police-he-cant-breathe. 0723.

Antonio Zambrano-Montes immigrated from Mexico to the U.S. with his wife and their two daughters. He worked as a fruit-picker in Pasco, Washington. https://www.theguardian.com/us-news/2015/feb/17/pasco-fatal-police-shooting-zambrano-montes-hispanic. 0723.

Denali Berries Stuckey lived in North Charleston, South Carolina. https://obits.postandcourier.com/us/obituaries/charleston/name/derrick-stuckey-obituary?id=2062726. 0723.

65: https://ropercenter.cornell.edu/shootings-guns-and-public-opinion. 0423.

"A day doesn't go by: Anonymous young person, as quoted in Obidah, "On Living (and Dying) with Violence," 52.

Hard to conceal: Madhubuti, *Taking Bullets*, 61.
"The 'official' killing, or modern day lynching, of Black boys, teenagers, and men, and out-of-proportion incarceration of Black teenagers, women and men are now hitting the front page of newspapers and being featured on the evening news. This is not due to any serious investigative reporting by mainstream media but by masses of people and their strategic use of *social media*. This cannot be minimized: young peoples' use of smart phones, tablets, laptops, and other personalized media and devices has kept much of the uninformed public informed and has driven major media to try to catch up with their coverage. This is truly social citizenship."

Hard to keep guns: Zimring, *American Youth Violence*, 95-96.
"To say that the prospect for restricting the availability of guns to minors is superior to the prospect for regulating adult use is by no means the equivalent of concluding that age-specific gun controls in the United States work well. Gun control for any target group is difficult to accomplish in an environment where available handguns might exceed 60 million."

50] • [51

Noel Aguilar. https://voicewaves.org/2016/05/residents-remember-noel-aguilar-killed-by-sheriffs-deputy-two-years-ago/. 0723.

Marvin Booker was 56. https://www.theguardian.com/us-news/2014/oct/14/denver-marvin-booker-police-brutality-family-award. 0723.

Emilie Parker was helping one of her younger sisters learn to read. https://www.ctinsider.com/news/article/emilie-parker-sandy-hook-17577224.php. 0223.

Cashay Henderson was born in Chicago. For more than five years she had been active with Sisters Helping Each Other Battle Adversity (SHEBA), a biweekly gathering for Black trans women. https://www.soundhealthandlastingwealth.com/people/who-was-cashay-henderson/. 0323.

Carrie Barnette lived in Riverside, CA, and worked as a cook at the Pacific Wharf Cafe, a waterfront restaurant at a Disney park in Anaheim. https://www.nytimes.com/2017/10/02/us/vegas-victims-names.html. 0523.

Sheneque Proctor was 18. https://www.theguardian.com/us-news/2015/jan/09/black-alabama-teenager-died-police-cell-sheneque-proctor. 0823.

Peggy Warden had one daughter and three grandchildren. https://people.com/crime/texas-church-shooting-victim-shielded-her-grandson/. 0523.

Carlos Alcis immigrated from Haiti to Brooklyn in 2000 in search for a better life for his family. He was 43 years old. https://www.learntheirstories.com/#/carlos-alcis/. 0623.

Mario Woods had a dry sense of humor, according to his mother, and a "nervous, goofy laugh." https://kpfa.org/blog/remembering-mario-woods/. 0823.

MaKayla Walker. https://www.articobits.com/obituaries/keith-p-clark-son-funeral-home/makayla-shybree-ann-walker-obituary. 0823.

2: https://www.local10.com/news/2015/01/24/man-dies-after-police-involved-shooting-in-lauderhill/. 0823.
2: https://www.theguardian.com/us-news/2015/apr/19/pennsylvania-police-homicide-taser-video-shooting-david-kassick. 0823.
4: https://www.howmyvoiceisheard.com/lives/tyisha-miller. 0723.

Long histories of violence: Deer, "Federal Indian Law," 18.
"Addressing 500 years of violence, maltreatment, and neglect requires major changes and adjustments to the current structure of federal laws, policies, and regulations affecting tribal nations. Decision-making authority and control over violent crime should be restored to indigenous nations to provide full accountability and justice to the victims."

"Breaking with the violent past: Bracha L. Ettinger, in Evans and Lennart, *Violence*, 115.

Until killing: Brittany Packnett, as quoted in Lowery, *They Can't Kill Us All*, 232.
"We have no choice but to keep going. If one of the central demands of the movement is to stop killing us, and they're still killing us, then we don't get to stop, either."

51] • [52

Sarah Gonzalez. https://www.reynoldsfuneralhomes.com/obituary/Sarah-Gonzalez. 0823.

Kyam Livingston was 37. https://bklyner.com/one-year-after-kyam-livingstons-death-family-and-friends-continue-push-for-investigation-ditmas-park/. 0823.

Kate Armand. https://www.dailymail.co.uk/news/article-4067262/Police-cadet-dad-two-murdered-wife-seriously-injured-trooper-police-shootout-shot-dead.html. 0823.

Royal Poetical Starz was a 26-year-old trans woman. Her favorite restaurant was the Longhorn Steakhouse, and her favorite drink was Hennessy and cranberry.
https://www.hrc.org/news/hrc-mourns-royal-poetical-starz-black-transgender-woman-killed-in-miami-gardens-florida. 0723. https://www.miaminewtimes.com/news/miami-gardens-police-deadnamed-murder-victim-royal-poetical-starz-13214188. 0723.
https://www.advocate.com/crime/2021/10/15/black-trans-woman-royal-poetical-starz-killed-florida. 0723.

Catherine Hubbard. https://www.newstimes.com/news/article/sandy-hook-catherine-hubbard-animal-sanctuary-17475244.php. 0223.

Daunte Wright had, as a high school freshman, been voted a class clown. https://www.nytimes.com/2021/12/08/us/who-was-daunte-wright.html. 0623.

John Phippen lived in Santa Clarita, California. He enjoyed traveling with his family to the sand dunes of Glamis, piloting his pontoon boat, and 4-wheeling. https://www.legacy.com/us/obituaries/signalscv/name/john-phippen-obituary?id=10284851. 0523.

Julio Joseph Bald Eagle graduated as valedictorian of his high school. https://www.findagrave.com/memorial/221616572/julio-joseph-bald_eagle. 0823.

Makenna Elrod liked softball and gymnastics. She liked to dance and sing, play with fidgets and spend time with her family. She was a member of the 4-H club and loved animals. https://www.tributearchive.com/obituaries/24944217/makenna-lee-elrod. 0523.

Rocio Lissette Vasquez. https://homicide.latimes.com/post/rocio-lissette-vasquez/. 0723.

>$7 billion: Jimenez, Helm, and Arndt, "Racial Prejudice Predicts," 2009.
12,440: Masera, "Police Safety," 6.
0.76 per million inhabitants: Masera, "Police Safety," 5.

Gun carriers: Carlson, *Citizen-Protectors*, 173.
"While gun carriers are private actors buttressed by the gun industry, they belong in a slightly different analytical category than market actors — they are not the citizen-consumer often envisioned in studies of neoliberal citizenship. Poised between the state and the market, gun carriers are political actors insofar as they are mobilized by a particular notion of policing and insofar as this becomes tethered to a particular understanding of 'good citizenship.' Enabled by the state and the market, this new kind of citizenship extends the punitive state beyond the market and onto the bodies of everyday Americans."

Gun owners: Gabor, *Confronting Gun Violence*, 280.
"The dogmatic pursuit of the freedoms of a minority of inflexible gun owners — probably accounting for less than a tenth of all adults — comes at the expense of the rights of Americans at large to be safe in their communities, work places, and recreational spaces. Ultimately, the lack of a balancing of gun owners' rights with public safety concerns comes at the cost of the liberties of all citizens."

Guns influence: Stroud, *Good Guys with Guns*, 27.
"The vast majority of CHL [concealed handgun license] holders will never need to draw their firearms in public. Thus what is most significant about CHLS and concealed firearms is not what happens in the moment a gun is drawn but in what they contribute to the cultural meaning systems that shape how we see ourselves and each other."

52] • [53

Stephen Young. https://www.azcentral.com/story/news/local/mesa-breaking/2023/05/28/suspect-identified-mesa-shooting-spree-linked-phoenix-homicide/70265292007/. 0723. https://www.azfamily.com/2023/05/30/family-remembers-one-mesa-shooting-spree-victims/. 0723.

Tyianna Alexander, a 28-year-old trans woman, was from Chicago. She lived with her mother. She was an aficionado of Chicago House music. She was a high school graduate, and worked in various retail and restaurant positions. https://www.windycitytimes.com/lgbt/Remembering-Tyianna-Alexander/71920.html. 0723.

Josephine Gay was on the autistic spectrum, and was unable to speak. Her family called her Joey. https://www.nbcconnecticut.com/news/newtown-school-shooting/family-of/1922103/. 0223.

Dominique Franklin Jr. was 23, and lived in Chicago. As an adult he had difficulties with alcohol and had accumulated a criminal record. https://www.chicagotribune.com/news/ct-xpm-2014-06-06-chi-father-remembers-son-who-died-after-taser-20140606-story.html. 0823.

Michelle Vo was 32, and had traveled extensively, "all over Europe and Southeast Asia." https://www.nytimes.com/2017/10/02/us/vegas-victims-names.html. 0523.

Antonio Guzman Lopez was an undocumented immigrant from Mexico who worked as a gardener and handyman. https://abc7news.com/archive/9449799/. 0723.

Annabell Rodriguez was in the fourth grade. She enjoyed watching TikTok and spending time with her sisters and family. https://www.tributearchive.com/obituaries/24954831/annabell-guadalupe-rodriguez. 0523.

Jamal Rollins. https://ebwiki.org/cases/jamal-rollins. 0823.

Loreal Tsingine dropped out of high school, and had a daughter when she was 18. She was 27, and had a history of mental health issues. https://www.phoenixnewtimes.com/news/navajo-womans-death-police-violence-against-native-americans-9595827. 0723.

Christian Siquieros. https://ebwiki.org/cases/christian-siqueiros. 0723.

11: In 2003, according to a Bureau of Justice Statistics study, as reported in Cornell, *School Violence*, 20-21.
103: For the period 1992-2000. Cornell, *School Violence*, 21.

Brutal enforcement: Gramsci, *Prison Notebooks* III, 300-301.
To understand "the growth of organized crime on a grand scale" in the U.S., "one has to look at the incredibly brutal methods of the American police; police brutality always creates 'brigandage.' This factor has a much greater effect that might appear: it is a catalyst for making professional criminals out of many individuals who would have otherwise carried on with their normal working lives.... The illegality of the executive organism raised to the level of a system leads the victims, etc., to wage a fierce battle."

Police use of deadly force: Taylor, "Beyond False Positives," 818-19.
"Each of the example cases discussed in this article and all of the shootings they exemplify could be, and indeed often are, for purposes of research, indiscriminately aggregated with all other available cases that fit under the heading of 'police use of deadly force' and then statistically analyzed for causal correlations. Yet the underlying causal mechanisms for each of these cases are much different and would be missed using such a coarse approach."

The higher the Social: Zare et al., "How Place and Race," 6.
"Police are more likely to use fatal force in counties with greater economic disadvantage, racial conflict, and high crime rates. Counties with a greater proportion of vulnerable populations are at a greater risk of experiencing police use of force."

53] • [54

Julian Cox. https://www.azcentral.com/story/news/local/mesa-breaking/2023/05/28/suspect-identified-mesa-shooting-spree-linked-phoenix-homicide/70265292007/. 0723.

Whispering Wind Bear Spirit loved dancing, singing, beading, playing sports, composing music and learning. Bear wore hearing aids because a case of meningitis in childhood had caused hearing impairment. Bear dropped out of high school but later got a GED. Bear was good with growing plants, good at handiwork and crafts. Bear's self-description on social media included the characterization "Shawnee by birth and Potawatomi by relations."
https://obits.mlive.com/us/obituaries/kalamazoo/name/jennifer-makos-obituary?id=14907658. 0723. https://www.yorkdispatch.com/story/news/2022/08/24/whispering-wind-bear-spirit-two-journeys-cut-short-one-night-york-city/7834325001/. 0723.
https://www.hrc.org/news/hrc-mourns-whispering-wind-bear-spirit-indigenous-non-binary-person-killed-in-pennsylvania. 0723.

Daniel Barden told other classmates about his friend, "I know she can't talk, but I know she can hear me." https://abcnews.go.com/blogs/headlines/2012/12/sandy-hook-elementary-victim-7-year-old-daniel-barden-was-old-soul. 0223. http://www.whatwoulddanieldo.com/daniels-story/. 0223.

Jack Beaton and his wife, whom he had married soon after her college graduation, had two children. https://www.legacy.com/us/obituaries/bakersfield/name/jack-beaton-obituary?id=10349967. 0523.

Xavier Lopez liked to play basketball and baseball and soccer. He was only in the fourth grade, but was already looking forward to middle school.
https://www.texastribune.org/2022/05/25/uvalde-school-shooting-victims/. 0523.
https://www.npr.org/2022/05/27/1101286508/what-we-know-about-the-victims-of-the-uvalde-school-shooting. 0523. https://www.nytimes.com/2022/05/27/briefing/uvalde-texas-shooting-victims.html. 0523.

Timothy Dawkins-El was the father of a young child. He lived in Washington, D.C., and as a community activist he was a leader in a faith-based program at Potomac Job Corps: the youth he mentored knew him as "Lil Daddy." https://nextlevelvision.org/about-us. 0323.

Antash'a English was a 38-year-old trans woman, originally from Albany, Georgia, who lived in Jacksonville, Florida. https://www.firstcoastnews.com/article/news/crime/slain-jacksonville-transgender-woman-remembered-for-being-bold-and-unapologetic/77-561117421. 0723. https://transgriot.blogspot.com/2018/06/number-12-rest-in-power-antasha-english.html. 0723.

Osmar Hernandez was 26. https://www.thecalifornian.com/story/news/crime/2015/07/10/officers-charged-osmar-hernandezs-salinas-death/29997183/. 0823.

Shayla Martin was a Seahawks fan and loved to cook, read, and go to the beach. https://www.seattletimes.com/seattle-news/law-justice/burlington-mall-shooting-victims-officially-identified/. 0323.

Derrick Scott. https://www.huffpost.com/entry/derrick-scott-oklahoma-city-police_n_5ee21230c5b6b39142ae0332. 0823.

15: https://www.prisonlegalnews.org/news/2018/apr/2/415000-settlement-lawsuit-over-tasered-prisoner-who-died-texas-jail/. 0823.

The heroic loner frontier gunfighter: Melzer, *Gun Crusaders*, 32-34.
"Firearms were unquestionably part of white westward expansion, for hunting and for forcibly taking land from indigenous populations. But the role of firearms in this expansion has been exaggerated, as it took a great deal more than firearms to 'settle' the West, notably ranchers and farmers…. Violence, including gun violence, generally decreased once displaced native groups were killed or removed and towns were established in the 1800s. Settlers then took steps to lessen violence. Quite the opposite of frontier individualism, new communities initiated forms of law and order that would encourage everyone to cooperate and benefit from mutual protection."

Good guys killing off bad guys: Utter, "Accessories Included," 371-72.
Re. statements made by Jack Wilson, one of those involved, in the incident "two days after Christmas, 2019, when armed members of a volunteer security unit at the West Highway Church of Christ in White Settlement, Texas, shot and killed a man after he had shot two parishioners with a shotgun he had concealed under his coat": "While his humility is admirable, his analysis of the situation is telling: 'I don't feel like I killed an individual, I killed evil.' Evil is precisely what the killing of one 'bad guy with a gun' failed to kill, at least inasmuch as gun violence is a systemic enemy requiring systemic transformation. Though Wilson is right to recognize the shooter as an emissary of a bigger issue, to describe him in terms that subsume his individuality within a sweeping sense of cosmic evil is indicative of how so much of White American Christianity individualizes the problem of gun violence, as if one could effectively attack it one dead 'bad guy' at a time."

Owning a gun: https://nationalpost.com/opinion/jonathan-kay-more-guns-arent-the-answer-americans-are-likelier-to-wet-their-pants-facing-a-mass-shooter. 0423.
"The America of the NRA's imagination is a mythic, death-match arena populated by 'good guys' and 'bad guys,' 'monsters' and 'patriots.' As in a videogame or superhero comic book, everyone apparently falls into one category or the other. And since the patriots are more numerous, the theory goes, life is arithmetically safest when Americans are all armed to the teeth, ready to rake others with gunfire at the slightest provocation. In reality, whether you are a 'monster,' or a 'patriot,' or (like most of us) something in between, having a gun in your home makes you more likely to die."

54] • [55

Sergio Navas. https://www.latimes.com/local/lanow/la-me-ln-lapd-burbank-shooting-family-20160203-story.html. 0823.

Dawn Hochsprung worked as an elementary school Principal. At her school, she introduced "Wacky Wednesdays," a day for coming to school in clothes that don't match, and sometimes she herself participated. https://www.theguardian.com/world/2012/dec/15/dawn-hochsprung-sandy-hook-elementary. 0223.

Victor Link had an adopted adult son. https://abcnews.go.com/US/las-vegas-shooting-mother-father-dead/story?id=50229707. 0523. https://www.nytimes.com/2017/10/02/us/vegas-victims-names.html. 0523. https://apnews.com/article/1432490102. 0523.

Layla Salazar ran track. She liked Koala bears and the Dallas Cowboys. She liked to sing and dance and make TikTok videos. https://www.rekfunerals.com/obituaries/Layla-Salazar. 0523.

Wendell Allen had recently graduated from a New Orleans high school, where he was a talented basketball player. He was attending Navarro College in Texas, but had recently returned to New Orleans to be closer to his family. https://www.learntheirstories.com/#/wendell-allen/. 0623.

Chavis Carter was 21 years old. https://www.washingtontimes.com/news/2012/aug/21/slain-mans-family-seeks-answers-on-ruling-of-suici/. 0623.

Savannah Graziano was homeschooled. She was 15, and had one brother. She enjoyed spending time with her family and friends. https://www.dignitymemorial.com/obituaries/bloomington-ca/savannah-graziano-10950186. 0723.

Pooh Johnson was a 25-year-old trans woman.
https://tdor.translivesmatter.info/reports/2021/08/23/pooh-johnson-titanizer-mua_shreveport-louisiana-usa_16aace3b. 0723.

Frank Shephard III. https://www.chron.com/houston/article/Shots-fired-at-end-of-police-chase-6201525.php. 0823.

Ricky Cobb II had a twin brother.
https://www.washingtonpost.com/nation/2023/08/03/video-shows-minnesota-trooper-fatally-shot-black-driver-traffic-stop/. 0823.

2.6: Grinshteyn and Hemenway, "Violent Death Rates," 22.
7.5: Grinshteyn and Hemenway, "Violent Death Rates," 23.

Militarization nudges: Lawson, "TRENDS," 177.
"[P]olice have a great deal of discretion in deciding how to handle situations they encounter, and militarization affects the decision making of police by moving their preferences toward more violent responses to suspects."

"[P]olice militarization: "Police Safety," 9. My italics.
Masera is explicitly countering the prevailing view. The sentence in its entirety reads: "Finally, I show that contrary to what is often argued in policy debates, police militarization decreases police safety."

Routine use of militarized policing: Mummolo, "Militarization Fails to Enhance," 9186.
"[T]he routine use of militarized police tactics by local agencies threatens to increase the historic tensions between marginalized groups and the state with no detectable public safety benefit."

55] • [56

Caroline Ireland lived in North Carolina. https://www.wnct.com/news/five-people-found-dead-inside-a-vanceboro-home-investigation-underway/. 0823.
https://www.dignitymemorial.com/obituaries/new-bern-nc/april-ireland-children-9015422. 0823.

Lauren Rousseau worked as a substitute elementary-school teacher, and also worked part-time at Starbuck's. https://www.newstimes.com/local/article/Lauren-Rousseau-The-best-year-of-her-life-4120850.php. 0223.

Neysa Tonks worked in technology sales, and lived in Las Vegas.
https://www.dignitymemorial.com/obituaries/las-vegas-nv/neysa-tonks-7586778. 0523.

Tamir Rice, 12, lived in Cleveland, and was the youngest of four siblings.
https://www.goodmorningamerica.com/news/story/12-year-son-tamir-rice-killed-police-im-71654873. 0723.

Maranda Mathis liked being outdoors: running during school field days, swimming in the river, and showing rocks she found to her mother. She liked to play Roblox on her tablet with her younger brother. https://www.rekfunerals.com/obituaries/Maranda-Mathis. 0523.
https://www.nytimes.com/article/uvalde-shooting-victims.html. 0523.

Bennie Edwards. https://freepressokc.com/bennie-edwards-was-a-victim-of-okc-police-gunfight-mentality/. 0623.

Danielle Keyes liked taking walks, shopping, and playing on her phone. https://rumsey-yost.com/2014/11/danielle-joanna-keyes/. 0923.

Kirk Mattson was a high school graduate. He enjoyed processing meats and produce, creating his own craft beers and wines, and reading books about history, his various creative interests, and select fiction. He enjoyed spending time with his siblings and nieces and nephews. https://www.carlsonlillemoen.com/obituary/Kirk-Mattson. 0923.

Jaylow McGlory was from Alexandria, Louisiana. https://www.findagrave.com/memorial/182190901/jeffrey-brad-mcglory. 0923.

Brandon Jones. https://www.cleveland.com/court-justice/2016/03/mother_of_unarmed_man_shot_dea.html. 0823.

953,613: Jones and Stone, "The U.S. Gun Control Paradox," 171.
3: Jones and Stone, "The U.S. Gun Control Paradox," 172.

Cool violence: McLaren, Leonardo, and Allen, "Rated 'CV' for Cool Violence," 89.
"So, where is violence? It exists not just in the regular forms of the occasional act or isolated condition, but in the cool violence perpetrated by the conceptual space of modernist epistemologies and their associated logics of whiteness, masculinity, and capitalism. Cool violence is slippery and cannot be easily regulated by bureaucratic solutions without committing more violence."

Invisible violence: Žižek, *Violence*, 2.
"Systemic violence is thus something like the notorious 'dark matter' of physics, the counterpart to an all-too-visible subjective violence. It may be invisible, but it has to be taken into account if one is to make sense of what otherwise seem to be 'irrational' explosions of subjective violence."

"Acceptable 'defensive' violence: Allen, "A Non-Defensive Gun," 218.
The quoted sentence occurs later in a paragraph that Allen begins in this way: "When people think of gun violence in the United States, they often think of mass shootings. Mass shootings in the United States, however, are a vanishingly small element in the far larger wildfire of US gun violence (to say nothing of our still greater problems). In contradistinction to mass shootings, which are terrifying because they are imagined as 'attacks,' the ubiquitous gun violences we more quietly live with are framed, at least somewhat effectively, as defensive."

56] • [57

Jason Ireland loved his younger brother and sister. https://www.wnct.com/news/five-people-found-dead-inside-a-vanceboro-home-investigation-underway/. 0823.
https://www.dignitymemorial.com/obituaries/new-bern-nc/april-ireland-children-9015422. 0823.

Tracy Single was a 22-year-old trans woman. She liked clothes, and wanted to work in a local resale shop. She grew up in New Orleans, but had recently moved to Houston, where she was insecurely housed. https://www.outsmartmagazine.com/2019/08/remembering-tracy-single/. 0723.

Rachel D'Avino worked as a behavioral therapist. She had completed coursework for a graduate certificate in Autism Spectrum Disorders. https://abcnews.go.com/US/newtown-shooting-teachers-aide-rachel-davinos-boyfriend-propose/story?id=17999719. 0223.

Steve Berger had played basketball on his college team. He was a Wisconsin native, and a University of Wisconsin football fan. https://www.reviewjournal.com/crime/homicides/las-vegas-shooting-victim-steve-berger-minneapolis/. 0523.

Timothy Stansbury was 19. His family called him "Tim-Tim," and his friends called him "Drag." He had recently earned his GED. https://www.blackpast.org/african-american-history/people-african-american-history/timothy-stansbury-jr-1984-2004/. 0623. https://www.learntheirstories.com/#/timothy-stansbury/. 0623.

Rojelio Torres. https://www.legacy.com/us/obituaries/name/rojelio-torres-obituary?id=34958659. 0523.

Jaquarrius Holland was an 18-year-old trans woman from Monroe, Louisiana. She enjoyed doing hair and makeup, and loved long false eyelashes so much that one friend nicknamed her the "eyelash queen." https://www.logotv.com/news/0ao83s/transgender-day-of-remembrance-memorial-2017. 0723. https://www.mic.com/articles/169896/jaquarius-holland-18-year-old-trans-woman-killed-in-louisiana-misgendered-in-reports#.tFBvE2plP. 0723.

Lewis DeWayne Green had two sisters and two brothers. https://greenlawnfuneralhome.com/obituary/lewis-dewayne-green-2/. 0923.

Briseis Aljumaily loved spending time with her friends and cutting up on SnapChat and Tik Tok. She especially loved shopping. https://www.tributearchive.com/obituaries/27188410/briseis-aaliyah-aljumaily. 0923.

John Paul Quintero. https://ebwiki.org/cases/john-paul-quintero. 0823.

57: https://ropercenter.cornell.edu/shootings-guns-and-public-opinion. 0423.
2001: *Fortune* magazine, as cited in Burbick, *Gun Show Nation*, xvi.
$2 million: Jones and Stone, "The U.S. Gun Control Paradox," 169. The precise figures given are: $1,960,899 and $276,903,028.
50: https://ropercenter.cornell.edu/shootings-guns-and-public-opinion. 0423.

Gun owners are: Joslyn, *The Gun Gap*, 190-91.
"[G]un owners are not merely a loose collection of individuals but a group exhibiting systematic patterns of political thinking and behavior…. [Also,] owning more firearms amplifies the

tendencies that owning one gun produces. In other words, stronger gun attachments further separate gun owners from nonowners."

Gun owners are not: Boine, Caffrey, and Siegel, "Who Are Gun Owners…?" 49.
"[T]he gun-owning population is far more complex than that depicted by stereotypes displayed in the media and sometimes found in existing scholarship on gun owners."

There is queer: Combs, "Queers with Guns?" 72.
"[T]his study shows that LGBT gun ownership is inextricably linked with the vulnerability of navigating public spaces as individual gender and/or sexual minorities. Moreover, this study illuminates that LGBT gun owners navigate two supposedly disparate communities as gender and/or sexual minorities. For these LGBTQ gun owners, firearms ownership is shaped by their perception of being erased from contemporary LGBT movement discourse and rejected by LGBT communities invested in pro-gun control measures, a preference to mitigate their individual vulnerability to violence through gun ownership, as well as their perspective of historical oppression against marginalized people overall in the United States."

57] • [58

Billy Collins lived in Louisa, Kentucky.
https://wilsonfuneralhomeky.com/tribute/details/371/Billy-Collins/obituary.html. 0823.

Troy Boyd lived in Jayess, Mississippi. He was 36.
https://www.findagrave.com/memorial/143807226/troy-ray-boyd. 0823.

Caroline Previdi wanted to give all the money in her piggy bank to her family's church at Christmas, to make sure all the other kids had a present under the tree.
http://carolineprevidifoundation.org/index.php/faqs/85-banner-articles/102. 0223.

Calla Medig had just been promoted to manager.
https://www.nytimes.com/2017/10/02/us/vegas-victims-names.html. 0523.

Eva Mireles' hobbies included Crossfit, hiking, and spending time with her dog, Kane.
https://www.legacy.com/us/obituaries/name/eva-mireles-obituary?id=34962239. 0523.

Muhammad Abdul Muhaymin had a service dog, Chiquita, to help relieve symptoms of post-traumatic stress disorder, acute claustrophobia, and schizophrenia.
https://www.huffpost.com/entry/newly-released-footage-shows-police-mocking-black-mans-faith-before-he-was-killed_n_5f3e94a2c5b6dd14014b3d51. 0723.

Tyre King was a 13-year-old eighth-grader. https://www.learntheirstories.com/#/tyre-king/. 0623.

Jon Stoffel and his wife had three children, with whom he enjoyed wrestling, playing soccer, and board games. He was very active in his church, including teaching Sunday School. He was 33.

https://www.wichmannfuneralhomes.com/obituaries/jonathan-stoffel. 0923.
https://www.wkrn.com/news/father-daughter-killed-in-random-wisconsin-shooting/. 0923.

Gabriella Aljumaily's family called her "Gabi." Her favorite pastimes were watching Cocomelon & Ryan's World shows on her tablet while chewing on a straw. https://www.tributearchive.com/obituaries/27188035/gabriella-annaleese-aljumaily/maynardville/tennessee/trinity-funeral-home-llc. 0923.

Salome Rodriguez Jr. https://homicide.latimes.com/post/salome-rodriguez-jr/. 0823.

3: Peeples, "What the Data Say," 24.
50: https://www.theguardian.com/us-news/2015/dec/31/the-counted-police-killings-2015-young-black-men. 0423.
8-10: Patrick Ball, "Violence in Blue." https://granta.com/violence-in-blue/. 0623.

"Racial/ethnic disparities: Zare et al., "Association between Neighborhood," 1-2.

"Police homicide risk: Edwards, Esposito, and Lee, "Risk of Police-Involved Death," 1241.

The policed trust the police: Lowery, *They Can't Kill Us All*, 18.
"The story of Ferguson, Cleveland, and Baltimore is that of the fractured and neglected relationship that exists between those who walk the streets without a badge and those who wear one. This gulf of trust only widens and becomes harder still to fill with each shooting…. The story of Ferguson remains the story of America."

58] • [59

Andy Lopez lived in Santa Rosa, California. https://www.ktvu.com/news/andy-lopez-family-say-they-never-saw-justice-for-son-killed-by-deputy. 0823.
https://www.pressdemocrat.com/article/news/andy-lopez-memorialized-5-years-after-sonoma-county-deputy-killed-him/. 0823.

Ben Wheeler was a Boy Scout, and was taking swimming lessons and piano lessons.
https://benslighthouse.org/ben-wheeler/. 0223.
https://screeningsandyhook.net/2018/01/03/benjamin-wheeler/. 0223.

George Floyd played high school basketball and football, and junior college basketball. After moving from Texas to Minnesota, he worked driving a truck and providing security at a restaurant. He had three children. https://www.howmyvoiceisheard.com/lives/george-floyd. 0723.

Bill Wolfe Jr. and his family lived in Shippensburg, Pennsylvania. He worked as an engineer for a consulting group based in Virginia. He coached youth in elementary wrestling and little league baseball. https://heavy.com/news/2017/10/bill-wolfe-las-vegas-shooting-victim-photos-shippensburg-coach/. 0523. https://www.findagrave.com/memorial/183935223/william-winfield-wolfe. 0523.

Li Lan Li lived in the U.S., but most of her family members lived in China. https://www.dailybreeze.com/2023/01/29/lilan-li-her-family-was-robbed-of-a-loving-grandmother/. 0623.

April Ireland was a high school graduate. https://www.wnct.com/news/five-people-found-dead-inside-a-vanceboro-home-investigation-underway/. 0823. https://www.dignitymemorial.com/obituaries/new-bern-nc/april-ireland-children-9015422. 0823.

Michael Sabbie. https://exhibits.stanford.edu/saytheirnames/feature/michael-sabbie. 0823.

Olivia Stoffel was 11, and in the fifth grade. She enjoyed Drama Club, swimming, and playing with her family's dog, Sammy. She was active in her family's church, including going on a mission trip with her father, and making bracelets to raise funds for a local prison ministry. https://www.wichmannfuneralhomes.com/obituaries/olivia-stoffel. 0923.

Audrie Quinn Cooper-Fortner was being home-schooled after going to public school through the 4th grade. She loved to draw, and had two fish, one named 640-East Right Here On The Road, and the other named Jason Vorhees. https://www.dignitymemorial.com/obituaries/knoxville-tn/audrie-cooper-fortner-11134284. 0923.

Phillip White was 32. https://www.courierpostonline.com/story/news/2022/01/05/vineland-indemnify-police-officer-federal-lawsuit-punitive-damages-phillip-white-death-215/9091655002/. 0823.

1: The 2018 figure is for the period through March 12 of that year. Wesleyan Media Project. http://mediaproject.wesleyan.edu/mar-guns-2018/. 0523.

E pluribus unum: Charles, *Armed in America*, 311.
"The history of gun rights — as is true of all historical subjects — speaks differently to different people. There is not one historical narrative of gun rights, but many. There is a constitutional narrative, civil rights narrative, social narrative, cultural narrative, political narrative, and a number of others."

The shooter's mental illness:
https://www.aacap.org/AACAP/zLatest_News/Statement_Gun_Violence_Crisis_from_60_National_Organizations.aspx. 0223.
"Attempts to connect mental illness to mass shootings are a distraction that inflicts enormous damage by taking attention from solutions that could actually prevent such events. This perpetuates a false narrative that encourages stigmatization of and discrimination against the millions of Americans living with mental health conditions who are more likely to be victims of violence than perpetrators of it. In fact, persons with mental illness account for a very small portion of gun violence. While mental health conditions are common in countries across the globe, the United States is the only country where mass shootings have become disturbingly commonplace. In fact, firearms are now the leading cause of death for children and adolescents

in the United States. Not coincidentally, the U.S. is also alone in making firearms widely available with few restrictions."

Our *stories* secure: Smith, "Civil Society and Violence," 111.
"The state risks losing public support when it cannot align its violent actions with legitimating narratives. For this reason, narrative frames deployed by civil society can exert a braking force on violent policies employed by the state."

59] • [60

Ivy Webster. https://www.kcra.com/article/remembering-mom-and-five-teenagers-killed-in-rural-oklahoma-mass-shooting/43787644. 0923.

Chase Kowalski was a baseball fan. https://cmakfoundation.org/about-cmak. 0223. https://www.ctpost.com/local/article/Chase-Kowalski-wanted-his-front-teeth-back-4122846.php. 0223.

Denise Cohen had recently begun a new job at a company that focused on homeowner association accounting. https://www.nytimes.com/2017/10/02/us/vegas-victims-names.html. 0523. https://www.reviewjournal.com/crime/homicides/las-vegas-shooting-victim-denise-cohen-carpinteria-california-1200012/. 0523.

Leonardo Campos had played goalie on his high school soccer team and kicker on the football team. He had a sister and two brothers, and he went by "Leo."
https://www.tributearchive.com/obituaries/5645323/Leonardo-Campos-Jr. 0523.
https://www.elpasotimes.com/story/news/2019/08/04/el-paso-shooting-texas-victims-identities-updates-and-details/1915050001/. 0523.

Bryson Ireland was 3 years old. https://www.wnct.com/news/five-people-found-dead-inside-a-vanceboro-home-investigation-underway/. 0823.
https://www.dignitymemorial.com/obituaries/new-bern-nc/april-ireland-children-9015422. 0823.

Jamie Lee Wounded Arrow was a two-spirit member of the Oglala Lakota, and had grown up on the Pine Ridge Reservation. After studying social work at Oglala Lakota College and nursing at a Georgetown University summer program, she lived in Sioux Falls.
https://www.logotv.com/news/0ao83s/transgender-day-of-remembrance-memorial-2017. 0723.

Adam Bentdahl lived in Wisconsin, but enjoyed travel and had visited Argentina and Canada. He liked camping, and also walking local trails. He was 31.
https://www.legacy.com/us/obituaries/fdlreporter/name/adam-bentdahl-obituary?id=18808594. 0923. https://archive.jsonline.com/news/crime/menasha-shooting-victim-led-simple-life-with-friends-and-family-b99495390z1-302785261.html/. 0923.

Trayvon Martin was a 17-year-old high school junior. He had graduated from a seven-week "Experience Aviation" summer program. He was good at assembling, repairing, and riding pocket bikes and dirt bikes. When he was nine years old, he pulled his father, who had been immobilized by burns to the legs, out of a fire in their apartment, saving his life. https://en.wikipedia.org/wiki/Trayvon_Martin. 0723.

Evelyn Rose Cooper-Fortner liked to find flowers, or sit out on the hammock and play games on her tablet. She loved unicorns and rainbows, but she also loved rocks and getting dirty. She wanted to be a traveling Veterinarian/Ballerina, because she loved animals and wanted to make them feel better but she also wanted to dance. https://www.dignitymemorial.com/obituaries/knoxville-tn/evelyn-cooper-fortner-11134292. 0923.

Tiara Banks. https://www.windycitytimes.com/lgbt/Remembering-Tiara-Banks/71910.html. 0923.

4: Stylianos, "Injuries and Deaths," 516. Stylianos is reporting the result of a study by A. L. Kellerman et al.

Opportunities for harmful: Hemenway et al., "Gun Use," 266.
"Certainly some self defense gun uses are legal and in the public interest. But many are not. The possibility of using a gun in a socially useful manner—against a criminal during the commission of a crime—will rarely, if ever, occur for the average gun owner. By contrast, at any other moment, the use of a gun against another human is illegal, and socially undesirable. Regular citizens with guns, who are sometimes tired, angry, drunk or afraid, and who are not trained in dispute resolution or on when it is proper to use a firearm, have many opportunities for inappropriate gun use. People engage in innumerable annoying and somewhat hostile interactions with others in the course of a lifetime. We might expect that unlawful 'self defense' gun uses will outnumber the legitimate and socially beneficial ones."

If I need a gun to be safe: Elisabeth Pearson Waugaman, "20 Children in Newtown." https://www.psychologytoday.com/intl/blog/whats-in-name/201212/20-children-in-newtown-116385-kids-killed-1979. 0423.
"What kind of society do we live in that citizens believe that they have to have a gun concealed in their pocket in order to be safe?"

If taking up arms: Nathenson, "Finding Your Inner Gun," 208.
"Guns are connected to the American Dream, to manifest destiny, the belief that we are culturally directed by God to achieve, to do, to succeed, regardless of cost. The gun provides us with the means to achieve, and a potential solution when we cannot. Taking up arms to solve our problems is seen as a norm, a positive way to reclaim power. We carry the archetypal image of the gun-toting cowboy, the myth of the American West to support this conquering mentality."

60] • [61

Gavin Haight "always wanted to be in the middle of whatever was going on." https://www.thespectrum.com/obituaries/sgs027098. 0923.

Jacqueline Salyers went by "Jackie." https://www.findagrave.com/memorial/164623229/jacqueline-daniell-salyers. 0723. https://revcom.us/en/a/429/justice-for-jaqueline-salyers-en.html. 0723.

Dylan Hockley replied, when his mother asked him once why he liked to flap his arms when he got excited, "Because I am a beautiful butterfly." https://www.sandyhookpromise.org/blog/stories/dylan-hockley-the-butterfly-effect/. 0223. https://nation.time.com/2012/12/22/sandy-hook-victim-dylan-hockley-a-beautiful-butterfly-whose-life-was-cut-short/. 0223.

Melissa Ramirez was a sports fan whose favorite teams included the Philadelphia Eagles, the L.A. Dodgers, the Mexican national soccer team, and the L.A. Lakers. She worked for a car insurance company. https://www.bustle.com/p/who-was-melissa-ramirez-the-las-vegas-shooting-victim-came-from-a-close-knit-family-2791381. 0523.

Juan Velazquez lived in Denver for 30 years before moving to El Paso. https://apnews.com/article/texas-shootings-immigration-us-news-el-paso-texas-mass-shooting-1aa03c4a153f4f6d9881f0f11cd2e89a. 0623.

Michael Barrera lived in Woodland, California. https://www.davisvanguard.org/2020/05/guest-commentary-woodland-police-killed-my-brother-and-i-will-not-be-silenced/. 0723.

Breonna Taylor had previously worked at a Steak & Shake, and held a job driving senior citizens to their appointments. Her family had nicknamed her "Breewayy" – because whatever she wanted, she found a way to make it happen. She and her boyfriend wanted a child, and she had a name picked out. She was 26. https://www.cnn.com/2020/09/06/us/breonna-taylor-louisville-trnd/index.html. 0723.

John Leehey was 67, and lived in Irvine, California. He worked for 35 years as an urban planner and landscape architect, and had recently opened his own consulting firm. https://www.ocregister.com/2023/08/25/at-cooks-corner-lives-remembered-a-hero-a-noted-urban-planner-and-a-mom-who-loved-to-dance/. 0923.

Tausha Haight earned her bachelor's degree in Child Development Studies from Southern Utah University. She enjoyed reading and traveling. She was 40. https://www.thespectrum.com/obituaries/sgs027098. 0923.

Muhlaysia Booker. https://www.cnn.com/2019/05/29/us/muhlaysia-booker-funeral/index.html. 0923.

8: https://www.cbsnews.com/news/destinee-thompson-family-lawsuit-pregnant-mother-3-fatally-shot-by-police-denver-suburb-arvada/. 0923.

8: https://www.theguardian.com/world/2015/may/31/jose-antonio-us-mexico-border-shooting-constitutional-rights. 0723.
9: https://en.wikipedia.org/wiki/Murder_of_Laquan_McDonald. 0723.

"No duty to retreat": Brown, *No Duty to Retreat*, 155, i.
"From the Industrial Society of the nineteenth and the early twentieth century to the Information Society of our own time, the factor of values has been crucial in regard to American violence and crime. Central to understanding the doctrine of no duty to retreat is the realm of values, for the notion of no duty to retreat is an expression of American values as well as American behavior…. [It] helps explain why the American homicide rate has been so much higher than that of England during the nineteenth and twentieth centuries. It also helps explain why our country has been the most violent among its peer group of the industrialized, urbanized democracies of the world."

"Stand your ground": Esposti, "Increasing Adolescent," 187.
"After adjusting for trends, the law was associated with a 44.6% increase in adolescent firearm homicide. Our analysis indicates that Florida's Stand Your Ground is associated with a significant increase in firearm homicide and may also exacerbate racial disparities."

Tell me again: Lewis, "The Arena of Suspension," 488-89.
"Use of the term 'ground' as a law-specified basis for a demand, complaint, suit, or defense occurs so often that there are countless examples…. Yet recently, the proliferation of Stand Your Ground (SYG) laws in the United States have thrown into high relief what we actually mean by 'ground' as both concept and concrete reality when faced with the hypervisibility of unequal legal outcomes and fatalities in the context of such laws…. The phrase 'stand your ground' makes the law seem natural and applicable to all, and yet it covers up the fact that the crucible of this definition was formed and is still shaped by the lingering effects of slavery and settler colonialism, which challenged any presumed juridical or conceptual neutrality about the idea of ground."

61] • [62

Joseph Slater lived in Highland, California.
https://www.legacy.com/us/obituaries/sbsun/name/joseph-slater-obituary?id=16921730. 0823.

Austin Cloyd had played high school basketball. She taught swimming to preschoolers, and worked as a lifeguard. She was majoring in international studies and French, and wanted to work in the United Nations. http://vt-memorial.org/profiles/Cloyd.html. 0223.
https://www.weremember.vt.edu/biographies/cloyd.html. 0223.

David Werblow was a graduate of Babson College. He had done market research for Stop and Shop and for various Connecticut banks. He suffered from schizophrenia.
https://www.legacy.com/us/obituaries/nhregister/name/david-werblow-obituary?id=16289027. 0823. https://www.nbcnewyork.com/news/local/man-shot-stun-gun-police-death-connecticut-homicide-medical-examiner-david-werblow/1350250/. 0823.

Denise Burditus was married to her high school sweetheart, with whom she had two children. She had recently enrolled at her local community college to study sports fitness and nutrition.

https://www.reviewjournal.com/crime/homicides/he-lost-his-wife-in-strip-shooting-now-has-2-guardian-angels/. 0523. https://www.brownfuneralhomeswv.com/memorials/denise-burditus/3199723/obituary.php. 0523.

Hector Arreola settled down in Columbus, Georgia as an adult. He was 30. https://www.legacy.com/us/obituaries/ledger-enquirer/name/hector-arreola-obituary?id=22300326. 0723.

Jorge Calvillo was originally from Gómez Palacio, Mexico, and had recently moved to El Paso. He and his wife had three children, and often would take used clothes to Juarez orphanages in need. https://www.gofundme.com/f/el-paso-strong-jorge-calvillo-garcia-memorial. 0523. https://www.theguardian.com/us-news/2019/aug/09/el-paso-shooting-victims. 0523.

Andrew Finch went by "Andy." He had one son and one daughter. He was 28, and lived in Wichita, Kansas. https://www.legacy.com/us/obituaries/kansas/name/andrew-finch-obituary?id=12284145. 0723.

Tonya Clark was 49. One friend said that "her favorite song was always the one that she was dancing to." https://www.ocregister.com/2023/08/25/at-cooks-corner-lives-remembered-a-hero-a-noted-urban-planner-and-a-mom-who-loved-to-dance/. 0923.

Macie Haight was set to graduate soon from high school, and simultaneously to receive her associate's degree from Southern Utah University, where she planned to pursue a further degree in digital marketing. She was 17. https://www.thespectrum.com/obituaries/sgs027098. 0923.

Alexus Braxton was a 45-year-old trans woman. https://www.insideedition.com/alexus-braxton-transgender-miami-woman-killed-in-violent-and-vicious-attack-was-6th-victim-of-2021. 0923.

4: Roth, *American Homicide*, 4.

State violence is not: Smith and Ross, "Introduction," 6.
"[B]ecause indigenous nations understand themselves as sovereign nations, they have been proactive in developing their own models for addressing violence within their communities. As such, they exist as models for other communities of color to develop their own programs for addressing violence within their communities that do not primarily rely upon the state for enforcement."

"[I]ntergenerational transmission: Widom, "The Cycle of Violence," 164.
"[P]revention programs and intervention strategies aimed at buffering at-risk children play a potentially important role in the reduction of further violent criminal behavior." Widom carefully observes that her findings do "indicate that abused and neglected children have significantly greater risk of becoming delinquents, criminal, and violent criminals," but do *not* show "that every abused or neglected child will become delinquent, criminal, or a violent criminal."

"We are not bound: Rood, *After Gun Violence*, 140.

Rood contextualizes the claim. "The cycle of violence and inaction at the national level," he writes, "has been imprinted on our consciousness. It has been made to seem unsurprising. Since little has changed, we assume that nothing will. We assume that the past predicts the future — or worse, that the cycle of violence and inaction is inescapable.... We need to challenge the gridlock narrative and offer an alternative in its place. I am not suggesting that gridlock is imaginary, without any basis in reality. Nor am I denying that there are structural forces that sustain gridlock. There are. My point, quite simply, is that gridlock is not inevitable."

62] • [63

Alonzo Bagley was 43. https://snbc13.com/alonzo-bagley-died-in-shreveport-officer-involved-shooting-in-louisiana-death-obituary/. 0923.

Julia Pryde wrote a feasibility study for a plan to have her university compost the leftovers from its dining halls. http://www.vt-memorial.org/profiles/Pryde.html. 0223.

Derrick Taylor, who went by "Bo," was a 29-year veteran of the California Department of Corrections and Rehabilitation. https://www.huffpost.com/entry/las-vegas-route-91-shooting-victims_n_59d235cde4b06791bb11d6b1. 0523.
https://www.nytimes.com/2017/10/02/us/vegas-victims-names.html. 0523.

Eleanor Bumpurs lived in the Bronx. She was 67, and mentally ill.
https://face2faceafrica.com/article/35-years-ago-mentally-ill-woman-eleanor-bumpurs-was-killed-by-nypd-cops-for-being-behind-on-rent. 0723.

Gloria Irma Márquez was born in Mexico, and had lived in the U.S. for more than twenty years. Her first two children were born in Mexico, her second two in the United States.
https://apnews.com/article/texas-shootings-immigration-us-news-el-paso-texas-mass-shooting-1aa03c4a153f4f6d9881f0f11cd2e89a. 0623.

Michael Lembhard had two children, one of whom had died of "crib death" in infancy.
https://www.findagrave.com/memorial/86664860/michael-lembhard. 0723.
https://www.recordonline.com/story/news/2012/03/18/lembhard-killed-by-newburgh-officers/49699383007/. 0723.

Brooklyn Deshuna was a 20-year-old trans woman. https://www.hrc.org/news/hrc-mourns-brooklyn-deshuna-black-trans-woman-killed-in-louisiana. 0923.

Glen Sprowl lived in California, and worked for an environmental recycling company, but planned to move to Arizona and start a motorcycle parts company, to be closer to his three children. He had previously worked as a bouncer and a band roadie. He liked to go on long road trips on his Harley. He was 53. https://www.ocregister.com/2023/08/25/at-cooks-corner-lives-remembered-a-hero-a-noted-urban-planner-and-a-mom-who-loved-to-dance/. 0923.

Briley Haight loved music, and played piano and cello. She was 12. https://www.thespectrum.com/obituaries/sgs027098. 0923.

DaJuan Graham lived in Burtonsville, Maryland. https://www.legacy.com/us/obituaries/washingtonpost/name/dajuan-graham-obituary?id=6051643. 0823.

920,000: Cassino and Besen-Cassino, "Sometimes," 15.
11: Turchan, Zeoli, and Kwiatkowski, "Reacting to the Improbable," 280.

Police use of excessive force: Gilbert and Ray, "Why Police," S133.
"Over time, the narrative remains the same: black males who die from excessive force at the hands of police officers become involuntary martyrs for the sustained legacy of institutional and interpersonal racism. Those who do not die carry significant health threats displayed by physical scars and mental stress that may shorten their telomeres and increase their risk of CVD, cerebrovascular disease, and hypertension. The concept of involuntary martyrdom suggests that some black males are persecuted not by choice or because they advocate for a particular belief, but because the visibility of their bodies in a particular space pose a threat to the normative social order. The social reality of involuntary martyrs is that these black men become representations of the most restrictive and constrained sense of democratic ideals, which are juxtaposed against the sensibilities that America is post-racial and colorblind."

Crime is not the only: Gaston, Fernandes, and DeShay, "A Macrolevel Study," 1093.
"Together, results from analyses of racial/ethnic composition and racial/ethnic income point to racial conflict, especially Hispanic threat, as shaping police use of fatal force, even when accounting for legally relevant factors, such as crime and social disorganization."

Racial bias in police shootings: Ross, "A Multi-Level Bayesian Analysis," 1.
"Finally, analysis of police shooting data as a function of county-level predictors suggests that racial bias in police shootings is most likely to emerge in police departments in larger metropolitan counties with low median incomes and a sizable portion of black residents, especially when there is high financial inequality in that county. There is no relationship between county-level racial bias in police shootings and crime rates (even race-specific crime rates), meaning that the racial bias observed in police shootings in this data set is not explainable as a response to local-level crime rates."

63] • [64

Amaree'ya Henderson was 25 years old. https://fox4kc.com/news/family-of-man-shot-killed-by-kck-police-says-he-was-unarmed-delivering-for-doordash/. 0923.

Kevin Granata was a runner and cyclist who often participated in biathlons and triathlons. He had three children, and had begun studying lacrosse when his sons' team needed a volunteer coach. http://www.vt-memorial.org/profiles/Granata.html. 0223.
https://www.weremember.vt.edu/biographies/granata.html. 0223.

Sandy Casey was born and raised in Vermont, where she had played high school basketball. She had a masters degree, and had recently become engaged. https://www.nytimes.com/2017/10/02/us/vegas-victims-names.html. 0523. https://www.burlingtonfreepress.com/story/news/local/vermont/2017/10/02/las-vegas-shooting-victim-dorset-vermont-native/724527001/. 0523.

Alexander Gerhard Hoffman met his future wife at a discothèque across the border from El Paso, where he was stationed. After his retirement from the military, they returned to Ciudad Juárez, where he worked as an engineer for several multinational companies. They had three children. https://www.ktsm.com/local/el-paso-news/who-is-impersonating-the-family-of-a-walmart-massacre-victim/. 0523. https://www.findagrave.com/memorial/201868120/alexander-gerhardt-hoffman_roth. 0523.

Luis Góngora Pat was born into a Yucatan Mayan family in Mexico, where his wife and three grown children still lived. https://justice4luis.org/luiss-story/. 0723.

Ariella Bell. https://www.legacy.com/us/obituaries/concordmonitor/name/nicole-bell-obituary?id=52179583. 0923.

Timothy Owens was from Illinois, and was 37. His service awards included three Army Commendation Medals and four Army Achievement Medals. https://www.kcentv.com/article/news/local/military/four-years-later-remembering-the-victims-of-the-2014-fort-hood-shooting/500-534235346. 0923.

Ammon Haight was fascinated with trains. He was 7 years old. https://www.thespectrum.com/obituaries/sgs027098. 0923.

Che Taylor. https://www.seattletimes.com/seattle-news/law-justice/spd-settles-che-taylor-wrongful-death-lawsuit-for-1-5-million-new-evidence-questioned-officers-claim-he-was-armed/. 0723. https://www.seattletimes.com/seattle-news/law-justice/newly-released-records-spd-officers-who-fatally-shot-che-taylor-feared-for-their-lives/. 0723.

Yenitza Arroyo Torres lived in Fayetteville, Arkansas. https://www.wral.com/story/its-still-shocking-daughter-mourns-loss-of-mother-killed-in-apparent-murder-suicide-by-fayetteville-police-officer/20849405/. 0923. https://www.fayobserver.com/story/news/crime/2023/04/29/fayetteville-deaths-of-police-officer-and-wife-under-investigation/70166233007/. 0923.

6.75: Brady Center to Prevent Gun Violence, as cited in Younge, *Another Day*, xiv.
2: Spina, "Introduction," 1.
350: https://everytownresearch.org/solution/responsible-gun-storage/. 0323.
35: Schuster et al., "Firearm Storage Patterns," 591.

"Public health: Reinhart, "Reconstructive Justice," 562.

Our advanced society: Morrison, *The Source of Self-Regard*, 19.

"It may be that the most defining characteristic of our times is that… walls and weapons feature as prominently now as they once did in medieval times."

Border Patrol: Ramirez, "The Normalization of State-Sponsored Violence," 185.
U.S. Customs and Border Protection "is the largest law enforcement agency in this country, with more than sixty thousand employees, twenty thousand of whom are Border Patrol agents." Agents have "extraordinary and unprecedented powers. Immigration officers are able to stop and frisk people, set up checkpoints in our communities, and racially profile border residents. They can stop, interrogate, and search children on their way to school, parents on their way to work, and families going to doctors' appointments or the grocery store — well inside the United States, and all done without a warrant or reasonable suspicion."

64] • [65

Darryl Tyree Williams had two sisters and four brothers.
https://www.legacy.com/us/obituaries/name/darryl-williams-obituary?id=38702418. 0923.

Mary Read was studying to become an elementary school teacher. Her favorite dessert was pumpkin pie. http://www.vt-memorial.org/profiles/Read.html. 0223.
https://www.weremember.vt.edu/biographies/read.html. 0223.

Lisa Patterson had three children. She volunteered in the local girls softball league.
https://people.com/crime/bob-patterson-las-vegas-shooting-anniversary-wife-lisa/. 0523.
https://www.bustle.com/p/who-was-lisa-patterson-the-las-vegas-shooting-victim-was-full-of-infectious-energy-fierce-love-2790944. 0523.

Ivan Filiberto Manzano worked in sales and marketing at a Juárez radio station.
https://people.com/crime/el-paso-mass-shooting-remembering-victims-2-year-later/. 0623.

Amia Tyrae Berryman was from Baton Rouge, Louisiana. https://avp.org/2018/03/27/ncavp-mourns-the-death-of-amia-tyrae-berryman-in-baton-rouge-la/. 0723.
https://www.wbrz.com/news/police-one-dead-after-early-morning-shooting. 0723.

Carlos Lazaney-Rodriguez was born in Puerto Rico, and his service had been recognized with four Army Commendation Medals and three Army Achievement Medals.
https://www.kcentv.com/article/news/local/military/four-years-later-remembering-the-victims-of-the-2014-fort-hood-shooting/500-534235346. 0923.

Sienna Haight was diligent with her schoolwork, and liked playing with friends and family.
https://www.thespectrum.com/obituaries/sgs027098. 0923.

Gwen Grimmette had hundreds of record albums, and her favorite artists included the Temptations, Al Green, Donny Hathaway, Jimi Hendrix, Marvin Gaye, and Tammi Terrell. Trethewey, *Memorial Drive.*

Jeremy Lett went by "Jed." He was a high school graduate, and a gospel musician who played the steel guitar. https://www.banksmemorial.com/obituary/Jeremy-Lett. 0823. https://s3.amazonaws.com/CFSV2/obituaries/media/5905/5905-639533JeremyLettObituary.pdf. 0823.

Jordan Davis was from Jacksonville, Florida. He had one brother. https://www.westcobbfuneralhome.com/obituaries/Jordan-Davis-22633/#!/Obituary. 0823.

56.6: Goldstick et al., "Current Epidemiological Trends," 241.
48,830: https://www.nytimes.com/2023/06/23/health/gun-violence-psychology.html?smid=em-share. 0623.

"Violence is a form: Rose, *On Violence*, 3.

White privilege: Cottom, *Thick*, 135.
"Originating as it does not from nation or kin but from the primordial ooze of capitalism, whiteness can only be defined by state power." It "requires a police state that can use violent force to defend its sovereignty."

White male anger: Kimmel, *Angry White Men*, 284.
"Addressing the anger of America's angry white men is a national political issue, not a therapeutic one."

65] • [66

Julius Hamilton had 3 children, ages 11, 8, and 3. He lived in Albany, Oregon. https://www.gofundme.com/f/funeral-costs-and-funds-for-his-3-children. 0923.

Serenity Hollis was a 24-year-old trans woman. She had been born in Orlando, Florida, and she lived in Albany, Georgia. https://www.pghlesbian.com/2021/05/black-trans-woman-serenity-hollis-24-killed-in-albany-georgia/. 0723.

Matthew Gwaltney had played high school baseball and basketball, and continued to be a sports fan, especially enjoying sports statistics and trivia. http://www.vt-memorial.org/profiles/Gwaltney.html. 0223. https://www.weremember.vt.edu/biographies/gwaltney.html. 0223.

Kurt Von Tillow and his wife took golfing trips to Scotland and Ireland, and their home overlooked the 13th green of their local country club. https://www.legacy.com/obituaries/name/kurt-von-tillow-obituary?pid=186868683. 0523. https://www.villagelife.com/news/cameron-park-man-killed-in-vegas-shooting-2/. 0523.

Luis Alfonzo Juarez emigrated from Mexico, and eventually became an American citizen. He had a long career as an iron worker, bought a home, and he and his wife raised seven children. https://apnews.com/article/texas-shootings-immigration-us-news-el-paso-texas-mass-shooting-1aa03c4a153f4f6d9881f0f11cd2e89a. 0623.

Korryn Gaines lived in Baltimore. https://exhibits.stanford.edu/saytheirnames/feature/korryn-gaines. 0823.

Daniel Ferguson was a transportation supervisor, and his awards included a Bronze Star, three Meritorious Service Medals, five Army Commendation Medals, and two Army Achievement Medals. He was from Florida, and was 39. https://www.kcentv.com/article/news/local/military/four-years-later-remembering-the-victims-of-the-2014-fort-hood-shooting/500-534235346. 0923.

Gail Earl taught piano, and enjoyed traveling, playing the piano, and making quilts. She was very active in her church. https://mvprogress.com/2023/01/10/obituary-gail-gubler-earl/. 0923.

Danton Munoz lived in Elkhart, Indiana. https://www.legacy.com/us/obituaries/elkharttruth/name/danton-munoz-obituary?id=23304976. 0823.

Shakiie Peters was a 31-year-old trans woman from Amite, Louisiana. https://www.them.us/story/suspect-arrested-in-murder-of-black-trans-woman-shaki-peters. 0923.

101,970: Diaz, *The Last Gun*, 2.

Better state laws: Madhavan et al., "Firearm Legislation Stringency," 150.
"Although more studies are needed to determine causality, state-level legislation could play an important role in reducing pediatric firearm-related deaths."

Accurate records: O'Donnell, "Monsters, Myths, and Mental Illness," 501.
For laws strengthening gun control to be effective, "both federal and state legislation must be changed to focus on the dangerousness of the individual as opposed to the mere presence of mental illness," and "the accuracy of the NICS must be improved…. These two steps must happen together, since one will not be able to effect any real change without the other."

Different polities: Wilson, "Let the Locals Decide," 228.
"Allowing different states and even school districts to adopt different policies regarding firearms seems to be a reasonable response to a problem which does not have a clear solution and which arouses strong and differing responses from different people."

66] • [67

Candace Towns was a 30-year-old trans woman. https://www.legacy.com/us/obituaries/macon/name/jontavious-towns-obituary?id=20339345. 0923.

Reema Samaha had decided to major in urban planning. http://www.vt-memorial.org/profiles/Samaha.html. 0223.

Laquan McDonald had learning disabilities and was diagnosed with complex mental health problems, including post-traumatic stress disorder. He had tattoos on each of his hands, one reading "Good Son" and the other a pair of dice and the acronym "YOLO" — "You only live once." https://www.chicagotribune.com/news/breaking/ct-laquan-mcdonald-trouble-met-20151211-story.html. 0723.

Thomas Day Jr. worked as an estimator for the family construction business. He had four adult children, and loved country music.
https://www.desertsun.com/story/news/nation/2017/10/06/lifelong-corona-resident-and-country-music-fan-thomas-day-jr-dies-las-vegas-shooting/740041001/. 0523.

Ashley Atwell. https://www.gofundme.com/f/nzvsjm-funeral-and-memorial. 0723.

Jack Keewatinawin had a criminal record as a sex offender.
https://mynorthwest.com/30120/stories-vary-about-mentally-ill-man-killed-by-seattle-police/. 0723.

Michael Cahill had worked in rural health clinics and at Veterans Affairs hospitals. He and his wife had been married 37 years, and had three adult children. He was 62.
https://www.cbsnews.com/news/profiles-of-ft-hood-shooters-victims/. 0923.

Miguel Flores and Kelly Baltazar. She was the mother of an adult daughter.
https://gunmemorial.org/2022/10/17/kelly-baltazar. 0923.

Jor'Dell Da'Shawn Richardson. https://www.cpr.org/2023/06/16/memorial-for-jordell-richardson-fatally-shot-by-aurora-police/. 0923.

Keri Washington was a 49-year-old trans woman.
https://tdor.translivesmatter.info/reports/2021/05/01/keri-washington-bobo_clearwater-florida-usa_11e46762. 0723.

5: Goldstick et al., "Current Epidemiological Trends," 241.
<20: Data for the period 2000-2011. Van Horne, "Institutional Correlates," 93.

If only violence *were* confined: Kurtz and Turpin, "Conclusion," 208.
"[T]he tendency to see violence as the consequence of aberrant behavior committed by deviant individuals at the margins of society obscures the central role violence plays in the very foundations of the social order and the fundamental dilemmas that humans face.... The problems created by violence will not be solved by acting on the margins but by rethinking the pervasive use of violence in contemporary cultures."

Abnormal violence: Tonso, "Violent Masculinities," 1281.

"[M]asculine supremacy ideologies that lie at the roots of rampage violence in schools, and that school practices contribute to forming and preserving in hierarchies of power, are anathema to a participatory equal educational opportunity. If schools took seriously the damage done by building hierarchies of power among students, students would suffer less marginalization, come to appreciate the diversity of their classmates, and develop ways to think about others without resorting to violent means to regain some undeserved privilege or another. Thus, social, cultural, and institutional normalities must be radically transformed if we are to stop rampage violence."

We don't have to change: Diaz, *The Last Gun*, 230-31.
"Once vehicle safety advocates stopped trying to reform people and started looking at the actual designs of vehicles and roads, enormous strides were made in saving lives and preventing injuries. This is precisely what needs to be done to turn around America's gun violence problem. We need to prevent injury before it happens. To do that, we need to look upstream at the gun industry, its products, and how they are distributed."

67] • [68

Gustav Montag was a student at East Los Angeles College. Cid, "'It Is Not a Question of Militancy,'" 171.

Alton Sterling worked as a CD vendor, which had earned him the nickname "CD Man." He had previously been incarcerated for a five-year term. He was 37.
https://www.blackpast.org/african-american-history/alton-sterling-1979-2016/. 0623.
https://www.learntheirstories.com/#/alton-sterling/. 0623.

Emily Hilscher was majoring in animal and poultry sciences, intending to become a veterinarian.
http://www.vt-memorial.org/profiles/Hilscher.html. 0223.
https://www.weremember.vt.edu/biographies/hilscher.html. 0223.

Erick Silva had recently received a promotion, and had just turned 21.
https://apnews.com/article/nv-state-wire-us-news-music-festivals-las-vegas-music-7312924a62f54727877745afc77fbce1. 0523. https://www.8newsnow.com/news/local-news/family-of-security-guard-who-died-saving-others-attends-1-october-ceremony/. 0523.

Annaway Mackey. https://www.gofundme.com/f/nzvsjm-funeral-and-memorial. 0723.

Jamarion Robinson was a student athlete, preparing for his final semester as a political science major and football player. He had recently been diagnosed with paranoid schizophrenia.
https://justiceforjamarion.org/who-was-jamarion. 0623.
https://www.learntheirstories.com/#/jamarion-robinson/. 0623.

Eduardo Caraveo arrived in the U.S. from Ciudad Juarez, Mexico, in his teens, knowing very little English, but earned a Ph.D. in psychology, and worked with bilingual special-needs students at Tucson-area schools before entering private practice. https://www.cbsnews.com/news/profiles-of-ft-hood-shooters-victims/. 0923.

Karrie Sotelo was a 19-year-old college student. https://patch.com/virginia/woodbridge-va/kind-loving-giving-families-remember-woodbridge-homicide-victims. 0923.

Shai Vanderpump was a 23-year-old trans woman who had grown up in New Jersey, raised by her maternal grandmother. She was a high school graduate.
https://www.hughesfuneralhome.net/obituary/Shaquil-Loftin. 0723.
https://tdor.translivesmatter.info/reports/2021/07/30/shai-vanderpump_trenton-new-jersey-usa_66c19f5c. 0723.

Hector Morejon was 19, the youngest of five children in his family.
https://www.presstelegram.com/2015/05/02/family-of-hector-morejon-teen-killed-by-long-beach-police-holds-vigil/. 0723. https://ebwiki.org/cases/hector-morejon. 0723.

3.8: Zimring, *When Police Kill*, 116. Zimring gives reason to think that the numbers used in calculating the ratio are based on substantial underreporting of the number of persons killed by police, and that "the true ratio is more than fifteen to one instead of 7.8 to one" (117).

Agreement that the gun: Jiobu and Curry, "Lack of Confidence," 87.
"[A]ny discourse about policy that focuses solely on the positive and negative consequences of gun ownership for the individual, community, and society may be valuable but will miss an essential point: namely, that for many people, the gun is an icon for evil and violence, whereas for others the same gun is an icon for democracy and personal empowerment. Until that is recognized and acted upon, neither side of the debate will be able to understand how the other side can be so blind to the 'truth.'"

As pacifiers console: Anker, "Mobile Sovereigns," 22.
"Gun ownership, I suggest, often carries the implicit promise of counteracting increasing economic and social insecurity. Owning, and especially carrying, a gun buffers against declining sovereignty. If sovereignty, classically defined, is the final authority to make decisions within a given sphere, then gun owners feel as if guns can restore their personal capacity for self-determination and success against a backdrop of waning economic and social sovereignty. Carrying a gun re-instantiates a type of individual sovereignty when other forms of sovereign power might seem out of reach."

To sell guns: Burbick, *Gun Show Nation*, 13-14.
"From the 1850s to today, Colt industries and many arms manufacturers like Winchester have not been so different from fashion designers who repackage, rename, and refit their models to create new product lines. A great challenge to Colt was to make the gun — a weapon designed to kill — a morally acceptable product…. To make the gun morally acceptable, Colt Firearms and the massive arms industry that followed to supply the domestic market needed to make the gun owner a simple moral hero who killed without nagging doubts and with the stamp of national approval. Dressed in a white hat and mounted on a white horse, he never hesitated in his call to duty. Enter the Buffalo Bills of the world, whose packaged morality created a checklist of enemies who could be shot with impunity."

Kawaski Trawick had been born and raised in Georgia, but lived in the Bronx, having moved to New York with the ambition of opening a dance studio. He had a degree in Business from Atlanta Tech, and had worked as a property manager in the Atlanta area. He was 32. https://en.wikipedia.org/wiki/Killing_of_Kawaski_Trawick. 0723. https://www.slatersfuneralhomeinc.com/obituary/Kawaski-Trawick. 0723.

Asia Jynaé Foster was a 22-year-old trans woman from Houston. She loved to sing. https://www.outsmartmagazine.com/2022/10/remembering-asia-jynae-foster/. 0923.

Waleed Shaalan. http://www.vt-memorial.org/profiles/Shaalan.html. 0223. https://www.weremember.vt.edu/biographies/shaalan.html. 0223.

Christiana Duarte had recently graduated from college with a degree in business and marketing. She was an avid runner, and loved the beach and country music. https://abc7.com/christiana-duarte-redondo-beach-funeral-las-vegas-mass-shooting/2552043/. 0523. https://www.legacy.com/us/obituaries/latimes/name/christiana-duarte-obituary?id=7591878. 0523. https://www.gofundme.com/f/christina-duarte-memorial. 0523.

Richard Nettleton had worked as a design and construction manager in his city's public utilities department for 28 years. He had two children and two stepchildren. He and his second wife had been married for 23 years. He had served for ten years in the U.S. Army 84th Engineering Battalion for ten years, ultimately at the rank of Captain. He had a masters degree in engineering, and an MBA. https://people.com/crime/virginia-beach-mass-shooting-victims-identified/. 0623. https://www.legacy.com/us/obituaries/pilotonline/name/richard-nettleton-obituary?id=15295317. 0623.

John T. Williams was 50 years old. He was hearing-impaired in one ear, and losing his eyesight. He had difficulties with alcohol abuse, and had been hospitalized for mental illness. https://ictnews.org/archive/the-shooting-death-of-john-t-williams. 0723. https://www.seattlemet.com/news-and-city-life/2020/08/the-shooting-of-john-t-williams. 0723.

Justin DeCrow was a 32-year-old Staff Sergeant in the Army, originally from Indiana. https://www.cbsnews.com/news/profiles-of-ft-hood-shooters-victims/. 0923.

Richard Corrales was nicknamed "Cheo." https://patch.com/virginia/woodbridge-va/kind-loving-giving-families-remember-woodbridge-homicide-victims. 0923.

Ahtalia Crayton worked after her military service as a small business owner, a certified public notary for the state of North Carolina, a certified Life Coach and a certified Interior Designer. She also attended North Carolina A&T as a psychology student. She was 46. https://www.bosticktompkinsinc.com/obituary/AthaliaAthena-Crayton. 0923.

Warren Bowman was 33. He and his wife had one daughter. https://www.echovita.com/us/obituaries/ky/richmond/warren-michael-bowman-16733087. 0823. https://www.lex18.com/news/she-was-taken-for-no-reason-family-remembers-woman-killed-in-richmond-double-homicide. 0823.

76: https://bjs.ojp.gov/female-murder-victims-and-victim-offender-relationship-2021. 0323.

To protect whom: Alcarz Ochoa and Alvarez Almendariz, "Under Trump" 186-87.
"Historically, police departments were not created to protect and serve the working class. In fact, they were created to do just the opposite: to protect the rich and elite from a poor, mainly immigrant, working class. Before that, law enforcement in the United States acted as slave patrols dedicated to capturing and 'deporting' free Black people in the North back to Southern enslavement. And today the police stand on the heels of an anti-Black and anti-immigrant legacy. Understanding this history allows us to be more critical of law enforcement and their spokespeople…. [W]hen interacting with law enforcement, our intention should be, not to collaborate or forge alliances, but rather to challenge them, hold them accountable, and demand justice when they kill members of the Black community or Latinxs and Indigenous people, who are often victims of police violence."

To protect how: Palmiotto, "Use of Deadly Force," 43-44.
"Evidence indicates that throughout America's history blacks have been treated poorly and in an unjust manner. History reveals that they have been treated more unjustly than any other racial or ethnic group. It seems realistic to expect that Afro-Americans have a distrust of the police. The police have functioned at times as an 'occupational army' rather than protectors of the community they police."

The streets are not: Woods, *Blackhood Against the Police Power*, 10.
"One of the most common ways in which white society ignores police violence is to accept what the police tell us: that the streets are a war zone, that they patrol the front lines, that they are in the trenches fighting hard on our behalf, making tough split-second decisions of lifes and death. This is not true."

69] • [70

Laura Ann Carleton lived in Cedar Glen, California. She was 67. Previously, she had been an executive for the fashion brand Kenneth Cole. Her passion was rescuing animals, and she was happiest on her boat. She had 9 children. https://www.cbsnews.com/news/laura-ann-carleton-magpi-store-owner-killed-pride-flag-best-friend-interview-melissa-lawton/. 0823.

Demixica Dunnette Coleman-Gipson had been active in sports in high school, including basketball, volleyball, and track. She worked first as a Certified Medical Assistant before being licensed as a cosmetologist and opening her own salon. She sang in her church choir. https://www.tributearchive.com/obituaries/24104269/demixica-denette-mosley/denver/colorado/pipkin-braswell. 0923.

Jarrett Lane was completing his college degree in civil engineering, and had been accepted into a graduate program in coastal engineering. https://www.weremember.vt.edu/biographies/lane.html. 0223. http://www.vt-memorial.org/profiles/Lane.html. 0223.

Kelsey Meadows was a graduate of Fresno State. https://www.nytimes.com/2017/10/02/us/vegas-victims-names.html. 0523.

Joshua Hardy worked as an engineering tech resident in his city's public utilities department for more than four years. He was 52. He was devoutly religious, and read the Bible every day. He had written and illustrated a children's book, *The ABC Book on Protecting Yourself from Strangers.* https://time.com/5599393/victims-viginia-beach-shooting/. 0623. https://people.com/crime/virginia-beach-mass-shooting-victims-identified/. 0623. https://www.legacy.com/us/obituaries/pilotonline/name/joshua-hardy-obituary?id=15297838. 0623.

Bianca "Muffin" Bankz was a 31-year-old trans woman. She and her roommate had recently moved into their own apartment. She had recently started her medical transition and had a dream of competing on RuPaul's Drag Race. https://www.pghlesbian.com/2021/01/black-trans-woman-bianca-muffin-bankzy-murdered-in-atlanta/. 0723.

John Gaffaney was a Captain in the Army Reserves. He had previously in the Navy and the National Guard. He had worked as a psychiatric nurse in San Diego for more than twenty years. He was San Diego Padres fan. He and his wife had one son. He was 56. https://www.cbsnews.com/news/profiles-of-ft-hood-shooters-victims/. 0923.

Bernadette Steadman went by "Bernie." She lived most of her life in Elyria, Ohio. She and her husband had been married for 69 years at the time of his death. She was an active church member, and enjoyed crafts and line dancing. https://www.findagrave.com/memorial/249876781/bernadette-a-steadman. 0923.

Kasim Crayton's firm, Only Chase Money Apparel, was a clothing and brand design company. https://www.bosticktompkinsinc.com/obituary/KasimAmaru-Crayton. 0923.

William Chapman's favorite books included *The Great Gatsby* and *The Last Olympian.* His favorite films included *The Shawshank Redemption* and *Blade Runner.* https://www.learntheirstories.com/#/william-chapman/. 0623.

3.1: Mike Males, "Who Are Police Killing?" as cited in Woodard, *American Apartheid*, 161.
515: Woodard, *American Apartheid*, 161.

"Most mass shootings: Geller, Booty, and Crifasi, "The Role of Domestic Violence," 1.

More mass shootings: Zeoli, "Multiple Victim Homicides," 3. https://www.preventdvgunviolence.org/multiple-killings-zeoli-updated-112918.pdf.

"Contrary to the portrayal of mass murders in the media as largely being committed in public places by strangers, familicides constitute half of mass murders in the U.S. These familicides sometimes include the killing of parents, siblings, or other close relatives and are most commonly committed with guns by middle-aged white males who are the husbands and fathers of their victims. In fact, from 2007 through 2011, 43% of mass murders involved only victims who were family members of the homicide offender, while 26% involved a combination of victim types."

In intimate partner homicides: Geller, Booty, and Crifasi, "The Role of Domestic Violence," 2. "It is not uncommon for IPH events to result in multiple victims, including perpetrator suicide and the death of family, friends, new dating partners of the victim, coworkers, children of the victim or perpetrator, strangers, or police officers. Research shows that around 40% of male-perpetrated IPHs result in multiple fatalities, either with the perpetrator dying by suicide or additional homicides."

70] • [71

Keke Collier was a 24-year-old trans woman who lived in Chicago, and also went by Tiara Richmond. https://www.chicagotribune.com/news/breaking/ct--tiara-richmond-transgender-woman-killed20170223-story.html. 0723.

Cindy Clouse lived in Lee Township, Michigan, and worked at an assisted living center in a nearby town. https://www.starksfamilyfh.com/obituaries/cindy-clouse. 0923.

Leslie Sherman was studying history and international relations, hoping first to serve in the Peace Corps and then to work in the Department of State. To pay for school, she worked twenty hours a week in one of her university's dining halls. https://www.weremember.vt.edu/biographies/sherman.html. 0223. http://www.vt-memorial.org/profiles/Sherman.html. 0223.

Stacee Etcheber had a degree in physical therapy and worked as a hairdresser. She and her husband had two children, a daughter and a son. https://www.nytimes.com/2017/10/02/us/vegas-victims-names.html. 0523. https://www.legacy.com/us/obituaries/sfgate/name/stacee-etcheber-obituary?id=8962559. 0523.

Shannan Gilbert was a 23-year-old sex worker from Jersey City, New Jersey. Before joining an escort agency, she worked as a hotel receptionist, a hostess at a chain restaurant, and a snack prepper at a senior center. https://www.washingtonpost.com/nation/2023/07/14/gilgo-beach-serial-killings-suspect-arrest/?utm_campaign=wp_post_most&utm_medium=email&utm_source=newsletter&wpisrc=nl_most. 0723. https://www.earnthenecklace.com/shannan-gilbert-wiki/. 0723.

Jonathan Ferrell had been a gymnast as a boy, and in high school had played football and run track. He played football at Florida A&M in 2009 and 2010. He was 24, and had just begun work-study programs that would pay for automotive-repair schooling at an area community college. https://www.learntheirstories.com/#/jonathan-ferrell/. 0623.

Frederick Greene went by "Freddie." He was in the U.S. Army. https://www.cbsnews.com/news/profiles-of-ft-hood-shooters-victims/. 0923.

Lisa Steadman was born in Wisconsin, and had lived in Florida before moving to Elyria, Ohio to seek professional care for her son. She had nine siblings, and was 60 years old. https://chroniclet.com/news/330943/lisa-terese-steadman/. 0923.

Nyla Crayton. https://www.bosticktompkinsinc.com/obituary/NylaAthenaJoyce-Crayton. 0923.

Derek Cruice especially liked Dagorhir battle games. He lived in Florida, and was 26. https://www.news-journalonline.com/story/news/2015/03/23/friends-hold-benefit-for-family-of-man-shot-by-sheriffs-deputy/30709596007/. 0823.
https://heavy.com/news/2015/03/derek-cruice-killed-police-shooting-shot-florida-volusia-deltona-todd-raible/. 0823.

10: https://www.thecalifornian.com/story/news/crime/2015/07/10/officers-charged-osmar-hernandezs-salinas-death/29997183/. 0823.
11: https://sfbayview.com/2013/01/manteca-killer-cop-cleared-of-any-wrongdoing/. 0723.
14: https://www.theguardian.com/us-news/2016/mar/21/death-by-gentrification-the-killing-that-shamed-san-francisco. 0723.

Good guys with guns: Rebecca Peters, as quoted in Gabor, *Confronting Gun Violence in America*, 48. "[R]elying on guys with guns to stop violence is a sign of a society where institutions have broken down."

Guns don't kill: Gabrielle Galimberti, in an interview about his book of photographs of gun owners. https://newsletters.theatlantic.com/galaxy-brain/62969b2d51acba0020910aed/gabriele-galimberti-gun-owner-photos-uvalde/. 0523.
"But I think when people use my photos to judge the people in them, that is a mistake. The real judgment in my work is on the society that allows this. The real problem isn't these 40 people I photographed; it is the regulations and the culture that permits it.... [I]f you are shocked by seeing this family with 200 guns, then maybe the real problem is there are no regulations that would keep them from obtaining these guns. And I want to be clear that it's not only guns I photographed, but also people with bazookas and flamethrowers, all legally obtained. They're free to buy them."

"People without guns: Baker, "Without Guns, Do People Kill People?" 588.

71] • [72

TeeTee Dangerfield was a 32-year-old trans woman who worked as a restaurant server and union shop steward. https://www.thedailybeast.com/transgender-murdered-and-missed-remembering-teetee-dangerfield. 0723.

Lauren McCain was studying German and international studies, and wanted to visit Germany. She was active in her university's chapter of Campus Crusade for Christ. https://www.weremember.vt.edu/biographies/mccain.html. 0223. http://vt-memorial.org/profiles/McCain.html. 0223.

Jordyn Rivera attended Cal State San Bernardino, and had participated in the university's study abroad program in London. https://www.nytimes.com/2017/10/02/us/vegas-victims-names.html. 0523.

Melissa Barthelemy graduated from South Park High School in Buffalo. She then got her cosmetology license and worked briefly at a Supercuts. She was physically small: 4'10" and 95 pounds. She was 24. https://www.oxygen.com/true-crime-buzz/lost-girls-who-were-the-victims-of-the-long-island-serial-killer. 0723.

Julian Lewis was 60. He and his wife had one son. https://www.cnn.com/2020/08/17/us/georgia-julian-lewis-death-family/index.html. 0623.

Autumn Hagger was in middle school. She played softball and loved riding horses. She wanted to be a dermatologist. She loved watching scary movies, sitting close and holding hands. She was nearing her 14th birthday. https://www.starksfamilyfh.com/obituaries/autumn-hagger#obit_anchor. 0923.

Jason Hunt was from Frederick, Oklahoma. He preferred video games to hunting or sports, and had recently gotten married. He was 22. https://www.cbsnews.com/news/profiles-of-ft-hood-shooters-victims/. 0923.

Matthew Steadman had autism spectrum disorder, and was 34 years old. He enjoyed singing and was a big fan of Martina McBride, whom he got to meet backstage once. https://chroniclet.com/news/330947/matthew-james-steadman/. 0923.

Nasir Crayton loved gaming, playing with his cousins and siblings, and family excursions. https://www.bosticktompkinsinc.com/obituary/NasirPeter-Crayton. 0923.

Brendon Glenn was 29, and had a drinking problem. He had grown up in Troy, New York, but lived unhoused in Venice, California. https://homicide.latimes.com/post/brendon-k-glenn/. 0823.

1,189: Morales, "Too Many Stolen Lives," 173.

"Violence is not generated: Collins, *Violence*, 413.

Thinking about violence: Milloy, *Blood, Sweat, and Fear*, 22.
"Beyond the conceptual challenges, thinking about violence means grappling with painful, traumatic events. It is a natural human response to trauma to try to forget, to dismiss it and move on, rather than examining it and bringing painful emotions to the surface again."

Violence reifies the fraudulence: Rose, *On Violence*, 179.
"Violence, then, is man's response to the fraudulence of his power and the limits of his knowledge." In this passage, Rose is characterizing a view of Hannah Arendt's, rather than declaring her own view.

72] • [73

Chyna Gibson was a 31-year-old trans woman who had been born and raised in New Orleans, but lived in California. She was also known by the name Chyna Doll Dupree. https://www.nola.com/news/crime_police/a-hole-in-our-hearts-family-friends-mourn-murder-victim-chyna-gibson/article_105599e9-dc36-53a7-b8f2-9e2f3d5205f4.html. 0723.

Mackenzie Hagger was 10 years old. She loved babies and wanted to have a big family. She sent nightly text messages to say I love you and good night to her family and cousins. She loved singing, swimming, softball, and cheer. https://www.starksfamilyfh.com/obituaries/mackenzie-grace-hagger-#obit_anchor. 0923.

Daniel O'Neil had run cross-country and track in high school. He was studying for his masters degree in environmental engineering. He had spent a semester in Brussels, and planned to live in Dublin after graduation. https://www.weremember.vt.edu/biographies/oneil.html. 0223. http://vt-memorial.org/profiles/ONeil.html. 0223.

Keri Galvan took her children to Disneyland once a month or so, continuing a family tradition begun by her father. https://www.reviewjournal.com/crime/homicides/las-vegas-shooting-victim-keri-lynn-galvan-thousand-oaks-california/. 0523.

Lucero Alcaraz had 5 sisters and one brother. She was on a full-tuition scholarship at her community college. https://www.findagrave.com/memorial/153150056/lucero-alcaraz. 0723.

Layleen Xtravaganza Cubilette-Polanco was 27. http://granvarones.com/layleen-xtravaganza-cubilette-polanco/. 0723.

Yvette Smith had a twin sister, and two sons. https://www.learntheirstories.com/#/yvette-smith/. 0623.

Amy Krueger was a high school graduate from Kiel, Wisconsin, who joined the Army after 9/11. She had been deployed once to Afghanistan, and was preparing for a second deployment there. She was 29, and had achieved the rank of Staff Sergeant. Friends nicknamed her "Kruegs." https://www.meiselwitzfh.com/obituary/454878. 0923. https://www.cbsnews.com/news/profiles-of-ft-hood-shooters-victims/. 0923.

Mary Beth Bergum was a registered nurse, and had nearly completed her bachelors degree to become an RN/BSN. She had one daughter and three sons. https://www.dignitymemorial.com/obituaries/east-amherst-ny/mary-elizabeth-bergum-10965600. 0923.

Deven Guilford was 17 years old, and a junior in high school. He had two older brothers. He had been adopted when he was 18 months old. He enjoyed camping with the family in the summer, playing with his four nieces and nephews and riding his bike. https://www.legacy.com/us/obituaries/lsj/name/deven-guilford-obituary?id=17781311. 0823. https://www.usatoday.com/story/news/nation-now/2015/10/22/michigan-family-teen-shot/74429034/. 0823.

76.5: Warner et al., "To Provide or Protect?" 105.
2011: Yamane, Yamane, and Ivory, "Targeted Advertising," 7.

"The sexualization: King, "Arming Desire," 89.
I have silently inserted the initial cap and full stop. In its entirety, the sentence reads: "Throughout, I set aside easy, individualistic assessments that might favor the language of the unconscious and the logic of fetishism, opting instead to integrate post-structural, queer, and feminist theories to highlight the ways in which the sexualization of guns arms deeper desires, namely hegemonic formulations of masculinity, heterosexuality, and domination."

Gun use has been gendered: Kreuter, Wilkes, and Skinnell, "Introduction," 5.
"From its beginning, gun ownership and use has been inextricably tied to gendered and racialized violence perpetrated primarily by white male European settler-colonists against Black, Indigenous, People of Color (BIPOC). This foundational gendered, racialized violence enacted through firearms has never ceased."

After one masculinity is lost: Cassino and Besen-Cassino, "Sometimes," 20.
"When some men are unable to fulfill the demands of hegemonic masculinities because of loss of income or some other perceived deficiency, they invent a perceived threat in order to justify their role as a protector and gun owner. As such, when economic conditions or other factors lead more men to be unable to meet the demands of hegemonic masculinities, they double down on other masculinities that they are better able to attain, leading to increased gun purchases."

73] • [74

Sheldon Haleck was born in Pago Pago, American Samoa, and lived in Kapolei, Hawai'i. He suffered from mental illness and had a history of drug use. He had a son and a stepson. https://www.dignitymemorial.com/obituaries/honolulu-hi/sheldon-haleck-6374057. 0823. https://www.civilbeat.org/2019/06/jury-no-excessive-force-in-sheldon-halecks-death/. 0823.

Queasha Hardy was a 24-year-old trans woman who lived in Baton Rouge, Louisiana. https://www.them.us/story/queasha-hardy-killing-transgender-violence. 0923. https://www.theadvocate.com/baton_rouge/news/crime_police/community-mourns-trans-woman-a-hairstylist-so-full-of-life-gunned-down-in-baton-rouge/article_00430942-de56-11ea-878e-17c199e8e1a6.html. 0923.

Juan Ortiz had two sisters and two brothers. He and his wife both were masters students in civil engineering. They watched action movies together when they needed a break from studying. https://www.weremember.vt.edu/biographies/ortiz.html. 0223. http://vt-memorial.org/profiles/Ortiz.html. 0223.

Dana Gardner had three children and two grandchildren. https://www.bustle.com/p/who-was-dana-gardner-the-las-vegas-shooting-victim-was-a-dedicated-public-servant-2780692. 0523. https://www.azcentral.com/story/news/nation/2017/10/04/las-vegas-shooting-victim-dana-gardner-san-bernardino/732922001/. 0523.

Lawrence Levine lived alone in a rented cabin on a river in Oregon. For a living he tended bar, taught English at a community college, and was a fly fishing guide. https://www.oregonlive.com/pacific-northwest-news/2015/10/oregon_college_shooting_lawren.html. 0723.

Steven Eugene Washington wanted to become a mechanic. He was 27. https://www.learntheirstories.com/#/steven-eugene-washington-27/. 0623.

Aaron Nemelka grew up in a suburb of Salt Lake City, the youngest of four children in his family. He had the rank of Private First Class. He was 19. https://www.cbsnews.com/news/profiles-of-ft-hood-shooters-victims/. 0923.

Jeremy McDole was 28. https://ebwiki.org/cases/jeremy-mcdole. 0723.

Nancy Bergum had climbed Mount Whitney, the highest peak in the continental United States. She and her husband had one child. https://www.dignitymemorial.com/obituaries/east-amherst-ny/nancy-bergum-10965629. 0923.

Angelina Harrison loved her dog Draco, and liked going to car meets and car shows. She liked doing her makeup, shopping, and hanging out with her mom and dad or her brother. https://www.thecheyennepost.com/obituaries/angelina-marie-harrison/article_bdbcd6ec-9367-11ed-b84b-dfbc2042218c.html. 0523.

4 million: Oklahoma figure as of 2020, probation figure as of 2014. https://www.brennancenter.org/our-work/analysis-opinion/just-facts-probation-nation. 0623.
70 million: https://www.brennancenter.org/our-work/analysis-opinion/just-facts-many-americans-have-criminal-records-college-diplomas. 0623.

Police threaten: Zimring, *When Police Kill*, 57.
"[T]he proliferation of concealable firearms in the civilian population is a major source of the singularly high rate of killings by the police in the United States. The major reason police shoot so often is that guns appear to be in the hands of civilians. Because firearms are also the cause of death in more than 90 percent of all fatal assaults on police, the dominant role of fear of

opponents with guns is easy to comprehend. The predominant instrument used in fatal force by American police is also the major threat to the lives of uniformed police."

Guns are used: Geller et al., "The Role of Domestic Violence," 2.
"While firearms are used in intimate relationships to kill, they are also used to threaten and intimidate. Around 4.5 million women in the U.S. have been threatened with a firearm, and nearly 1 million women have been shot or shot at by an intimate partner."

The more effective the tool: Kleck, *Point Blank*, 154.
"[T]he single most important factor that sets human violence apart from aggression among lower animals is arguably man's greater technological capacity to inflict harm. The tools of death available to humans are vastly more lethal than even the most deadly natural equipment of animals. Whereas interpersonal conflict of some sort is inevitable and universal, it may be factors such as use of weaponry that determine whether verbal conflict escalates to violence, whether physical attacks are completed by reaching their target, and whether they inflict serious injury or death when they do."

74] • [75

José Mendez had been a good soccer player as a child, but he had dropped out of school during his freshman year of high school. He was 16. https://www.laweekly.com/video-shows-boyle-heights-teen-shot-by-cops-was-dragged-from-scene/. 0723.

Sean Bell grew up in Queens, NY, and was a pitcher on his high school team. In his senior year he had an 11-0 record with a 2.30 E.R.A. and 97 strikeouts in 62.2 innings. He met his girlfriend in high school and after about six years of dating, they decided to get married. They had two daughters. https://www.learntheirstories.com/#/sean-bell/. 0623.

Minal Panchal liked the books *Little Women* and *To Kill a Mockingbird*, and the movies *When Harry Met Sally* and *The Way We Were*. https://www.weremember.vt.edu/biographies/panchal.html. 0223.

Susan Smith and her husband had two children. She had worked in her local school district for over fifteen years. https://www.bustle.com/p/who-was-susan-smith-the-las-vegas-shooting-victim-was-a-beloved-elementary-school-employee-2758876. 0523.

Treven Anspach went by "Trev." He had played high school basketball and soccer, and was on the basketball team at his college. His summer job was at a lumber company. He was 20. https://www.findagrave.com/memorial/153473081/treven-taylor-anspach. 0723. http://trevensfund.org/. 0723.

Melvin Pérez lived in Colorado Springs, Colorado his whole life. He liked to spend time with his family, and loved camping and fishing.
https://www.tributearchive.com/obituaries/21142977/Melvin-Antonio-Perez. 0823.

https://gazette.com/news/neighbors-in-colorado-springs-mass-shooting-mourn-the-6-slain-identified-by-family-member/article_4c15d008-b1c2-11eb-b8cf-6735c450f9fa.html. 0823.

Michael Pearson was a Private First Class in the Army. He was from Bolingbroke, Illinois, and had previously worked for a furniture company. He was 22. https://www.cbsnews.com/news/profiles-of-ft-hood-shooters-victims/. 0923.

Mark Bergum worked as an engineer at Calspan and then Fisher Price until his retirement. https://www.dignitymemorial.com/obituaries/east-amherst-ny/mark-bergum-10965632. 0923.

Gigi Eugene-Pierce was a 28-year-old trans woman. She grew up in Boise, Idaho, and later moved to Spokane, Washington, and then to Portland, Oregon. Before her transition, she had performed as a drag queen named Jeliza Rose, and one friend called her "a performer through and through." https://www.wweek.com/news/2018/05/29/friends-remember-gigi-eugene-pierce-for-her-vivacious-spirit-even-as-she-struggled-with-addiction-and-homelessness-in-portland/. 0723.

Don Myrick played the saxophone as a recording and touring artist, playing with such performers as Louis Armstrong, Diana Ross, and Carlos Santana. His nickname, "Hippmo," was given him in childhood by peers who called him "Hippmo-potamus" for being obese, but in adulthood it referred to his music, designating him as "mo' hip." He had three daughters, and was 53 years old. https://www.learntheirstories.com/#/don-myrick/. 0623.
https://eurweb.com/2020/remembering-don-myrick-the-man-behind-epic-horn-riffs-from-your-childhood-from-sun-goddess-to-sussudio-eur-video-throwback/. 0623.

16 October 1860: Haag, *The Gunning of America*, 63.
9,800: Haag, *The Gunning of America*, xviii.
292,400: Haag, *The Gunning of America*, xv.
225 million +: Burbick, *Gun Show Nation*, xx.

Punitive ≠: Muschert, "School Shootings," 35.
"School shooters have become the poster children for violent youth offenders and school antiviolence policies often address worst-case scenarios. Though not exclusively so, control responses in the United States tend to be punitive in the form of zero tolerance policies, use of police, and surveillance practices. Such punitive responses are in contrast to the restorative/ integrative measures available, including mediation programs, conflict resolution, and anti-bullying programming."

Detained by a police officer: https://www.nytimes.com/2015/01/05/opinion/charles-blow-privilege-of-arrest-without-incident.html. 0523.
"Everyone needs to be treated as though his or her life matters. More suspected criminals need to be detained and tried in a court of law and not sentenced on the street to a rain of bullets."

Dangerous + accessible to children =: Erdman, "Promoting Gun Safety," 88.
"Adults should expect that children are drawn to guns, will play with them if they find them, don't understand what guns really do, and can't understand the consequences of shooting a living

being. Given that children's understanding is very limited and given that children can't be expected to leave a gun alone if they find it, it is dangerous for guns to be unlocked and accessible."

75] • [76

Irvo Otieno was 28. He had a passion for music. Originally from Kenya, he came to the United States when he was 4. https://www.cnn.com/2023/03/17/us/irvo-otieno-death-what-we-know/index.html. 0723.

Daniel Pérez was majoring in international relations, with the goal of becoming a diplomat. http://www.vt-memorial.org/profiles/Cueva.html. 0223.

Angela Gomez had participated in children's theater, was involved in choir in both middle and high school, and was a cheerleader in high school. https://www.reviewjournal.com/videos/las-vegas-shooting-victim-angela-gomez-california/. 0523. https://www.nytimes.com/2017/10/02/us/vegas-victims-names.html. 0523.

Medgar Evers worked for several years as a traveling insurance salesman before being appointed Mississippi field secretary for the NAACP. He and his wife had three children. Zacek, "Evers, Medgar," n.p.

Rebecka Ann Carnes was 18. She was in her first semester on scholarship at community college, studying to become a dental assistant. She loved soccer and softball, liked to camp and go four-wheeling. https://people.com/human-interest/oregon-shooting-rebecka-carnes-family-releases-statement/. 0723.

Mayra Pérez, 32, was born in Gómez Palacio, Mexico, but had lived in Colorado Springs, Colorado for 25 years. She and her husband had 3 children. She liked to spend time with her family and friends. https://www.angelusfuneraldirectors.com/obituaries/Mayra-Ibarra-de-Perez?obId=21142944#/celebrationWall. 0823. https://gazette.com/news/neighbors-in-colorado-springs-mass-shooting-mourn-the-6-slain-identified-by-family-member/article_4c15d008-b1c2-11eb-b8cf-6735c450f9fa.html. 0823.

George Jackson was the second of five children. He liked to hunt. https://www.blackpast.org/african-american-history/jackson-george-1941-1971/. 0323.

Russell Seager was from Racine, Wisconsin. He had worked at the Veterans Affairs hospital in Milwaukee treating soldiers experiencing PTSD. He was 51. He and his wife had a 20-year-old son. https://www.cbsnews.com/news/profiles-of-ft-hood-shooters-victims/. 0923.

Carlos Mejia. https://www.altavistamortuary.com/obituary/5336545. 0823.

Marcus-David Peters was a magna cum laude graduate of VCU. Friends and family called him "Poppy." He was 24. https://www.findagrave.com/memorial/198763342/marcus-david-peters. 0723.

16: https://www.usatoday.com/story/news/2021/02/12/video-highlights-death-man-who-told-police-i-cant-breathe/6737819002/. 0723.

Violence can't just be: Gilligan, *Preventing Violence*, 9.
"[W]hen we talk about preventing violence, we are not talking about something that can be solved with gimmicks; we are not talking about 'techniques.' We are talking about *whether, and how, we and other human beings can learn to live with each other, and even to want to live with each other* — and I mean live as opposed to die, for that is the only other choice where violence is concerned. But that is too profound a question to be answered by anything other than a radical rethinking of the most basic principles on which our social life is based."

Violence is complex: Gellert, *Confronting Violence*, 272.
"Violence in America is a problem with diverse causes and upon which act numerous social, economic, family and psychological influences. Violence is not only a problem associated with an incompletely effective law enforcement or judicial system. These are critical to any effort to control violence. Violence is also not a problem that can be considered solely as a public health issue and approached in isolation from its origins in social and gender inequities, in failures of the educational system, or in the responsibilities of families in how they resolve conflicts and raise nonviolent children. Guns alone are not the source of this epidemic. Like most human behaviors, violence is a complex phenomenon that resists simple solutions. No single strategy can but modestly reduce violence."

The question is not: Goldberg et al., "The Smoking Gun," 2.
"Since allowing the federal assault weapons ban of 1994 to expire a decade later, we have seen an alarming increase in the number of mass shootings in the United States with assault weapons playing a large role in these horrific events. On the basis of these and other data, and believing what our eyes and common sense tells us, we no longer need additional research into whether having a gun in a home is a risk factor for these mass casualties or whether civilian access to assault weapons leads to more mass casualty events. The evidence is in front of our collective noses about our need for action on gun control. The research that we do need, however, is about providing insights into which population-based interventions could be designed and delivered to prevent gun-related violence and alter the trajectory of gun-related deaths in the United States."

76] • [77

Nina Pop was a 28-year-old trans woman who worked in a restaurant. https://www.pghlesbian.com/2020/05/black-trans-woman-nina-pop-28-murdered-in-missouri/. 0723.

Elijah McClain often spent his lunch breaks at local animal shelters, putting on concerts for cats and dogs because he believed music would help soothe their anxiety. He was 23. https://www.thecut.com/2021/09/the-killing-of-elijah-mcclain-everything-we-know.html. 0723.

Erin Peterson had been captain of her high school basketball team, and in marker had written on her shoe "I can do all things through Christ who strengthens me." http://www.vt-memorial.org/profiles/Peterson.html. 0223.

Bailey Schweitzer's favorite color was teal. She started at the age of 10 working the concession stand at the family business, Bakersfield Speedway, a dirt track racing oval, standing on a stool to sell hot dogs and popcorn. https://www.kget.com/news/local-news/remembering-bailey-schweitzer-youngest-victim-of-las-vegas-tragedy/. 0523.

Jason Johnson was born in Hawai'i and grew up in California. He had recently completed a six-month drug rehab program, he had earned his GED. He had a twin brother. https://umpqua.edu/we-remember/jason-dale-johnson-we-will-always-remember/. 0723. https://www.oregonlive.com/pacific-northwest-news/2015/10/oregon_shooting_victim_jason_j.html. 0723.

Joana Cruz was born in El Salvador, but had lived in Colorado Springs, Colorado for 26 years. She liked spending time with her family and friends. https://gazette.com/news/neighbors-in-colorado-springs-mass-shooting-mourn-the-6-slain-identified-by-family-member/article_4c15d008-b1c2-11eb-b8cf-6735c450f9fa.html. 0823. https://www.tributearchive.com/obituaries/21142966/Juana-DeJesus-Cruz. 0823.

Francheska Velez was preparing to return home from a tour in Iraq for maternity leave. She intended to continue in the military for her entire career. She was 21. https://www.cbsnews.com/news/profiles-of-ft-hood-shooters-victims/. 0923.

Duanna Johnson was a 43-year-old trans woman who struggled with unemployment, a crack addiction and frequent arrests for prostitution. https://www.queerty.com/duanna-johnson-murdered-execution-style-in-memphis-20081111. 0723. https://www.nytimes.com/2008/11/18/us/18memphis.html?searchResultPosition=1. 0723.

Ta'Kiya Young was 21. She lived in Columbus, Ohio. https://apnews.com/article/pregnant-woman-killed-police-shooting-ohio-c012c53ca8d11fbb839d593a724da288. 0823.

Richard Ramirez was an avid basketball player and comedian. https://www.legacy.com/us/obituaries/billingsgazette/name/richard-ramirez-obituary?id=9250937. 0723.

9: Drexel University Urban Health Collaborative, citing Big Cities Health Inventory data. https://drexel.edu/uhc/resources/briefs/BCHC%20Gun%20Deaths/. 0323. Other & Belonging Institute, citing U.S. Census data. https://belonging.berkeley.edu/most-least-segregated-cities-in-2020. 0323.

It is not self-evident: Johnson, "Guns as a Symbol," 113.
"Risks are socially constructed, and all risks are mediated by a social context and the technologies of communication. Positive action and constructive progress on gun violence has been hampered by the interests linking gun violence and Second Amendment gun rights. These issues are not the

same, and the failure to distinguish them has led to failures such as President Obama's bill proposed in the aftermath of Sandy Hook. If future proposals are successful, they will have to distinguish these issues."

Gun rights and gun control: Utter and True, "The Evolving Gun Culture," 69.
"Public opinion on the sale and ownership of handguns in America is broad enough and complex enough for both gun rights and gun control groups to believe that they represent mainstream opinion, even though the images and beliefs of the two groups starkly contrast with each other. Similarly, each group can argue about the authenticity of its historical and mythic ties to the roots of this country…. Both cultures focus on issues of crime, violence, and the call for various government-initiated controls on the possession and use of firearms. The two contending sides play a significant role in defining each other."

Between compromising rights: Southwick, "Government Options," 220.
Re. school shootings, "There appear to be no easy answers. Knives, hammers, guns, and explosives are available. They are not going away. Mental illness is always a problem. There is no magic cure or even an always correct diagnosis. Whatever is done implies steering a course between violating people's rights and allowing bad things to happen. We are discussing rather rare events at a probable cost of ignoring other problems that may have higher costs."

77] • [78

Walter Wallace was an aspiring rapper whose lyrics "featured guns and rhymes about shooting people, including police." He had bipolar disorder. He had an extensive criminal record that included convictions for resisting arrest and robbery. https://nypost.com/2020/10/28/walter-wallace-had-a-long-history-of-violent-run-ins-with-cops/. 0323.

Kayla Moore had a history of paranoid schizophrenia. https://www.huffpost.com/entry/kayla-moore-death_n_3000575. 0523.

Mike Pohle had played football and lacrosse in high school. He was a Phillies fan, and was studying biology. http://www.vt-memorial.org/profiles/Pohle.html. 0223.

Rocio Guillen had four children, one of whom she carried to term despite complications that meant spinal surgery, paralysis, and months of rehabilitation to learn to walk again, then years of effort culminating in the completion of three marathons. https://thergfoundation.org/rocios-story. 0523.

Quinn Cooper was 18. He loved the music of Louis Armstrong. He loved to dance and perform voice acting, and was studying theater at his local community college. He and his brother Cody liked playing the video game "Ingress" together. https://www.opb.org/news/article/quinn-cooper-a-gentle-giant-missed-by-many/. 0723. https://www.cnn.com/2015/10/02/us/oregon-umpqua-community-college-shooting-victims/index.html. 0723.

Jose Gutierrez, 21, lived in Colorado Springs, Colorado. https://www.tributearchive.com/obituaries/21142987/Jose-Luis-Gutierrez-Cruz. 0823.

Juanita Warman came from a military family, and was herself a military physician assistant. She had the rank of Lt. Col. She volunteered with Beyond the Yellow Ribbon, a reintegration program for Maryland National Guard soldiers returning from deployment overseas. https://www.cbsnews.com/news/profiles-of-ft-hood-shooters-victims/. 0923.

Russell Sharrer. https://www.tri-cityherald.com/news/local/obituaries/article32217702.html. 0823. https://www.tri-cityherald.com/news/local/crime/article32217312.html. 0823.

Tamara Wilson-Seidle went by "Tami." She had nine children, and was a five-year breast cancer survivor. She served as Coordinator of Religious Education for her parish. She was 51. She had been born in Germany, but moved with her family to the U.S. in her childhood. https://www.app.com/story/news/local/eatontown-asbury-park/asbury-park/2015/06/22/seidle-funeral/29116849/. 0823. https://www.legacy.com/us/obituaries/mycentraljersey/name/tamara-wilson-seidle-obituary?id=18024826. 0823.

Samuel Brightmon liked TV cop shows such as *Criminal Minds*, and he had an app on his phone that followed police activity. His family shortened his middle name, Courde-Bernard, into the nickname DaDa. Younge, *Another Day in the Death of America.*

251,000: Naghavi et al., "Global Mortality from Firearms," 792.

Persons killed in shootings: Fast, *Ceremonial Violence*, 10.
Re. school shootings: "And what of the wounded? Exposure to cinematic gun fights, where the just-shot engage in strenuous activity, scaling walls and performing acrobatic leaps from rooftops as though they have suffered nothing worse than an insect bite, has desensitized us all to the havoc a bullet creates in human tissue and bone. While a few lucky victims may leave the hospital the same day, more endure dozens of operations and years of occupational therapy before they recover the use of an arm or a leg. Some who avoided the bullets but witnessed the shooting are too traumatized to ever set foot in a school again, and suffer from panic attacks and flashbacks; over time, untreated, many victims become substance abusers or engage in self-destructive behaviors such as self-mutilation or promiscuous, unprotected sex."

Lives ended by police violence: Powers, "Killing the Future," 14.
"The old racial line between 'Black' and 'white' has been redrawn as the line between criminal and citizen…. Most of us [persons of color] aren't killed by cops. Most of us 'survive' racism. But every day another person of color is shot by police, and the holes left inside families are where loved ones used to breath. The cops not only steal the lives of our children; they steal the lives of everyone who loved them."

Harm from police killings: Mehra, et al., "'Police shootings...," 2.

"[P]olice killings of Black people also affect the health of pregnant and postpartum Black people…. Anticipated racism from police, specifically police brutality towards their children, may be a distinct factor contributing to chronic stress among Black women. Understanding Black women's experiences and perceptions of police brutality in relation to their pregnancies and children provides new insights to inform policy and clinical guidelines that may reduce racial inequities in health outcomes."

78] • [79

Calvin Cains had recently graduated from high school. https://www.nola.com/news/jefferson_parish/calvin-cains-jpso-metairie-shooting-trey/article_af73bdf4-0634-11ee-9a7a-03f58414d938.html. 0923.

Jessica Hernandez ended up buying *two* puppies, Simba and Precious, one for her and one for her sister. https://thefreethoughtproject.com/cop-watch/family-friends-jessica-hernandez-teen-slain-denver-pd-speak-challenging-official-story. 0723.

Oscar Aracena-Montero worked as a manager at McDonald's, and was studying for a business management degree. He had been born in the Dominican Republic, and wanted to bring his mother to the U.S. https://www.orlandoweekly.com/news/remembering-the-orlando-49-oscar-ambiorix-aracena-montero-2547558. 0323.

Cameron Robinson lived in southwestern Utah but commuted to Las Vegas. He had created a smartphone app that eased navigation for attendees of the city government's annual conferences. https://www.cnn.com/2017/10/02/us/las-vegas-shooting-victims/index.html. 0523. https://www.nytimes.com/2017/10/02/us/vegas-victims-names.html. 0523.

Kim Dietz did ceramics. She hoped the family's two Great Pyrenees could one day serve as therapy dogs for the local veteran's hospital. She was 59, and was attending the same community college as her 19-year-old daughter. https://people.com/crime/oregon-shooting-husband-and-daughter-of-victim-kim-dietz-describe-tragic-loss/. 0723.

Kalief Browder grew up in the Bronx. He had completed his first semester in college with a 3.562 GPA. https://exhibits.stanford.edu/saytheirnames/feature/kalief-browder. 0623.

Sandra Ibarra was 28. She liked spending time with her family. https://www.tributearchive.com/obituaries/21142957/Sandra-Cecilia-Ibarra/Colorado-Springs/Colorado/Angelus-Funeral-Home. 0823.

Kham Xiong had 10 siblings. He immigrated to the U.S. from Vietnam with his family when he was a toddler, and grew up in California but had lived in Minnesota for about ten years. He and his wife had three young children. https://www.cbsnews.com/news/profiles-of-ft-hood-shooters-victims/. 0923.

Valeria Tachiquin Alvarado. https://www.southernborder.org/valeria-tachiquin. 0723. https://sandiegofreepress.org/2012/10/vigil-for-valeria-munique-alvarado-young-mother-killed-by-border-patrol/. 0723.

Amadou Diallo had come to the U.S. from Guinea to pursue a degree in computer science. He sold socks, gloves and videos on 14th Street in Manhattan. He sent much of the money he earned to his parents back home. https://www.learntheirstories.com/#/amadou-diallo/. 0623.

>300: Springwood, "Gunscapes," 17.

If blaming you: Johnston, "Mass Shooters and Mental Illness," 13.
"[O]ur tendency to assume that mass shooters must be bad apples down to the core or deeply disturbed individuals with mental illnesses that we can only shudder to imagine (and sometimes we merge the two) is a common psychological tendency," namely the *fundamental attribution error.* "It serves to distance us from thinking we too are capable of 'evil,' protecting our self-esteem and preserving a holistic 'good' sense of self. The media further reinforces these ideas."

Cultural anesthesia: Allen Feldman, in Evans and Lennart, *Violence*, 293-94.
"Cultural anesthesia stratifies and preempts the capacity to publicly circulate the sensory experience of violence along lines of race, class, gender, religion, and ethnicity. Such state practice prepares the sociocultural conditions of political apperception — the violence of politically blanking out violence and the collective capacity for its public witness and seditious de-justification. This pattern of deleting sensorial difference and the dissimulating planting of originary violence onto the Black, Muslim, or immigrant body informs the current structure of counterinsurgent governance linking Trump anti-immigration rallies and torture at Abu Ghraib to the judicial murder of African Americans."

We're killing each other: Schildkraut and Elsass, *Mass Shootings*, 161.
"We all agree that the loss of even one life to a mass shooter is too great, but still find ourselves locked in a fight over topics such as gun control while ignoring the bigger picture. Statutes, policies, and procedures drafted for the purpose of helping to prevent mass shootings and reduce their lethality when they do occur that are based upon inaccurate stereotypes, uninformed political agenda, inflated fear, and raw emotion cannot be successful."

79] • [80

Shelly Frey moved from New Orleans to Houston after Hurricane Katrina. https://mommyish.com/shelly-frey-walmart-shoplifting. 0723.

Willie McCoy dropped out of high school, but earned his GED. Both his parents had died of cancer by the time he was 12 years old. He was 20. https://www.nbcnews.com/news/us-news/california-rapper-willie-mccoy-was-finding-his-voice-police-encounter-n979076. 0723.

Darryl Burt worked as a university financial aid officer. https://people.com/crime/orlando-pulse-shooting-tributes-to-49-victims/. 0323.

Charleston Hartfield had served for 11 years as a Las Vegas police officer. Friends called him "Charlie." He volunteered with a local youth football club, posting highlight reels on social media for the players. https://taskandpurpose.com/news/charleston-hartfield-funeral-las-vegas/. 0523. https://www.nytimes.com/2017/10/02/us/vegas-victims-names.html. 0523.

Nicholas Arnstad was 41, and lived in Mesa, Arizona. https://www.azcentral.com/story/news/local/mesa-breaking/2023/05/28/suspect-identified-mesa-shooting-spree-linked-phoenix-homicide/70265292007/. 0723. https://www.azcentral.com/obituaries/par070099. 0723.

Mary Stanton was 49. https://www.wdrb.com/news/nothing-seemed-off-family-devastated-after-father-kills-wife-daughters-at-home-near-valley-station/article_609c7656-7423-11ed-b351-3f4acc168715.html. 0923.

Jose Ibarra was 26. https://www.tributearchive.com/obituaries/21142953/Jose-Ibarra. 0823.

Carson Holmquist had played defensive back on his high school football team in Grantsburg, Wisconsin. His Marine Corps service included one deployment to Afghanistan. https://www.washingtonpost.com/graphics/national/chattanooga-tennessee-shooting-victims/. 0923.

Jasleen Kaur lived with extended family in Merced, California. She was 27. https://www.cnn.com/2022/10/07/us/merced-murders-american-nightmare/index.html. 0923.

Anthony Hill had been medically discharged from the Air Force after being diagnosed with bipolar disorder. https://www.ajc.com/news/local/who-was-anthony-hill/tKFWur32jtFFdHQgHbtBgP/. 0823. https://www.nytimes.com/2015/03/11/us/chamblee-georgia-police-shooting-anthony-hill.html. 0823.

19: Klarevas, *Rampage Nation*, 242.

"School shootings: Altheide, "The Columbine Shootings," 1355.

A school shooting: Webber, *Beyond Columbine*, 82-83, 85.
"[A] new kind of massacre has entered into the methectic script: lone attackers, largely stylizing and reasoning in a similar fashion to second-generation school violence like Columbine, Red Lake, Jokela, Rio de Janeiro, Quebec, Virginia Tech and Northern Illinois have become detached from the 'school' referent and now circulate around more recognizably political sites: a labor camp, parliament buildings, military bases, the Boston Marathon, and the office Christmas party…. [M]any of these acts are artificially separated from their connections to each other by the media. Usually they use the age of the perpetrator or the target of the attack as a way of distinguishing them. Yet, if we focus on the violence and cruelty itself, we can see that they are profoundly related."

Another child shot: Goldstick, et al., "Current Causes of Death," 1956.
"[I]ncreasing firearm-related mortality reflects a longer-term trend and shows that we continue to fail to protect our youth from a preventable cause of death."

80] • [81

Michael Brown's aspirations included learning sound engineering, playing college football, and becoming a rap artist. Hill, *Nobody.*

Idriss Stelley tutored math, English, French, and Spanish in a community college Day Labor Program that helped undocumented immigrants find jobs. He was maintaining a 4.0 GPA in his computer science studies at college.
https://www.indybay.org/newsitems/2006/06/13/18280438.php. 0623.
https://www.sfgate.com/news/article/STELLEY-Idriss-E-2904335.php. 0623.
https://www.learntheirstories.com/#/idriss-stelley/. 0623.

Juan Chevez-Martinez was born in Hidalgo, Mexico. He loved makeup and hairstyling. https://www.clickorlando.com/news/2017/06/07/juan-chavez-martinez-left-his-mark-with-everything-he-did/. 0323. https://www.nytimes.com/interactive/projects/cp/us/orlando-shooting-victims/juan-chavez-martinez. 0323.

Laura Shipp was a regular at the restaurant where her son tended bar and served. She and her son were close enough that his friends called her "Mama Shipp."
https://www.nytimes.com/2017/10/02/us/vegas-victims-names.html. 0523.

John Swain was 40, and lived in Mesa, Arizona. He at one time had a job and family, including a wife and four daughters in Atlanta. https://www.azcentral.com/story/news/local/mesa-breaking/2023/05/28/suspect-identified-mesa-shooting-spree-linked-phoenix-homicide/70265292007/. 0723. https://www.themesatribune.com/news/killing-spree-ended-mesa-man-s-struggle-for-sobriety/article_997ac76e-01c4-11ee-9cfa-e32b3bb59e6c.html. 0723.

Samuel DuBose was a rapper, music producer, entrepreneur, and motorcycle enthusiast.
https://www.learntheirstories.com/#/samuel-dubose/. 0623.

Miriam Carey was born and raised in Brooklyn, and had a degree in dental hygiene and a degree in health nutrition. She worked as a dental hygienist, and lived in Stamford, Connecticut.
https://en.wikipedia.org/wiki/Killing_of_Miriam_Carey. 0723.

Randall Smith had been a pitcher on his high school baseball team, and was a fan of the Houston Astros. He was 26. https://www.washingtonpost.com/graphics/national/chattanooga-tennessee-shooting-victims/. 0923.

Aroohi Dheri. https://www.cnn.com/2022/10/07/us/merced-murders-american-nightmare/index.html. 0923.

Kiwane Carrington was born in Champaign, Illinois. He was a student at the READY Program school. He lived with his aunt. He was 15 years old. https://www.learntheirstories.com/#/kiwane-carrington/. 0623.

<1%: https://www.nbcnews.com/data-graphics/6-charts-show-rise-guns-us-people-dying-rcna30537. 0523.
>6%: https://www.motherjones.com/politics/2016/06/fully-loaded-ten-biggest-gun-manufacturers-america/. 0623.

No single remedy: Keane, *Violence and Democracy*, 13.
To "think democratically about the various possible remedies for violence… requires the recognition that there is in fact no one substance (like sodium bicarbonate or plutonium 239) that is called violence. It comes in a very wide range of forms…. It is more or less mediated by technical instruments, ranging from rocks and Molotov cocktails and rubber bullets to Stealth bombers, tanks and precision-guided nuclear weapons. And violence can also have many functions."

No simple solution: Mogul et al., *Queer (In)justice*, xx.
"The 'bad apple' theory — the idea that few rogue individuals are responsible for poisoning the barrel, and their identification and removal is the simple cure — cannot account for the historically pervasive, consistent, and persistent systemic violence that characterizes the criminal legal system. The barrel itself is rotten — that is to say, foundationally and systemically violent and unjust."

Violence, like any other: Frazer et al., "The Violence Epidemic," 13.
"By recognizing violence as a public health disorder and implementing key intervention and prevention strategies we can and will reduce the ramifications of this devastating disease in our communities."

81] • [82

Naeschylus Carter enjoyed family, friends, restoring cars and cooking. He had eight children and two stepchildren. https://taylormortuary.com/tribute/details/756/Naeschylus-Carter-Vinzant/obituary.html. 0823.

Tevin Crosby grew up in North Carolina, where he had been president of his high school's Future Business Leaders of America, and he lived in Saginaw, Michigan. https://www.clickorlando.com/news/2017/06/07/tevin-crosby-entrepreneur-always-there-with-advice-a-helping-hand/. 0323. https://www.nytimes.com/interactive/projects/cp/us/orlando-shooting-victims/tevin-eugene-crosby. 0323.

Carly Kreibaum studied art education at Wayne State College in Nebraska and worked at Walmart. https://www.nytimes.com/2017/10/02/us/vegas-victims-names.html. 0523.

Barbara Hawthorne was 68. She earned an Associate Degree in Computer Science, and a Bachelor Degree in Education. She worked at the Kellogg Company for more than 20 years. https://www.huffpost.com/entry/kalamazoo-michigan-shooting-victims_n_56ca49d9e4b041136f176d3a. 0723. https://www.legacy.com/us/obituaries/battlecreek/name/barbara-hawthorne-obituary?id=16834879. 0723.

Jonny Gammage had been born and raised in Syracuse, New York, but lived in Pittsburgh. He worked for his cousin, a professional football player. He had back trouble that limited his mobility. https://www.pittsburghmagazine.com/im-only-31-the-legacy-of-jonny-gammage/. 0623. https://www.syracuse.com/opinion/2020/06/remember-jonny-gammage-who-never-got-justice-commentary.html. 0623.

Danyale Johnson was part of a large extended family. She graduated from Booker T. Washington High School in 2002 and studied at University of Memphis. https://www.pghlesbian.com/2021/11/black-trans-woman-danyale-johnson-35-killed-in-memphis/. 0723.

Richard Linyard Jr. was 23, and had started writing raps when he was 8. https://www.sfgate.com/crime/article/Man-who-died-during-Oakland-police-chase-mourned-6398121.php. 0623. https://www.learntheirstories.com/#/richard-linyard-jr/. 0623.

Thomas Sullivan had served two tours in Iraq, and received two purple hearts. He was originally from Springfield, Massachusetts, went by "Tommy," and was 40 years old. https://www.washingtonpost.com/graphics/national/chattanooga-tennessee-shooting-victims/. 0923.

Jasdeep Singh and his brother owned and operated a trucking and dispatch company in Merced, California. https://www.cnn.com/2022/10/07/us/merced-murders-american-nightmare/index.html. 0923.

Reginald Clay Jr. was known to his loved ones as "Lil Red." He was 24, and had a three-year-old daughter. https://blockclubchicago.org/2023/04/18/after-cops-kill-24-year-old-west-side-man-during-chase-devastated-family-demands-answers/. 0923.

11: https://news.yahoo.com/police-killing-anthony-lowe-double-163346472.html. 0723.
17: https://abc7.com/eduardo-edwin-rodriguez-lawsuit-filed-la-county-sheriffs-department-lasd-east-man-killed-by-deputies/1416509/. 0723.
34: https://www.theguardian.com/us-news/2019/aug/15/police-shootings-los-angeles-sheriffs-department-ryan-twyman. 0723.
39: https://en.wikipedia.org/wiki/Killing_of_Kathryn_Johnston. 0723.

Bullets kill: Kreuter, "Muzzle Velocity," 36-37.
"[K]illing power is generally determined by two factors: the mass of the projectile and the velocity as which the projectile is traveling. There are limits to how much mass can exist in a bullet.

Bullets are sized precisely for their firearms.... The AR-15, implicated in many recent mass-shooting events, is a somewhat unusual weapon in that instead of balancing bullet mass and muzzle velocity, it utilizes a relatively unmassive projectile but sends it downrange at a very high speed.... [T]he AR-15 is a particularly deadly weapon not because of its power, but because of its velocity."

"The most effective guns: Browder, *Her Best Shot*, 231-32.
In its original context, the passage ends in a colon rather than a period. Its author continues: "real guns are highly destructive to women and their worlds.... Guns are perhaps the best cultural example of how the imaginary and the real cannot be conflated: there is a fatal world of difference between props in fantasies and real guns that have the power to kill."

"[W]here there are no guns: Boss, *Guns and College Homicide*, 128.

82] • [83

Nicholas Dyksma was 18. He had one sister, and lived in Columbus, Georgia. https://www.wrbl.com/news/local-news/parents-of-nicholas-dyksma-speak-on-sons-police-involved-death/. 0723.

Joseph Murphy was born and raised in Alaska. He worked various jobs, at his local housing authority, school district, and fire department, and with the National Park Service. After his military service he suffered from PTSD and substance abuse. He loved hunting and fishing, playing cards with his mother-in-law, eating his wife's home cooking, his black lab Buster Joe, Christmas lights, driving his Silverado, dancing, good music, snowstorms, the NFL and the NBA, the Denver Broncos, snowmobiling, the U.S. military, cowboy movies, playing pool, TV and anything electronic, his Yupik culture and God. https://www.legacy.com/us/obituaries/juneauempire/name/joseph-murphy-obituary?id=21885683. 0723.

Deonka Drayton's fashion tastes included Michael Kors and Air Jordans. She liked poetry and music and basketball. https://thompsonsfuneral.com/tribute/details/51378/Deonka-Drayton/obituary.html. 0323. https://www.npr.org/2017/06/09/531945236/what-one-family-lost-in-pulse-nightclub-a-year-ago. 0323.

Christopher Roybal worked as a manager in a gym. He loved to sing, and enjoyed karaoke. His favorite singers were Luis Miguel and Christian Castro. https://www.reuters.com/article/us-lasvegas-shooting-veteran-idUSKCN1C82TG. 0523. https://www.findagrave.com/memorial/183925374/christopher-louis-roybal. 0523.

Tyler Smith was 17, and a senior in high school. His passion was soccer, and he played goalie and forward on several travel soccer clubs. He loved cars, and he loved pulling all-nighters watching movies, drinking energy drinks, listening to music and playing video games with his cousins. https://people.com/crime/kalamazoo-shooting-family-and-friends-remember-tyler-and-richard-smith/. 0723. https://obits.mlive.com/us/obituaries/kalamazoo/name/tyler-smith-obituary?id=16826590. 0723.

CoCo Chanel Wortham was also known as "Miss CoCo." She was frequently in encampment areas of downtown Dallas with other unhoused persons. https://www.hrc.org/news/hrc-mourns-miss-coco-transgender-woman-of-color-killed-in-dallas. 0723.

Dante Parker was 36. He and his wife had five children. https://www.learntheirstories.com/#/dante-parker/. 0623.

Squire Wells went by "Skip." In high school he had played clarinet in marching band and concert band. He held the rank of Lance Corporal. He was a devout Christian. He was 21. https://www.washingtonpost.com/graphics/national/chattanooga-tennessee-shooting-victims/. 0923.

Amandeep Singh came to the U.S. from Punjab, India. With his brother, he owned and operated a trucking and dispatch company in Merced, California. He and his wife had two children. He was 39. https://www.cnn.com/2022/10/07/us/merced-murders-american-nightmare/index.html. 0923.

Shereese Francis was 30, and studied at Nassau Community College in Queens, NY, hoping to become a physical therapist. She had been diagnosed with schizophrenia. https://www.learntheirstories.com/#/shereese-francis/. 0623.

4: Children's Defense Fund, *Protect Children, Not Guns 2019*.

L'état: Gramsci, *Prison Notebooks* I, 361.
"What is the police? It certainly is not just that particular official organization which is juridically recognized and empowered to carry out the public function of public safety, as it is normally understood. This organism is the central and formally responsible nucleus of the 'police,' which is a much larger organization in which a large part of the state's population participates directly or indirectly through links that are more or less precise and limited, permanent or occasional, etc. The analysis of these relations, much more than many philosophical juridical dissertations, helps one understand what the 'state' is."

Police shooting: Farrell and Monk-Turner, "Placing Police Shootings in Context," 454.
"It is surprising that, in a country known for demanding official accountability and governmental transparency, there is little empirical data on police shootings. These incidents are the manifestation of the ultimate form of coercion available to the state: the ability to invoke death to assure compliance."

It is a *task* to come to see: Ritchie, *Invisible No More*, 11, 15.
"Black women, and their responses to white male authority, have been policed in brutal and deadly ways ever since the formation of slave patrols in the mid-eighteenth century….
Expanding our understanding of the forms and contexts of police violence experienced by

women and gender-nonconforming people of color enables us to better understand the full shape and reach of state violence in ways essential to countering it."

83] • [84

Kaylin Gillis loved animals, especially goats and dolphins. She was a Disney fan, and her favorite characters were Mickey Mouse and Stitch. Her favorite foods included tacos, cheeseburgers, and ice cream. She was 20, and had two sisters. https://www.legacy.com/us/obituaries/saratogian/name/kaylin-gillis-obituary?id=51669458. 0723.

Leroy Fernandez went by Roy. On social media he described himself as a dancer, stylist, and fashion enthusiast. https://www.npr.org/sections/thetwo-way/2016/06/12/481785763/heres-what-we-know-about-the-orlando-shooting-victims. 0323.

Alprentice Carter was born in Shreveport, Louisiana, but in childhood moved with his family to Los Angeles. He attended UCLA, and worked for a period for the Teen Post anti-poverty program in L.A. Umoja, "Carter, Alprentice," n.p.

Jordan McIldoon rode a Harley, and drove a diesel pickup. He liked to play hockey, snowboard, and snowmobile in the winter, and ride dirt bikes or wakeboard in the summer. https://www.bustle.com/p/who-was-jordan-mcildoon-the-23-year-old-died-in-a-bystanders-arms-2754238. 0523. https://macleans.ca/news/canada/how-las-vegas-shooting-victim-jordan-mcildoon-didnt-die-alone/. 0523. https://www.theglobeandmail.com/news/national/family-and-friends-of-four-canadian-victims-of-las-vegas-shooting-share-their-losses/article36466880/. 0523.

Mary Lou Nye worked part time at a preschool and childcare program. Mary Jo Nye had been retired for four years from her work at an alternative high school teaching English to at-risk teens. https://www.huffpost.com/entry/kalamazoo-michigan-shooting-victims_n_56ca49d9e4b041136f176d3a. 0723.

Jessica Nelson Williams had five children, who were being raised by a sister. https://www.sfgate.com/bayarea/article/SFPD-sergeant-in-fatal-shooting-of-woman-is-7950410.php. 0723.

Edwin Rajo liked "chilling" with friends: playing soccer, smoking marijuana, drinking, and playing the video game Grand Theft Auto. Younge, *Another Day in the Death of America.*

David Wyatt's deployments included Iraq and Afghanistan. He and his wife had one daughter and one son. He was 35. https://www.legacy.com/us/obituaries/legacyremembers/david-wyatt-obituary?id=17276991. 0923. https://www.washingtonpost.com/graphics/national/chattanooga-tennessee-shooting-victims/. 0923.

Monica Delgado had two sons and a daughter. https://www.legacy.com/us/obituaries/name/monica-aviles-obituary?id=36702586. 0923.

Ramarley Graham was born in the Bronx and went to school at the Young Scholars Academy. He aspired to eventually travel the world and become a veterinarian. He loved watching Animal Planet, and as a child had asked for a pet monkey. He often walked his younger brother home from school. He was 18. https://www.learntheirstories.com/#/ramarley-graham/. 0623. https://www.theguardian.com/world/2019/aug/24/police-killings-families-ramarley-graham-terence-crutcher-tamir-rice. 0623.

51.6: Imai et al., "Firearm Presence," 783.
31: U.S. General Accounting Office, 1991 study, as cited in Younge, *Another Day*, 115.

The myth of heroic power: Utter, "Accessories Included," 372.
"This national failure of imagination has doomed us to try to reproduce at the personal level the same old mythology of heroic power through violence. The individual armed hero is not a solution to national malaise, but a symptom of it, and the tragedy of our current situation is that to strike the noble pose of assuming individual responsibility for protection of the people is to abnegate responsibility for larger and much more courageous societal change."

Rampant violence: Toplin, *Unchallenged Violence*, 12.
"The more uncontrolled violence grows, the more obsessed individuals become with two extreme options: to run away completely or to make a stand by 'fighting fire with fire.'"

The violence we use: Elias, "A Culture of Violent Solutions," 118.
"On various levels, violence is standard behavior in U.S. society.... [V]iolence is viewed as a legitimate means of solving problems, even if the problem is violence itself. To address a problem seriously, we must declare war. Arguably, we are a culture of violent solutions. Indeed, the usue of violence to solve social and other problems comprises a large portion of the violence we commit in U.S. society."

84] • [85

Aiyana Jones. https://en.wikipedia.org/wiki/Killing_of_Aiyana_Jones. 0323. https://sayhernamenow.wordpress.com/2020/09/07/aiyana-monay-stanley-jones/. 0323.

Novaa Watson was a 23-year-old trans man who had been born and raised in Baltimore, but lived in Lynchburg, Virginia. He was a student at Morgan State University. https://www.hrc.org/news/hrc-mourns-ej-boykin-aka-novaa-watson-black-transgender-man-killed-in-lynchburg-virginia. 0923. https://www.gaysonoma.com/2021/06/trans-man-shot-dead-in-the-street-in-broad-daylight-his-name-was-novaa-ru-watson/. 0923.

Peter Gonzalez-Cruz lived in Orlando, Florida, where he had grown up. https://www.orlandoweekly.com/news/remembering-the-orlando-49-peter-o-gonzalez-cruz-4309598. 0323.

Tara Roe worked as an education assistant in her local school district in Okotoks, Alberta, and as a model for a modelling and talent agency. https://calgaryherald.com/news/local-news/okotoks-mother-tara-roe-is-third-albertan-killed-in-las-vegas-attack/. 0523. https://www.findagrave.com/memorial/184474930/tara-ann-roe. 0523.

Richard Smith was 53. He was a high school graduate, and attended Denver Automotive & Diesel College before returning to his home state of Michigan. He and his wife had two children. His specialties as a chef were cheesy potatoes, brookies, and a secret BBQ rib recipe that only he knew. He grew up on the Silver Lake Sand Dunes riding motorcycles, ATVs and dune buggies. He also enjoyed downhill skiing, snowmobiling and jet skiing anything with a throttle. https://obits.mlive.com/us/obituaries/kalamazoo/name/richard-smith-obituary?id=16837205. 0723.

Andrew Alan Myers did three tours in Iraq, achieved the rank of Sergeant, and was awarded two Army Commendation Medals. https://www.findagrave.com/memorial/154912065/andrew-alan-myers. 0823.

Denis Reyes was born in Puerto Rico, but was raised in the Bronx. He was 40. https://www.theguardian.com/us-news/2015/jun/03/denis-reyes-the-counted-nypd. 0823. https://www.theguardian.com/us-news/2015/jun/14/denis-reyes-nypd-the-counted-family-mourns. 0823.

William Love was a retired Army First Sergeant with 27 years of service, including one tour in Vietnam. He and his wife had two daughters, eight grandchildren, and six great-grandchildren. He was 73. https://www.cnn.com/2022/06/02/us/tulsa-shooting-victims-what-we-know/index.html. 0923. https://www.tributearchive.com/obituaries/25031306/william-lee-love. 0923.

Miguel Avila was nearing his 16th birthday. https://www.legacy.com/us/obituaries/name/miguel-avila-obituary?id=36702590. 0923.

Marquiisha Lawrence was a 28-year-old trans woman who lived in Greenville, South Carolina. https://www.wyff4.com/article/family-friends-remember-murdered-trans-woman-who-loved-hair-nails-travel-and-cooking/38337986#. 0923.

60: Dahlberg, et al., "Guns in the Home," 929.
2/3: Pirelli, Wechsler, and Cramer, *The Behavioral Science of Firearms*, 458.

Communities pay less: "The Report of Governor Bill Owens' Columbine Review Commission (2001)," as presented in Schildkraut, *Mass Shootings in America*, 254.
"The task of coping with school rage is rendered even more difficult by the fact that our schools have become larger and larger in both number of students and building capacity. Large schools are generally preferred by state and local governments because of their fiscal advantages in terms of land and construction costs; one large school facility is less expensive to a community than two or three smaller facilities. Nevertheless, recent studies document the fact that a community pays a

price for larger schools: Students at large schools tend to feel marginalized and less a part of a school community in comparison to their counterparts in smaller facilities."

Patterns of violence: Spina, "Introduction," 5.
"American schools, like American cities, are segregated racially, politically, and economically. Ethnic and racial minorities have always been disproportionately represented in the incidence and depiction of violence."

To cut down on school shootings: Klein and Chancer, "Masculinity Matters," 152-3, 155.
"Recent school shootings are only extreme ramifications of the stark divisions between what is considered 'feminine' and what is considered 'masculine.' Alternative emotional expressions have been virtually inaccessible to many young boys.... [We need to] address the destructive hierarchies, overpowering needs, homophobic abuse, and unattainable masculine expectations the boys [who perpetrated these shootings] at one level set out to destroy. Though they did so wrongfully and criminally, the boys vented their rage and demanded a change in the social structures that oppressed them. They made their anguish painfully clear. Ignoring their words and deeds jeopardizes the future of all our children."

85] • [86

Chyna Carrillo was a trans woman who was also known as Chyna Cardena. She was a certified nursing assistant, and had recently moved from Arkansas to Pennsylvania. https://www.advocate.com/crime/2021/2/22/transgender-woman-chyna-carrillo-beaten-death-pennsylvania. 0923.

Keaton Farris grew up on Lopez and Whidbey islands in Washington. He suffered from mental health issues, and had been diagnosed with bipolar disorder. https://www.heraldnet.com/news/former-jail-guards-sentenced-in-dehydration-death-of-inmate/. 0823. https://www.whidbeynewstimes.com/news/family-holds-vigil-for-man-who-died-in-island-county-jail/. 0823.

Juan Guerrero was from a Dominican family, and was in his third year at the University of Central Florida. He worked as a service representative in the credit card department of a bank. https://www.orlandoweekly.com/news/remembering-the-orlando-49-juan-ramon-guerrero-2521176. 0323. https://www.nytimes.com/interactive/projects/cp/us/orlando-shooting-victims/juan-ramon-guerrero. 0323.

Sonny Melton and his wife, to whom he had been married for one year, lived in Tennessee. https://people.com/human-interest/vegas-shooting-heather-melton-remembers-husband-sonny/. 0523.

Dorothy Brown was 74, and had two adult sons. She had a B.A. from Western Michigan University. For a period, she worked as a caseworker for the Area Agency on Aging. https://www.huffpost.com/entry/kalamazoo-michigan-shooting-victims_n_56ca49d9e4b041136f176d3a. 0723.

https://www.legacy.com/us/obituaries/battlecreek/name/dorothy-brown-obituary?id=16834940. 0723.

Sinthanouxay Khottavongsa was 57. He made a living over the years as a cook and handyman, working manufacturing jobs and rehabbing houses. He settled in St. Paul's Frogtown neighborhood 20 years ago and was fond of gardening, cooking traditional Laotian laab, going to church, and teaching his children about the building trades. https://www.startribune.com/re-traumatized-family-of-man-killed-in-2015-brooklyn-center-police-encounter-calls-for-change/600047013/. 0823.

Christy Galella lived in a sobriety house, recovering from addiction to painkillers that started after she underwent gastric bypass surgery. https://www.cbsnews.com/colorado/news/colorado-springs-gunman-was-33-year-old-recovering-alcoholic/. 0823. https://apnews.com/article/d6813bb883024167b40fe31952947018. 0823.

Preston Phillips worked as an orthopedic surgeon specializing in spinal surgery, joint reconstruction, and fracture treatment. He went annually on a medical mission to Africa with a nonprofit organization, providing medical care to underserved populations. He enjoyed jazz. He was 59 years old. https://www.cnn.com/2022/06/02/us/tulsa-shooting-victims-what-we-know/index.html. 0923. https://news.yahoo.com/doctor-loved-jazz-mother-two-182731164.html. 0923.

Natallie Avila was 14. https://www.tributearchive.com/obituaries/26043969/natallie-nicole-avila. 0923.

Kenneth Chamberlain was a retired Marine who had worked for the Westchester County Department of Corrections for 20 years. He lived in White Plains, New York. https://www.learntheirstories.com/#/kenneth-chamberlain/. 0623.

55: https://washingtonsblog.com/youre-55-times-more-likely-to-be-killed-by-a-police-officer-than-a-terrorist/. 0423.

Violence is not essence: Guattari, *The Three Ecologies*, 38.
"Violence and negativity are the products of complex subjective assemblages; they are not intrinsically inscribed in the essence of the human species, but are constructed and maintained by multiple assemblages of enunciation."

Violence is *made*: Henry A. Giroux, in Evans and Lennart, *Violence*, 67.
"Once ignorance is weaponized, violence seems to be a tragic inevitability. The mass shooting in Orlando is yet another example of an emerging global political and cultural climate of violence fed by hate and mass hysteria. Such violence legitimates not only a kind of inflammatory rhetoric and ideological fundamentalism that views violence as the only solution to addressing social issues, it also provokes further irrational acts of violence against others. Spurred on by a complete disrespect for those who affirm different ways of living, this massacre points to a growing climate of hate and bigotry that is unapologetic in its political nihilism."

Being legitimated: Gayatri Chakravorty Spivak, in Evans and Lennart, *Violence*, 79.
"When dealing with violence deemed unreasonable, the dominating groups demonize violent responses, saying that 'those other people are just like that,' not just that they are worth less but also that they are essentially evil, essentially criminal, or essentially have a religion that is prone to killing.

Yet, on the other side, state-legitimized violence, considered 'reasonable' by many, is altogether more frightening. Such violence argues that if a person wears a certain kind of clothing or belongs to a particular background, he or she is legally killable. Such violence is more alarming because it is continuously justified by those in power."

86] • [87

Alvin Haynes had been participating in a drug treatment program while he was incarcerated. He was 57. https://www.sfgate.com/crime/article/Inmate-s-family-seeks-answer-in-his-jail-death-6427028.php. 0823.

Victor Villalpando had been accepted into a state-chartered high school for the arts after successfully auditioning for its dance program. He was an instructor for a performing arts education nonprofit in his hometown.
https://www.santafenewmexican.com/news/local_news/family-friends-question-boy-s-death-at-hands-of-police/article_85c7167b-48f9-5efa-993e-f46711a01ee6.html. 0723.

Frank Hernández grew up in Weslaco, Texas, and worked as a manager at a designer clothing store in Florida. He loved Beyoncé, dancing, traveling to South Padre Island, and Mexican food. https://www.orlandoweekly.com/news/remembering-the-orlando-49-frank-hernandez-escalante-3467057. 0323.

Lisa Romero-Muniz had worked most recently as a high school secretary. She was the mother of three grown children. https://www.nytimes.com/2017/10/02/us/vegas-victims-names.html. 0523.

Leonard Deadwyler was born in Gainesville, Georgia, and grew up as the oldest of three siblings in his family. https://en.wikipedia.org/wiki/Shooting_of_Leonard_Deadwyler. 0323.

Kellie Pyle and her high school sweetheart planned to marry. She had two adult children in their 20s and a young granddaughter. She was 52. https://www.nbcconnecticut.com/news/national-international/these-are-the-victims-of-the-virginia-walmart-shooting/2922633/. 0723.

Jennifer Vasquez was 42, and a lifelong resident of Colorado Springs, Colorado.
https://obits.gazette.com/us/obituaries/gazette/name/jennifer-vasquez-obituary?id=15676402. 0823.

Stephanie Husen's rescue dogs had been named Boomer and Sooner. She had one niece and four nephews. https://www.cnn.com/2022/06/02/us/tulsa-shooting-victims-what-we-know/index.html. 0923. https://www.hayhurstfuneralhome.com/obituaries/Stephanie-Husen/#!/Obituary. 0923.

Lorena Aviles was active with the American Cancer Society. After it helped her uninsured brother-in-law with medical expenses, she became a Board member and helped raise funds for the organization so it could help another family. https://meaww.com/texas-shooting-family-of-lori-aviles-natalie-pay-heartbreaking-tribute-to-victims-killed. 0923.

Vickie Lee Jones was 67, a widow with two sons and many grandchildren. She liked to travel and was a dedicated member of her church. https://www.legacy.com/news/celebrity-deaths/jeffersontown-kentucky-shooting-victims-2018/. 0823.

68.2: By "involving domestic violence," meaning specifically "the perpetrator either shot or killed at least one partner or family member or had a history of DV." Geller, Booty, and Crifasi, "The Role of Domestic Violence," 5.
83.7: For the years 2014-2019. By "case fatality rate" meaning the percentage of injuries that result in death. Geller, Booty, and Crifasi, "The Role of Domestic Violence," 5.

"[G]uns transform: Obert, Poe, and Sarat, "The Lives of Guns," 4.

"Gun and gunner: Luke, "Counting Up AR-51s," 87.
Luke elaborates: "The shooter and the gun are perhaps symbionts. Gun and gunner are co-constituting subjectivities, once readied, prepared, and joined by ownership, instruction, and use. Neither can really come to be fully without the other. As some suggest, weapons define subjects. So human subjects armed with different weapon objects gain varied capacities, powers, and identities, as well as diverse allies, deterrents, and targets by becoming spearmen, swordsmen, axemen, clubmen, bowmen, or gunmen."

Its being *strong* does not prevent: Blithe and Lanterman, "Subcultural Variability," 163-64.
"Members of stigmatized or hidden collectives can manage stigma reduction through schizo- and protean identifications. Individuals maintain a positive self-identity by disidentifying with some aspects of gun culture that conflict with their personal values, or by identifying specifically with their chosen subculture, disidentifying from others. At the same time, they can enjoy the benefits, which come from a strong identification with a collective, such as increased self-esteem, self-distinctiveness, and safety. By selectively disidentifying with some aspects of the collective, individuals can avoid the stigma attached to it. At the same time, they can avoid disidentifying with the entire collective and still enjoy a strongly identified position. Because belonging is so important to individuals, practices that help individuals manage conflicting identities are useful to identify and cultivate, particularly for individuals with attachments to controversial collectives. It is important for people who feel belonging with stigmatized groups to have a means through which to both identify and also to distance themselves from the stigma."

87] • [88

Anthony Lee, 39, had an extensive acting career that included stage productions and guest roles on television shows, such as *ER* and *Brooklyn South*, and in films, such as *Liar Liar*.

https://www.learntheirstories.com/#/anthony-lee/. 0623.
https://en.wikipedia.org/wiki/Anthony_Lee_(actor). 0623.

Miguel Honorato's family businesses included a restaurant and catering business. He enjoyed soccer. https://www.orlandoweekly.com/news/remembering-the-pulse-49-miguel-andaacutengel-honorato-2555180. 0323.

Deborah Danner had a BS in computer science from the New York Institute of Technology. She was 66, and lived in the Bronx. https://www.blackpast.org/african-american-history/people-african-american-history/deborah-j-danner-1950-2016/. 0723.
https://www.nytimes.com/interactive/2016/10/19/nyregion/document-Living-With-Schizophrenia-by-Deborah-Danner.html. 0723.

Pati Mestas loved country music. She spent all the time she could with her three children, eight grandchildren, and one great-grandchild. https://www.nytimes.com/2017/10/02/us/vegas-victims-names.html. 0523.

Randy Blevins began working at Walmart after it put the five-and-dime he owned with his wife out of business. He worked the overnight shift as a stocker. He attended Norfolk Admirals hockey games. He had three stepdaughters. https://www.nbcconnecticut.com/news/national-international/these-are-the-victims-of-the-virginia-walmart-shooting/2922633/. 0723.

Jose Romero's wife and four children still lived in Mexico.
https://www.reuters.com/world/us/california-shooting-victims-who-died-monterey-park-half-moon-bay-attacks-2023-01-26/. 0823.

LaVena Johnson was stationed in Iraq. She was from Florrisant, Missouri, and had enlisted in the military to earn money for college. She had been an honor student in high school. She had four siblings. https://exhibits.stanford.edu/saytheirnames/feature/lavena-johnson. 0823.
https://news.stlpublicradio.org/government-politics-issues/2015-07-19/10-years-later-a-soldiers-family-still-grieves-and-questions-the-armys-version-of-her-death. 0823.

Amanda Glenn and her husband had two sons. They lived in Tulsa, Oklahoma. She was a fan of University of Oklahoma football and St. Louis Cardinals baseball. She was 40 years old.
https://www.cnn.com/2022/06/02/us/tulsa-shooting-victims-what-we-know/index.html. 0923.
https://news.yahoo.com/doctor-loved-jazz-mother-two-182731164.html. 0923.

Natalie Aviles had used her banana bread as a fundraiser to help a local family who had lost their sole financial provider. https://meaww.com/texas-shooting-family-of-lori-aviles-natalie-pay-heartbreaking-tribute-to-victims-killed. 0923.

Jesse LePore was 9. https://www.gofundme.com/f/in-memory-of-jennifer-sean-and-jesse-lepore. 0923. https://www.al.com/news/huntsville/2023/01/alabama-child-dead-in-tennessee-murder-suicide-recalled-as-exceptional-racer-with-stern-father.html. 0923.

25: https://www.businessinsider.com/insider-investigation-5-years-of-transgender-homicides-2022-12#insider-compiled-a-comprehensive-account-of-the-rising-fatal-violence-targeting-transgender-people-1. 0323.

The more wars the state fights: Balko, *Rise of the Warrior Cop*, 42.
"No one made a decision to militarize the police in America. The change has come slowly, the result of a generation of politicians and public officials fanning and exploiting public fears by declaring war on abstractions like crime, drug use, and terrorism. The resulting policies have made those war metaphors increasingly real."

Police *have* partnered: Gebo, "Intersectoral Violence," 1.
"Community violence prevention is both a public health and criminal justice issue. Public health systems emphasize primary prevention and criminal justice systems address violence at secondary and tertiary levels. Better partnering between public health and criminal justice may be one way to leverage benefits of both approaches to realize violence reduction gains."

To end police violence: Ritchie, "Say Her Name," 88-89.
"Centering women and trans people's experiences… will push us beyond police reform to a radical reimagination of public safety. When we begin to understand that police are a significant source of violence against women and LGBTQ people of color — even as they are promoted as our protectors — we must question whether countering police violence is really a question of dealing with a few 'bad apples' or problematic policies. Challenging police violence requires a challenge to the institutional structure itself, which is deeply rooted in policing the boundaries of race, gender, sexuality, poverty and nation."

88] • [89

Donovan Lewis was a high school graduate who had played middle linebacker and tight end on his high school football team. https://news.yahoo.com/columbus-police-change-warrant-policy-161011639.html. 0723.

Javier Jorge-Reyes worked as a manager at a Gucci store. He had been born in Puerto Rico. His friends called him "Javi." https://www.orlandoweekly.com/news/remembering-the-orlando-49-javier-jorge-reyes-2914592. 0323.
https://www.nytimes.com/interactive/projects/cp/us/orlando-shooting-victims/javier-jorge-reyes. 0323.

Quinton Robbins worked for the for the Henderson, Nevada Parks and Recreation Department, where he was in charge of setting up recreational leagues for children.
https://lasvegassun.com/news/2021/oct/01/family-legacy-son-mass-shooting-playing-forward/. 0523.

Brian Pendleton had been a Walmart employee for 10 years, and worked the overnight shift as a custodian. He was 38. https://www.nbcconnecticut.com/news/national-international/these-are-the-victims-of-the-virginia-walmart-shooting/2922633/. 0723.

Marciano Martinez-Jimenez was born in Oaxaca, Mexico, but had lived in California for more than twenty years. He was 50. https://www.reuters.com/world/us/california-shooting-victims-who-died-monterey-park-half-moon-bay-attacks-2023-01-26/. 0823. https://www.kron4.com/news/bay-area/what-we-know-about-the-half-moon-bay-mass-shooting-victims/. 0823.

Rikkey Outumuro was 39, and the oldest of three siblings. She attended the Centralia Beauty College, and earned her Cosmetology license, and then later attended Centralia College, where she earned her General Studies Degree. After working for various upscale salons, she worked out of her home. She was once the reigning Miss Gay Olympia. https://www.legacy.com/us/obituaries/name/rikkey-outumuro-obituary?id=31773811. 0723.

Melissa Dunham was a partner in an accounting firm, and specialized in corporate tax returns. She had earned an MBA from Kent State University, and an MTax from the University of Akron. She was certified to teach archery. She was 42, and the mother of three children. https://www.cantonrep.com/story/news/2023/08/25/carnation-ave-uniontown-ohio-lake-township-murder-suicide-five-people-found/70676411007/. 0923. https://www.hopkinslawver.com/obituaries/melissa-renee-amber-and-evan-dunham. 0923.

Abdoulaye Thiam had moved with his family from Senegal to the U.S. when he was 10. https://www.lhamar.org/say-their-names-biography/abdoulaye-thiam. 0623.

Douglas Dulmage and his wife owned a farm in Leeds, North Dakota. https://www.thenelsonfuneralhome.com/obituary/douglas-doug-dulmage. 0923.

Keith Lamont Scott had worked as a security guard at a mall before suffering multiple injuries in a severe motorcycle accident. He liked to read while he waited for his son's school bus. https://www.cnn.com/2016/09/22/us/keith-lamont-scott/index.html. 0623. https://www.learntheirstories.com/#/keith-lamont-scott/. 0623.

21: https://www.propublica.org/article/deadly-force-in-black-and-white. 0423.
28: Eisen-Martin, "We Charge Genocide Again!" 3. http://www.operationghettostorm.org/uploads/1/9/1/1/19110795/we_charge_genocide_again_final.pdf. 0423.

Gun violence is shameless: Scheff and Retzinger, *Emotions and Violence*, 187.
"[T]he social system creates destructive violence to the extent that *alienation and shame go unacknowledged*."

Tragedy resists: Simon Critchley, in Evans and Lennart, *Violence*, 24-25.
"The great virtue of ancient tragedy is that it allowed the Greeks to see their role in a history of violence and war that was to some extent of their own making. It also allowed them to imagine a suspension of that cycle of violence.... The slim sliver of hope I have is that the same could be true of us. To see the bloody events of the contemporary world in a tragic light exposes us to a disorder that is not just someone else's disorder."

Exclusive attention: Gilligan, *Violence*, 6.
"If we limit ourselves to the mode of discourse of the criminal legal process in the courtroom, only two questions about violence are admissible: how to distinguish the innocent from the guilty (the 'good guys' from the 'bad guys'); and the guilty from the criminally insane (the 'bad guys' from the 'mad guys'). The problem with this discourse is that it limits our capacity both to understand violence and to prevent it. This moral, legal framework, which is the existing arena of jurisprudence, judgment, and punishment, often leads to the aggravation of violence and its perpetuation, rather than deterring it."

89] • [90

Alberto Sepulveda was 11 years old, and in the seventh grade.
https://www.latimes.com/archives/la-xpm-2001-feb-23-mn-29219-story.html. 0723.
http://www.theppsc.org/Archives/Firearms-Safety/swat_officer_kills_boy.htm. 0723.

Jason Josaphat graduated from high school in Arizona. He had a business office specialist certificate from a technical institute, and he liked photography.
https://www.orlandoweekly.com/news/remembering-the-orlando-49-jason-benjamin-josaphat-2538320. 0323.

Austin Meyer wanted one day to have his own auto repair shop.
https://www.nytimes.com/2017/10/02/us/vegas-victims-names.html. 0523.

Fernando Jesus Chavez was 16, and had recently gotten his drivers license. He was an honor student in his junior year of high school. He had three brothers and a sister.
https://www.nbcconnecticut.com/news/national-international/these-are-the-victims-of-the-virginia-walmart-shooting/2922633/. 0723.
https://www.tributearchive.com/obituaries/26478004/fernando-jesus-chavez/chesapeake/virginia/oman-funeral-home. 0723.

Yetao Bing was an only child. He had immigrated from China to the U.S. He had a son in college, and a 4-year-old daughter. https://www.kron4.com/news/bay-area/what-we-know-about-the-half-moon-bay-mass-shooting-victims/. 0823.

Sean LePore was 11. https://www.gofundme.com/f/in-memory-of-jennifer-sean-and-jesse-lepore. 0923. https://www.al.com/news/huntsville/2023/01/alabama-child-dead-in-tennessee-murder-suicide-recalled-as-exceptional-racer-with-stern-father.html. 0923.

Renee Dunham was 15, and in the ninth grade. She loved reading, videogames, and drawing.
https://www.cantonrep.com/story/news/2023/08/25/carnation-ave-uniontown-ohio-lake-township-murder-suicide-five-people-found/70676411007/. 0923.
https://www.hopkinslawyer.com/obituaries/melissa-renee-amber-and-evan-dunham. 0923.

Bich Cau Thi Tran immigrated to America in 1997. She had worked at an automobile manufacturing company. She was petite: 4' 9" tall, and 98 pounds. She spoke little English. She had a history of mental health problems, and had been hospitalized at least three times for mental health issues. https://asamnews.com/2021/11/29/a-grand-jury-cleared-a-san-jose-police-officer-of-any-wrongdoing-for-shooting-a-woman-waving-a-vegetable-peeler/. 0723. https://en.wikipedia.org/wiki/Shooting_of_Bich_Cau_Thi_Tran. 0723.

Justin Bracken enjoyed snowmobiling, fishing, annual sausage making, gardening, and cooking and spending time at the lake. https://www.thenelsonfuneralhome.com/obituary/justin-r-bracken. 0923.

Joseph Taylor was 33, and lived in Shreveport, Louisiana. https://www.ksla.com/2023/04/25/officers-involved-killing-my-son-i-want-justice-says-mother-man-killed-during-traffic-stop/. 0923.

44: Zimring, *When Police Kill*, 8. Zimring notes that "the volume of police killings is understated probably by half."

Mass murder: Simpson, "Breaking the Mirror," 1109.
"Mass murder can be understood as the ecstasy of simulated experience, its violent countertransference, constituting a zone of indistinction between the spectacle and the real, killing and being killed."

Violence feeds: Keane, *Reflections on Violence*, 116.
"Among the least obvious ways in which the fragile openness of civil societies contributes to their apparently violent character is the way in which their sophisticated means of public and private communication ensure images of violence are circulated more or less freely to large numbers of people. That is to say, freedom of communication within civil society ensures that violence can [be] and is often turned into entertainment, that is, made the object of popular fascination, thrill and pleasure. The anomic violence that is regularly produced within civil societies is not always, and sometimes rarely, experienced as loss or a lapse into nothingness. The hard fact is that violence can be experienced as pleasure, as fulfilment, as a form of excitement that tickles the fancy of not only the violated — expressed in masochistic pleasure — but also the violent and the witnesses of acts of violence. Individuals who are violent, alone with their victims, sometimes treat their actions as entertainment."

Too much too-visible violence: Strain, *Reload*, 115.
"In casting a blind eye on the violence that surrounds us, we have in fact perfected a kind of superviolence, actualized in gun deaths and honed in ultraviolent entertainment, that desensitizes empathy — so much so, that it becomes nearly impossible to see how destructive this violence really is."

90] • [91

Patrick Warren started his business after he was laid off from his factory job during the Coronavirus pandemic. He was 52.
https://www.legacy.com/us/obituaries/theeagle/name/patrick-warren-obituary?id=7417758.

0623. https://www.nbcnews.com/news/us-news/texas-family-calls-officer-s-arrest-after-man-fatally-shot-n1254297. 0623.

Eddie Justice went by a nickname he created for himself, Brycen Banks. He lived, in his mother's words, "in a sky house, like the Jeffersons." https://www.orlandoweekly.com/news/remembering-the-orlando-49-eddie-justice-2505698. 0323.

Jennifer Parks went by "Jenny." She coached volleyball. She had married her high school sweetheart, and they had two children. https://people.com/crime/las-vegas-shooting-jenny-parks-bobby-perfect-family/. 0523. https://www.nytimes.com/2017/10/02/us/vegas-victims-names.html. 0523.

Chance Ross had been diagnosed with paranoid schizophrenia and other mental illnesses. https://www.findagrave.com/memorial/143539084/tony-chance-ross. 0823. https://www.prisonlegalnews.org/news/2018/apr/2/415000-settlement-lawsuit-over-tasered-prisoner-who-died-texas-jail/. 0823.

Tyneka Johnson was a 22-year-old high school graduate who had recently begun working at Walmart. She lived with her mother, with whom she was close. https://www.nbcconnecticut.com/news/national-international/these-are-the-victims-of-the-virginia-walmart-shooting/2922633/. 0723. https://thevirginiabeachobserver.com/local-news/remembering-tyneka-johnson-chesapeake-walmart-shooting-victim-was-just-beginning-to-live-her-dreams/. 0723.

Zhishen Liu was 73, and Aixiang Zhang was 74. They were a married couple who had immigrated from China to the U.S. https://www.kron4.com/news/bay-area/what-we-know-about-the-half-moon-bay-mass-shooting-victims/. 0823.

Amber Dunham was a Girl Scout, and ran cross country. She loved baking, and sometimes made cookies or cupcakes for her neighbors. https://www.cantonrep.com/story/news/2023/08/25/carnation-ave-uniontown-ohio-lake-township-murder-suicide-five-people-found/70676411007/. 0923. https://www.hopkinslawyer.com/obituaries/melissa-renee-amber-and-evan-dunham. 0923.

Valerie Jackson, Dwayne Jackson, Nathaniel Conley, Dewayne Jackson, Honesty Jackson, Caleb Jackson, Trinity Jackson, and Jonah Jackson were a family, and lived in Houston. https://www.nbcdfw.com/news/local/texas-news/man-accused-of-killing-8-wont-face-death-penalty-in-texas/2760543/. 0723. Their ages were: Valerie Jackson, 40; Dwayne Jackson, 50; Nathaniel Conley, 13; Honesty Jackson, 11; Dwayne Jackson, 10; Caleb Jackson, 9; Trinity Jackson, 7; and Jonah Jackson, 6. Valerie was the mother of all six children; Dwayne was the biological father of the youngest five.

Richard Bracken was 64. https://www.thenelsonfuneralhome.com/obituary/richard-d-bracken. 0923.

Dan Brown worked at FreightCar America in Roanoke, Virginia. He loved the Buffalo Bills and the New York Yankees, and was a fan of NASCAR driver Mark Martin. He had served in Iraq and Desert Storm as a U.S. Army Sergeant. He and his girlfriend had two puppies, named Samson and Misty. https://www.legacy.com/obituaries/batesville/name/daniel-brown-obituary?id=7568693. 0323.

43: https://ropercenter.cornell.edu/shootings-guns-and-public-opinion. 0423.

Anger ≠: Whitmer, *The Violence Mythos*, 11.
"The belief in the innateness of violence to human beings seems to indicate a collapse in the distinction between anger the emotion and violence the behavior, which has led to an equation between anger and violence such that anger has been perceived both to be violent and to have violence as its 'natural' means of expression. The result of this misnomer of 'violent anger' is the location of violence within the human being and to position control of violence in external collective authority. This is 'legitimate violence' because it rationalizes control of 'illegitimate' violence as socially acceptable."

Ability + desire: Rahtz, *Shots Fired*, 3.
"Keeping guns out of the hands of those with violent intent thwarts their ability to murder. Extinguishing the desire to kill makes these individuals less dangerous. Modifying the opportunity to kill acts to safeguard potential victims."

Fewer guns toted =: Hureau and Wilson, "The Co-Occurrence of Illegal Gun Carrying," 2550.
"Within a policy context that has sought to reduce illegal gun carrying almost exclusively through criminal justice punishment, our findings suggest an important opportunity for public health intervention. The primary implication of this study is that even for those at highest exposure to gun violence, individuals commonly experience changes in their patterns of gun carrying—and these changes are highly consequential. Reducing gun carrying can reduce experiences of gun violence."

91] • [92

John Collado was the primary caregiver for his mother, who has from Alzheimer's disease. He had worked as a building superintendent and later in a hotel before resigning because of a spinal injury. He lived in New York City. https://news.yahoo.com/killed-two-men-line-duty-083247228.html. 0723. https://www.nytimes.com/2019/10/25/nyregion/james-connolly-john-collado-police-settlement.html. 0723.

Anthony Laureano Disla had moved from Puerto Rico to Florida, to pursue a career as a dancer and choreographer. https://www.npr.org/sections/thetwo-way/2016/06/12/481785763/heres-what-we-know-about-the-orlando-shooting-victims. 0323.

Adrian Murfitt had played defenseman on his high school hockey team. He worked summers as a commercial salmon fisherman in his home state of Alaska, and the rest of the year as a car mechanic. https://www.nytimes.com/2017/10/02/us/vegas-victims-names.html. 0523. https://www.legacy.com/us/obituaries/adn/name/adrian-murfitt-obituary?id=40006701. 0523.

Lorenzo Gamble was 43. He had two sons, and enjoyed going to his 19-year-old's football games and cheering for the Washington Commanders NFL team. https://www.nbcconnecticut.com/news/national-international/these-are-the-victims-of-the-virginia-walmart-shooting/2922633/. 0723.

Mya Hall was a 27-year-old trans woman. She had been convicted of assault, and had violated the terms of her probation often enough to have been placed in Maryland's Violence Prevention Initiative, the state's strictest probation monitoring. https://www.washingtonpost.com/local/crime/baltimores-transgender-community-mourns-one-of-their-own-slain-by-police/2015/04/03/2f657da4-d88f-11e4-8103-fa84725dbf9d_story.html. 0723.

Qizhong Cheng was 66. https://abcnews.go.com/US/names-half-moon-bay-mass-shooting-victims-released/story?id=96632050. 0823.

Evan Dunham was a Cub Scout, and enjoyed Legos, baseball, videogames, and reading. https://www.cantonrep.com/story/news/2023/08/25/carnation-ave-uniontown-ohio-lake-township-murder-suicide-five-people-found/70676411007/. 0923. https://www.hopkinslawyer.com/obituaries/melissa-renee-amber-and-evan-dunham. 0923.

Cameron Tillman was 14. He had a 3.7 GPA. He helped his grandmother with her computer, and he helped her cook, so he could learn to cook. https://www.learntheirstories.com/#/cameron-tillman/. 0623.

George Keene was 34. https://baytownsun.com/local/article_b3c7279c-4901-11ed-bde1-63411cd57cd5.html?fbclid=IwAR3tXB_3k9L6vzDC4u7HCp2b4fiJWzWTgMexJeKgBqn4nwePo--NEthj-tU. 0923. https://www.echovita.com/us/obituaries/tx/baytown/george-anthony-keene-15338405. 0923.

Daniel Covarrubias was 37, and the father of seven children. He worked as a mechanic, and was studying for a college degree to certify his skills. He was a member of the Suquamish Tribe. He struggled with alcoholism. https://truthout.org/articles/a-wound-that-will-never-heal-organizing-after-the-death-of-daniel-covarrubias-at-the-hands-of-police/. 0823.

46: https://www.howmyvoiceisheard.com/lives/jayland-walker. 0623.
48: https://www.learntheirstories.com/#/idriss-stelley/. 0623.
55: https://www.theguardian.com/us-news/2019/jun/12/willie-mccoy-shooting-vallejo-police-55-shots. 0723.
59: https://www.nytimes.com/2021/10/27/us/jamarion-robinson-shooting-officers-charged.html. 0623.

Polarizing approaches: Pirelli, Wechsler, and Cramer, *The Behavioral Science of Firearms*, 488. "Confirmation biases are strong…. Continuance of a broad-based, polarizing approach to addressing firearm-related issues will only strengthen our biases and interfere with our ability to develop evidence-based processes beneficial to our society, such as those designed to reduce firearm-involved violence and suicide."

Introducing the binary: Roberts-Miller, "The Only Thing," 30.
"Characterizing gun owners as irrational and irresponsible yahoos whose views on gun policy can be dismissed because of their motives confirms the NRA presentation of gun policy debates as *really* a zero-sum contest between two groups.... I am not saying that 'both sides' engage in demagoguery about guns, but that any 'side' that frames any issue related to guns as a binary of gun owners versus non-gun owners is engaged in demagoguery. Identity is not policy, and if we hope to deliberate well about guns, we'd be wise to argue about the latter rather than the former."

The gun culture war: Campbell, *America's Gun Wars*, 153.
"The struggle over guns and gun regulations is merely the external manifestation of a much deeper struggle around sharply different national visions for the country and two distinct value systems.... The gun culture war is a proxy war fought around fundamental philosophical, social, and political beliefs...."

92] • [93

David Dehmann had a 5-year-old daughter. He lived in Mt. Vernon, Ohio. https://thefreethoughtproject.com/cop-watch/deputy-kills-autistic-man-disorderly-conduct-smashing-skull. 0823.

Christopher Leinonen, whose middle name was Andrew, went by "Drew." He worked as a counselor at a mental health facility. He liked foreign film, Star Trek, and Dance Dance Revolution. https://www.nytimes.com/interactive/projects/cp/us/orlando-shooting-victims/christopher-andrew-leinonen. 0323.

Rachael Parker had attended Eastern Washington University. She worked for ten years as a records technician at the Manhattan Beach Police Department.
https://www.khq.com/news/remembering-las-vegas-shooting-victim-rachael-parker/article_ab5dd712-26f1-521c-b7c9-d8991aa7a34b.html. 0523.
https://www.legacy.com/us/obituaries/spokesman/name/rachael-parker-obituary?id=17812949. 0523.

Rexdale Henry was 53. https://www.bustle.com/articles/99920-what-happened-to-rexdale-henry-a-native-american-activist-his-death-is-drawing-comparisons-to-sandra. 0723.

Jingzhi Lu was 64. https://abcnews.go.com/US/names-half-moon-bay-mass-shooting-victims-released/story?id=96632050. 0823.

A.J. Laguerre, 19, was the youngest of five siblings, all raised by their grandmother after their mother died. He worked at a Dollar General store to help his grandmother pay the bills. He played Fortnite and other video games on Twitch, and was working to build a large enough online following to be a professional streamer. https://apnews.com/article/jacksonville-shooting-victims-racist-5e66c7e4baf504de08d73a3857b78490. 0823.

Clayton Doerman had a dog named Gatlin, and he looked out for his two younger brothers. https://www.rohdefuneral.com/obituary/clayton-hunter-and-chase-doerman. 0923.

Bryan Gradney had two stepdaughters and an adopted son. He was 54. He was a high school graduate, and lived in Baytown, Texas. https://www.crespoandjirrels.com/tributes/Bryan-Gradney. 0923.

Alonzo Smith was 27. He attended Morgan University, where he had completed his associate's degree and was about to go back for his bachelor's in social work. In his spare time, he also made money modeling. https://www.lhamar.org/say-their-names-biography/alonzo-smith. 0623. https://truthout.org/articles/justice-for-alonzo-smith-beverly-smith-reflects-on-her-son-s-life-before-he-was-killed-by-special-police/. 0623.

Chuck Eagan was planning to retire soon. He had two daughters. https://www.seattletimes.com/seattle-news/law-justice/burlington-mall-shooting-victims-officially-identified/. 0323.

<200: Figures from 2014. https://www.brennancenter.org/our-work/analysis-opinion/just-facts-probation-nation. 0623.

Capital keeps itself safe: Rose, *On Violence*, 6.
"Not naming violence — its often undercover path of destruction, its random disposal of the bodies it needs and does not need — is one of the ways that capitalism has always preserved and perpetuated itself."

Rampage killers: Berardi, *Heroes*, 3.
The perpetrators of "spectacular murderous suicides" such as those at Columbine and Virginia Tech are "the extreme manifestation of one of the main trends of our age. I see them as the heroes of an age of nihilism and spectacular stupidity: the age of financial capitalism."

Violence brings financial benefits: Kapadia, "Gun Control for Health," 1710.
"The commercial interests of the gun lobby and the gun industry that limit research and drive laws and practices to sustain the availability and presence of guns in the United States cause immediate and horrific public health harms—mass shootings, mass murders, homicides, suicides, and unintentional gun-related injuries and deaths. The physical and emotional costs of gun-related injuries and deaths to survivors, their friends, and families are staggering."

93] • [94

Andre Hill earned college certification in business management and culinary arts. He worked for years a chef or restaurant manager. During the Coronavirus pandemic he worked as a subcontractor, and he had just put together his own crew to do independent contracting. Friends called him "Dre" and his three grandchildren called him "Big Daddy." He liked to play chess.

He was 47. https://www.pbs.org/newshour/nation/andre-hills-loved-ones-mourn-loss-of-a-chess-playing-mind. 0623.

Maurice Stallard was 69. https://www.legacy.com/news/celebrity-deaths/jeffersontown-kentucky-shooting-victims-2018/. 0823. https://www.legacy.com/us/obituaries/louisville/name/maurice-stallard-obituary?id=2113367. 0823.

Brenda McCool had 11 children and 6 grandchildren. https://www.self.com/story/orlando-victim-brenda-lee-marquez-mccool. 0323. https://www.nytimes.com/interactive/projects/cp/us/orlando-shooting-victims/brenda-lee-marquez-mccool. 0323. https://www.romper.com/p/who-is-brenda-lee-marquez-mccool-the-orlando-victim-mother-of-11-lived-a-brave-life-12522. 0323.

Carrie Parsons grew up on Bainbridge Island, and worked as a manager at the Seattle office of an employment firm. She had recently gotten engaged in Hawaii. https://komonews.com/news/local/seattle-woman-among-victims-of-las-vegas-massacre. 0523. https://abcnews.go.com/US/las-vegas-shooting-mother-father-dead/story?id=50229707. 0523.

Yitzian Torres Garcia was from Puerto Rico, and had grandparents in Florida. https://www.nbcnews.com/news/us-news/7-year-old-shot-killed-fourth-july-jet-ski-dispute-florida-rcna92896. 0823. https://www.the-sun.com/news/8886940/boy-shot-dead-yitzian-torres-garcia-tampa-florida/. 0823. https://www.fox13news.com/news/child-shot-on-courtney-campbell-causeway-remembered-on-birthday-as-killer-remains-loose. 0823.

John Crawford III was 22, had been born and raised in Cincinnati, Ohio, and was a high school graduate. He and his girlfriend had two young sons. https://www.learntheirstories.com/#/john-crawford-iii/. 0623.

Angela Michelle Carr was 52, and had been a member of the St. Stephen AME church in Jacksonville since she was 3. https://apnews.com/article/jacksonville-shooting-victims-racist-5e66c7e4baf504de08d73a3857b78490. 0823.

Hunter Doerman's nickname was "Hunter Dog." He called his mother and sister "Pretty Girls." https://www.rohdefuneral.com/obituary/clayton-hunter-and-chase-doerman. 0923.

Scott Nolet had played football and run track in high school. He was 34, and had three children. https://www.dignitymemorial.com/obituaries/pasadena-tx/scott-nolet-10996991. 0923.

Eddie Irizarry was known to friends and family as "Junito." He was 27. He liked riding dirt bikes. He experienced mental health issues, including schizophrenia and bipolar disorder. https://www.inquirer.com/crime/eddie-irizarry-funeral-mark-dial-philadelphia-20230824.html. 0923. https://www.inquirer.com/crime/eddie-irizarry-memorial-obituary-philadelphia-police-20230817.html. 0923.

9: Testimony of James Johnson, Baltimore County Police Department chief and chair of the National Law Enforcement Partnership to Prevent Gun Violence, "U.S. Senate Judiciary Committee Hearing on Gun Violence (2013)," as presented in Schildkraut, *Mass Shootings in America*, 279.

Free rein to police: Schmidt, "Police Violence, Public Response," 158.
"When the larger society views police violence as justified, the political response is muted or nonexistent. But when the violence offends established middle class social norms, politicians are more likely to respond with public statements, policy initiatives, or other responses that will bring real change to communities."

Racialized police violence: Rivera and Ward, "Developing a Comparativist Ethics," 255.
"Racialized police violence represents a failure of public administration and therefore of the state itself.... Public administration as an epistemic community and community of practice is obliged to address the multilayered, complex, and daunting problems involved, in the interest of social equity and justice, in the public interest. It needs to do so integrally, nonreductively, and also in a way that rejects the equivalency of value positions when it comes to human rights."

Police killings, eruptions: Lee and Ifill, "Do Black Lives Matter to the Courts?" 260.
"The police-involved killings of black individuals are merely the tip of the iceberg in terms of the systemic racial discrimination in law enforcement agencies across the country. At the heart of this discrimination is the automatic association between 'blackness' and criminality that is the product of the longstanding dehumanization of black people throughout American history. Burgeoning scientific studies on 'implicit bias' have proven this to be the case: people unconsciously connect black people with dangerous weapons, animals, and aggressive behavior. The activist cry that 'Black Lives Matter,' therefore, urges a fundamental reconfiguring of the societal hardwiring that presumes the dangerousness and criminality of black people by virtue of their race."

94] • [95

Prince Jones Jr. was a 25-year-old student at Howard University. He planned to join the Navy after graduation, and hoped to become either a doctor or a diplomat. He and his fiancée had an 11-month-old daughter. https://exhibits.stanford.edu/saytheirnames/feature/prince-c-jones-jr. 0623. https://www.findagrave.com/memorial/184967394/prince-carmen-jones. 0623.

Maxwell Emerson's father had been a school principal, and his mother had been a teacher. He had a twin brother, and was a new uncle to his sister's 11-month-old son. He was 25. https://www.washingtonpost.com/dc-md-va/2023/07/06/dc-killings-lyft-driver-refugee-teacher/?utm_campaign=wp_post_most&utm_medium=email&utm_source=newsletter&wpisrc=nl_most. 0723.

Gilberto Silva Menéndez was born in Puerto Rico. With friends, he went by "Culi" and "Junito." https://www.nytimes.com/interactive/projects/cp/us/orlando-shooting-victims/gilberto-ramon-silva-menendez. 0323. https://www.orlandoweekly.com/news/remembering-the-orlando-49-4833144. 0323.

Alyssa Alhadeff was a 14-year-old high school freshman. She was on her school's soccer team; she planned to play soccer in college, and dreamed of being a member of the U.S. women's national team. Her favorite song was "The Climb" by Miley Cyrus. https://www.fallenheroesproject.org/post/alyssa-alhadeff. 0723. https://www.northjersey.com/story/news/bergen/waldwick/2018/03/19/alyssa-alhadeff-teen-killed-parkland-shooting-celebrated-superdome-sports/436368002/. 0723.

Gustin Hinnant had started a record label with his friends, called Green Team. His parents were separated, and he lived with his father. His Facebook page identified his favorite movies as *Happy Feet* and *Toy Story*. Younge, *Another Day in the Death of America.*

Jerrald Gallion's jobs included one as a restaurant manager. https://apnews.com/article/jacksonville-shooting-victims-racist-5e66c7e4baf504de08d73a3857b78490. 0823.

Chase Doerman had the nickname "Chasers." https://www.rohdefuneral.com/obituary/clayton-hunter-and-chase-doerman. 0923.

Donald Ivy was 39, and lived in Albany, New York. He served two years in the Navy, and graduated from Virginia State University. He had a nightly ritual of walking from his home to a nearby convenience store for a pack of cigarettes. https://www.timesunion.com/news/article/Taser-victim-Dontay-Ivy-to-be-laid-to-rest-6187858.php. 0823.

Violet Parrish was a high school graduate who had grown up in New Jersey, and lived in Texas. https://www.bradleystow.com/obituary/Violet-Parrish. 0923.

Charly Leundeu Keunang was born in Cameroon. He moved to France to find work to support his family at home, then to the U.S., wanting to become an actor. He went by "Africa." https://www.gq.com/story/skid-row-police-shooting-charly-keunang. 0823.

27: https://www.motherjones.com/politics/2016/06/fully-loaded-ten-biggest-gun-manufacturers-america/. 0623.

Men disproportionately: Cukier and Cairns, "Gender, Attitudes and … Small Arms," 18. "Women represent a very small proportion of gun owners, but are a disproportionate number of gun-violence victims. This imbalance has been one of the arguments advanced for positioning the debate on small-arms control in the context of human rights and equity. Small arms affect women differently to men, and this shapes the solutions needed to address the problem. While men represent the majority of small-arms victims, they are also the majority of small-arms users. Women, in contrast, represent a higher percentage of victims of small arms than users. In addition, while women are victimized by combatants and criminals, they are also at risk of being victimized by their intimate partners. Statistics show that the number of small arms in civilian possession is far greater than those in the possession of states and police. The evidence is clear: civilian-owned small arms represent a particular threat to women."

Violence: Campbell, *End of Equality*, 61.
"Militarism, crime and violence are contexts for doing or making masculinity. Unsafe cities and war zones multiply the arenas for rape and repudiation of women. Violence is not a sign of primitive masculinity or the collapse of civilization; it is its hardened heart."

Make America: Kellner, *Guys and Guns Amok*, 97.
"The crisis in masculinity drove many men to seek solace in guns and weapons. Gun and military culture in particular fetishize weapons as an important part of male virility and power, treating guns as objects of almost religious veneration and devotion. In this constellation, the expression of violence through guns and the use of weapons is perceived as an expression of manhood."

95] • [96

Larry Kobuk was originally from Norton Sound, Alaska. He had been convicted of multiple misdemeanors. https://www.adn.com/alaska-news/article/doc-report-describes-prisoner-deaths-rare-ugly-detail/2015/11/17/. 0723.

Kendrec McDade was 19, and had two younger siblings. https://www.learntheirstories.com/#/kendrec-mcdade/. 0623. https://www.lhamar.org/say-their-names-biography/kendrec-mcdade. 0623.

Jean Méndez Pérez was born in Puerto Rico, and had lived in the U.S. since he was a teenager. https://www.npr.org/sections/thetwo-way/2016/06/12/481785763/heres-what-we-know-about-the-orlando-shooting-victims. 033. https://www.orlandoweekly.com/news/remembering-the-orlando-49-4833144. 0323.

Cara Loughran was a 14-year-old high school freshman. She loved the beach. https://caradanceson.net/. 0723.

Katherine Goldstein was 64, and the mother of two adult daughters. https://abcnews.go.com/US/victims-july-4th-highland-park-parade-shooting/story?id=86205738. 0823.

Stephen Romero had just graduated from kindergarten, and was excited to start first grade. https://www.latimes.com/california/story/2019-07-29/gilroy-garlic-festival-shooting-what-we-know-about-the-victims. 0923.

John Sawyer was a native of San Bernardino, California. He was 35, and had two sons and two daughters. https://www.newsmirror.net/obituaries/john-s-sawyer/article_6ea5f8c6-b85b-11e4-818b-870661475108.html. 0823.

Rob Hiaasen worked as an assistant editor and Sunday columnist for the Capital Gazette newspaper in Annapolis, Maryland. He had worked previously at the Baltimore Sun. https://www.cnn.com/2018/06/29/us/maryland-shooting-victims/index.html. 0923.

Glenn Edward Bennett was born in Wyoming, and had lived in Bend, Oregon for 28 years. He was 84. https://www.tributearchive.com/obituaries/25813393/glenn-edward-bennett/bend/oregon/bend-funeral-homes. 0923.

Michael Stewart was an art school student who lived with his parents in Clinton Hill, Brooklyn. He was 25. https://www.learntheirstories.com/#/michael-stewart/. 0623.

3,410: Children's Defense Fund, *Protect Children, Not Guns 2019*.
2020: Goldstick, et al., "Current Causes of Death," 1955.

Even violence that happens: Kelleher, *When Good Kids Kill*, xiv.
"When violence strikes at our family, our nation, or us, there are reasons waiting to be understood and motivations crying out to be discovered. Without an effort to move beyond the mere punishment of an individual or group who has violated our societal norms, we run the risk of never coming to an understanding of why violence so plagues our nation. Worse, we overlook opportunities to create a better, safer society for our children and ourselves."

Proximate causes of killing: Roth, *American Homicide*, 3.
"Why, if humans have roughly the same capacity for violence, does murder claim 1 in 10,000 adults in some societies, and 1 in 20 in others? To find out why homicide rates rise and fall over time, we have to try to get beyond generalizations based on proximate causes to discover the ultimate causes of murder. The Centers for Disease Control monitor homicide statistics because homicide rates behave like disease rates. Like cases of the flu, they increase at certain times and in certain places, sometimes very rapidly.... [H]omicide rates among adults are not determined by proximate causes such as poverty, drugs, unemployment, alcohol, race, or ethnicity, but by factors that seem on the face of it to be impossibly remote, like the feelings that people have toward their government, the degree to which they identify with members of their own communities, and the opportunities they have to earn respect without resorting to violence."

Power the exercised: Larkin, "Masculinity, School Shooters, and the Control of Violence," 338.
"The resort to physical violence is primarily a male prerogative, even an aspect of male social privilege, because it is the ultimate method for enforcing relationships of dominance and subordination. Violence is literally the exercise of power."

96] • [97

Stanley Taylor's friends nicknamed him MadMaxx, for his high-top fade crowned with small dreads. He liked to hang out on the corner with his friends. Younge, *Another Day in the Death of America.*

Kimberly Morris had recently moved from Hawai'i to Florida to help her mother and grandmother. She had played small forward on her college basketball team in Connecticut. https://www.nytimes.com/interactive/projects/cp/us/orlando-shooting-victims/kimberly-morris. 0323. https://www.orlandoweekly.com/news/remembering-the-orlando-49-4833144. 0323. https://www.npr.org/sections/thetwo-way/2016/06/12/481785763/heres-what-we-know-about-the-orlando-shooting-victims. 0323.

Helena Ramsay was a 17-year-old high school senior. She was active in such extra-curricular activites as UN club and First Priority Group. She enjoyed arts and crafts, and dancing. https://www.dignitymemorial.com/obituaries/tamarac-fl/helena-ramsay-7765085. 0723. https://abcnews.go.com/US/teacher-coach14-year-freshman-florida-high-school-massacre/story?id=53092879. 0723.

Reggie Doucet Jr. was born and raised in Prunedale, California. After graduating from Middle Tennessee State University, where he had played football, he returned to the Playa Vista section of Los Angeles. His nickname was "Gametime." He had a three-year-old daughter. https://www.learntheirstories.com/#/reggie-doucet-jr/. 0623.

Irina McCarthy studied taekwando. She and her husband lived in Highland Park, Illinois, and had a 2-year-old son. https://abcnews.go.com/US/victims-july-4th-highland-park-parade-shooting/story?id=86205738. 0823. https://chicago.suntimes.com/2022/7/12/23205730/highland-park-parade-shooting-funeral-irina-mccarthy. 0823. https://www.chicagotribune.com/news/breaking/ct-irina-kevin-mccarthy-two-year-old-son-20220706-egrkrv5unjfjfdy3u73tfuzfsi-story.html. 0823.

Christina Tahhahwah had worked at a chain grocery store, and then at a child care center. In her youth, she had been Little Miss Comanche Gourd Clan Princess and a member of the Comanche Youth Dancers. She was 37, and had a daughter. https://www.findagrave.com/memorial/139444291/christina-dawn-tahhahwah. 0723.

Keyla Salazar was 13, and lived in San Jose. She had autism but had just graduated from middle school. Her favorite animation character was Stitch, from the movie *Lilo & Stitch.* https://www.latimes.com/california/story/2019-07-29/gilroy-garlic-festival-shooting-what-we-know-about-the-victims. 0923. https://www.latimes.com/california/story/2019-08-05/gilory-shooting-victim-keyla-salazar. 0923.

Gerald Fischman was the editorial page editor for the Capital Gazette in Annapolis, Maryland. He was 61, and had worked at the paper for more than 25 years. https://www.cnn.com/2018/06/29/us/maryland-shooting-victims/index.html. 0923. https://people.com/crime/newsroom-maryland-shooting-victims-identified/. 0923.

Donald Ray Surrett Jr. had 3 children, 7 grandchildren, and 3 great-grandchildren. He worked for six seasons with the U.S. Forest Service. He was active in his Seventh-day Adventist church and his local Disabled American Veterans chapter. https://www.fs.usda.gov/inside-fs/memorial/remembering-don-surrett-jr. 0923. https://www.deschutesmemorial.com/obituaries/Donald-Ray-Surrett-Jr?obId=25863632. 0923.

Donnell Thompson, Jr. liked to play Uno at El Camino College's Compton Center, where he also attended classes for people with mental disabilities. He was the youngest of four siblings, and lived with his father. https://homicide.latimes.com/post/donnell-thompson-jr/. 0723.

15: https://www.theguardian.com/us-news/2015/jun/01/black-americans-killed-by-police-analysis. 0423.

No gun rights: Testimony of Captain Mark Kelly, United States Navy (Ret.) and Americans for Responsible Solutions, "U.S. Senate Judiciary Committee Hearing on Gun Violence (2013)," as presented in Schildkraut, *Mass Shootings in America*, 274.
"One of our messages is simple: The breadth and complexity of the problem of gun violence is great, but it is not an excuse for inaction.... We believe wholly and completely in the Second Amendment of our Constitution — and that it confers upon all Americans the right to own a firearm for protection, collection, and recreation.... Our rights are paramount. But our responsibilities are serious. And as a nation we are not taking responsibility for the gun rights our founders conferred upon us."

What of your violence: Auden, *The Prolific*, 60.
"The trouble about violence is that most of the punishment falls on the innocent. That is why, even if you imagine you are fighting for the noblest of ends, the knowledge that it is more your children than yourself who will have to pay for your violence, that should make you hesitate."

"Gun control": McMillan and Bernstein, "Beyond Gun Control," 181.
"Theoretically, by conceiving of the movement as gun control rather than GVP [gun violence prevention], scholars limit their focus to organizations trying to influence laws and policies, assuming that this is the only or most important way to reduce gun violence, ignoring the breadth of activism by racially oppressed people and others who focus on the roots of gun violence."

97] • [98

Ashley Carpenter was an 18-year-old high school senior who was active in band. She enjoyed hanging out with friends and listening to music.
https://www.legacy.com/us/obituaries/ohio/name/ashley-carpenter-carpenter-kohler-obituary?id=13895767. 0723.

Clifford Glover lived in Queens. He was 10 years old, and in fourth grade. He and his family watched cowboy shows on TV after dinner.
https://www.theblackamericanmuslim.com/clifford-g. 0623.

Jean Nieves Rodriguez, originally from Puerto Rico, lived in Florida, and worked as the manager of a check-cashing store. https://www.orlandoweekly.com/news/remembering-the-orlando-49-4833144. 0323. https://www.npr.org/sections/thetwo-way/2016/06/12/481785763/heres-what-we-know-about-the-orlando-shooting-victims. 0323.

Martin Duque Anguiano, a 14-year-old high school freshman, was born in a small town in Mexico. He liked "Star Wars," and was an FC Barcelona fan.
https://www.fallenheroesproject.org/post/martin-duque-anguiano. 0723.
https://www.nbcmiami.com/news/local/reflection-remembering-the-17-parkland-victims/2690110/. 0723.

Stephen Straus was born in Chicago, but lived in Highland Park, Illinois for decades. https://abcnews.go.com/US/victims-july-4th-highland-park-parade-shooting/story?id=86205738. 0823.

Dominique Lucious was born in St. Louis, and lived in Springfield, Missouri. https://www.advocate.com/crime/2021/4/12/dominique-lucious-black-trans-woman-killed-missouri. 0723.

Trevor Irby was an alum of Keuka College, where he had majored in biology. He was 25. https://www.latimes.com/california/story/2019-07-29/gilroy-garlic-festival-shooting-what-we-know-about-the-victims. 0923. https://apnews.com/d4870276877243f2b21432960639598e. 0923.

John McNamara loved covering sports, and had written two books about University of Maryland sports history. He was 56. https://www.cnn.com/2018/06/29/us/maryland-shooting-victims/index.html. 0923.

Deborah Martinez-Garibay's Army service included multiple tours in Afghanistan. She volunteered with the PGA Hope program, which unites golf pros and veterans with disabilities. She had one daughter, and a dog named Haji that she took on "walks" in a wagon. https://www.cbsnews.com/news/tucson-shooting-deborah-martinez-garibay-pima-county-constable-4-killed-eviction-arizona/. 0923. https://www.legacy.com/us/obituaries/tucson/name/deborah-martinez-garibay-obituary?id=36355445. 0923.

Dominique Jackson was 30, and had come out as trans as a teenager. She was born in Detroit, and had been placed into foster care after her mother's death. She went by "DeDe." She and others in her chosen family did hair as a side job out of their apartment. https://www.clarionledger.com/story/news/local/2021/03/11/friends-black-transgender-woman-killed-jackson-had-life-cut-short/4423312001/. 0723.

9.1: Eterno and Barrow, "Contemporary Police and Minorities," 43, 44.

In use of force: Boylstein, *When Police Use Force*, 127.
"The theoretical premise that a state must at its foundation monopolize the use of legitimate force against a populace ties directly into the societal importance of ensuring police use of force is justified and equitable across all groups of citizens, or at a minimum ensuring no member of society faces a higher risk of having force used against him due to noncriminal aspects of his personhood (race, ethnicity, age, sex, social class, area of residence)."

To diminish police brutality: Holmes and Smith, *Race and Police Brutality*, 151.
"Police brutality seems inevitable in America's current social milieu. Its roots are deeply embedded in fundamental psychological processes and in a social structure that deeply divides America along racial and ethnic lines. Human emotional and cognitive processes are not readily amenable to change. These mental mechanisms make humans acutely aware of and responsive to

intergroup differences, psychological processes not easily overcome when huge sociocultural differences separate people. Social and cultural contexts, particularly the concentration of certain minorities into impoverished neighborhoods, provide the substance for the operation of these processes. Thus to meaningfully combat the problem of police brutality, as well as to alleviate the many other afflictions of poverty, America must commit itself to reversing the inexorable social trends certain to further erode police-minority relations."

The number of police killings: Zimring, *When Police Kill*, 12.
"This [police use of lethal force] is a serious problem we can fix. Clear administrative restrictions on when police can shoot can eliminate 50 to 80 percent of killings by police without causing substantial risk to the lives of police officers or major changes in how police do their jobs. A thousand killings a year are not the unavoidable result of community conditions or of the nature of policing in the United States."

98] • [99

David Carpenter-Kohler was 14, and in the eighth grade. He enjoyed hanging out with friends, listening to music, and playing video games and football.
https://www.legacy.com/us/obituaries/ohio/name/ashley-carpenter-carpenter-kohler-obituary?id=13895767. 0723.

Francisco Serna had numerous grandchildren and greatgrandchildren. He had begun experiencing dementia, and when he had trouble sleeping he sometimes took walks to make himself tired. https://heavy.com/news/2016/12/francisco-serna-73-year-old-unarmed-man-dementia-shot-police-bakersfield-california-photos-video/. 0523.

Ke'Yahonna Stone was born and raised in Indianapolis, and had a brother and two sisters. She attended Brown Mackie College in Indianapolis for two years. Friends called her "Yaya."
https://www.windycitytimes.com/lgbt/PASSAGES-Black-trans-activist-KeYahonna-Stone-victim-of-gun-violence-dies/72111.html. 0723.

Luis Ocasio-Capo was born in Puerto Rico, and had lived with his family in Ohio, Tennessee, and Florida. He worked in a coffee shop located in a department store, and he wanted to become an actor. https://time.com/one-year-after-pulse/. 0323.
https://www.orlandoweekly.com/news/remembering-the-orlando-49-luis-omar-ocasio-capo-2532809. 0323.

Gina Montalto was a 14-year-old high school freshman. She was an avid reader and loved Harry Potter books, Hunger Games, and Wonder Woman. She had a younger brother.
https://ginarosemontaltomemorialfoundation.org/aboutgina/. 0723.

Eduardo Uvaldo was retired. He had worked at various jobs, including maintenance at Abbott Labs. He and his wife had just celebrated their 50th anniversary. He was 69.
https://abcnews.go.com/US/victims-july-4th-highland-park-parade-shooting/story?id=86205738. 0823.

Aaliyah Gonzalez was 18. She worked at Starbucks. She loved plants, and loved to draw. Her family nicknamed her "Sweet Face" because her cheeks rose when she smiled. https://www.washingtonpost.com/dc-md-va/2023/07/15/funeral-baltimore-shooting-aaliyah-gonzalez/. 0923.

Rebecca Smith was 34. On social media, she described herself as a "Dog Mom. Softball Fiance. Bonus Mom to the best kid ever." https://www.cnn.com/2018/06/29/us/maryland-shooting-victims/index.html. 0923.

Angela Fox and her husband had three children. She was 28. https://www.kgun9.com/news/local-news/remembering-angela-fox-heath-one-of-four-lives-taken-in-lind-commons-shooting. 0923.

Jeremy Linhart lived in Findlay, Ohio. He was a high school graduate. In childhood and youth he had played hockey. He was 30, and had one daughter. https://www.findagrave.com/memorial/188080971/jeremy-john-linhart. 0823.

53: https://ropercenter.cornell.edu/shootings-guns-and-public-opinion. 0423.

Depicted aggression: Congressional Public Health Summit, July 26, 2000. https://images.procon.org/wp-content/uploads/sites/36/jointstatement.pdf. 0423.
"At this time, well over 1000 studies – including reports from the Surgeon General's office, the National Institute of Mental Health, and numerous studies conducted by leading figures within our medical and public health organizations – our own members – point overwhelmingly to a causal connection between media violence and aggressive behavior in some children. The conclusion of the public health community, based on over 30 years of research, is that viewing entertainment violence can lead to increases in aggressive attitudes, values and behavior, particularly in children.

Its effects are measurable and long-lasting. Moreover, prolonged viewing of media violence can lead to emotional desensitization toward violence in real life."

Action films mythologize: Arjet, "Man to Man," 129.
"The power that flows through guns in action films has particular forms and expressions. However, any power that a man wields in a gunplay film — whether sexual, familial or legal in origin — must eventually be proved or defended by engaging in gunplay with other men. This is the central truth of the gunplay film, and one vigorously propagated by the gun culture at large: nothing that a man has — not his possessions, not his family, not his power — is truly his unless he can defend it in gun combat with other men."

"Violence as entertainment: Kearney, *Optic Subwoof*, 103.

99] • [100

Taylin Roland lived in Columbus, Ohio. She enjoyed rap music, cooking, and comedy. She was 28, and had two daughters. https://www.tributearchive.com/obituaries/27901085/taylin-roland. 0923.

Manuel Ellis was the middle child of three siblings. He was 33, and lived in Tacoma, Washington. With family and friends he went by "Manny." He had two children, an 11-year old son and an infant daughter, and he lived off-and-on with his sister, helping care for her five children. https://www.blackpast.org/african-american-history/people-african-american-history/manuel-ellis-1987-2020/. 0823.

Fred Hampton. https://www.howmyvoiceisheard.com/lives/fred-hampton. 0723.

Geraldo Ortiz-Jimenez was born in the Dominican Republic, had graduated from high school in Pennsylvania, and was studying law at a university in Puerto Rico. His favorite singer was Selena Gomez. https://www.orlandoweekly.com/news/remembering-the-orlando-49-geraldo-a-ortiz-jimenez-4033264. 0323. https://www.nytimes.com/interactive/projects/cp/us/orlando-shooting-victims/geraldoa-ortiz-jimenez. 0323.

Meadow Pollack was an 18-year-old high school senior who planned to attend Lynn University. https://sinceparkland.org/people/meadow-pollack/. 0723.

Kevin McCarthy worked for a gene therapy company. He was 37. https://www.chicagotribune.com/news/breaking/ct-highland-park-shooting-kevin-mccarthy-funeral-20220718-7uk35grk2zexdeugqpzf5oddna-story.html. 0823.

Kylis Fagbemi worked as a forklift operator for Amazon and Kohl's. His nickname was "Mooka," and he loved video games, music, motorcycles and playing with his dogs. He was 20. https://www.thebaltimorebanner.com/community/criminal-justice/kylis-fagbemi-brooklyn-shooting-victim-funeral-IQBLW7DBORAUNDYKF5TDRKU3B4/. 0923.

Wendi Winters worked as an editor and community reporter for the Capital Gazette in Annapolis, Maryland, after previously working for public relations firms and owning her own boutique PR agency. She was 65. https://www.cnn.com/2018/06/29/us/maryland-shooting-victims/index.html. 0923.

Elijah Miranda was 25, and a member of the Pascua Yaqui Tribe. As a youth, he had been a student of ballet, very active in the Dancing in the Streets AZ performing arts organization. He lived in Tucson. https://www.azcentral.com/story/news/local/arizona/2023/06/10/friends-family-grieve-elijah-miranda-who-died-in-shooting/70308124007/. 0923. https://www.kgun9.com/news/local-news/former-ballet-instructors-of-elijah-miranda-describe-2022-shooting-victim-as-a-sweet-gentle-giant. 0923.

Diamond Sanders was a 23-year-old trans woman from Cincinnati. As a child, she had enjoyed weekends with an aunt and grandmother, especially baking cookies and making "pigs in a blanket." Family report her explaining her always-coordinated attire with "I have to be cute, honey!" https://www.prestoncharlesfuneralhome.com/obituary/DiamondKyree-Sanders. 0723.

50: O'Brien et al., "Racism, Gun Ownership and Gun Control," e77552. On the same page, the authors give this account of symbolic racism: "Symbolic racism is a belief structure underpinned by both antiblack affect and traditional values. The anti-black affect (racism) component of symbolic racism is said to be established in pre-adult years through exposure to negative black stereotypes (e.g. blacks as dangerous, blacks are lazy), to the point that phenomena such as crime and physical violence have become typified as black phenomena. The anti-black affect is not necessarily conscious or deliberative, but may be felt as fear, anger, unease, and hostility towards blacks. The symbolic component reflects the abstract view of blacks as a collective rather than as individuals, as well as its basis in abstract white moralistic reasoning and traditions. Because symbolic racism represents an ingrained schema, individuals high in symbolic racism will react in a negative manner, often unconsciously, to issues perceived to involve a racial (i.e. black) component."
106.3: Holmes, Painter, and Smith, "Race, Place, and Police-Caused Homicide," 770.
44.4: Siegel et al., "The Relationship between Racial," 582.
24: Mesic et al., "The Relationship between Structural Racism," 112.

Toward reducing violence: Obidah, "On Living (and Dying) with Violence," 65.
"Current discourses and consequent policies on youth violence obviate the narratives of the youth living in the midst yet not a part of the violence. To legislate effective policy addressing youth violence it is necessary to hear — to listen to — the voices of those most affected by the issues: the youth themselves."

Toward reducing gun violence: Squires, "Afterword," 257.
"We would do well to continue investigating how the gun acts in public memory and imagination, to ask why there are so many people who cannot imagine life without the gun — either the threat of its power or its alleged protection against imagined enemies."

Violence is everywhere: Brian Massumi, in Evans and Lennart, *Violence*, 255.
Violence "is everywhere all the time, effectively in potential — but so is resistance. There is primary resistance that is always churning, always vying, always pushing toward the augmentation of powers of life. And this can be performed. It can be enacted in a way that it is attuned to the ingression of violence in that particular situation, countering it head-on or clandestinely evading it."

100] • [101

Adrianna Stanton lived in Louisville, Kentucky. https://www.wdrb.com/news/family-of-kenyan-immigrants-saw-no-signs-of-trouble-before-murder-suicide-in-south-louisville/article_80598a02-74c7-11ed-be6f-7b3aeb1306e7.html. 0923.

Anthony Lamar Smith was the oldest of four brothers. He attended but did not complete high school. He was interested in fashion, and wanted to become a clothing designer. He enjoyed reading books and playing many sports; including football, swimming, basketball, and racquetball. https://www.blackpast.org/african-american-history/smith-anthony-lamar-1987-2011/. 0623.
https://www.learntheirstories.com/#/anthony-lamar-smith/. 0623.

Eric Ivan Ortiz-Rivera and his husband were married on the very day that the U.S. Supreme Court ruled that same-sex couples have a right to marry. He was born and raised in Puerto Rico, and had studied communications in college. https://www.orlandoweekly.com/news/remembering-the-orlando-49-eric-ivan-ortiz-rivera-2563336. 0323.

Nicholas Dworet went by "Nick." He was a 17-year-old high school senior. He dreamed of competing in the Olympics. https://sinceparkland.org/people/nicholas-dworet/. 0723.

Jacki Sundheim lived in Highland Park, Illinois, and her synagogue was in neighboring Glencoe. https://abcnews.go.com/US/victims-july-4th-highland-park-parade-shooting/story?id=86205738. 0823.

Sean Adler worked as a security guard, and had previously coached high school wrestling. His earlier ambition to become a police officer had been ended by a heart attack suffered during training. He was 48. He and his wife had two sons. https://time.com/5449995/california-borderline-bar-shooting-victims/. 0923.

Shirly Voita and her husband were married for 57 years, and had five children. She earned her BS in Nursing from Arizona State University. She volunteered each year at her local Senior Center as a tax preparer. She and her husband enjoyed traveling together to visit their children and grandchildren. She was 79. https://www.legacy.com/us/obituaries/name/shirley-voita-obituary?id=51974712. 0923.

Natasha McKenna was a high school graduate who had played on her school basketball team. She was 37, and had a 7-year-old daughter. She lived in Alexandria, Virginia. https://www.blackpast.org/african-american-history/mckenna-natasha-1978-2015/. 0823. https://exhibits.stanford.edu/saytheirnames/feature/natasha-mckenna. 0823.

Clyde and Sally Knox lived in Butler Township, Ohio. He was 82 and she was 78. https://www.mortonwhetstonefh.com/obituary/ClydeandSally-Knox. 0923.

Brianna Stanton lived in Louisville, Kentucky. https://www.wdrb.com/news/family-of-kenyan-immigrants-saw-no-signs-of-trouble-before-murder-suicide-in-south-louisville/article_80598a02-74c7-11ed-be6f-7b3aeb1306e7.html. 0923.

7,391: Leventhal, Gaither, and Sege, "Hospitalizations Due to Firearm Injuries," 219.

Effective preventive measures: Schildkraut, Elsass, and Muschert, "Satirizing Mass Murder," 249. "It is simply not enough to look for a 'quick fix' to the problem of mass shootings or even homicide in a broader sense, nor is it enough to address one event at a time.... In order to implement effective preventative measures, we must look beyond a single place and time to all like events, connect the dots, and see where improvement really is needed.... [W]hat is needed is cognizant and intelligent analysis of events among a variety of disciplines, collaborative efforts between academics, the media, and politicians, and the creation of responsible, well-informed legislation, in addition to the enforcement of existing laws and policies."

About guns, too, it matters: Shapira, Liang, and Lin, "How Attitudes About Guns Develop," 12. "Changes in attitudes about guns can take place in terms of both the content (what young adults think about guns) and the form (how young adults think about guns)."

My perceiving threat: Davis, "Introduction," xiii.
"Many unarmed black men and boys have been killed since Trayvon Martin's tragic death five years ago. Many of the killings occurred after police officers arguably engaged in racial profiling — stopping and harassing these men for no explainable reason other than the color of their skin. In all of the cases where black men were shot and killed, the officers claimed that they felt threatened, even though the men were unarmed and often running away or retreating. In almost all of the cases, the police officers were never arrested or charged with a crime."

101] • [102

Bryant Tennell won his school's chili cook-off, and when his bicycle was stolen he restored an antique lowrider trike and customized it with a speaker box and battery cage. He made brownies and cookies at home and sold them to classmates at school. Leovy, *Ghettoside*, 99-102.

Malcolm Ferguson, when he was a child, had helped his legally blind mother with paperwork and bills and kitchen chores. He had especially liked to shop for the family because he could buy spaghetti. https://www.workers.org/2007/us/ferguson-0621/. 0623.

Botham Jean was born in Castries, Saint Lucia. His friends and co-workers nicknamed him "Bo." He moved to the U.S. to attend Harding University, a Christian school in Arkansas. He lived in Dallas, and worked as an accountant for Price Waterhouse Coopers. He was 26. https://www.blackpast.org/african-american-history/people-african-american-history/botham-shem-jean-1991-2018/. 0723.

Joel Rayon Paniagua worked in Florida; his family lived in Veracruz. He loved to dance. https://www.orlandoweekly.com/news/remembering-the-orlando-49-joel-rayon-paniagua-4447640. 0323.

Luke Hoyer was a 15-year-old high school freshman. He had two older siblings. He planned to try out for football in his sophomore year, and one classmate had nicknamed him "king of the one-word answers." https://people.com/crime/15-year-old-freshman-among-those-killed-in-florida-school-shooting-he-was-just-a-good-boy/. 0723. https://sinceparkland.org/people/luke-hoyer/. 0723.

Nicolas Toledo-Zaragoza spent most of his life in Morelos, Mexico. https://abcnews.go.com/US/victims-july-4th-highland-park-parade-shooting/story?id=86205738. 0823. https://chicago.suntimes.com/metro-state/2022/7/4/23194745/highland-park-victim-nicolas-toledo-mass-shooting-fourth-of-july-parade-homicide. 0823.

Cody Coffman planned to enter the military. He was 22. https://time.com/5449995/california-borderline-bar-shooting-victims/. 0923.

Melody Ivie and her husband had eight children. She was active in her church, and ran a preschool. She was 63. https://www.serenityandcompany.com/obituaries/melody-deanivie. 0923.

Sarah Anderson and her husband had two daughters. She lived in Butler Township, Ohio, and was 41. https://www.mortonwhetstonefh.com/obituary/SarahandKayla-Anderson. 0923.

Ben A. C de Baca was a Pittsburgh Steelers fan. He had a history of mental illness. He was a high school graduate who had been in JROTC.
https://www.legacy.com/us/obituaries/santafenewmexican/name/ben-c-de-baca-obituary?id=17795038. 0723. https://www.thedailybeast.com/cops-gagged-and-smothered-a-man-to-death-then-fist-bumped. 0723.

20: https://www.theguardian.com/uk-news/2016/feb/12/mario-woods-autopsy-san-francisco-police-fatal-shooting. 0723.

With every push: Jones and Stone, "The U.S. Gun Control Paradox," 172.
"Cause-oriented marketing efforts, as well as political initiatives by gun-control advocates in the U.S. face a paradox: the more advocates push for increased regulation to limit gun sales, the more guns that are sold."

Guns compensate: Mencken and Froese, "Gun Culture in Action," 24.
"[G]uns provide moral purpose to white males who have lost, or fear losing, their economic footing. Our findings also indicate that Americans' attachment to guns is not explained by religious or political cultures.... [O]nly a subset of religious conservatives find emotional solace in guns, for reasons neither religious nor partisan. Specifically, less religious white men in economic distress find comfort in guns as a means to reestablish a sense of individual power and moral certitude in the face of changing times."

Guns help the rich: Monzó, McLaren, and Rodriguez, "Deploying Guns," 92.
"[T]he gun industry, as part of the broader military industrial complex, serves a specific function of both producing and securing capital interests, U.S. imperialism, and racism and that these work together to support the capital accumulation of the transnational capitalist class."

102] • [103

JoAnna Cottle was 39. https://www.wtvr.com/news/local-news/cottle-family-murder-chesterfield-mother-joanna-loved-her-kids-had-huge-heart. 0923.

Jared Forsyth had wanted, even in childhood, to be a policeman or a fireman. In youth he had been active in the Boy Scouts, DeMolay, drama club, and choir. He loved spending time with his family and friends, children, and animals. He had five siblings, and eight nieces and nephews. https://www.wesh.com/article/family-of-ocala-police-officer-accidentally-killed-speaks-to-wesh-2/4441411#. 0823. https://www.legacy.com/us/obituaries/ocala/name/jared-forsyth-obituary?id=11466627. 0823.

Enrique Rios lived with his grandmother, for whom he served as primary caretaker. He worked as a coordinator at a home health care agency. https://www.nytimes.com/interactive/projects/cp/us/orlando-shooting-victims/enriquel-rios-jr. 0323. https://www.orlandoweekly.com/news/remembering-the-orlando-49-enrique-l-rios-jr-3184155. 0323.

Aaron Feis was 37. He and his wife had one daughter. https://t2t.org/first_responders/aaron-feis/. 0723.

Patrick Dorismond was 26. His parents immigrated to the U.S. from Haiti. He and his fiancée had a one-year-old daughter. https://www.learntheirstories.com/#/patrick-dorismond/. 0623.

Blake Dingman was 21, and lived in Newbury Park, California. https://time.com/5449995/california-borderline-bar-shooting-victims/. 0923. https://www.uscannenbergmedia.com/2018/11/08/borderline-shooting-victims-who-they-were/. 0923.

Gwendolyn Schofield was the fourth of seven daughters in her family. She and her first husband had four children, and converted as adults to the Church of Jesus Christ of Latter-day Saints. She earned her BA in Education from Utah State, and taught school for more than thirty years. She went by "Gwen," and was 97. https://www.daily-times.com/obituaries/tnm075393. 0923.

Kayla Anderson was on her school's JV soccer team, and worked part-time at a local restaurant and ice cream parlor. https://www.mortonwhetstonefh.com/obituary/SarahandKayla-Anderson. 0923.

Jonathan Pierce was 37. In high school, he had been a member of the marching band, and the football and track teams. He was an employee of FairPoint Communications and a member of his local First Baptist Church. https://www.legacy.com/us/obituaries/newsherald/name/jonathan-pierce-obituary?id=44357011. 0823.

Lorenzo Hayes was a high school graduate who had seven children and lived in Spokane, Washington. https://www.legacy.com/us/obituaries/spokesman/name/lorenzo-hayes-obituary?id=22106230. 0823.

15: https://www.huffpost.com/entry/mass-shootings-domestic-violence-women_n_55d3806ce4b07addcb44542a. 0523.

The spread of violent behavior: Frazer et al., "The Violence Epidemic," 6.
"Violent behavior has the ability to transmit, spread and cluster based on exposure consistent with an epidemic disease. Thus, the presence of violence in a community increases not only the potential number of victims of violence but also increases the likely number of perpetrators of violence, fostering an ongoing cycle of violence in the communities afflicted by this public health disease."

Violence-proneness: Toch, *Violent Men*, 183.
"The willingness to adopt the violence-prone mythology of survival distinguishes the [violent men who make up] our sample from other inmates or police officers or slum children or unhappily married men…. [Violence-proneness] appears to be insidious in its cumulative character. Once a person discovers that the ego can be buttressed at the expense of others, the discovery seems to be recurrently applied. The routine, moreover, gains from both success and failure; its stability rests on the fact that it feeds on personal insecurity, rather than on the reactions of victims and the sanctions of authority."

We must be ever: Rose, *On Violence*, 31.
"There can be no 'being done' with violence. Reckoning with violence has to be enacted over and over again."

103] • [104

Kaelyn Person was a 13-year-old middle school student. https://www.wtvr.com/news/local-news/cottle-family-murder-chesterfield-mother-joanna-loved-her-kids-had-huge-heart. 0923.

Juan Pablo Rivera Velázquez was born in Puerto Rico and lived in Florida. https://www.nytimes.com/interactive/projects/cp/us/orlando-shooting-victims/juanp-rivera-velazquez. 0323. https://www.orlandoweekly.com/news/the-pulse-shooting-took-juan-pablo-rivera-velazquezs-life-but-now-his-mother-and-sister-carry-on-his-dreams-2551235. 0323.

Chris Hixon worked as Athletic Director and Security Monitor at a high school, where he was also the wrestling coach. He and his wife had two sons. He was 49. https://www.legacy.com/us/obituaries/sunsentinel/name/christopher-hixon-obituary?id=9497067. 0723.

Kiwi Herring. https://www.bustle.com/p/who-was-kiwi-herring-the-transgender-woman-was-fatally-shot-by-st-louis-police-78723. 0723.

Tierramarie Lewis had three siblings and two stepsiblings. She was from Coshocton, Ohio, but had moved to Cleveland looking for programs to help her break away from sex work and recover from addiction. https://thelandcle.org/stories/she-was-just-ready-to-turn-her-life-around-advocates-and-trans-community-remember-the-life-of-tierramarie-lewis/. 0923. https://www.dignitymemorial.com/obituaries/coshocton-oh/tyrone-lewis-10240625. 0923.

Miles Hall was a high school graduate. He had schizoaffective disorder. He was 23, and had a younger sister. He loved camping and snowboarding. https://www.themileshallfoundation.org/about-miles. 0723. https://www.insider.com/miles-halls-killed-by-police-california-2020-11. 0723.

Jake Dunham. https://time.com/5449995/california-borderline-bar-shooting-victims/. 0923. https://www.uscannenbergmedia.com/2018/11/08/borderline-shooting-victims-who-they-were/. 0923.

Hilda Marshall and Susie Arnold worked at the same assisted living home. Hilda had worked there for 18 years, Susie for almost 6. https://www.walb.com/2023/06/29/new-details-emerge-deadly-may-moultrie-shootings-gbi-still-investigating/. 0923.

Tyler Schmidt had played trumpet, been on the cross-country and swim teams, and been an Eagle Scout in high school. He earned a degree in computer science from Truman State University. He and his wife had two children. He was on the Board of his church. https://www.legacy.com/us/obituaries/wcfcourier/name/tyler-schmidt-obituary?id=36092705. 0923.

Zachee Imanitwitaho was a Black transgender woman who moved with her family from Rwanda to the U.S. She was a fan of Rwandan rapper Ngabo Meddy, and loved fashion. https://www.courier-journal.com/story/news/local/2023/02/10/zachee-imanitwitaho-louisville-fatal-shooting-mourned-remembered/69887863007/. 0723. https://www.advocate.com/crime/transgender-2659391559. 0723. https://www.pghlesbian.com/2023/02/26-year-old-trans-woman-zachee-imanitwitaho-killed-in-louisville/. 0723.

26: Klinger, "The Consequences of Using Deadly Force," 155-56.

Guns exist: Ballentine, "Hunting Firearms," 49.
"As both a technology and an agent, guns are bound up in complex networks of other actors, rules, regulations, and codes that may shape and guide their use."

Police decide: Edwards, Esposito, and Lee, "Risk of Police-Involved Death," 1246.
"Police-involved deaths are often interpreted as being driven entirely by individual-level behaviors and choices. Narratives around fatal interactions between officers and civilians, as reported in the news, often reduce encounters to moments of crisis…. Individualizing narratives, however, masks the broader social forces that lead to distinct geographic and racial inequalities in police homicide risk. Our results suggest that the risk of being killed in a violent interaction with the police depends not only on idiosyncratic circumstances and individual choices but also on the interplay between one's race/ethnicity and the broader contextual environment in which policing occurs."

Assign the use: Justin Nix, as cited in Peeples, "What the Data Say," 24-25.

Use of deadly force "is this awesome power that [police officers] have that no other profession has. Let's keep track of it."

104] • [105

KC Johnson was a 27-year-old trans woman. She was passionate about anime and manga, and sharing images and art on social media of characters from the shows *Demon Slayer* and *Naruto.* https://www.them.us/story/kc-johnson-trans-woman-killed. 0723.

Yilmary Rodriguez Solivan was born in Puerto Rico, and lived in Florida. https://www.orlandoweekly.com/news/remembering-the-orlando-49-yilmary-rodriguez-solivan-2531113. 0323.

Joaquin Oliver was a fan of the musician Frank Ocean and the basketball player Dwyane Wade. He immigrated to the U.S. with his family when he was a toddler, and became a U.S. citizen when he was a teen. https://heavy.com/news/2018/02/joaquin-oliver-school-shooting-victim/. 0723.

Matthew Ajibade was born in Nigeria. Under the name of his creative alter ego, Matt Black, he owned and operated a print design company called Afridale. https://atlantablackstar.com/2015/01/08/family-matthew-ajibade-22-year-old-savannah-college-student-want-know-died-georgia-jail-cell/. 0823.

Alaina Housley was a co-founder of a soccer outreach program that provided soccer materials and gear to teens and children around the world. She was a musician who could play several instruments. https://time.com/5449995/california-borderline-bar-shooting-victims/. 0923. https://www.uscannenbergmedia.com/2018/11/08/borderline-shooting-victims-who-they-were/. 0923.

Kinsey Cottle and Jayson Cottle. https://www.wtvr.com/news/local-news/cottle-family-murder-chesterfield-mother-joanna-loved-her-kids-had-huge-heart. 0923.

Antwon Rose Jr. coached children in after-school classes at the Pittsburgh Gymnastics Club, and at age 14 he began volunteering at the Free Store, which provides surplus and donated items to those in need. https://www.blackpast.org/african-american-history/people-african-american-history/antwon-rose-jr-2000-2018/. 0723.

Amia Smith lived in Moultrie, Georgia. She had attended her local technical college. She was 41. https://heavy.com/news/kentavious-white-amia-smith/. 0923.

Sarah Schmidt had a Masters degree from the University of Kansas. She and her husband had two children. She enjoyed knitting, sewing Halloween costumes, crafting, making hand made greeting cards, being outdoors, birding, entomology, gardening, snowshoeing, cake decorating, and pottery. https://www.legacy.com/us/obituaries/wcfcourier/name/tyler-schmidt-obituary?id=36092705. 0923.

Nicole Kelly had been active in sports in school, including flag football, basketball, soccer, and volleyball. She earned an associate's degree in early childhood education, and held various jobs waitressing and as a teacher's aide, before becoming a stay-at-home mom. She was 35. https://www.legacy.com/us/obituaries/concordmonitor/name/nicole-bell-obituary?id=52179583. 0923.

15, 16, 22: https://us.glock.com/en/pistols/g22. 0723.
16: https://www.santafenewmexican.com/news/local_news/mother-of-jeanette-anaya-speaks-out-on-daughter-s-death-at-hands-of-police/article_72eb7e0f-e885-5c5d-b003-e359a70b969c.html. 0723.
16: https://en.wikipedia.org/wiki/Murder_of_Laquan_McDonald. 0723.

"America is: Moya-Smith, "Killing Indians Since 1492," 189.

Americans are no more: Younge, *Another Day*, 240.
"Americans are no more inherently violent than anybody else. What makes its society more deadly is the widespread availability of firearms."

The U.S. does not keep: Lindsay-Poland, "Understanding Police Militarization," 153.
"The U.S. exceptionalism—the belief that it is an 'indispensable nation' with standards of democracy superior to those in the rest of the world—coupled with its coercive power in the international arena also leads inexorably to the export of U.S. policing methods, protocols, and equipment to other nations."

105] • [106

Nancy Lanza lived as an adult next door to the house she had lived in as a child. She had worked as a stock broker for John Hancock, and after retiring from that career had developed an interest in target shooting. https://www.npr.org/sections/thetwo-way/2012/12/18/167527771/nancy-lanza-gunmans-mother-from-charmed-upbringing-to-first-victim. 0323.

Jarrell Garris was 37. He was born and raised in New Rochelle, New York, and had recently moved to Greensboro, North Carolina. He lived with his girlfriend. He was a fan of the Los Angeles Rams and the New York Knicks.
https://www.nytimes.com/2023/07/13/nyregion/new-rochelle-police-shooting-jarrell-garris.html. 0723.

Christopher Joseph Sanfeliz was born into a Cuban-American family, and worked as a personal banker at JPMorgan Chase. His favorite foods included restaurant bread baskets and mac and cheese. https://www.orlandoweekly.com/news/remembering-the-orlando-49-christopher-joseph-sanfeliz-2561394. 0323.

Alaina Petty was 14. She was an active volunteer for the "Helping Hands" program of The Church of Jesus Christ of Latter-day Saints.
https://www.findagrave.com/memorial/187346603/alaina-joann-petty. 0723.
https://www.churchofjesuschrist.org/church/news/shooting-victim-alaina-petty-remembered-as-a-very-nice-good-person?lang=eng. 0723.

Dominique Fells, who went by "Rem'mie," was a 27-year-old trans woman from Philadelphia. She loved music, and her sewing skills enabled her to take old clothes and transform them into something fashionable. https://exhibits.stanford.edu/saytheirnames/feature/dominique-fells. 0823.

Daniel Manrique served six years in Afghanistan as a Marine Corps radio operator. He worked for a veterans nonprofit called Team Red White & Blue. https://time.com/5449995/california-borderline-bar-shooting-victims/. 0923.

Holly Guess was 35, and had been born in El Paso, Texas, but lived in Henryetta, Oklahoma. https://www.kcra.com/article/remembering-mom-and-five-teenagers-killed-in-rural-oklahoma-mass-shooting/43787644. 0923.

Alex Nieto was the son of immigrants from Mexico. As a teen he had worked as a youth counsellor for almost five years at the Neighborhood Center in his local community. He had graduated from community college with a focus on criminal justice, and hoped to help young people as a probation officer. He had an internship with the city's juvenile probation department. He was 28. https://www.theguardian.com/us-news/2016/mar/21/death-by-gentrification-the-killing-that-shamed-san-francisco. 0723.

Lula Schmidt enjoyed outdoor activities, playing with her cousins, art, reading, and animals. She loved being at school with her teachers and friends.
https://www.legacy.com/us/obituaries/wcfcourier/name/tyler-schmidt-obituary?id=36092705. 0923.

David Lynch was a 33-year-old high school graduate. He and his wife had one son and two daughters. https://www.findagrave.com/memorial/144585400/david-cody-lynch. 0823.

92,000: The Brookings Institution. https://www.brookings.edu/blog/up-front/2020/07/13/three-million-more-guns-the-spring-2020-spike-in-firearm-sales/. 0323.
29.3: Schleimer et al., "Neighborhood Racial and Economic Segregation," 147.
3.8 million: https://www.thetrace.org/newsletter/who-bought-during-the-pandemic-gun-buying-surge/. 0423.

Gun ownership: Yamane, "Awash in a Sea of Faith and Firearms," 634.
"America's gun arsenal, like so many other phenomena, is not randomly distributed through religious, social, and geographic space."

"[W]hat matters most: Rogna and Nguyen, "Firearms Law," 3121.
The quoted sentence is from the article's abstract. In fuller context, the passage reads: "Our results confirm the negative impact of stricter firearms regulations on deadly use of force by police officers found in previous cross–sectional studies. However, in contrast with previous findings, we show that such impact is not mediated by gun availability. We also show that regulations pertaining to gun owner accountability are most effective in reducing fatal police

shooting incidence. These results suggest that, from a public health perspective, what matters most is who owns guns rather than how many guns are owned."

No demographic: Douglas Kellner, in Katz and Kellner, "A Conversation," 180.
"A multicausal analysis needs to look at multiple factors of class, race, gender, and specific social environments in which shootings take place. So far, research suggests that black and Latino shootings tend to be specific-target incidents that are related to particular issues or personal conflicts. The striking thing about many of the shootings from Columbine to the present was that it was white middle-class school shooters who tended to attack their victims indiscriminately, showing that alienation and violence is expanding through all classes, races, and sectors of contemporary U.S. society." Kellner is answering Katz's question, "How do factors of class and race enter into the problem of school shootings?"

106] • [107

Thomas May Jr. and his wife had one daughter and one son. He lived in Johnston, Rhode Island, and was 45. https://www.echovita.com/us/obituaries/ri/johnston/thomas-may-jr-16458796. 0923.

Malice Green was a high school graduate with two children and three stepchildren. He and his wife had plans to move to North Carolina. He was 35.
https://www.learntheirstories.com/#/malice-green/. 0623.
https://allthatsinteresting.com/malice-green. 0623.

Rhiannon Layendecker was a 51-year-old trans woman who lived in Englewood, Florida. She had two brothers. https://www.hrc.org/news/hrc-mourns-rhiannon-layendecker-a-transgender-woman-killed-in-florida. 0723.
https://www.tributearchive.com/obituaries/24218752/rhiannon-winter-layendecker. 0723.

Xavier Serrano Rosado lived in Florida. He had given up his career as a professional dancer in order to have more regular hours and be able to spend more time with his young son.
https://www.orlandoweekly.com/news/remembering-the-orlando-49-xavier-emmanuel-serrano-rosado-2551244. 0323.

Dennis Johnson had served in the US Navy Reserves and the Army National Guard. He was an elder at his church. https://www.cnn.com/2017/11/06/us/texas-church-shooting-victims-list/index.html. 0523.

Oscar Grant had a 4-year-old daughter. In his childhood, he had enjoyed fishing, baseball, chess and dominoes. https://www.findagrave.com/memorial/71246233/oscar-julius-grant. 0623.
https://www.blackpast.org/african-american-history/grant-oscar-juliuss-iii-1986-2009/. 0623.

Justin Meek was a recent college graduate who sang in choir. He moonlighted at a local bar. He planned to join the Coast Guard. He was 23. https://time.com/5449995/california-borderline-bar-shooting-victims/. 0923.

Rylee Allen. https://www.kcra.com/article/remembering-mom-and-five-teenagers-killed-in-rural-oklahoma-mass-shooting/43787644. 0923.

Pedro Piñeda was 56. https://www.indystar.com/story/news/crime/2022/07/18/indiana-greenwood-park-mall-shooting-victims-pedro-rosa-pineda-victor-gomez/65375925007/. 0923.

Feras Morad was a 20-year-old college student. He had been in ROTC in high school, and planned to attend Harvard Law School. https://www.theguardian.com/us-news/2015/jun/01/student-shot-california-long-beach-police-feras-morad. 0823. https://www.latimes.com/local/lanow/la-me-ln-feras-morad-vigil-woodland-hills-20150604-story.html. 0823.

79: https://ropercenter.cornell.edu/shootings-guns-and-public-opinion. 0423.

The most visible: DeKeseredy, "Men's Rights," 5.
"When one is talking about mass shootings and intimate femicide, one is often talking about the same events. In fact, the typical mass shooting does not take place in a shopping mall, but at home behind closed doors, with most victims being women and children."

Complete prevention: Schildkraut and Elsass, "Preventing Mass Shootings," 202.
"It is impossible to completely prevent mass shootings because, due to the unpredictability of human nature, the risk never can be completely eliminated. Yet, it is possible to institute techniques that either reduce the opportunity for these events to occur or minimize their subsequent lethality if they do take place. Proposed tactics must be firmly grounded in academic research rather than based upon emotion or politics. Criminological theory, specifically routine activities theory, aids in such an undertaking as it offers testable propositions to determine if a particular proposed solution is, in fact, effective."

More mass shootings: Melissa Jeltsen, "We're Missing the Big Picture on Mass Shootings." https://www.huffpost.com/entry/mass-shootings-domestic-violence-women_n_55d3806ce4b07addcb44542a. 0523.
"The majority of mass shootings in the U.S. take place in private. They occur in the home, and the victims are predominantly women and children.

The untold story of mass shootings in America is one of domestic violence. It is one of men (yes, mostly men) targeting and killing their wives or ex-girlfriends or families. The victims are intimately familiar to the shooters, not random strangers. This kind of violence is not indiscriminate — though friends, neighbors and bystanders are often killed alongside the intended targets."

107] • [108

Frank Petro was 62. He wrestled in high school. He worked for a time as an Emergency Response and Training Specialist with the Pennsylvania Department of Environmental Protection. He enjoyed hunting and fishing, and loved spending time with his grandchildren. He was a member of the Indiana (PA) Rod & Gun Club, Indiana County Beagle Club, and the Saltsburg Fire Company. https://www.curranfuneralhome.com/obituaries/obituary-listings?obId=62422. 0723.

Sarai Lara had been diagnosed with cancer at age 8, but had survived. She had a 5-year-old sister. She liked the colors pink and purple. https://www.seattletimes.com/seattle-news/law-justice/burlington-mall-shooting-victims-officially-identified/. 0323.

Shane Tomlinson was born in New York, and lived in Florida. His favorite performers included Jazmine Sullivan, John Legend, Janet Jackson, and Brandy Norwood. https://www.orlandoweekly.com/news/remembering-the-orlando-49-shane-evan-tomlinson-2536351. 0423.

Robert Marshall. https://www.nytimes.com/2017/11/07/us/sutherland-springs-texas-victims.html. 0523.

Franklin Lynch. https://www.bostonmagazine.com/news/frank-lynch-death/. 0723.

Amilcar Perez-Lopez was 21. He had arrived in the U.S. when he was 17. He worked at construction sites and restaurants in San Francisco, to send money back home. https://justice4amilcar.org/amilcar-story/. 0723.

Kristina Morisette had saved for, and recently purchased, her first car. https://time.com/5449995/california-borderline-bar-shooting-victims/. 0923.

Tiffany Guess was 13. Her nickname was "Tiffasaurus." https://www.kcra.com/article/remembering-mom-and-five-teenagers-killed-in-rural-oklahoma-mass-shooting/43787644. 0923.

Victor Gomez was 30, and lived in Indianapolis. He and his wife had one son and two daughters. https://www.wishtv.com/news/local-news/friend-of-greenwood-park-shooting-victim-victor-gomez-saw-him-moments-before-he-died/. 0923. https://www.legacy.com/us/obituaries/name/victor-gomez-obituary?id=35925306. 0923.

Egypt Powers loved cooking, and worked for a friend's catering company. They had experienced substance abuse and housing insecurity for much of their adult life, but had been sober for seven months. https://www.beaconjournal.com/story/news/local/2020/07/23/who-killed-brian-powers-police-have-no-leads-loved-ones-want-answers-in-death-of-black-trans-man/113376374/. 0723.

28: Boine, Caffrey, and Siegel, "Who Are Gun Owners in the United States?" 35.

"Peaceful violence": Trask, "The Color of Violence," 9-10. The "we" to whom Trask refers is Native people, by contrast with non-Native settlers.

"We exist in a violent and violated world, a world characterized by 'peaceful violence,' as Frantz Fanon so astutely observed. This is the peaceful violence of historical dispossession, of racial, cultural, and economic subjugation and stigmatization. Our psychological suffering and our physical impairments are a direct result of this peaceful violence, of the ordered realities of confinement, degradation, ill health, and early death."

Obedience can be: Keane, *Violence and Democracy*, 36.
"[A]cts of violence are not always face-to-face, hand-to-hand conflicts. In our times, people kill and are killed by proxy. Violence seems increasingly to be mediated by large-scale institutions, like armies equipped with state-of-the-art surveillance and monitoring and killing equipment. These institutions of violence have the effect of blurring the intentions and camouflaging the culpable negligence and responsibility of the violent. Those who inflict physical pain and suffering upon others do so not because they are thugs and sadists (although they may be this), but because they are trained in the habits and skills of behaving in accordance with the logic and imperatives of the institutional system in which they are operating."

Violence overpowers: Girard, *Violence and the Sacred*, 2.
"Violence is frequently called irrational. It has its reasons, however, and can marshal some rather convincing ones when the need arises. Yet these reasons cannot be taken seriously, no matter how valid they may appear. Violence itself will discard them if the initial object remains persistently out of reach and continues to provoke hostility. When unappeased, violence seeks and always finds a surrogate victim. The creature that excited its fury is abruptly replaced by another, chosen only because it is vulnerable and close at hand."

108] • [109

Alfred Olango had arrived in the U.S. as a refugee from Uganda in 1991, with his mother and eight siblings. He later married, and he and his wife had one child. He worked at Toro manufacturing and McDonald's. https://www.lhamar.org/say-their-names-biography/alfred-olango. 0623.

Martin Benitez Torres was born in Puerto Rico and lived in Florida. https://www.orlandoweekly.com/news/remembering-the-orlando-49-martin-benitez-torres-3614707. 0423.

Tony Terrell Robinson Jr. went by Tony with friends and Terrell with family. He was 19. He dealt with anxiety issues, depression and ADHD. He had to live with friends after his father lost his job and then his apartment. https://www.cnn.com/2015/03/10/us/wisconsin-police-shooting-tony-robinson/index.html. 0723.

Crystal Holcombe raised goats and made cheese. She was 8 months pregnant with what would have been her first child with her second husband. https://people.com/crime/holcombe-family-killed-texas-church-shooting/. 0523. https://heavy.com/news/2017/11/sutherland-springs-texas-church-shooting-victims-list-names-photos-pictures/. 0523.

Atatiana Jefferson, who went by "Tay," earned her B.A. in biology from Xavier University. She was 28. https://www.blackpast.org/african-american-history/people-african-american-history/atatiana-jefferson-1990-2019/. 0623.

Mark Meza was originally from Santa Barbara and studied photography at Santa Barbara City College. He was 20. https://www.uscannenbergmedia.com/2018/11/08/borderline-shooting-victims-who-they-were/. 0923.

Michael Mayo was 15. https://www.kcra.com/article/remembering-mom-and-five-teenagers-killed-in-rural-oklahoma-mass-shooting/43787644. 0923.

Rosa Mirian Rivera de Piñeda was born in El Salvador, and lived in Indianapolis, Indiana. https://www.indystar.com/story/news/crime/2022/07/18/indiana-greenwood-park-mall-shooting-victims-pedro-rosa-pineda-victor-gomez/65375925007/. 0923.

Akai Gurley moved to New York when he was a child. As a kid, he had loved fashion and dreamed of becoming a rapper; he carried a karaoke machine from room to room, practicing. https://www.learntheirstories.com/#/akai-gurley/. 0623.

Melissa Perez was 46. She had four children and two grandchildren. She loved to dance and listen to music. She had been diagnosed with schizophrenia.
https://www.dignitymemorial.com/obituaries/san-antonio-tx/melissa-perez-11346992. 0823.
https://www.nytimes.com/2023/07/22/us/melissa-perez-police-shooting-san-antonio.html. 0823.

92: UN Committee Against Torture, *We Charge Genocide*, 2.

Gun violence has analogies: Carlson, *Policing the Second Amendment*, 174.
"Gun violence, after all, is not an epidemic that can strike anyone, anywhere, with the same force. It is patterned, concentrated, systematic."

Meaningful early: Taxman, "Gun Violence in America," 121-22.
"There are currently instruments and standardized evaluative observation tools used to assess empathy and mentalizing. Creating and utilizing a program – not unlike President John Kennedy's program for youth physical fitness – to evaluate young children's developmental progress toward stable, robust mentalizing capacity may allow us to identify children in need of help before they are marginalized or socially lost…. Aside from potentially decreasing future violent actors such a program may benefit the emotional health of future generations of Americans. A program that could increase empathy, mentalizing, and attachment, may improve the well-being of individuals, couples, and large group systems."

If gun violence is: Sheley and Wright, *In the Line of Fire*, 157.
"There is a useful analogy to be drawn between the violence problem and the yellow fever problem that plagued many southern cities in the nineteenth century. The vector for the yellow fever infection was eventually found to be the mosquito; once that essential fact was learned, it

became possible to control yellow fever by eradicating the conditions under which mosquitoes bred. No one suggested that the solution to yellow fever was to wander through the swamps of Louisiana removing the mouthparts of mosquitoes with little tweezers, so they could no longer bite people and thereby spread the infection. Guns, we suggest, are the 'mouthparts' of our contemporary epidemic of violence; as such, 'gun control' has no better chance of solving the violence problem than 'proboscis control' had to solve the yellow fever problem."

109] • [110

Calvon Reid was 39, and had two sons. He was born in South Carolina, but lived in Florida. https://www.legacy.com/us/obituaries/greenvilleonline/name/calvon-reid-obituary?id=11487902. 0823. https://news.yahoo.com/death-florida-man-tased-police-deemed-homicide-200324421.html. 0823.

Janet Harrison had lived in Johnston, Rhode Island for 31 years. She worked as a civil servant for the federal government for 34 years until her retirement as an Immigration Services Officer. Her hobbies included cooking and spending time with her grandchildren. https://www.woodlawnri.com/obituary/Janet-Harrison. 0923.

Jonathan Camuy Vega was active in the National Association of Hispanic Journalists. He had moved from Puerto Rico to Florida to work for the Spanish-language television network Telemundo, on the production team for talent show "La Voz Kids." https://www.cbsnews.com/newyork/news/orlando-nightclub-shooting-victims-2/. 0323. https://www.orlandoweekly.com/news/remembering-the-orlando-49-jonathan-camuy-vega-2526809. 0423.

Joann Ward worked at a daycare center. She had three daughters and a stepson, and was active in het church. She liked riding horses. https://www.findagrave.com/memorial/184994621/jo_ann-ward. 0523. https://www.mysanantonio.com/news/local/article/Shooting-victim-Joann-Ward-s-life-was-all-about-12338429.php. 0523.

Jonathon Salcido. https://www.legacy.com/us/obituaries/legacyremembers/jonathon-salcido-obituary?id=11524080. 0523. https://www.nbclosangeles.com/news/local/family-lawsuit-death-of-mentally-ill-man-whittier-police/148337/. 0523.

Telemachus Orfanos was 27. https://time.com/5449995/california-borderline-bar-shooting-victims/. 0923. https://www.uscannenbergmedia.com/2018/11/08/borderline-shooting-victims-who-they-were/. 0923.

Henry James Hunter was a lifelong resident of Anadarko, Oklahoma. He attended school there, and played football and baseball. He was 34. https://www.findagrave.com/memorial/176207138/henry-james-hunter. 0823.

Brittany Brewer had been selected as "Miss Henryetta," and was to represent her hometown of Henryetta, Oklahoma in the upcoming "National Miss" pageant in Tulsa. https://www.kcra.com/article/remembering-mom-and-five-teenagers-killed-in-rural-oklahoma-mass-shooting/43787644. 0923.

Ryan Bolinger was originally from St. Joseph, Missouri, but had lived for two years in Des Moines, Iowa. He liked to have family and friends around. He was a high school graduate, and was engaged. https://www.legacy.com/us/obituaries/desmoinesregister/name/ryan-bolinger-obituary?id=17720776. 0823.

Daniel Prude had four siblings and five children. He grew up in a public housing complex. https://www.nytimes.com/article/what-happened-daniel-prude.html. 0723.

75,000+: https://solitarywatch.org/2022/06/16/long-awaited-prison-census-shows-more-than-75000-people-in-solitary-confinement/. 0623.
10: Reinhart, "Reconstructive Justice," 559.
11: Pullen-Blasnik, Simes, and Western, "The population prevalence of solitary confinement," as cited in Reinhart, "Reconstructive Justice."

How one thinks about guns: Shapira and Simon, "Learning to Need a Gun," 18.
"Our data revealed that the practice of gun carrying is connected to: (1) thinking that guns are needed for one's safety; (2) thinking that guns are safe objects; (3) thinking that killing someone else is sometimes a necessary and moral action; and lastly, (4) developing physical comfort with holding, carrying, and shooting guns. We showed that these schemes and dispositions are learned, and that the cognitive schemes (how people think about guns and gun carrying) and embodied experiences (how people physically experience guns and gun carrying) of gun carrying appear to be co-constitutive."

How we talk about guns: Anisin, "Antagonisms," 135.
"[G]iven the consistent occurrence of gun violence and citizen shootings, the United States theoretically should have the ability to transform politically, socially, and economically when it comes to the numerous horrors that are constantly brought about by guns. For this to occur, the discursive sedimentation of salient elements in American discourse has to be dislocated, and then rearticulated."

The rubber band's snap: "Federal Bureau of Investigation's Report on Threat Assessment of School Shooters (2000)," as presented in Schildkraut, *Mass Shootings in America*, 248.
"In general, people do not switch instantly from nonviolence to violence. Nonviolent people do not 'snap' or decide on the spur of the moment to meet a problem by using violence. Instead, the path toward violence is an evolutionary one, with signposts along the way. A threat is one observable behavior; others may be brooding about frustration or disappointment, fantasies of destruction or revenge, in conversations, writings, drawings, or other actions."

110] • [111

Kindra Chapman was 18. She was in a relationship with a woman who was pregnant, and she was "very excited about the baby." https://www.workers.org/2015/07/21179/. 0823.

Edward Morris Jr. had 5 brothers and 3 sisters. He enjoyed music, video games, basketball, was an avid Golden State Warriors fan. https://www.wkbn.com/my-valley-tributes/edward-maurice-morris-jr-obituary/. 0723.

Luis Vielma had two siblings, a younger brother and a younger sister for whom he was planning to be the chambelán at her Cinderella-themed quinceañera. https://www.nytimes.com/interactive/projects/cp/us/orlando-shooting-victims/luiss-vielma. 0423. https://www.orlandoweekly.com/news/remembering-the-orlando-49-luis-vielma-2522807. 0423.

Robert Corrigan had three sons, two of whom joined the Air Force. https://www.nytimes.com/2017/11/07/us/sutherland-springs-texas-victims.html. 0523.

Phillip Vallejo was 30, and lived in Fort Worth. https://www.legacy.com/us/obituaries/dfw/name/phillip-vallejo-obituary?id=18480915. 0723.

Noel Sparks was a 21-year-old college student, majoring in art. https://time.com/5449995/california-borderline-bar-shooting-victims/. 0923. https://www.uscannenbergmedia.com/2018/11/08/borderline-shooting-victims-who-they-were/. 0923.

Tracy Martinez was born in Belize, but grew up and graduated from high school in Fontana, California. She had one daughter and one son. https://www.dignitymemorial.com/obituaries/bloomington-ca/tracy-martinez-10950160. 0723.

Darrell Mattson was a Vietnam Veteran. After his military service, he had a career in transportation. He and his wife had three children and six grandchildren. He was 73. https://www.carlsonlillemoen.com/obituary/DarrellJandDeniseL-Mattson. 0923.

Cassandra Geschke was the mother of one daughter. She was a high school graduate, and loved being around children and hanging out with her friends. She lived in Elkhart, Indiana. https://www.echovita.com/us/obituaries/in/elkhart/cassandra-geschke-14719049. 0823. https://www.tributearchive.com/obituaries/24963993/cassandra-cassie-geschke. 0823.

Jaiden Dixon wanted to try out for pitcher on his Little League team. At the local YMCA, he liked to play Battleship, hide and seek, and cops and robbers. Younge, *Another Day in the Death of America*.

7: Brady Center to Prevent Gun Violence, as cited in Younge, *Another Day*, xxii.

Militarization: Caporale, "On State Violence," 177.

"The militarization of police agencies further demonstrates that legislators and justices are not addressing the issue of police brutality and that they are running away from its causes. In fact, the extra-armament of police agencies not only signifies the distrust against communities of color especially but also that all branches of government may share the same views."

In a militarized world: Camus, *The Rebel*, 183.

Enemies are not: Schwitters, *Myself and My Aims*, 152.
"There are no values worth defending. Our enemies are just like us. We should not fight them; we should fight our mistakes. The enemy's right to live is greater than your right to kill him."

111] • [112

David Felix immigrated to New York City from Haiti at age 16. He liked strawberry milkshakes, and gave friends fashion makeovers. https://www.theguardian.com/commentisfree/2015/jun/10/david-felix-immigration-mental-illness-killed-by-police. 0823.

Luis Daniel Wilson-Leon was born in Puerto Rico, and lived in Florida. He and his partner had met at a perfume shop. https://heavy.com/news/2016/06/luis-daniel-wilson-leon-tribute-obituary-memorial-jean-carlos-mendez-perez-florida-pulse-night-club-nightclub-shooting-omar-mateen-club/. 0423.

Lula White. https://heavy.com/news/2017/11/lula-woicinski-white-texas-church-shooting/. 0523.

Meagan Hockaday had been captain of her high school JV cheerleading squad. She and her fiancé had wedding plans. She was 26. https://www.learntheirstories.com/#/meagan-hockaday/. 0623. https://www.edhat.com/news/let-s-scream-our-sister-s-name-the-story-of-meagan-hockaday. 0623.

Rubén García Villalpando was born in Mexico, and had lived in the United States for 15 years. https://www.cnn.com/2015/03/08/us/texas-police-shooting/index.html. 0723.

Ron Helus planned to retire after one more year at his work. He was 54. He and his wife had one son. https://time.com/5449995/california-borderline-bar-shooting-victims/. 0923.

Bianca Roberson had graduated from high school, and had received a 4-year merit scholarship to Jacksonville University, where she planned to major in criminal justice, with the ambition of becoming an FBI forensic agent. She loved drawing. She was 18. https://www.legacy.com/us/obituaries/dailylocal/name/bianca-roberson-obituary?id=6824823. 0723.

Denise Mattson worked as a health care professional while she and her husband raised their three children. She was 68. https://www.carlsonlillemoen.com/obituary/DarrellJandDeniseL-Mattson. 0923.

Kiér Laprí Kartier was a 21-year-old trans woman. https://www.advocate.com/crime/2021/10/04/kier-solomon-texan-black-trans-woman-shot-death-car. 0923.

Jennifer LePore lived in Hazel Green, Alabama, and worked in the elementary school there. She was 44, and had four children. https://www.gofundme.com/f/in-memory-of-jennifer-sean-and-jesse-lepore. 0923. https://www.al.com/news/huntsville/2023/01/alabama-child-dead-in-tennessee-murder-suicide-recalled-as-exceptional-racer-with-stern-father.html. 0923.

40: https://www.huffpost.com/entry/americans-know-gun-violence-victims_n_56169834e4b0e66ad4c6bd2b. 0423.

Empathy after violence: White, *Survivor's Guilt*, 5, 8-9.
"[S]ympathy for a gunned-down stranger does not necessarily translate into tolerance for the same body alive and in need of civil rights.... [E]mpathy for those who are different shouldn't just happen after a body has been gunned down and is no longer seen as a political threat."

Forgiveness may supplement: Rodríguez, *Yolqui*, 25.
"I truly believe the ability to forgive is something that makes us human. Forgiveness, however, is not a substitute for justice. In most cases of police violence, justice includes imprisoning the perpetrators and requiring them to pay restitution to their victims. It is especially important that restitution comes out of their own pockets rather than from the institutions they work for, the taxpayer, or insurance companies."

Recognition of the life: Wieviorka, *Violence*, 64.
"[T]he conspicuous public presence of the figure of the victim... implies a demand for justice which would otherwise not be satisfied or would be inadequately satisfied. It also implies a recognition of a lived experience that the courts previously tried to cover up or minimize."

112] • [Websites

Online sources are given as a url linking to a specific web page, followed by the date of access, given as a four-digit designation of month: e.g. 0323 = March 2023. That form of citation is exhaustive, identifying every web *page* on which I have directly drawn.

As a supplement to that form of citation, here are some web *sites* on which I have drawn for multiple entries. This listing is partial, not exhaustive.

Black Past. https://www.blackpast.org/.
The Brookings Institution. https://www.brookings.edu/.
CNN: https://www.cnn.com/.
Everytown Research & Policy. https://everytownresearch.org/.

Fallen Heroes Project. https://www.fallenheroesproject.org/.
Find a Grave. https://www.findagrave.com/.
The Guardian. https://www.theguardian.com/.
How My Voice Is Heard. https://www.howmyvoiceisheard.com/.
Mapping Police Violence. https://mappingpoliceviolence.org/.
Mass Shooting Tracker. https://www.massshootingtracker.site/.
Mother Jones. https://www.motherjones.com/.
NBC News: https://www.nbcnews.com/.
The New York Times. https://www.nytimes.com/.
People Magazine. https://people.com/.
Pew Research Center. https://www.pewresearch.org/.
Say Their Names, Learn Their Stories. https://www.learntheirstories.com/.
Sikh Temple of Wisconsin. http://sikhtempleofwisconsin.com/welcome.
Small Arms Survey. https://www.smallarmssurvey.org/.
The Virginia Tech Online Memorial. http://www.vt-memorial.org/.
We Remember. https://www.weremember.vt.edu/.

Websites] • [Articles and Books

Sources native to the net are embedded above. This list identifies sources with print provenance.

Ahmed, Sara. *The Promise of Happiness*. Duke Univ. Press, 2010.
AlAmmar, Layla. *Silence Is a Sense: A Novel*. Algonquin Books, 2021.
Alcaraz Ochoa, Raúl, and Citlalli Alvarez Almendariz. "Under Trump, Can Law Enforcement Work for Us?" In Rodríguez, *Yolqui*, 186-87.
Alexander, Michelle. *The New Jim Crow: Mass Incarceration in the Age of Colorblindness*. 10th anniv. ed. The New Press, 2020.
Allen, Ira J. "A Non-Defensive Gun: Violence, Climate Catastrophe, and Rhetorical Education." In Wilkes, Kreuter, and Skinnell, *Rhetoric and Guns*. 218-35.
Altheide, David L. "The Columbine Shootings and the Discourse of Fear." *The American Behavioral Scientist (Beverly Hills)* 52:10 (June 2009): 1354-1370.
Andrews, Annie L., et al. "Pediatric Firearm Injury Mortality Epidemiology." *Pediatrics* 149:3 (March 2022): 36-43.
Anisin, Alexei. "Antagonisms and the Discursive Sedimentation of American Gun Culture: A New Framework." *Cultural Studies, Critical Methodologies* 17:2 (2017): 133-139.
Anker, Elisabeth. "Mobile Sovereigns: Agency Panic and the Feeling of Gun Ownership." In Obert, Poe, and Sarat, *The Lives of Guns*. 21-42.
Arendt, Hannah. *On Violence*. Harcourt, 1970.
Arjet, Robert. " 'Man to Man': Power and Male Relationships in the Gunplay Film." In Springwood, *Open Fire*. 125-37.
Auden, W. H. *The Prolific and the Devourer*. *Antaeus* 42 (Summer 1981): 5-65.
Balko, Radley. *Rise of the Warrior Cop: The Militarization of America's Police Forces*. PublicAffairs, 2013.
Baker, Susan P. "Without Guns, do People Kill People?" *American Journal of Public Health* 75:6 (1985): 587-588.

Ballentine, Brian. "Hunting Firearms: Rhetorical Pursuits of Range and Power." In Wilkes, Kreuter, and Skinnell, *Rhetoric and Guns*. 49-68.

Barlow, David E. and Melissa Hickman Barlow. *Police in a Multicultural Society: An American Story*. 2nd ed. Waveland Press, 2018.

Beckman, James A. "A Problem Entailing Many Policy Ideas — But Few Likely to Have Complete Success." In Schildkraut, *Mass Shootings in America*, 203-211.

Berardi, Franco "Bifo." *Heroes: Mass Murder and Suicide*. Verso, 2015.

----------. *The Uprising: On Poetry and Finance*. Semiotext(e), 2012.

Berry, Wendell. *Imagination in Place: Essays*. Counterpoint, 2010.

Blithe, Sarah Jane, and Jennifer L. Lanterman. "Subcultural Variability and Protean-Identification in Gun Culture." *Culture and Organization* 28:2 (2022): 148-166.

Blocher, Joseph. "Firearm Localism." *The Yale Law Journal* 123:1 (2013): 82-146.

Boine, Claire, Kevin Caffrey, and Michael Siegel. "Who are Gun Owners in the United States? A Latent Class Analysis of the 2019 National Lawful use of Guns Survey." *Sociological Perspectives* 65:1 (2022): 35-57.

Borum, Randy, et al. "What can be done about School Shootings? A Review of the Evidence." *Educational Researcher* 39:1 (2010): 27-37.

Boss, Stephen K. *Guns and College Homicide: The Case to Prohibit Firearms on Campus*. McFarland & Co., 2019.

Boylstein, Craig. *When Police Use Force: Context, Methods, Outcomes*. Lynne Rienner Publishers, 2018.

Braman, Donald and Dan M. Kahan. "Overcoming the Fear of Guns, the Fear of Gun Control, and the Fear of Cultural Politics: Constructing a Better Gun Debate." *Emory Law Journal* 55"4 (2006): 569-607.

Branas, Charles C., et al. "Investigating the Link Between Gun Possession and Gun Assault." *American Journal of Public Health* 99:11 (November 2009): 2034-2040.

Browder, Laura. *Her Best Shot: Women and Guns in America*. Univ. of North Carolina Press, 2006.

Brown, Richard Maxwell. *No Duty to Retreat: Violence and Values in American History and Society*. Oxford Univ. Press, 1991.

Bubar, Roe, and Pamela Jumper Thurman. "Violence Against Native Women." *Social Justice* 31:4 (2004): 70-86.

Burbick, Joan. *Gun Show Nation: Gun Culture and American Democracy*. The New Press, 2006.

Butler, Judith. *Precarious Life: The Powers of Mourning and Violence*. Verso, 2004.

Butler, Paul. *Chokehold: Policing Black Men*. The New Press, 2017.

Campbell, Beatrix. *End of Equality: The Only Way Is Women's Liberation*. Seagull Books, 2013.

Campbell, Donald J. *America's Gun Wars: A Cultural History of Gun Control in the United States*. Praeger, 2019.

Camus, Albert. *The Plague*. Trans. Stuart Gilbert. Vintage, 1991.

----------. *The Rebel: An Essay on Man in Revolt*. Trans. Anthony Bower. Vintage, 1954.

Caporale, Juvenal. "On State Violence Against People of Color: A Systemic Cycle." In Rodríguez, *Yolqui*, 176-78.

Carlson, Jennifer. *Citizen-Protectors: The Everyday Politics of Guns in an Age of Decline*. Oxford Univ. Press, 2015.

Carlson, Jennifer. *Policing the Second Amendment: Guns, Law Enforcement, and the Politics of Race*. Princeton Univ. Press, 2020.

Carlson, Jennifer, and Rina James. "Conspicuously Concealed: Federal Funding, Knowledge Production, and the Criminalization of Gun Research." *Sociological Perspectives* 65:1 (2022): 196-215.

Cassino, Dan and Yasemin Besen-Cassino. "Sometimes (but Not this Time), a Gun is just a Gun: Masculinity Threat and Guns in the United States, 1999–2018." *Sociological Forum* 35:1 (2020): 5-23.

Caulfield, Susan L. "Militarism, Feminism, and Criminal Justice: Challenging Institutionalized Ideologies." In Kraska, *Militarizing the American Criminal Justice System.* 120-40.

Charbonneau, Amanda, Katherine Spencer, and Jack Glaser. "Understanding Racial Disparities in Police use of Lethal Force: Lessons from Fatal Police-on-Police Shootings." *Journal of Social Issues* 73:4 (2017): 744-767.

Charles, Patrick J. *Armed in America: A History of Gun Rights from Colonial Militias to Concealed Carry.* Prometheus Books, 2018.

Children's Defense Fund. *Protect Children, Not Guns 2019.* Children's Defense Fund, 2019.

Cid, David. "'It Is Not a Question of Militancy, but of Survival: Police-State Violence During the L.A. Chicano Movement, 1967-1971." In Rodríguez, *Yolqui*, 169-71.

Cobbina-Dungy, Jennifer E. and Delores Jones-Brown. "Too Much Policing: Why Calls are made to Defund the Police." *Punishment & Society* 25:1 (2023): 3-20.

Collins, Randall. *Violence: A Micro-sociological Theory.* Princeton Univ. Press, 2008.

Combs, Thatcher Phoenix. "Queers with Guns?: Against the LGBT Grain." *Sociological Perspectives* 65:1 (2022): 58-76.

Cornell, Dewey G. *School Violence: Fears Versus Facts.* Lawrence Erlbaum Associates, 2006.

Corrigan, Lisa M. "The Gun as (Race/Gender) Technê." In Wilkes, Kreuter, and Skinnell, *Rhetoric and Guns.* 69-82.

Couch, Todd C. "A Qualitative Analysis of the Vulnerability Narratives of Student Gun Rights Advocates." *Sociological Research Online* 26:2 (2021): 394-409.

Cukier, Wendy, and James Cairns. "Gender, Attitudes and the Regulation of Small Arms: Implications for Action." In Farr, Vanessa, Henri Myrttinen, and Albrecht Schnabel, eds. *Sexed Pistols: The Gendered Impact of Small Arms and Light Weapons.* United Nations Univ. Press, 2009. 18-48.

Dahlberg, Linda L., Robin M. Ikeda, and Marcie-jo Kresnow. "Guns in the Home and Risk of a Violent Death in the Home: Findings from a National Study." *American Journal of Epidemiology* 160:10 (15 November 2004): 929-936.

Davis, Angela J., ed. *Policing the Black Man: Arrest, Prosecution, and Imprisonment.* Pantheon Books, 2017.

----------. "Introduction." In Davis, *Policing the Black Man.* xi-xxiv.

Davis, Brandon R. "Predation in State and Nation." *Race and Justice* 11:2 (2021): 205-225.

Dawson, Jessica. "Shall Not be Infringed: How the NRA used Religious Language to Transform the Meaning of the Second Amendment." *Palgrave Communications* 5:1 (2019): 58.

Deer, Sarah. "Federal Indian Law and Violent Crime: Native Women and Children at the Mercy of the State." *Social Justice* 31:4 (2004): 17-30.

DeKeseredy, Walter S. "Men's Rights, Gun Ownership, Racism, and the Assault on Women's Reproductive Health Rights: Hidden Connections." *Dignity* 7:3 (2022).

Diaz, Tom. *The Last Gun: How Changes in the Gun Industry Are Killing Americans and What It Will Take to Stop It.* The New Press, 2013.

----------. *Making a Killing: The Business of Guns in America.* The New Press, 1999.

Dizard, Jan E., Robert Merrill Muth, and Stephen P. Andrews, Jr., eds. *Guns in America: A Reader.* New York Univ. Press, 1999.

Dubber, Markus Kirk. *The Police Power: Patriarchy and the Foundations of American Government.* Columbia Univ. Press, 2005.

Dunbar-Ortiz, Roxanne. *Loaded: A Disarming History of the Second Amendment.* City Lights Books, 2018.

Dunlap, Col. Charles J., Jr. "The Thick Green Line: The Growing Involvement of Military Forces in Domestic Law Enforcement." In Kraska, *Militarizing the American Criminal Justice System.* 29-42.

Dunn, Timothy J. "Waging a War on Immigrants at the U.S.-Mexico Border: Human Rights Implications." In Kraska, *Militarizing the American Criminal Justice System.* 65-81.

Eargle, Lisa A. and Ashraf Esmail, eds. *Gun Violence in American Society: Crime, Justice, and Public Policy.* University Press of America, 2016.

Edwards, Frank, Michael H. Esposito, and Hedwig Lee. "Risk of Police-Involved Death by Race/Ethnicity and Place, United States, 2012-2018." *American Journal of Public Health* 108:9 (2018): 1241-1248.

Elias, Robert. "A Culture of Violent Solutions." In Turpin and Kurtz, *The Web of Violence*, 117-47.

Erdman, Sarah. "Promoting Gun Safety: Sharing Knowledge of Child Development to Support Informed Decisions." *YC Young Children* 73:1 (March 2018): 86-89.

Esposti, Michelle Degli, et al. "Increasing Adolescent Firearm Homicides and Racial Disparities Following Florida's 'Stand Your Ground' Self-Defence Law." *Injury Prevention* 26:2 (2020): 187-190.

Eterno, John A., and Christine S. Barrow. "Contemporary Police and Minorities in the United States: Causes, Theories, and Solutions." In Ward, *Policing and Race in America.* 31-53.

Evans, Brad, and Natasha Lennart. *Violence: Humans in Dark Times.* City Lights Books, 2018.

----------. "Introduction: Humans in Dark Times." In Evans and Lennart, *Violence.* 1-6.

Farah, Mirna M., Harold K. Simon, and Arthur L. Kellermann. "Firearms in the Home: Parental Perceptions." *Pediatrics* 104:5 (1999): 1059-1063.

Farrell, Amanda L. and Elizabeth Monk-Turner. "Placing Police Shootings in Context and Implications for Evidence Based Policy: An Exploration and Descriptive Analysis of these Incidents in the Hampton Roads Region of Virginia from 1990-2010." *Police Practice & Research* 20:5 (2019): 444-459.

Farrell, Amanda L., et al. "'There's no Crying in Police Work:' Exploring Police Shootings with Feminist Methods." *Gender Issues* 35:3 (2018): 220-235.

Fast, Jonathan. *Ceremonial Violence: A Psychological Explanation of School Shootings.* The Overlook Press, 2008.

Fisher, Jim. *SWAT Madness and the Militarization of the American Police: A National Dilemma.* Praeger, 2010.

Frazer, Eva, et al. "The Violence Epidemic in the African American Community: A Call by the National Medical Association for Comprehensive Reform." *Journal of the National Medical Association* 110:1 (February 2018): 4-15.

Fridell, Lorie A. "Racial Aspects of Police Shootings: Reducing both Bias and Counter Bias." *Criminology & Public Policy* 15:2 (2016): 481-489.

Gabor, Thomas. *Confronting Gun Violence in America.* Palgrave Macmillan, 2016.
Gage, Scott. "National News Coverage of White Mass Shooters: Perpetuating White Supremacy through Strategic Rhetoric." In Wilkes, Kreuter, and Skinnell, *Rhetoric and Guns.* 169-84.
Gamal, Fanna. "The Racial Politics of Protection: A Critical Race Examination of Police Militarization." *California Law Review* 104:4 (2016): 979-1008.
Garza, Alicia. "Foreword." To Schenwar, Macaré, and Price, *Who Do You Serve, Who Do You Protect?* vii-x.
Gaston, Shytierra, April D. Fernandes, and Rashaan A. DeShay. "A Macrolevel Study of Police Killings at the Intersection of Race, Ethnicity, and Gender." *Crime and Delinquency* 67:8 (2021): 1075-1102.
Gebo, Erika. "Intersectoral Violence Prevention: The Potential of Public Health-Criminal Justice Partnerships." *Health Promotion International* 37:3 (2022).
Geller, Lisa B., Marisa Booty, and Cassandra K. Crifasi. "The Role of Domestic Violence in Fatal Mass Shootings in the United States, 2014–2019." *Injury Epidemiology* 8:1 (2021): 38-38.
Gellert, George A. *Confronting Violence: Answers to Questions About the Epidemic Destroying America's Homes and Communities.* Westview Press, 1997.
Gilbert, Keon L. and Rashawn Ray. "Why Police Kill Black Males with Impunity: Applying Public Health Critical Race Praxis (PHCRP) to Address the Determinants of Policing Behaviors and 'Justifiable' Homicides in the USA." *Journal of Urban Health* 93:1 (2016): 122-140.
Gilligan, James. *Preventing Violence.* Thames and Hudson, 2001.
----------. *Violence: Our Deadly Epidemic and Its Causes.* G. P. Putnam's Sons, 1996.
Girard, René. *Violence and the Sacred.* Trans. Patrick Gregory. Johns Hopkins Univ. Press, 1977.
Goldberg, Robert J., et al. "The Smoking Gun: Can we do for Gun Control what we are Doing to Control the Vaping and E-Cigarettes Epidemic?" *Medical Care* 58:1 (January 2020): 1-3.
Goldstick, Jason E., Patrick M. Carter, and Rebecca M. Cunningham. "Current Epidemiological Trends in Firearm Mortality in the United States." *JAMA Psychiatry* 78:3 (March 2021): 241-242.
Goldstick, Jason E., Rebecca M. Cunningham, and Patrick M. Carter. "Current Causes of Death in Children and Adolescents in the United States." *New England Journal of Medicine* 386:20 (19 May 2022): 1955-56.
González, Roberto J. *Militarizing Culture: Essays on the Warfare State.* Routledge, 2010.
Gramsci, Antonio. *Prison Notebooks.* Vol. I. Ed. Joseph A. Buttigieg. Trans. Joseph A. Buttigieg and Antonio Callari. Columbia Univ. Press, 1992.
----------. *Prison Notebooks.* Vol. III. Ed. and trans. Joseph A. Buttigieg. Columbia Univ. Press, 1991.
Grinshteyn, Erin, and David Hemenway. "Violent Death Rates: The US Compared with Other High-Income OECD Countries, 2010." *The American Journal of Medicine* 129:3 (2016): 266-273.
Grossman, Allen. *The Sighted Singer.* Johns Hopkins Univ. Press, 1992.
Grossman, Dave. *On Killing: The Psychological Cost of Learning to Kill in War and Society.* Rev. ed. Back Bay Books, 2009.
Guattari, Félix. *The Three Ecologies.* Trans. Ian Pindar and Paul Sutton. Continuum, 2008.
Haag, Pamela. *The Gunning of America: Business and the Making of American Gun Culture.* Basic Books, 2016.

Harmon, Josephine. "U.S. Gun Culture as a Martial Culture within a Weberian Framework: Disrupting the State's Monopoly on Force." *Cultural Studies, Critical Methodologies* 22:5 (2022): 520-532.

Hayes, Heather Ashley. "The Thriving Life of Racialized Weaponry: Violence and Sonic Capacities from the Drone to the Gun." In Obert, Poe, and Sarat, *The Lives of Guns.* 95-121.

Hemenway, D., D. Azrael, and M. Miller. "Gun use in the United States: Results from Two National Surveys." *Injury Prevention* 6:4 (2000): 263-267.

Herbert, Jenna Katherine. "Arming the Settler Colony: Visualizing White Gun Culture in the American Suburban Home." ProQuest Dissertations Publishing, 2021.

Hill, Marc Lamont. *Nobody: Casualties of America's War on the Vulnerable, from Ferguson to Flint and Beyond.* Atria Books, 2016.

Holmes, Malcolm D., and Brad W. Smith. *Race and Police Brutality: Roots of an Urban Dilemma.* SUNY Press, 2008.

Holmes, Malcolm D., Matthew A. Painter, and Brad W. Smith. "Race, Place, and Police-Caused Homicide in U.S. Municipalities." *Justice Quarterly* 36:5 (2019): 751-786.

Horwitz, Joshua, and Casey Anderson. *Guns, Democracy, and the Insurrectionist Idea.* Univ. of Michigan Press, 2009.

Hureau, David and Theodore Wilson. "The Co-Occurrence of Illegal Gun Carrying and Gun Violence Exposure: Evidence for Practitioners from Young People Adjudicated for Serious Involvement in Crime." *American Journal of Epidemiology* 190:12 (December 2021): 2544-2551.

Imai, Satomi, et al. "Firearm Presence and Storage Practices in North Carolina Homes." *Journal of Human Behavior in the Social Environment* 27:7 (2017): 779-788.

Jackman, Geoffrey A., et al. "Seeing Is Believing: What Do Boys Do When They Find a Real Gun?" *Pediatrics* 107:6 (June 2001): 1247-50.

Jimenez, Tyler, Peter J. Helm, and Jamie Arndt. "Racial Prejudice Predicts Police Militarization." *Psychological Science* 33:12 (2022): 2009-2026.

Jiobu, Robert M. and Timothy J. Curry. "Lack of Confidence in the Federal Government and the Ownership of Firearms." *Social Science Quarterly* 82:1 (2001): 77-88.

Johnson, John M. "Guns as a Symbol of (Fill-in-the-Blank)." *Cultural Studies, Critical Methodologies* 17:2 (2017): 110-113.

Johnston, Jennifer. "Mass Shooters and Mental Illness." In Schildkraut, *Mass Shootings in America*, 13-21.

Jones, Michael A. and George W. Stone. "The U.S. Gun-Control Paradox: Gun Buyer Response to Congressional Gun-Control Initiatives." *Journal of Business & Economics Research* 13:4 (Fourth Quarter 2015): 167-74.

Joslyn, Mark R. *The Gun Gap: The Influence of Gun Ownership on Political Behavior and Attitudes.* Oxford Univ. Press, 2020.

Kaminer, Wendy. "Second Thoughts on the Second Amendment." In Dizard, Muth, and Andrews, *Guns in America.* 490-99.

Kapadia, Farzana. "Gun Control for Health: A Public Health of Consequence, December 2022." *American Journal of Public Health* 112:12 (December 2022): 1710-1712.

Katz, Jackson, and Douglas Kellner. "A conversation between Jackson Katz and Douglas Kellner on Guns, Masculinities, and School Shootings." *Fast Capitalism* 4:1 (2008): 179-83.

Kautzer, Chad. "Good Guys with Guns: From Popular Sovereignty to Self-Defensive Subjectivity." *Law and Critique* 26:2 (2015): 173-187.

Keane, John. *Reflections on Violence.* Verso, 1996.
----------. *Violence and Democracy.* Cambridge Univ. Press, 2004.
Kearney, Douglas. *Optic Subwoof.* Wave Books, 2022.
Kelleher, Michael D. *When Good Kids Kill.* Praeger, 1998.
Kellner, Douglas. *Guys and Guns Amok: Domestic Terrorism and School Shootings from the Oklahoma City Bombing to the Virginia Tech Massacre.* Paradigm Publishers, 2008.
Kendi, Ibram X. *Stamped from the Beginning: The Definitive History of Racist Ideas in America.* Nation Books, 2016.
Kierkegaard, Søren. *Eighteen Upbuilding Discourses.* Trans. Howard V. Hong and Edna H. Hong. Princeton Univ. Press, 1990.
Kimmel, Michael. *Angry White Men: American Masculinity at the End of an Era.* Nation Books, 2013.
King, C. Richard. "Arming Desire: The Sexual Force of Guns in the United States." In Springwood, *Open Fire.* 87-97.
Klarevas, Louis. *Rampage Nation: Securing America from Mass Shootings.* Prometheus Books, 2016.
Kleck, Gary. *Point Blank: Guns and Violence in America.* Aldine de Gruyter, 1991.
Klein, Jessie, and Lynn S. Chancer. "Masculinity Matters: The Omission of Gender from High-Profile School Violence Cases." In Spina, *Smoke and Mirrors.* 129-62.
Klinger, David A. "The Consequences of Using Deadly Force." In Joseph B. Kuhns and Johannes Knutsson, eds., *Police Use of Force: A Global Perspective* (Praeger, 2010), 152-61.
Kraska, Peter B., ed. *Militarizing the American Criminal Justice System: The Changing Roles of the Armed Forces and the Police.* Northeastern Univ. Press, 2001.
----------. "The Military-Criminal Justice Blur: An Introduction." In Kraska, *Militarizing the American Criminal Justice System.* 3-13.
----------. "Crime Control as Warfare: Language Matters." In Kraska, *Militarizing the American Criminal Justice System.* 14-25.
Kraska, Peter B. and Victor E. Kappeler. "Militarizing American Police: The Rise and Normalization of Paramilitary Units." *Social Problems* 44:1 (1997): 1-18.
Kreuter, Nate. "Muzzle Velocity, Rhetorical Mass, and Rhetorical Force." In Wilkes, Kreuter, and Skinnell, *Rhetoric and Guns.* 32-48.
Kreuter, Nate, Lydia Wilkes, and Ryan Skinnell. "Introduction: Rhetoric and Guns." In Wilkes, Kreuter, and Skinnell, *Rhetoric and Guns.* 3-18.
Kriegel, Leonard. "A Loaded Question: What Is It about Americans and Guns?" In Dizard, Muth, and Andrews, *Guns in America.* 145-53.
Kurtz, Lester R., and Jennifer Turpin. "Conclusion: Untangling the Web of Violence." In Turpin and Kurtz, *The Web of Violence*, 207-232.
Lane, Roger. *Murder in America: A History.* Ohio State Univ. Press, 1997.
Lankford, Adam and Eric Madfis. "Don't Name Them, Don't Show Them, But Report Everything Else: A Pragmatic Proposal for Denying Mass Killers the Attention They Seek and Deterring Future Offenders." *The American Behavioral Scientist* 62:2 (February 2018): 260-279.
Larkin, Ralph W. "Masculinity, School Shooters, and the Control of Violence." In Heitmeyer, William, et al., eds. *Control of Violence: Historical and International Perspectives on Violence in Modern Societies.* Springer, 2011. 315-44.
Lawson, Edward. "TRENDS: Police Militarization and the use of Lethal Force." *Political Research Quarterly* 72:1 (2019): 177-189.

Lee, Jin Hee, and Sherrilyn A. Ifill. "Do Black Lives Matter to the Courts?" In Davis, *Policing the Black Man.* 255-93.

Leventhal, John M., Julie R. Gaither, and Robert Sege. "Hospitalizations due to Firearm Injuries in Children and Adolescents." *Pediatrics* 133:2 (2014): 219-225.

Lewis, Sarah Elizabeth. "The Arena of Suspension: Carrie Mae Weems, Bryan Stevenson, and the 'Ground' in the Stand Your Ground Law Era." *Law and Literature* 33:3 (2021): 487-518.

Lindsay-Poland, John. "Understanding Police Militarization in the Global Superpower." *Peace Review* 28:2 (2016): 151-157.

Lowery, Wesley. *They Can't Kill Us All: Ferguson, Baltimore, and a New Era in America's Racial Justice Movement.* Little, Brown and Co., 2016.

Luke, Timothy W. "Counting Up AR-15s: The Subject of Assault Rifles and the Assault Rifle as Subject." In Obert, Poe, and Sarat, *The Lives of Guns.* 70-92.

Macaraeg, Sarah, and Alison Flowers. "Amid Shootings, Chicago Police Department Upholds Culture of Impunity." In Schenwar, Macaré, and Price, *Who Do You Serve, Who Do You Protect?* 33-46.

Madhavan, Sriraman, et al. "Firearm Legislation Stringency and Firearm-Related Fatalities among Children in the US." *Journal of the American College of Surgeons* 229:2 (August 2019): 150-157.

Madhubuti, Haki R. *Taking Bullets: Terrorism and Black Life in Twenty-first Century America.* Third World Press Foundation, 2016.

Mahmood, Cynthia Keppley. "Gun Cultures, Majority Nationalism, and the Prominence of Fear: Reflections on Anti-Sikh Hate Crimes." *Sikh Formations* 8:3 (2012): 275-279.

Marganski, Alison J. "Making a Murderer: The Importance of Gender and Violence Against Women in Mass Murder Events." *Sociology Compass* 13:9 (2019): n/a.

Martin, Dawn Lundy. "Introduction." In Aleshea Harris, *Is God Is* (3 Hole Press, 2018).

Masera, Federico. "Police Safety, Killings by the Police, and the Militarization of US Law Enforcement." *Journal of Urban Economics* 124 (2021): 103365.

McGinty, Emma E., et al. "News Media Framing of Serious Mental Illness and Gun Violence in the United States, 1997-2012." *American Journal of Public Health* 104:3 (March 2014): 406-413.

McLaren, Peter, Zeus Leonardo, and Ricky Lee Allen. "Rated 'CV' for Cool Violence." In Spina, *Smoke and Mirrors.* 67-92.

McMillan, Jordan, and Mary Bernstein. "Beyond Gun Control: Mapping Gun Violence Prevention Logics." *Sociological Perspectives* 65:1 (2022): 177-95.

Mehra, Renee, et al. "'Police Shootings, Now that Seems to be the Main Issue' - Black Pregnant Women's Anticipation of Police Brutality Towards their Children." *BMC Public Health* 22:1 (2022): 146-154.

Melzer, Scott. *Gun Crusaders: The NRA's Culture Wars.* New York Univ. Press, 2009.

Mencken, F. Carson and Paul Froese. "Gun Culture in Action." *Social Problems* 66:1 (2019): 3.

Mesic, Aldina, et al. "The Relationship between Structural Racism and Black-White Disparities in Fatal Police Shootings at the State Level." *Journal of the National Medical Association* 110:2 (2018): 106-116.

Milloy, Jeremy. *Blood, Sweat, and Fear: Violence at Work in the North American Auto Industry, 1960-80.* UBC Press, 2017.

Milosz, Czeslaw. *Nobel Lecture.* Farrar Straus Giroux, 1981.

Mingus, William and Bradley Zopf. "White Means Never having to Say You're Sorry: The Racial Project in Explaining Mass Shootings." *Social Thought & Research* 31 (2010): 57-77.

Moeller, Matthew. "Cycle Breakers: How People, Not Systems, are Ending the Cycle of Violence in Prison and Society." *Journal of Contemporary Criminal Justice* 38:2 (2022): 197-199.

Mogul, Joey L, Andrea J. Ritchie, and Kay Whitlock. *Queer (In)justice: The Criminalization of LGBT People in the United States*. Beacon Press, 2011.

Monzó, Lilia D., Peter McLaren, and Arturo Rodriguez. "Deploying Guns to Expendable Communities: Bloodshed in Mexico, U.S. Imperialism, and Transnational Capital—A Call for Revolutionary Critical Pedagogy." *Cultural Studies, Critical Methodologies* 17:2 (2017): 91-100.

Morales, Travis. "Too Many Stolen Lives — This Must Stop." In Rodríguez, *Yolqui*, 172-73.

Morrison, Toni. *The Source of Self-Regard: Selected Essays, Speeches, and Meditations*. Alfred A. Knopf, 2019.

Moya-Smith, Simon. "Killing Indians Since 1492." In Rodríguez, *Yolqui*, 188-89.

Mummolo, Jonathan. "Militarization Fails to Enhance Police Safety Or Reduce Crime but May Harm Police Reputation." *Proceedings of the National Academy of Sciences - PNAS* 115:37 (2018): 9181-9186.

Murdoch, Iris. *The Sovereignty of Good*. Ark, 1985.

Muschert, Glenn W. "School Shootings." In Schildkraut, *Mass Shootings in America*, 31-37.

Naghavi, Mohsen, et al. "Global Mortality from Firearms, 1990-2016." *JAMA : The Journal of the American Medical Association* 320:8 (2018): 792-814.

Nathenson, Randi Gross. "Finding Your Inner Gun: A Jungian Perspective on Mass Shootings and American Gun Culture." *Psychological Perspectives* 63:2 (2020): 204-215.

Neville-Shepard, Ryan and Casey Ryan Kelly. "Whipping it Out: Guns, Campaign Advertising, and the White Masculine Spectacle." *Critical Studies in Media Communication* 37:5 (2020): 466-479.

Obert, Jonathan, Andrew Poe, and Austin Sarat, eds. *The Lives of Guns*. Oxford Univ. Press, 2019.

----------. "The Lives of Guns: An Introduction." In Obert, Poe, and Sarat, *The Lives of Guns*. 1-17.

Obidah, Jennifer. "On Living (and Dying) with Violence: Entering Young Voices in the Discourse." In Spina, *Smoke and Mirrors*. 49-66.

O'Brien, Kerry, et al. "Racism, Gun Ownership and Gun Control: Biased Attitudes in US Whites may Influence Policy Decisions." *PloS One* 8:10 (2013): e77552-e77552.

O'Donnell, Alyssa Dale. "Monsters, Myths, and Mental Illness: A Two-Step Approach to Reducing Gun Violence in the United States," *Southern California Interdisciplinary Law Journal* 25:2 (Spring 2016): 475-501.

Palmiotto, Michael J., ed. *Police Use of Force: Important Issues Facing the Police and the Communities They Serve*. CRC Press, 2017.

Palmiotto, Michael J. "Use of Deadly Force." In Palmiotto, *Police Use of Force*, 35-49.

Pawlett, William. *Violence, Society and Radical Theory: Bataille, Baudrillard and Contemporary Society*. Ashgate, 2014.

Pearl, Sharrona. "Staying Angry: Black Women's Resistance to Racialized Forgiveness in U.S. Police Shootings." *Women's Studies in Communication* 43:3 (2020): 271-291.

Peeples, Lynne. "What the Data Say about Police Shootings." *Nature* 573:7772 (2019): 24-26.

Phelps, Michelle S., Christopher E. Robertson, and Amber Joy Powell. "'We're Still Dying Quicker than we can Effect Change': #BlackLivesMatter and the Limits of 21st-Century Policing Reform1." *The American Journal of Sociology* 127:3 (2021): 867-903.

Pierre, Joseph M. "The Psychology of Guns: Risk, Fear, and Motivated Reasoning." *Palgrave Communications* 5:1 (2019): 159-66.

Pirelli, Gianni, Hayley Wechsler, and Robert J. Cramer. *The Behavioral Science of Firearms: A Mental Health Perspective on Guns, Suicide, and Violence.* Oxford Univ. Press, 2019.

Powers, Nicholas. "Killing the Future: The Theft of Black Life." In Schenwar, Macaré, and Price, *Who Do You Serve, Who Do You Protect?* 9-20.

Prokos, Anastasia and Irene Padavic. "'There Oughtta be a Law Against Bitches': Masculinity Lessons in Police Academy Training." *Gender, Work, and Organization* 9:4 (2002): 439-459.

Poudrier, Almira F. "The Virtue of the Weaponed Hero." *The Humanist* 61:4 (2001): 35-35.

Rahtz, Howard. *Shots Fired: Gun Violence in the United States.* Lynne Rienner Publishers, 2020.

Ramey, David M. and Trent Steidley. "Policing through Subsidized Firepower: An Assessment of Rational Choice and Minority Threat Explanations of Police Participation in the 1033 Program." *Criminology* 56:4 (2018): 812-856.

Ramirez, Christian. "The Normalization of State-Sponsored Violence in the U.S. Southern Border Region." In Rodríguez, *Yolqui*, 185.

Ramirez, Renya. "Healing, Violence, and Native American Women." *Social Justice* 31:4 (2004): 103-16.

Rascon-Canales, Michelle. "'Brokenheartedness' or Systematic Killings: *Testimonios* and Sequelae Violence." In Rodríguez, *Yolqui*, 160-63.

Reinhart, Eric. "Reconstructive Justice — Public Health Policy to End Mass Incarceration." *The New England Journal of Medicine* 388:6 (2023): 559-564.

Ritchie, Andrea J. *Invisible No More: Police Violence Against Black Women and Women of Color.* Beacon Press, 2017.

----------. "Say Her Name: What It Means to Center Black Women's Experiences of Police Violence." In Schenwar, Macaré, and Price, *Who Do You Serve, Who Do You Protect?* 79-89.

Rivera, Mario A., and James D. Ward. "Developing a Comparativist Ethics for the Evaluative Study of Racialized Political Violence." In Ward, *Policing and Race in America.* 241-61.

Roberts-Miller, Patricia. "The Only Thing That Stops a Bad Guy with Rhetoric Is a Good Guy with Rhetoric." In Wilkes, Kreuter, and Skinnell, *Rhetoric and Guns.* 19-31.

Robertson, Ray Von, and Cassandra D. Chaney. *Police Use of Excessive Force against African Americans: Historical Antecedents and Community Perceptions.* Lexington Books, 2019.

Rodríguez, Roberto Cintli. *Yolqui: A Warrior Summoned from the Spirit World.* Univ. of Arizona Press, 2019.

Rogna, Marco and Bich Diep Nguyen. "Firearms Law and Fatal Police Shootings: A Panel Data Analysis." *Applied Economics* 54:27 (2022): 3121-3137.

Rood, Craig. *After Gun Violence: Deliberation and Memory in an Age of Political Gridlock.* Penn State Univ. Press, 2019.

Rosa, Asha, Monica Trinidad, and Page May. "We Charge Genocide: The Emergence of a Movement." In Schenwar, Macaré, and Price, *Who Do You Serve, Who Do You Protect?* 119-23.

Rose, Jacqueline. *On Violence and On Violence Against Women.* Farrar, Straus and Giroux, 2021.

Ross, Cody T. "A Multi-Level Bayesian Analysis of Racial Bias in Police Shootings at the County-Level in the United States, 2011-2014." *PloS One* 10:11 (2015): e0141854.

Roth, Randolph. *American Homicide.* Harvard Univ. Press, 2009.

Russell-Brown, Katheryn. "Making Implicit Bias Explicit: Black Men and the Police." In Davis, *Policing the Black Man.* 135-60.

Rutherford, Alison, et al. "Violence: A Glossary." *Journal of Epidemiology and Community Health* 61:8 (2007): 676-680.

------------. "Violence: A Priority for Public Health? (Part 2)." *Journal of Epidemiology and Community Health* 61:9 (2007): 764-770.

Scheff, Thomas J., and Suzanne M. Retzinger. *Emotions and Violence: Shame and Rage in Destructive Conflicts.* Lexington Books, 1991.

Schenwar, Maya, Joe Macaré, and Alana Yu-lan Price, eds. *Who Do You Serve, Who Do You Protect?: Police Violence and Resistance in the United States.* Haymarket Books, 2016.

Schildkraut, Jaclyn, ed. *Mass Shootings in America: Understanding the Debates, Causes, and Responses.* ABC-CLIO, 2018.

Schildkraut, Jaclyn, and H. Jaymi Elsass. *Mass Shootings: Media, Myths, and Realities.* Praeger, 2016.

----------. "Preventing Mass Shootings: Using Theory to Drive Evidence-Based Practice." In Schildkraut, *Mass Shootings in America*, 197-202.

Schildkraut, Jaclyn, H. Jaymi Elsass, and Glenn W. Muschert. "Satirizing Mass Murder: What Many Think, Yet Few Will Say." In Eargle and Esmail, *Gun Violence in American Society.* 233-55.

Schleimer, Julia P., et al. "Neighborhood Racial and Economic Segregation and Disparities in Violence during the COVID-19 Pandemic." *American Journal of Public Health* 112:1 (2022): 144-153.

Schmidt, Carolyn Speer. "Police Violence, Public Response: The Public Gets What It Tolerates." In Palmiotto, *Police Use of Force*, 157-67.

Schuster, M. A., et al. "Firearm Storage Patterns in US Homes with Children." *American Journal of Public Health* 90:4 (April 2000): 588-594.

Schutten, Nathaniel M., et al. "Are Guns the New Dog Whistle? Gun Control, Racial Resentment, and Vote Choice." *Criminology* 60:1 (2022): 90-123.

Schwitters, Kurt. *Myself and My Aims: Writing on Art and Criticism.* Ed. Megan R. Luke. Trans. Timothy Grundy. Univ. of Chicago Press, 2021.

Settembrino, Marc. "Mass Shootings as Hate Crimes." In Schildkraut, *Mass Shootings in America*, 55-61.

Shanafelt, Robert, and Nathan W. Pino. *Rethinking Serial Murder, Spree Killing, and Atrocities.* Routledge, 2015.

Shapira, Harel. "How to Use the Bathroom with a Gun and Other Techniques of the Armed Body." In Obert, Poe, and Sarat, *The Lives of Guns.* 194-206.

Shapira, Harel, Chen Liang, and Ken-Hou Lin. "How Attitudes about Guns Develop over Time." *Sociological Perspectives* 65:1 (2022): 12-34.

Shapira, Harel and Samantha J. Simon. "Learning to Need a Gun." *Qualitative Sociology* 41:1 (2018): 1-20.

Sheley, Joseph F., and James D. Wright. *In the Line of Fire: Youth, Guns, and Violence in Urban America.* Aldine de Gruyter, 1995.

Shrikant, Natasha and Rahul Sambaraju. "'A Police Officer Shot a Black Man': Racial Categorization, Racism, and Mundane Culpability in news Reports of Police Shootings of Black people in the United States of America." *British Journal of Social Psychology* 60:4 (2021): 1196-1217.

Siegel, Michael, et al. "The Interaction of Race and Place: Predictors of Fatal Police Shootings of Black Victims at the Incident, Census Tract, City, and State Levels, 2013–2018." *Race and Social Problems* 13:3 (2021): 245-265.

Siegel, Michael, et al. "The Relationship between Racial Residential Segregation and Black-White Disparities in Fatal Police Shootings at the City Level, 2013–2017." *Journal of the National Medical Association* 111:6 (2019): 580-587.

Simpson, Oliver. "Breaking the Mirror of the Spectacle: Mass Murder/Suicide as the Ecstasy of Simulated Experience." *Critical Sociology* 46: 7-8 (2020): 1109-1120.

Skolnick, Jerome H. and James J. Fyfe. *Above the Law: Police and the Excessive Use of Force.* The Free Press, 1993.

Smith, Andrea and Luana Ross. "Introduction: Native Women and State Violence." *Social Justice* 31:4 (2004): 1-7.

Smith, Philip. "Civil Society and Violence: Narrative Forms and the Regulation of Social Conduct." In Turpin and Kurtz, *The Web of Violence*, 91-116.

Southwick, Lawrence Jr. "Government Options to Stop School Shootings." In Schildkraut, *Mass Shootings in America*, 213-21.

Spencer, J. William. *The Paradox of Youth Violence.* Lynne Rienner Publishers, 2011.

Spina, Stephanie Urso, ed. *Smoke and Mirrors: The Hidden Context of Violence in Schools and Society.* Rowman & Littlefield, 2000.

----------. "Introduction: Violence in Schools: Expanding the Dialogue." In Spina, *Smoke and Mirrors.* 1-39.

----------. "When the Smoke Clears: Revisualizing Responses to Violence in Schools." In Spina, *Smoke and Mirrors.* 229-59.

Springwood, Charles Frueling, ed. *Open Fire: Understanding Global Gun Cultures.* Berg, 2007.

Springwood, Charles Frueling. "The Social Life of Guns: An Introduction." In Springwood, *Open Fire.* 1-11.

----------. "Gunscapes: Toward a Global Geography of the Firearm." In Springwood, *Open Fire.* 15-27.

Squires, Catherine R. "Afterword." In Wilkes, Kreuter, and Skinnell, *Rhetoric and Guns.* 252-59.

Stewart, Susan. *The Open Studio: Essays on Art and Aesthetics.* Univ. of Chicago Press, 2005.

Strain, Christopher B. *Reload: Rethinking Violence in American Life.* Vanderbilt Univ. Press, 2010.

Stroud, Angela. *Good Guys with Guns: The Appeal and Consequences of Concealed Carry.* Univ. of North Carolina Press, 2016.

----------. "Guns don't Kill People…: Good Guys and the Legitimization of Gun Violence." *Humanities & Social Sciences Communications* 7:1 (2020): 1-7.

Stylianos, Steven. "Injuries and Deaths due to Firearms in the Home: A.L. Kellerman, G. Somes, F.P. Rivara, Et Al. J Trauma 45:263–267, (August), 1998." *Journal of Pediatric Surgery* 34:3 (1999): 516.

Swanson, Jeffrey W., et al. "Mental Illness and Reduction of Gun Violence and Suicide: Bringing Epidemiologic Research to Policy." *Annals of Epidemiology* 25:5 (May 2015): 366-376.

Taxman, Jeffrey. "Gun Violence in America — A Tri-Vector Model: Perspectives on Gun Violence: National and International Views." *International Journal of Applied Psychoanalytic Studies* 13:2 (2016): 113-123.

Taylor, Jimmy D. *American Gun Culture: Collectors, Shows, and the Story of the Gun.* LFB Scholarly Publishing, 2009.

Taylor, Paul L. "Beyond False Positives: A Typology of Police Shooting Errors." *Criminology & Public Policy* 18:4 (2019): 807-822.

Toch, Hans. *Violent Men: An Inquiry Into the Psychology of Violence.* 25th Anniversary Ed. American Psychological Association, 2017.

Tonso, Karen L. "Violent Masculinities as Tropes for School Shooters: The Montréal Massacre, the Columbine Attack, and Rethinking Schools." *The American Behavioral Scientist* 52:9 (2009): 1266-1285.

Toplin, Robert Brent. *Unchallenged Violence: An American Ordeal.* Greenwood Press, 1975.

Trask, Haunani Kay. "The Color of Violence." *Social Justice* 31:4 (2004): 8-16.

Trethewey, Natasha. *Memorial Drive: A Daughter's Memoir.* Ecco, 2020.

Turchan, Brandon, April M. Zeoli, and Christine Kwiatkowski. "Reacting to the Improbable: Handgun Carrying Permit Application Rates in the Wake of High-Profile Mass Shootings." *Homicide Studies* 21:4 (2017): 267-286.

Turpin, Jennifer, and Lester R. Kurtz, eds. *The Web of Violence: From Interpersonal to Global.* Univ. of Illinois Press, 1997.

United Nations Committee Against Torture. *We Charge Genocide: Police Violence Against Chicago's Youth of Color.* Report. Sept. 2014.

Utter, Benjamin D. "'Accessories Included': Armed Christians and the Mythos of Heroic Violence." *Review and Expositor* 117:3 (2020): 358-372.

Utter, Glenn H. and James L. True. "The Evolving Gun Culture in America." *Journal of American Culture* 23:2 (2000): 67-79.

Van Horne, Sheryl L. "Institutional Correlates of Intimate Partner Gun Homicides." In Eargle and Esmail, *Gun Violence in American Society.* 82-112.

Vizzard, William. "Our Gun Laws Are Fine, the System That Implements Them Is Broken." In Schildkraut, *Mass Shootings in America*, 189-90.

Wallace, Lacey N. "Responding to Violence with Guns: Mass Shootings and Gun Acquisition." *The Social Science Journal* 52:2 (2015): 156-167.

Ward, James D., ed. *Policing and Race in America: Economic, Political, and Social Dynamics.* Lexington Books, 2018.

Warner, Tara D., et al. "To Provide or Protect? Masculinity, Economic Precarity, and Protective Gun Ownership in the United States." *Sociological Perspectives* 65:1 (2022): 97-118.

Waugaman, Elisabeth. "Understanding America's Obsession with Guns: How Did We Get Where We Are?" *Psychoanalytic Inquiry* 36:6 (2016): 440-453.

Webber, Julie A. *Beyond Columbine: School Violence and the Virtual.* Peter Lang, 2017.

Weil, Simone. *Gravity and Grace.* Trans. Arthur Wills. Univ. of Nebraska Press, 1997.

White, Artress Bethany. *Survivor's Guilt: Essays on Race and American Identity.* New Rivers Press, 2022.

Whitmer, Barbara. *The Violence Mythos.* SUNY Press, 1997.

Widom, Cathy Spatz. "The Cycle of Violence." *Science* 244:4901 (1989): 160-166.

Wieviorka, Michel. *Violence: A New Approach.* Trans. David Macey. SAGE, 2009.

Wilkes, Lydia, Nate Kreuter, and Ryan Skinnell, eds. *Rhetoric and Guns.* Utah St. Univ. Press, 2022.

Wilkes, Lydia. "This Is America on Guns: Rhetorics of Acquiescence and Resistance to Privatized Gun Violence." In Wilkes, Kreuter, and Skinnell, *Rhetoric and Guns.* 118-34.

Williams, Kristian. *Our Enemies in Blue: Police and Power in America.* AK Press, 2015.

Wilson, Harry L. "Let the Locals Decide How to Stop School Shootings." In Schildkraut, *Mass Shootings in America*, 223-28.

Witkowski, Terrence H. "Mythical Moments in Remington Brand History." *Culture and Organization* 22:1 (2016): 44-66.

Woodard, Stephanie. *American Apartheid: The Native American Struggle for Self-Determination and Inclusion*. Ig Publishing, 2018.

Woods, Tryon P. *Blackhood Against the Police Power: Punishment and Disavowal in the "Post-Racial" Era.* Michigan St. Univ. Press, 2019.

Yamane, David. "Awash in a Sea of Faith and Firearms: Rediscovering the Connection between Religion and Gun Ownership in America." *Journal for the Scientific Study of Religion* 55:3 (2016): 622-636.

Yamane, David, Paul Yamane, and Sebastian L. Ivory. "Targeted Advertising: Documenting the Emergence of Gun Culture 2.0 in Guns Magazine, 1955–2019." *Palgrave Communications* 6:1 (2020).

Younge, Gary. *Another Day in the Death of America: A Chronicle of Ten Short Lives.* Nation Books, 2016.

Zare, Hossein, et al. "How Place and Race Drive the Numbers of Fatal Police Shootings in the US: 2015–2020." *Preventive Medicine* 161 (2022): 107132-107132.

----------. "Association between Neighborhood and Racial Composition of Victims on Fatal Police Shooting and Police Violence: An Integrated Review (2000–2022)." *Social Sciences* 11:4 (2022): 153.

Zimring, Franklin E. *American Youth Violence.* Oxford Univ. Press, 1998.

----------. *When Police Kill.* Harvard Univ. Press, 2017.

Žižek, Slavoj. *Violence: Six Sideways Reflections.* Picador, 2008.

About the Author

H. L. Hix's other recent books include *Bored In Arcane Cursive Under Lodgepole Bark*, *Moral Tales*, *Constellation*, and another BlazeVOX book, *Say It Into My Mouth.* His earlier books include an "evidentiary" called *American Anger*, and an edition and translation of *The Gospel* that merges canonical with noncanonical sources in a single narrative, and refers to God and Jesus without assigning them gender. He lives and works in the Mountain West.

Made in the USA
Middletown, DE
29 June 2024